CALAMUS

CALAMUS

MALE HOMOSEXUALITY IN TWENTIETH-CENTURY LITERATURE

AN INTERNATIONAL ANTHOLOGY

Edited by

David Galloway and

Christian Sabisch

QUILL

New York   1982

Library of Congress Cataloging in Publication Data
Main entry under title:

Calamus : male homosexuality in twentieth-century
    literature.

    1. Homosexuality, Male—Literary collections.
2. Literature, Modern—20th century. I. Galloway,
David D. II. Sabisch, Christian.
[PN6071.H724C3 1982b]   808.8'0353   81-13790
ISBN 0-688-00797-X   AACR2
ISBN 0-688-00606-X (pbk.)

Printed in the United States of America

First Quill Edition

1 2 3 4 5 6 7 8 9 10

BOOK DESIGN BY MICHAEL MAUCERI

For permission to reprint copyrighted material, we should like to make the following grateful acknowledgments:

B.V. Uitgeverij De Arbeiderspers: pages 175-186 from *Ik had een Wapenbroeder* by Maarten 't Hart. Copyright © 1973, 1978 by Maarten 't Hart. Originally published by B.V. Uitgeverij De Arbeiderspers, Amsterdam.

Ardis Publishers: "Aunt Sonja's Sofa" by Mikhail Kuzmin. Reprinted from *Wings: Prose & Poetry of Mikhail Kuzmin*. Copyright © 1972 by Ardis.

Giorgio Bassani and Erich Linder, Agenzia Letteraria Internazionale: pages 58-91 from *The Gold-Rimmed Spectacles* by Giorgio Bassani. Copyright © 1960 by Atheneum House, Inc., and Faber & Faber, Ltd. Originally published in Italian under the title *Gli Occiali D'Oro*. Copyright © 1958 by Giulio Einaudi Editore, S.p.A., Turin.

Marion Boyars Publishers, Ltd.: a selection from *Trans-Atlantyk* by Witold Gombrowicz. Originally published in Polish under the title *Trans-Atlantyk*.

John Calder (Publishers) Ltd. and Riverrun Press, Inc.: a selection from the pages 139-167 from *Sweet Tooth* by Yves Navarre. English translation copyright © 1976 by Donald Watson, Ltd. Originally published under the title *Les Loukoums*. Copyright © 1973 by Editions Flammarion.

Ronald Christ: "A Sinner's Guidebook" by Eduardo Gudiño Kieffer. Copyright © 1975 by Ronald Christ. Reprinted from *New Directions in Prose and Poetry*, 36. Originally published in Spanish under the title *Guia de pecadores* by Editorial Losada S.A., Buenos Aires.

City Lights Books: "A Supermarket in California" by Allen Ginsberg. Reprinted from *Howl* by Allen Ginsberg. Copyright © 1956, 1959 by Allen Ginsberg. "Please Master," "Rain-wet asphalt" by Allen Ginsberg. Reprinted from *The Fall of America* by Allen Ginsberg. Copyright © 1971 by Allen Ginsberg.

Lonnie Coleman and Curtis Brown, Ltd.: "Theban Warriors" by Lonnie Coleman. Copyright © 1955 by Lonnie Coleman. Reprinted from *Ship's Company*, published by Little, Brown & Co.

Candida Donadio & Assoc., Inc.: "On Ruegen Island" by Christopher Isherwood. Reprinted from *Goodbye to Berlin* by Christopher Isherwood. Copyright 1945 by New Directions, renewed © 1973 by Christopher Isherwood.

Gleerup Publishers and Anne-Marie Ekelund: "Nothing, Nothing Else in the World," "October" by Vilhelm Ekelund. Originally published in Swedish in

*This volume is dedicated
to
Douglas Johnson and Derek Yeld*

FOREWORD

The scope of this volume can only begin to suggest the immense complexity of homosexual experience and the rich variety of its literary expression. The designation "homosexual literature" cannot be avoided in these pages, but it is a thematic description that should not be automatically equated with the sexual preferences of an individual author. Heterosexual writers have sometimes addressed the theme of homosexual love with insight and compassion; many known homosexuals, on the other hand, have rigorously avoided the subject. Women have frequently portrayed the love of man for man in their writings—in part, no doubt, for the light it sheds on the entire problem of sexual role-playing. Thus, without reference to the author's biography, we have sought works of literary consequence that focus on the problems, the stereotypes, the poetry and psychology of homosexual relationships between men.

Our focus is on work produced in the twentieth century, when many writers have enjoyed a new freedom to explore sexuality in a direct, explicit manner. The development of this freedom is neither constant nor universal, but its tendency has been to reject the "coding" and the circumventions many earlier writers adapted in order to screen their real intentions. We have, in addition, limited ourselves to the theme of male homosexuality, despite persuasive arguments from the Gay Liberation Movement that male and female homosexuals must unite in a common front. For the purposes of this work, however, both social and legal actualities argue for the separation. However cruelly censored and suppressed they may have been, Lesbian relationships have seldom been actively, systematically persecuted by church or state. The particular institutionalized discrimination against male homosexuality has, inevitably, left a deep stamp on the manner of its literary expression; this reality demands a volume of its own. In making our selections we have sought to reflect a broad range of cultural backgrounds, though there is an inevitable concentration on the Western hemisphere—in particular, on Europe and the Americas. There, thanks to the growing consciousness and self-confidence produced by various homosexual and libertarian movements, the theme has been handled with particular frequency and assurance.

Every anthology is the product of numerous compromises. Often it was necessary to exclude works because of their excessive length, and some texts appear only in extracts; other selections were eliminated by problems of copyright, or because they were otherwise readily available to the interested reader. Certain well-known texts had to be included in order to establish the necessary historical dimension, but we have sought to complement these with a number of lesser-known pieces—works formerly suppressed, long out of print, or never before translated into English. We regret that, in the end, so little space could be apportioned for younger writers, but we have seen our primary obligation as establishing a foundation on which further work can be done. If our choices prompt the reader to compose his own, alternative table of contents, our goal has been achieved.

We hope that *Calamus* can make some contribution to restoring the blighted and obscured heritage of the homosexual, and that it can simultaneously offer the heterosexual a deeper insight. But above all we would welcome an audience that could approach the works presented here without recourse to labels and stereotypes, but as significant achievements of the literary imagination.

—David Galloway
—Christian Sabisch

ACKNOWLEDGMENTS

For their generous advice and assistance in the making of this book, we should like to thank:

Zoltán Abádi-Nagy
Vincent Balitas
Margret Büscher
John Calder
Ann Carter
Ronald Christ
Javier Coy
Louis Crompton
Jonathan Cutbill
S.M. Daly
Henriette Dornenberg
Lit Fischer
Armand de Fluvià
Hans-Peter Förding
Warren French
Jonathan Fryer
Stephen Gray

Page F. Grubb
Richard Hall
Ute Henneberg
Alison Hennegan
Michael Holm
Francis Howard
Joachim S. Hohmann
Raoul Hübner
Dieter Ingenschay
Josef Jarab
Douglas James Johnson
Jerzy Kutnik
Denis Lemon
Winston Leyland
Jürgen Loos
Franek Lyra
Ross McGregor

CALAMUS

Julian Meldrum
Barbara Shelby Merello
Norbert Messler
Ron Mooser
Zdzisaw Najder
Bruno Peterson
Walter J. Phillips
Angela Praesent
James Purdy
Antonio Jorge Consalves
 Rodrigues

Georges-Michel Sarotte
Klaus Scherpe
Ed Schraepen
Richard Senate
Sven Sponberg
Bill Swainson
James Wootton
Derek Yeld
Ian Young
Thekla Zachrau

CONTENTS

17

CALAMUS

Contents

CALAMUS

FULL OF LIFE NOW

Full of life now, compact, visible,
I, forty years old the eighty-third year of the States,
To one a century hence or any number of centuries hence,
To you yet unborn these, seeking you.

When you read these I that was visible am become invisible,
Now it is you, compact, visible, realizing my poems, seeking me,
Fancying how happy you were if I could be with you and become your
    comrade;
Be it as if I were with you. (Be not too certain but I am now with
    you.)

—WALT WHITMAN, Calamus

INTRODUCTION

The right to speak frankly and approvingly of homosexual love is still denied to many writers, but remarkable progress has been made in reversing the effects of centuries of suppression and hypocrisy, and in giving voice to a persecuted minority. Though pioneering work had in fact been accomplished three decades before, the beginnings can be symbolically dated from 1895, when the Brazilian writer Adolfo Caminha published the first sympathetic and accomplished novel of homosexual love. *Bon-Crioulo* (*Good Nigger*) explored the passionate sexual relationship between a mature black sailor and a fifteen-year-old ship's boy, "a beautiful little sailor with blue eyes, much liked by all, about whom 'certain things' were said." The novel concludes with the violence that would become obligatory for countless later works, but its descriptions of the love of an older man for a cherished boy are presented with tender compassion.

In 1895 the courageous German pioneer of homosexual liberation, Karl Heinrich Ulrichs, died in self-imposed Italian exile; Havelock Ellis began to publish in American periodicals the studies of homosexual and bisexual conduct that would form part of *The Psychology of Sex*; and Edward Carpenter

23

completed the manuscript of *Love's Coming of Age.* The English poet, socialist and reformer championed women's rights and sex education; he also called, in "The Intermediate Sex," for a new, important role for the homosexual in society. Arguing in the manner of Walt Whitman—whom he had met and devoutly admired—that homosexuals can best rise above mere sex to spiritual comradeship, Carpenter insisted that they were thus especially well fitted for leadership in a progressive, democratic society.

In the history of homosexual literature, however, the most sensational and consequential event of 1895 was the trial of Oscar Wilde. Wilde was a married man and the father of two children; his writings had been internationally acclaimed, and two of his plays were enjoying successful runs in London theaters. He was also a well-known public figure, notorious for his wit, aesthetics and dandyism. For some years he had freely indulged in homosexual liaisons, including a romantic affair with his beloved "Bosie," Lord Alfred Douglas. A few days after the triumphant premiere of *The Importance of Being Earnest,* Wilde received an insulting card from Bosie's father, Lord Queensberry, accusing him of sodomy. At the insistence of his young lover, Wilde sued Queensberry for criminal libel. When the court ruled against Oscar Wilde, the spectators broke into cheers of approval. Wilde's books immediately disappeared from libraries and shops, his plays were closed, and the author bankrupted. A second trial, in which soiled bedsheets were entered as evidence and a professional blackmailer testified against Wilde, resulted in a maximum prison sentence of two years at hard labor.

There had been such scandals before—as when the Unitarian minister Horatio Alger, who went on to become the most influential writer of boys' books in America, was dismissed from the church for "the abominable and revolting crime of unnatural familiarity with *boys* . . ." Other, more publicized scandals would follow—the Krupp and Eulenberg-Moltke affairs in Germany, the purges of Senator Joseph McCarthy in the United States, the indictment of Liberal Party leader Jeremy Thorpe in England. The Wilde affair remains almost unique, however, in the depth of the shock waves it produced. Spotlighted in the international press, it provoked people to speak about the "unspeakable," and to debate the possible relationship between sexual preference and artistic temperament.

Reaction to the Wilde affair delayed publication of Edward Carpenter's *Love's Coming of Age* until 1896, the year in which Adolf Brand began to publish the German magazine *Der Eigene*, devoted to "art and masculine culture." In 1897 the world's first homosexual liberation organization was formed in Germany, under the leadership of Magnus Hirschfeld, and a petition campaign was launched to amend the notorious paragraph 175 of the German penal code, which made all sexual acts between males a criminal offense. More than 6,000 prominent Germans signed the petition—including Hermann Hesse, George Grosz, Krafft-Ebing, Martin Buber, Käthe Kollwitz, Thomas Mann, Stefan Zweig and Rainer Maria Rilke. Hirschfeld's work with the Scientific Humanitarian Committee further eroded the code of silence surrounding the problem of homosexuality, and gradually won major support from members of the Reichstag.

In 1929 the Committee on Criminal Law of the German Parliament recommended abolition of anti-homosexual legislation, but before that recommendation could become law, the nation was plunged into the economic and political chaos that brought about the rise of Adolf Hitler. On a May morning in 1933, Nazi youths sacked the Institute for Sexual Research where Hirschfeld's Scientific Humanitarian Committee was housed. A few days later, more than 10,000 volumes from the Institute's library, as well as extensive files, charts and photographs, fed an enormous bonfire on Opera Square. The bust of Hirschfeld, carried in a torchlight procession through the streets, was thrown into the flames. It was the beginning of a horror story that continued with the bloody Röhm-Putsch and the deaths of tens of thousands of homosexuals in Nazi concentration camps. In post-war, democratic Germany, those homosexuals who survived the barbarities of Auschwitz and Dachau would be repeatedly denied restitution for their sufferings on the grounds that they had been criminal and not political prisoners. Such events make tragically clear that homosexual emancipation cannot be charted on a simple curve. Furthermore, if progress in reform movements becomes too visible, the victors too jubilant, it may well trigger reactionary impulses—as in the self-righteous campaign of Anita Bryant. Nonetheless, the homosexual imagination has gradually won rights of self-expression that would have been unthinkable in the nineteenth century.

The selections included in this volume can only hint at the immense range of technique and thematic concern that characterize the literature of male homosexuality. To be sure, certain patterns recur: adolescent sexual initiation, transvestism, voyeurism, the fantasy figure of the handsome sailor, sexuality as religious ritual and as revolt. Particular settings are also archetypal: the prison, the ship at sea, the gay bar, the boarding school, the theater. In part, such patterns derive from the ghetto existence to which many homosexuals have been tacitly condemned; in part, they are reflections (or inversions) of behavior sanctioned by the dominant heterosexual culture. To this degree, at least, homosexual writing fits the basic patterns of minority literature, though with the important qualification that unlike other minorities, which are tolerated somewhere at least, homosexuals suffer a discrimination that is absolutely international.

Despite yawning differences in the legal status and social recognition of homosexuals themselves, their literature reveals numerous configurations that cut across political and cultural boundaries. Comparative anthropology suggests that some of these may be rooted in ancient rites of adolescent initiation and the all-male rituals of warrior societies. The image of the supermale may be embodied in Samurai warrior, Prussian officer, booted cowboy or black-jacketed motorcyclist. The female ideal takes romantic or comic or tragic form in the cherished "wife" of a German nobleman, a Brooklyn dragqueen, a Kabuki actor, a Brazilian soda-jerk, a confused Dutch soldier on holiday leave. Such recurrent prototypes, far from suggesting some implicit limitation of the homosexual imagination, underscore its universality; furthermore, the patterns implied here all have their counterparts in the established literatures of the heterosexual majorities. If Chekhov and Ibsen and Simone de Beauvoir offer alternative views of woman's role in society, so too do the transvestites portrayed by Kieffer, Genet and Selby. As Robert Duncan has argued about fellow-poet and fellow-homosexual Hart Crane, "Crane's suffering, his rebellion, and his love are sources of poetry for him not because they are different to, superior to, mankind, but because he saw in them a link with man; he saw in them his sharing in universal human experience."

A minority has the opportunity to develop a radical perspective on the dominant society, and this perspective has, in turn, allowed homosexuals to address certain themes with particular authority. Western literature in the twentieth century has repeatedly anatomized the figure of the lonely individual, alienated from his own culture—the impotent Fisher King of T.S. Eliot's *The Waste Land*, the aimless wanderers portrayed by Borges and Beckett, the estranged heroes of Albert Camus' *The Stranger,* Saul Bellow's *Dangling Man,* Ralph Ellison's *Invisible Man*—titles symbolic of a fundamental existentialist dread. The homosexual, so often compelled to cultivate invisibility, to live in what novelist John Rechy terms a *City of Night,* has been able to express the search for a viable identity with particular insight.

It is also frequently argued that homosexuals possess unique artistic gifts, that something in the presumed blending of male and female temperaments broadens their creative vision. Such arguments are commonly accompanied by a list of accomplished homosexuals, from Socrates through Michelangelo and DaVinci, to Proust, Gide and an encyclopedic company of actors, composers, painters and dancers. If one subscribes to the neurosis theory of art, it is, of course, entirely plausible that the friction and frustration of his life might encourage the homosexual to seek expression through aesthetic forms. It is also true that in many cultures the performing arts and Bohemian circles of the big cities have frequently been unusually tolerant of sexual difference, encouraging homosexual expression and rewarding it. But all such arguments are highly speculative. More persuasive is

27

the contention of the American psychiatrist Colin J. Williams that "homosexuals are usually marginal to society and this marginality ... seems to have something to do with a creative person's ability to tolerate ambiguity, project varying points of view, and strike out in new directions."

One thing remains certain: the homosexual sensibility has made a vital contribution to the arts, despite the efforts of prudery, religious dogmatism and official censorship to mask those achievements. For generations, American Blacks suffered from a similar conspiracy to conceal their unique cultural heritage. Such repression cruelly diminishes the self-identity of a group, but it is also a deprivation for the entire literate community. Male homosexuality has an ancient and accomplished literary tradition which is gradually being redeemed from centuries of suppression and outright falsification. Censorship has not always been so perverse as in the case of John Benson, the first important editor of Shakespeare's sonnets, who replaced the pronoun "he" with "she" in those sonnets addressed to the mysterious "Mr. W.H." On the other hand, generations of literary historians have ransacked the cupboards of metaphor to prove that these impassioned love poems were merely a courtly Renaissance tradition, utterly devoid of sexual implication. Conveniently, they ignore the entire pastoral tradition of homoerotic love elaborated by Theocritus and Virgil from which such Elizabethan conventions derived.

In 1684 an erotic play entitled *Sodom, or the Quintessence of Debauchery,* attributed to the satirist John Wilmot, Earl of Rochester, won the distinction of being the first work censored by the English government for obscenity and pornography. It was symbolic that this enraptured paean to the joys of homosexual love should be thus singled out. From the Middle Ages until the early twentieth century, the writer who wished to give positive expression to the love of men for their own sex was repeatedly compelled to disguise his intention with metaphor and encoded allusion, or to publish his works privately or anonymously. Perhaps more sinister than official censorship was the implicit censorship of publishers and public which frequently led the writer to falsify or deny his own art. Even Walt Whitman, so joyfully bold in projecting an entire politics of homosexual experience, felt compelled to modify later editions of *The Leaves of Grass* to blunt the poem's erotic content. Similarly, the "fair slim boy" who inspired Oscar Wilde's "Wasted Days" (1877) was heterosexualized into the inferior tribute to "a lily girl" in "Madonna Mia."

Jean Cocteau's remarkably graceful little novella, *The White Paper*, was published anonymously in 1928, and even today its authorship is rarely acknowledged in official literary histories. This lyric study of homosexual passion contained such transparently autobiographical references that its authorship was scarcely disguised, and the elegantly simplified line-drawings for the second edition bore Cocteau's unmistakable stamp. In fashionable Parisian circles, neither Cocteau's homosexuality nor his experiments with opium were secret; indeed, they helped establish his glamorous credentials as inheritor of the *fin de siècle* Decadents. On the other hand, it was neither fashionable nor wise to advertise such exotic preferences too blatantly. Cocteau may, as well, have enjoyed the private joke of this transparent anonymity. Far more extreme was E.M. Forster's unhappy decision to withhold his own homosexual short stories and the novel *Maurice*, which only appeared in print after the author's death. In our own time the English poet Stephen Spender has included in the official collected edition of his verse a poem concluding with the lines, "Whatever happens, I shall never be alone. I shall always have an affair, a railway fare, or a revolution." It is doubtful that the revision is a genuine improvement over the poem's original wording: "I shall always have a boy, a railway fare, or a revolution."

Even such self-censorship was not always sufficient to pacify audiences. Although Oscar Wilde never specified the "vices" of his decadent hero Dorian Gray, enough readers were scandalized by the mere implication of sexual waywardness for the bookseller W.H. Smith to withdraw from their newsstands the June, 1890, issue of *Lippincott's Monthly Magazine* in which *The Portrait of Dorian Gray* first appeared. Not coincidentally, and with unintentional prophecy, in the same year Wilde composed a short story centering on the riddle of the identity of Shakespeare's beloved "W.H." For two of the three characters involved, solution of the puzzle brings death. Oscar Wilde himself would soon stand trial for gross offenses against nature; dissolute, impoverished and abandoned by most of his friends, Wilde died in 1900 in Paris, where he lived after his release from prison under the pseudonym of Sebastian Melmoth. The allusion to the martyred St. Sebastian, later an idol of Japanese novelist Yukio Mishima, was suggested by arrows on the prison uniform Wilde wore in Reading Gaol. "Melmoth" was borrowed from a famous nineteenth-century novel, *Melmoth the Wanderer*, whose tormented hero has made a Faustian pact with the devil in order to gain eternal life, and who wanders the earth as an outcast, seeking someone who will relieve him from his painful bargain.

Wilde's affair with Lord Alfred Douglas and the legal persecution it provoked form the subject of Eric Bentley's historical drama, *Lord Alfred's Lover* (1978). In the opening of the play, the author tells his children the story of Dr. Jekyll and Mr. Hyde, converting it into a psychodrama of the tormented secret life of the homosexual:

> Dr. Hyde must have an alter ego. . . . A second personality. Called Mr. Jekyll. We'll simply keep Dr. Hyde from public view. He must live only at night, and have his nice times then. By day, coming out at his front door, only Mr. Jekyll will be seen, and he won't be nice and have a nice time, he will be respectable and have a respectable time. Now, all the crimes of London, all the vices, can be imputed to Dr. Hyde!

Bentley's parable neatly describes the double life countless homosexuals have been compelled to lead, and it is hardly surprising that motifs of disguise, impersonation and transformation should recur throughout homosexual literature. Often this takes the form of literal transvestism, recalling the pastoral tradition in which such disguises were a common device, as they were in Shakespeare's comedies and romances, and in the entire tradition of boy-actors playing female roles on the

Elizabethan stage. A writer may also subsume a male within a female character—as Proust shaped Albert into Albertine, or as Tennessee Williams has incorporated much of his own homosexual yearning into portraits of neurotic women, or as Edward Albee, according to some critics, presented a study of homosexual marriage in *Who's Afraid of Virginia Woolf?*

It would be naive to presume that such techniques of inversion automatically undermine the authority of the work of art. Blanche Dubois, the emotionally scarred and fragile heroine of Tennessee Williams' *Streetcar Named Desire,* may express the author's feeling of vulnerable isolation as a homosexual, but she is also an entirely credible female character. And to rewrite Proust by changing the name Albertine to Albert and *elle* to *il* would entirely falsify the aesthetic structure of *À la recherche du temps perdu.* Homosexual writers, furthermore, are hardly unique in having to resort to nuance and symbol and artful substitutions in their work. Political pressures and social conventions, the fear of censors or the guillotine or jealous wives, may give rise to similar techniques; it is necessary, always, to distinguish between transformation of the "real" subject—as in Swift's *Gulliver's Travels* or Alexander Solzhenitsyn's *Cancer Ward*—and evasion or conscious falsification.

Erotic subject matter was long under an equal ban for both heterosexual and homosexual authors; the explicit description of genital sex gave notoriety to John Cleland's *The Adventures of Fanny Hill,* D.H. Lawrence's *Lady Chatterley's Lover* and James Joyce's *Ulysses.* The right to depict the full sexual dimension of human relationships had to be won as part of a far broader struggle against the iniquities of censorship. Until the early twentieth century, deviations from the norm of sexual propriety could be portrayed only if the offender eventually underwent miraculous conversion, was murdered, or committed suicide. Stephen Crane's Maggie drowns herself, Tolstoy's adulterous Anna Karenina throws herself in front of a train, Flaubert's Madame Bovary drinks arsenic, and generations of confused homosexuals drown or poison or hang or shoot themselves in order to confirm the superior social order.

Nonetheless, the proscriptions on homosexual literature have had a particularly sinister quality. Readers, for example, take it for granted that the relationship between a man and a woman can be rendered in an infinite variety of ways, and that the given elements in a character's situation—gender, class or heredity—are diversely tempered by personal experience. But this assumption of uniqueness is rarely extended to those individuals who happen to make emotional and sexual attachments to members of their own sex. One does not find it necessary to classify *Othello* or *Buddenbrooks* as "heterosexual" literature, but the frank treatment of intimacy between members of the same sex guarantees such labeling. So long as the homosexual is isolated from the mainstream of his society, the label is perhaps necessary; he or she belongs to a sub-culture that has no option but to develop its own life-styles and codes. Minority literature itself has become a favorite theme of modern criticism, but there is no implicit moral judgment in a study of the working-class novel in Britain, Black or Jewish writing in the United States, Zulu poetry in South Africa, or French-Canadian drama. In marked contrast to such objectivity, in her provocative and influential study of "camp" as a homosexual style, Susan Sontag asserts that the homosexual viewpoint is incompatible with moral seriousness. And the gifted critic Philip Thody remarks that "Genet's homosexuals are unfaithful to one another because homosexuality is, of itself, a disappointing form of sexual activity." The same critics would quite rightly be resourceful in identifying extenuating circumstances to account, say, for the high illegitimacy rate among American Blacks, but homosexuality can be summed up in tired and untested clichés.

The presumption that the intimate attachment of male to male (or female to female) can only be viewed in sexual terms is, of course, a patent absurdity. It is another simplification of what Christopher Isherwood terms "the heterosexual dictatorship," and its pervasiveness has often had the unfortunate effect of determining the self-image of the homosexual himself. So long as he accepts this discriminating definition, he is unlikely to develop the crucial implications of sexual choice as they manifest themselves in the orientation to friendship, tradition, social mores, authority and the imagination. The homoerotic rituals of the football field and of all-male bands of spectators are sanctioned as part of the masculine role, but homogenital contact remains taboo. Thus, the homosexual is repeatedly told that his unacceptable difference is entirely and indelibly defined by his sexual performance. If he accepts that judgment, the homosexual artist who struggles to express his own identity may be compelled to place unreasonable stress on the sexual act itself. To the extent that this limits or trivializes his art, he is once more a victim of the heterosexual dictatorship.

Rather than speaking of homosexuality in literature, it would be more appropriate to examine "homosexualities," for homosexuals in fact express their relationships in infinitely variable and subtle ways. In the sixteenth century the essayist Montaigne reasoned that if a truly intimate bond could be established between men, "where not only the souls might have entire fruition, but the bodies also might share in this alliance, and a man be engaged throughout, the friendship would certainly be more full and perfect." What Walt Whitman termed "adhesiveness," the devotion of man to man, was the central emotional fact of his life; it was also the basis of his philosophical, political and spiritual beliefs, the cornerstone of his faith in a new human partnership. For a number of contemporary poets—including Allen Ginsberg, Robert Duncan and Thom Gunn—the physical love of men promises the way back to spiritual values that have gone out of modern industrialized cultures. Orgasm becomes the equivalent of religious ecstasy. For Jean Genet, homosexuality is a cherished expression of revolt against the state, for defining the individual in a mass culture. Consequently, he has argued that "I would like the world not to change so that I can be against the world." More characteristic of contemporary writers, particularly those influenced by the Gay Liberation Movement, is the desire to bring about fundamental alterations in law, social custom and popular attitudes. Feminists have often supported such arguments because they, too, have suffered the tyranny of traditional roles. To reduce that spectrum of homosexual attitudes to the motions a person performs in bed is blatant sophistry.

One way to curtail pernicious stereotyping is to restore to the homosexual his lost cultural heritage—and with it, his pride. The task is hardly simple, for so much of the ancient literary tradition has been bowdlerized, lost or destroyed by prudent guardians of heterosexual supremacy. The compass of these introductory remarks is not sufficient to explore the intricate implications of that heritage, but certain recurrent motifs should be underscored for the insight they offer into twentieth-century literary conventions. Warrior-lovers, for example, were frequently celebrated in ancient literature, as in the Babylonian epic of Gilgamesh, who with his lover Enbidu roamed the earth in search of the herb of immortality. Their counterparts include not only Achilles and Patroclus, Damon and Pythias or David and Jonathan, but the entire Sacred Band of Thebes, a Greek army consisting of 150 pairs of warriors, who remained invincible in battle until their defeat by Philip of Macedon. In Sparta, according to Xenophon's short essay *The Lacedaemonian Constitution,* the homosexual relationship between such comrades was treated as a conjugal union. Far from being regarded as "unmanly," male couples were widely believed to make exceptionally good citizens and soldiers. "Once Eros has entered into the souls of a pair of lovers," Plutarch argued, "no enemy ever succeeds in separating them. They display their ardor and risk their lives even when there is no need of it."

Frequently, the soldierly bond was not between equals but between officer and underling, as in the case of Achilles and Patroclus, or the Knights Templar and their body servants. Strabo, in his *Geography,* records that in nearly all the Celtic tribes of early England, the warriors not only slept with their squires, but valued them more highly than their wives. Such comradeship is praised as *comitatus* in the Anglo-Saxon world of *Beowulf;* and in the medieval period every knight had his squire. Wrestling ceremonies like those recorded by Pindar are an integral part of male education and the rituals of bonding; in its Greek root *gymnasium* means, literally, "to train naked," and described an institution where such manly arts as wrestling could be mastered. In *Men in Groups* Lionel Tiger argues that for primitive societies wrestling-initiation and homoerotic love were part of the intimate bond necessary to make the activities of all-male hunting tribes more efficient. Transformed, those contacts re-emerge in the complex rites, secret rituals and diverse all-male activities that constitute "blood brotherhood" (*Blutsbrüderschaft*).

An awareness of this traditional background enriches the implication of the powerful scene in Thomas Mann's *Death in Venice* when Jaschin and Tadzio wrestle, semi-naked, on the beach of the Lido. It also illuminates the wrestling match between Gerald and Birkin in D.H. Lawrence's *Women in Love*, restoring the explicit homoerotic dimension which Lawrence obscured by suppressing the novel's original introductory chapter. The love of warriors is repeatedly evoked in modern homosexual literature—obliquely and somewhat abstractly in the First World War poetry of Wilfred Owen and Siegfrid Sassoon, explicitly in Simon Raven's *Feathers of Death* (1959), Susan Hill's *Strange Meeting* (1971), Maarten 't Hart's *I Had a Brother in Arms* (1973) and Jennifer Johnston's *How Many Miles to Babylon?* (1974). It is raised to a point of religious ecstasy in the Samurai code elaborated by Yukio Mishima, and has provided the focus for numerous novels by Mary Renault.

As the legends of Achilles and Patroclus or Alexander and the slave-boy Bagoas make clear, differences in rank or in social standing were once no barrier to love. In early Rome, on the other hand, the first attempts to regulate homosexual conduct were specifically designed to promote a caste system; homosexual acts were not condemned, but the *Lex Scautinia* strictly prohibited freeborn men to have intercourse with slaves. As one consequence of the Hebraic-Christian campaign against homosexuality, the metaphor of class or caste taboo also attaches to the warrior bond as a further barrier to so-called sins against nature. In D.H. Lawrence's violent, compelling story "The Prussian Officer," a class struggle underlines the unspoken sexual conflict. Lawrence's neurotic, aggressive officer is a direct if distorted descendent of the Spartan ideal; his unwitting orderly, sensual and instinctive, is described as having "strong, heavy limbs, was swarthy, with a soft, black, young moustache." Similarly, Hemingway's "A Simple Enquiry" creates tension in the opposition of an elegant, disciplined, but somewhat effete officer with his "dark-faced" peasant orderly. The terms "swarthy" and "dark-faced" imply an ethnic difference as well as one of rank—thus adding yet another taboo to the classical warrior bond. From very different viewpoints, racial and sexual discrimination would be seen as corollaries by writers like LeRoi Jones and James Baldwin. Meanwhile, the "primitive" dark man and the working-class boy would become special objects of desire in the eyes of many homosexuals.

In Norman Mailer's *Why Are We in Viet Nam?* two American adolescents undergo ceremonial preparation for war; alone in the Alaskan wilderness they discover deep homosexual longings, but sublimate them into the mentality of the killer. In a score of other novels, repression of the sexual dimension between comrades at arms brings about senseless violence—in Mailer's *The Naked and the Dead*, Carson McCullers' *Reflections in a Golden Eye* and, most savagely, in James Purdy's *Eustace Chisolm and the Works*. Purdy's novel concludes with a grotesque scene in which an enlisted man and an officer, maddened by guilt, self-hatred and repressed love, enact a cruel parody of the blood-letting ceremony of *Blutsbrüderschaft*.

Even more pervasive than the soldier as a prototype in the literature of male homosexuality is the figure of the sailor, though he, too, has a complex classical inheritance. The sailor is often, as in Cocteau's *The White Paper*, a source of erotic fantasy; frequently, too, he evokes myths of the sea's boundless fertility, and of freedom from the strictures of land-bound society. In Lonnie Coleman's *Ship's Company* (1955), a collection of stories set on board a battleship during World War II, a young seaman is dazzled and intrigued by Montgomery, a new, athletically masculine crew member who openly indicates his sexual preference for other men. At the conclusion of the story, the narrator yields to Montgomery's pleading:

Don't you know that most women hate men and use their sex to insult them and dominate them? I'm offering you something better than that, you damned fool. I'm offering you myself, and I promise you that I'll take you and hold you and keep you as long as such promises last. I love you, Barney.

With a nod to classical predecessors, Coleman entitled his story "The Theban Warriors." The tempestuous love of two sailors also forms the subject of "Divorce in Naples," a surprisingly tender and sympathetic story by William Faulkner.

In *The Enchafèd Flood* the English poet W.H. Auden remarked that:

It is not an accident that many homosexuals should show a special preference for sailors, for the sailor on shore is symbolically the innocent god from the sea who is not bound by the law of the land and therefore can do anything without guilt. Indeed, in a book like *Querelle de Brest,* the hero is at once god and the devil. He is adored because, though he is a murderer and a police informer and sexually promiscuous in every sense, though, that is, he loves no one but himself, is in fact Judas, yet he remains Billy Budd, the beautiful god who feels neither guilt nor remorse, and whose very crimes, therefore, are a proof of his divinity.

Genet has more than once hymned the mysterious and sensuous charm, the sadomasochistic virility of "those shoulders, profiles, mouths, those sinuous, turbulent rumps, those strong and supple boys," but the definitive image of the handsome sailor is indeed Melville's Billy Budd.

The blond and innocent seaman, whose "rustic beauty" is universally admired, is executed to reaffirm and renew the existing social order; his death recalls innumerable primitive rituals of the sacrifice of surrogates representing kings or gods. Behind his agony are the rites of Osiris and Adonis, the sea voyages and trials of Hercules and Odysseus, and of spiritual leaders like Moses symbolically resurrected from the water. He is related to Hylas, the boy-lover of Hercules drowned by water-nymphs, and to the near-universal harvest ritual described in Sir James Frazer's *The Golden Bough*, in which the young corn god is sacrificed. His literary peers include the character in William Burroughs' *The Soft Machine* identified as "young Corn God" and the various adolescents put to violent death in *The Naked Lunch*. They also include the young homosexual anthropologist murdered and eaten by cannibals in Tennessee Williams' *Suddenly Last Summer,* and the executed Maurice Pilorge whose beauty is celebrated in Jean Genet's poem *Le Condamné a Mort*.

Though *Billy Budd* never alludes directly to physical contact between men, Melville was more explicit in other writings of the sea—referring to sailing ships in *White Jacket* as the "wooden-walled Gomorrahs of the deep," the setting of "sins for which the cities of the plains were overthrown." Like other military figures, the sailor wears a uniform whose cut stresses classically masculine dimensions, and even more than the soldier, he inhabits a predominantly male world in which homoerotic contacts are not uncommon. In their letters and journals, both Walt Whitman and Hart Crane revealed the powerful attraction sailors had for them; in *Howl* Allen Ginsberg hymns men "who let themselves be . . . . . . in the . . . by saintly motorcyclists,/and screamed with joy,/who blew and were blown by those human seraphim, the sailors,/caresses of Atlantic and Caribbean love."

"The Obelisk," E.M. Forster's wryly comic tale of marital infidelity, shows a husband and wife equally incapable of resisting the appeal of a common seaman. In a short story by William Carlos Williams, the homosexual theme is signaled by the very title—"The Sailor's Son," and the visiting lover is a motorcyclist, another figure whose uniform and masculine control frequently associate him with the Spartan ideal. When the hero of James Baldwin's *Giovanni's Room* finally abandons his heterosexual charade, he spends three days with a sailor picked up in a bar on the the Côte d'Azur. Yukio Mishima explores the recurrent and seemingly universal ideal in *The Sailor Who Fell from Grace with the Sea,* and the Colombian poet Porfirio Barba-Jacob concluded his moving "Elegy to an Imaginary Sailor" with the lyric plea, "Give me your honey, child of the perfumed mouth!" It is thus particularly fitting that the first serious homosexual novel, Adolfo Caminha's *Bon-Crioulo,* is the story of the love between a sailor and a ship's boy.

In Caminha's novel, as in a number of the writings referred to above, there is a marked discrepancy between the ages of the lovers—a variation on the pederastic tradition commemorated in Greek mythology but practiced, in fact, in numerous ancient cultures as an established, integrated aspect of adolescent education. As in the ritual sacrifice of the young corn god, the conventions of pedagogic pederasty may well derive from primitive rituals in which a boy-surrogate was sacrificially murdered to renew the life of the king. This, in turn, takes the form of ceremonial rape of the boy-surrogate in a forcible rite of initiation. Later, when the use of force is forbidden, certain theatrical elements of the earlier rites still remain. According to Strabo's *Geography,* after the mock capture of a pubescent boy by an older man in Crete, the two spent sixty days together in the wilderness, hunting, fishing and making love— but always with the tacit approval of the boy's family. On their return from this "honeymoon," the older man was required to present his boy-lover with three gifts—a military outfit, an ox and a drinking cup. Cretan and Dorian homosexuality thus created the essential link between pedagogy and pederasty elaborated in Plato's *Symposium.* Comparative anthropology indicates that similar relationships played a part in the ancient civilizations of Egypt and Babylon, in South America, much of the Orient, and among numerous Indian tribes of North America. A homosexual bond of deep and consequential intimacy may not always have been homogenital, but it is difficult to read the praises of the Persian poet Hafiz for his smooth-cheeked cupbearers or descriptions of the *siang kong* academies for boy-actors in China without acknowledging their implicit sexuality.

The Virgilian *formosus puer,* the archetypal beautiful boy, figures prominently in Greek and early Roman mythology. Zeus had innumerable boy-lovers, all of whom coalesce in the enchanting person of Ganymede. Hercules, the ideal manly figure of the Greek imagination, was famed not only for his

39

strength, but for transvestism and pederastic amours; according to Plutarch, he had so many male lovers that it would be impossible to name them all, but the favorites were Iolas and Hylas. Hylas accompanied Hercules on his voyages with the Argonauts, and is repeatedly referred to as his "squire" and "minion." Drawing on numerous ancient accounts, including those of Theocritus and Herodotus, Robert Graves summarizes the circumstances of Hylas' death in *The Greek Myths*. During a rowing contest, Hercules broke his oar, and the Argo had to be beached while he fashioned a new one. Leaving the crew to prepare the evening meal, Hercules went in search of a suitable tree, uprooted it, and dragged it back to the camp. Hylas, meanwhile, had set out to fetch water from a nearby pool and had not returned. Frantically crying, "Hylas! Hylas!", Hercules plunged into the wood where he encountered Polyphemus, who reported, "Alas, I heard Hylas shouting for help; and ran towards his voice. But when I reached Pegae I found no signs of a struggle . . . There was only his water-pitcher lying abandoned by the pool side." Hylas had been drowned by water-nymphs who, entranced by his beauty, persuaded him to live with them in an underwater grotto. Hercules' grief was so extreme that cults were established to honor the lamented water-bearer; they closely resemble the cults of Bormus, an extraordinarily beautiful youth who at harvest time went to fetch water for the reapers and was dragged into the well by water-nymphs. Once more, the young corn god, the idealized lover, the sacrificial youth draw together, as in the story of *Billy Budd*.

Both the praise for a young lover and the lament for his death become central elements of the pastoral tradition; the love of two youthful shepherds was also a common device. Theocritus, in the third century B.C., composed a series of sentimental *Idylls* that showed boy-love as a natural, healthy expression of virility. Virgil's second "Ecologue" commemorated the love of Corydon and Alexis, and André Gide would recall their devotion in giving his fictionalized dialogue on homosexuality the title *Corydon*. Eventually, such motifs made their way into the literature of the Renaissance—in Daphnis' love for Ganymede in Richard Barnfield's *The*

Affectionate Shephearde (1594) and in the more muted devotion of Hobbinol and Colin in Edmund Spenser's *The Shepheardes Calender* (1579). In *Hero and Leander* (1598), Christopher Marlowe compares Leander—another drowned hero—to both Ganymede and Adonis. And in his play about the fall of the homosexual Edward II, when the nobles accuse the king's minion of wearing a jewel in his cap worth more than the crown, Queen Isabella complains, "Never doted Jove on Ganymede/So much as he on cursèd Gaveston." In the early years of our own century, the Dutch poet Willem de Merode languished in something very like house-arrest on the isolated farm to which his family removed him when his preference for adolescents threatened to cause scandal. His repressed tenderness and yearning flowed out in a poem entitled "Ganymede."

Though pastoral conventions were often heterosexualized, presenting exclusively the adoration of shepherd and shepherdess, the homosexual dimension would never be entirely suppressed. It emerges in the modern period in poems by Whitman and Gerard Manley Hopkins on boys bathing, in Proust's lyric explorations of "Bee and Orchid," and in such semi-pornographic classics as Richard Amory's *Loon Trilogy,* subtitled "a gay pastoral." García Lorca's "Ode to Walt Whitman" creates erotic beauty in the image of "the sun singing in the navels of boys playing baseball under the bridges." The sexual initiation of the narrator of Cocteau's *The White Paper* occurs in the sylvan park surrounding his father's château; significantly, his first awareness of homosexuality comes through the love-making of two dark-skinned gypsy boys; equally significantly, his own adored Dargello dies after swimming in the Seine. The idealized sexual memory of Gore Vidal's *The City and the Pillar* is set in a woodland retreat, on the bank of a river, where "the air was gold." In James Baldwin's *Giovanni's Room* the hero's most fulfilling sexual encounters occur in a room whose wallpaper recalls a dream of Eden, and where life "seemed to be occurring beneath the sea"; after murdering a wealthy homosexual, Giovanni is captured hiding under one of the bridges of the Seine.

Thus, as with the motif of warrior-lovers, classical elements

41

persist—though metamorphosed, sometimes corrupted or tainted by taboos—in the literature of male homosexuality. The initiation of a boy by an older man (often of darker race) is central to such works as James Fenimore Cooper's "Leatherstocking" novels, Herman Melville's *Moby Dick*, Mark Twain's *The Adventures of Huckleberry Finn* and William Faulkner's *The Bear*—an element which led critic Leslie Fiedler to assert that classic American literature contains a deep strain of latent homosexuality. The pederastic theme becomes overt in Thomas Mann's *Death in Venice,* Giorgio Bassani's *The Gold-Rimmed Spectacles* and many of the writings of Christopher Isherwood. It also emerges with nightmarish irony in Paul Bowles' story, "Pages from Cold Point." In William Inge's crude but powerful short play, "The Boy in the Basement" (1950), the cherished youth is a corpse awaiting the embalmer's art, and a ghastly symbol of the repression of homosexual desire.

Taking various form as the relationship between tyro and initiate, priest and acolyte, teacher and pupil, the ancient pederastic-pedagogic tradition yields such modern psychological studies as Stefan Zweig's *Episode in the Early Life of Privy Councillor D.* or Fritz Peters' *Finistere.* Peters' novel, which caused a sensation when it appeared in 1951, tells the story of a lonely American teenager who falls in love with the ruggedly handsome athletic director at his French boarding school. Their sexual affair begins soon after the teacher saves his pupil from drowning; emotionally, intellectually and physically, their intense relationship is a model of the Hellenic ideal. When the affair is revealed, the tormented boy drowns himself off the Brittany coast, thus once more re-enacting the death of Hylas, companion to the super-athlete Hercules. Vastly trivialized, the relationship of an athletic coach and a brilliant young track star becomes the subject of Patricia Nell Warren's *The Front Runner* (1974), commercially one of the most successful novels published in the wake of the Gay Liberation Movement in the United States. Numerous other novels and autobiographies have dealt with the prevalence of homosexuality among athletes, but few if any have the canny per-

suasiveness of "The Zenner Trophy," a story published by
Gore Vidal in 1956.

Boy-love remains, meanwhile, the most heavily tabooed
form of homosexual expression, and its defenders almost
invariably point to the Hellenic ideal—as in the ingenuously
"literary" photographs of semi-naked Greek and Sicilian
boys made by the Baron von Glöden. Both Jean Genet and
Allen Ginsberg have given impassioned arguments for intimate relations between men and boys, the latter stressing
psychic renewal for the man and education for the young
lover. But twentieth-century reality is better represented by
Alexander Ziegler's documentary novel, *The Consequence*
(1975), in which the Swiss author describes his own persecution for love of a teenager, and the far more grotesque sufferings of the boy himself.

It would, however, be naive to counter such contemporary
realities with images of the Greek world as an untroubled paradise for men who loved youths or other men. The exclusively
homosexual male was often pictured as laughable and despic-
able by the ancients. Solon condemned to death men who
sneaked into gymnasiums in Athens; in Sparta, Lycurgus
made sexual relations with a youth punishable by exile. Aris-
tophanes anticipated numberless modern critics in arguing
that the homosexual lacked the "spunk" to produce great
poetry, and even Plato in his later writings became increasingly critical of homosexual conduct. No doubt much homosexual activity then, as now, took place in secret and with a brand
of shame, but in certain institutionalized forms it was not only
permissible but, often, fully integrated into contemporary
social and ethical standards.

In the modern period Freudian psychology called special
attention to the "transitory" homosexual phase common to
adolescent boys, and consequently provoked fears that outright indulgence of such passions might curb the later evolu-
tion into heterosexuality. In fact, adolescent sexual ambiguity
—often reminiscent of the androgynous traditions of Greek
mythology and Renaissance poetry and drama—proved a rela-

43

tively safe theme for writers who would have felt intimidated by the portrayal of adult homosexuality. It was thus responsible for the creation of an entire sub-genre of homosexual fiction. The boarding school has been particularly important in the English literary tradition, but an early example—*Bertram Cope's Year* (1919) by Henry Blake Fuller—was published in the United States, and Robert Musil's tense scenes of sexual initiation in *Young Törless* (1906) have rarely been surpassed. Like Lawrence, Genet and the English playwright Joe Orton, Musil was acutely sensitive to the relationships between sexuality and power. A similar pathology is observable in much homosexual prison literature, including John Herbert's play *Fortune and Men's Eyes* (1967). But the confined environment of prison, school or army barracks may also offer alternatives to the conformist values of the outside world—as it does in Genet's *Thief's Journal* (1949), Manuel Puig's *Kiss of the Spider Woman* (1976) or Martin Sherman's drama *Bent* (1979), set in a Nazi concentration camp.

Nearly all the archetypes discussed in these pages flow together immediately beneath the surface of John Knowles' school novel, *A Separate Peace* (1959), which describes the adoration of a fellow pupil for the school athletic star. Overt sexuality is never described, since friendship is transformed into hatred before it can manifest itself as corporal love. The narrator proposes a "test" for his athletic friend, and in conforming to it the handsome and virile idol is mutilated and dies. Like countless other works, the novel illustrates the perils that beset the homosexual's pursuit of identity in a society that brands his intuitive longings as perverse and degraded.

The homosexual impulse turns inward, becomes neurotic, violent and self-destructive under the burden of guilt heaped on it by the Hebraic-Christian tradition. It was not homosexuality itself that the early Hebrews condemned, but the particular form of homosexual practice—including temple prostitution—they had known during their captivity in Babylon. Sexual acts between men were not regarded as a crime or a perversion or sickness, but as heresy—adherence to an unorthodox religious institution associated with the mystical cult of the Canaanite priests. Throughout the Old Testament the homosexual lover is excommunicated as a practitioner of the pagan rituals of the city of Sodom and the cult of Artemis. In early Rome homosexuality was not condemned but regulated; in 249 A.D., for example, the Emperor Philip attempted with limited success to outlaw the *exsoleti*, mercenary catamites who followed the legions. But when Christianity was adopted as the official state religion, heresy immediately became treason. During the fourth-century reign of Emperor Constantine, homosexuals were beheaded; under the fifth-century Emperor Valentinian, they were burned at the stake—supposedly by fire and brimstone. Such acts of "purification" would reach a frenzy during the Inquisition, when fully one-quarter of those burned at the stake were condemned for sodomy. Centuries later, the enlightened democrat Thomas Jefferson recommended substituting castration for capital punishment. It is noteworthy that in the long, grim history of torture, banishment and execution, it was almost exclusively homosexual acts between men that were officially condemned; the fact suggests that homosexual love itself was not initially the "abomination" in question, but the heresy of male temple prostitutes.

By the end of the twelfth century anti-homosexual prejudice had almost entirely usurped the humanistic tradition of Greek love. In Canto XV of the *Inferno*, Dante meets his former cherished comrade Brunetto Latine, condemned to eternal suffering for his "violence against nature." When questioned about his homosexual companions in the underworld, Latine responds that "all were clerks, and great scholars, and of great renown; by the same crime on earth defiled." Their number includes a distinguished grammarian, Priscian, whose position as a teacher of youth made him particularly liable to such vice. Boccaccio's *Decameron* offers a similar image in the ghost of Prince Lycidas, damned for thievery and homosexual affairs. The most repulsive characters in Chaucer's *Canterbury Tales* are the Summoner and the Pardoner—the one with scruffy hair, scabs and pimples on his face, the other effeminate in voice and manner. Riding together, they form a parody of knight and squire, and they sing an obscene love-song that almost certainly has homosexual implications. The Summoner is sexually promiscuous, and perhaps likes boys as well as girls; the Pardoner is described as a "gelding," but the charge of unmanliness may have to do with perversity rather than literal castration. While elements of an earlier tradition would persist in the sonnet and the pastoral lament, the homosexual as villain had now moved to center-stage. Even Christopher Marlowe's sympathetic portrayal of Edward II's homosexuality could not reverse the pattern. Based on Holinshed's *Chronicles,* from which Shakespeare drew many of his plots, it demonstrates how the king so doted on his French minion Gaveston that the court was corrupted, the land despoiled, and the people brought to the brink of civil war. In the centuries to follow—including our own—the homosexual would be acceptable in literature only as villain, corrupter of youth, effeminate clown, criminal or corpse.

A further consequence of Judeo-Christian prohibitions is that homosexual practice (and particularly sodomy) is increasingly associated with the decadence and exoticism of an imaginary Orient. By the mid-nineteenth century this never-never land had become a highly elaborated cultural abstraction, of such potency that its distortions persist to the present day. The publishing sensation of 1885 in England was the appearance of the first ten volumes of the *Book of the Thousand and One Nights,* translated by Sir Richard Burton. An inveterate traveler and anthropological scholar, his early researches had included an official report on male bordellos in Karachi. Burton's amazing adventures made him the most famous travel writer of all time, and wherever he went, he gathered information on local sexual customs. His translation of what was popularly known as *The Arabian Nights* included entire erotic passages omitted by previous translators—including those dealing with pederasty, bestiality and female orgasm. Even more sensational, however, was the rambling "Terminal Essay" summarizing his observations on sexual customs. One part of the essay was devoted to homosexual practices, and out of the jumble of gossip, genuine scholarship and wild hypothesis emerged the influential theory of the "Sotadic Zone.'' Homosexuality, Burton argued, was ''geographic and climatic,'' located approximately between the latitudes of 43 and 30 degrees, within which homosexuality flourished without social restraint. Including southern Spain, France and Italy, the zone stretched from Greece across Turkey and Afghanistan and ultimately took in not only most of the Near and Far East, but by some geographical *reductio ad absurdam,* the entire hemisphere of pre-Columbian America. Burton insisted that:

> Within the Sotadic Zone, the vice is popular and endemic, held at the worst to be a mere peccadillo, while the races to the north and south of the limits here defined practise it only sporadically amid the opprobrium of their fellows who, as a rule, are physically incapable of performing the operation and look upon it with the liveliest disgust.

Even Burton sensed that what he was actually describing was not a geographic distinction but a theological boundary erected by Christendom.

Sir Richard Burton was scarcely alone in forming the popular concept of homosexuality as a ''vice'' of heathen and hot-blooded men, but his ''Terminal Essay'' unintentionally served to authenticate a superstition that had theological origins. The Arab became a common symbol of pederastic excess, but it was Italy that became the Sotadic ''capital'' in the Occidental imagination, and above all Venice, with its trading ties to the East. In *The Unfortunate Traveler* (1594), Thomas Nashe called Venice ''the Sodom of Italy,'' and Byron termed it ''the sea-Sodom of Italy.'' For countless homosexuals, Italy was an ideal; significantly, when Karl Heinrich Ulrichs fled Germany, he went directly to Naples, and then to Aquila, where he spent the last twelve years of his life. Baron Corvo's ''disguised'' idyll of the love of an English traveler for an Italian boy, *The Desire and Pursuit of the Whole,* composed shortly before the author's death in 1913, is subtitled ''A Romance of Modern Venice.'' In Donald Windham's *Two People* (1965) a young American businessman, estranged from his wife, falls in love with an Italian boy during a visit to Rome. The definitive link between Italy and homosexual awakening is, of course, to be found on every page of Thomas Mann's *Death in Venice*. The explicit homosexual scenes in John Horne Burns' *The Gallery* (1946) take place in Naples, and the expatriated American hero of *Giovanni's Room* has his first adult homosexual experience with a handsome, sensuous Italian. In linking homosexuality, death and the Italian setting, Wolfgang Koeppen's *Death in Rome* (1954) pointedly echoes the dominant motifs of *Death in Venice*. As a comic variation on the theme, in Bernard Malamud's *Pictures of Fidelman* (1969), the American schlemiel is sodomized by a lusty Venetian glass-blower.

Homosexual literature is, indeed, filled with characters who might in this context be regarded as "symbolic Italians," congenital representatives of the Sotadic temperament. The men of darker skin who so frequently appear as objects of erotic fantasy or sexual experimentation add racial taboo to religious proscription; the taboo of class compounds the forbidden aspect of homosexual love, and as Christopher Isherwood has pointed out, it was almost a fetish for upper-class Englishmen to pursue working-class boys—between the wars, in Germany and Austria, but most frequently in France, Italy and North Africa. Implicit in such obsessions is the myth of the superior virility of "primitive" or working-class men. The guilt produced by the violation of multiple taboos frequently produces grotesque and tragic results, as the earlier rites of initiation become savage rites of exorcism. In Tennessee Williams' "Desire and the Black Masseur," a timid, frail, middle-aged man submits to sadomasochistic tortures at the hands of a massive Negro who ultimately kills and eats him. In the final scenes, the voice of a neighborhood preacher is heard shouting, "Suffer, suffer, suffer!" The beautiful Luc, a French visitor to New York in Yves Navarre's *Sweet Tooth* (1973), undergoes an even more brutal death at the hands of a handsome Negro. When Andrew first strikes him, Luc remembers a book he had read as a child in which a black man dies in the arms of a Missionary Priest: "Luc tries to sit up. Andrew clobbers him with a good resounding slap. Luc falls back on the Missionary's lap. The Missionary blesses him. . . .

Ceremonial." In a room that "smells like hell," two potential lovers—one black, the other white—beat each other into unconsciousness in Le Roi Jones' *The Toilet* (1967).

The cherished "dark companion" of earlier initiation rites thus becomes the dark avenger, often satanic in his manifestations. Corrupted and faded, the beautiful Hylas becomes the fop, the hustler, the agonized adolescent driven to suicide, or the anarchic "angels" of Genet's twilight world. Similarly, and though many transvestites are exclusively heterosexual, transvestism degenerates into a parody of the effeminate and ineffectual male, a subject for cheap farce, burlesque comedies of errors and "safe" glimpses of homosexual waywardness. It becomes, as well, a cherished cinematic device, as in Billy Wilder's *Some Like It Hot*, whose title recalls Shakespeare's *As You Like It*, in which Rosalind appears disguised as the celebrated Ganymede.

In an essay entitled "The Homosexual Villain" written in 1954, Norman Mailer sought to analyze the unpleasant, often sinister presentation of homosexual characters in his own early writings. "At the time I wrote these novels," he remarked, "I was consciously sincere. I did believe—as so many heterosexuals believe—that there was an intrinsic relation between homosexuality and 'evil,' and it seemed perfectly natural to me, as well as *symbolically* just, to treat the subject in such a way." In attempting to come to terms with these clichés, the author himself achieved a new awareness of the sinister correlations between sexual repression and political oppression: "I suppose I can say that for the first time I understood homosexual persecution to be a political act and a reactionary act, and I was properly ashamed of myself." Unhappily, even the most committed defenders of homosexuality are likely to embrace similar stereotypes. Mart Crowley's *The Boys in the Band,* which opened in New York in 1968, became the first play dealing exclusively with a homosexual milieu to achieve broad popular success; it was acclaimed as "the frankest and funniest homosexual play ever put on a stage," and enjoyed similar esteem as a popular motion picture. Yet *Boys in the Band* parades the very clichés of vicious queen, closet-case, brainless hustler, promiscuity and insecurity under which homosexuals have suffered for centuries. That such types and such patterns of behavior "really" exist is unquestionable, as do the heterosexual sterotypes of the jealous husband, absentminded professor, overbearing mother and power-hungry tycoon. The difference between soap opera and art, however, is that the latter probes sterotypes to reveal the depth and uniqueness of the individual character. This is what Tennessee Williams achieves with the figure of the hustler in "One Arm" or the study of promiscuity in "Two on a Party." In Ernest Hemingway's "Mother of a Queen" the effeminate male is a vicious, one-dimensional caricature, but in Yukio Mishima's "Onnagata" transvestism is depicted as an art of ultimate grace and refinement, and in Hubert Selby's "The Queen is Dead," from *Last Exit to Brooklyn* (1964), Georgette's monologue moves from shrill hysteria to genuinely tragic passion.

A rich body of literature has been created on the theme of the "tragic queen," a figure whose wit and superficial gaiety are often the mask for profound despair. Here one is not concerned with simple transvestism, which may be a passing fancy or a carnival joke, but a man in flight from his own virility—in flight, often, from the coarse, insensitive image that the heterosexual majority approves as "a man's man." Such persons may not, literally, want to *be* women; in fact, few homosexual transvestites are actually transsexuals. But they embrace a feminine ideal and, with it, notions of delicacy and tenderness and vulnerability that are typically labeled as "feminine" by societies that insist only women should be sexually attracted to men. In Nathanael West's novel of Hollywood sham and imposture, *The Day of the Locust* (1939), the only convincingly womanly character is a female-impersonator who sings in a night-club; this compassionate portrayal by a heterosexual writer is worth quoting for its rare insight:

He had a soft, throbbing voice and his gestures were matronly, tender and aborted, a series of unconscious caresses. What he was doing was in no sense parody; it was too simple and restrained. It wasn't even theatrical. This dark young man with his thin, hairless arms and soft, rounded shoulders, who rocked an imaginary cradle as he crooned, was really a woman.

John Rechy's *City of Night* (1963) presents two queens who are equally successful in presenting womanliness rather than a parody of woman. One is the celebrated "Miss Destiny," whose Hollywood wedding, complete with flowing white gown and veil, becomes a legend for the other characters in the novel. The second is Trudi, who "has most accurately been able to duplicate the female stance so that, unlike most other queens, she has not become the parody of a woman." But parody is often present in the figure of the bitchy queen who consciously cultivates the coarseness of a fishwife as well as the possessive and mercenary qualities that are part of an accepted heterosexual stereotype of the wife's negative attributes. Again, whether as "evil queen" or "tragic queen," the homosexual is reflecting or inverting patterns imposed by the heterosexual dictatorship. The full range of transvestite responses is examined in the films of Andy Warhol.

The despair felt by Selby's Georgette or by the nameless narrator of Eduardo Gudiño Kieffer's "A Sinner's Notebook" at belonging to neither sex is a moving symbol of the identity-crisis suffered by countless homosexuals. Rarely is a male able to embrace a female identity without guilt or anxiety; Mishima's Onnagata is an exception because his "impersonation" is within a respected tradition, and in "Snow White Revisited," a short story by Brazilian writer Darcy Penteado, the transvestite hero finally succeeds in being "enshrined" as a princess only after decades of persecution and rejection. More typical of the transvestite's dilemma is the anonymous tale of "The Marquis de Saint-Brissac," in which the impersonation ends in suicide. The universality of the phenomenon symbolized by such figures is underscored in "Miss Knight," one of the stories Robert McAlmon published in *Distinguished Air* in 1925, and which presents a compulsive, cocaine-sniffing, vulgar American tourist in Berlin; despite burly shoulders and the repeated boast that "I'm so glad I'm a real man,"

51

Charlie Knight has a particular fondness for elegant evening dresses. Miss Knight disappears unexpectedly from Berlin, but a few weeks later sends her friends a postcard from Paris. "That one!" a character remarks. "If she was run over by a truck or a steam roller she'd turn up, about to appear in Paris, or London, or Madrid, or Singapore. She's just that international."

In the selections that follow, numerous other figures emerge as "international." They highlight common elements in homosexual experience, but they also suggest an even more universal dimension: the search for self, the hunger for love and recognition, the conflict between instinct and convention, the need for ritual. These motifs occur and reoccur in all literatures. Centuries of persecution and misrepresentation give the homosexual writer a particular mandate, but that must not obscure his ties and his obligations to a larger community of suffering and joy and aspiration. The relatively new liberties of expression available to many writers sometimes obscure that wider dimension; intoxicated by the freedom to explore sexual experience, homosexual and heterosexual alike may end by reducing human relationships to genital contacts. And the recent mode of creating homosexual versions of such cookie-cutter clichés of popular literature as the western, science fiction, the detective story and the sentimental romance does no service either to literature or to sexual liberation. The right openly to embrace a homosexual life-style can paradoxically end by creating self-styled ghettos as isolating as the old conspiracies of repression and silence. There is a danger, too, that homosexuality becomes merely another "fashion" in liberal societies; indeed, the feminist Kate Millett has described the homosexual as "our current nigger of love."

The new freedoms clearly bring new dangers and responsibilities in their wake. Prophetically, Norman Mailer concluded his essay on "The Homosexual as Villain" with the following paragraph:

If the homosexual is ever to achieve real social equality and acceptance, he too will have to work the hard row of shedding his own prejudices. Driven into defiance, it is natural if regrettable, that many homosexuals go to the direction of assuming that there is something intrinsically superior in homosexuality, and carried far enough it is a viewpoint which is as stultifying, as ridiculous, and as anti-human as the heterosexual's prejudice. Finally, heterosexuals are people too, and the hope of acceptance, tolerance and sympathy must rest on this mutual appreciation.

The challenge implicit in Mailer's remarks is immense, but homosexuals know only too well what it means to struggle against seemingly impossible odds. Many have been broken by the struggle; but the survivors have often developed a remarkable muscularity of spirit. This volume commemorates both the victims and the victors.

VILHELM EKELUND

THE FRIENDS

O auch mir ist das Andenken an unsere
Spaziergänge das heiligste das ich kenne.

—Heinrich Wackenroder
Briefe an L. Tieck

O hour of melancholy in the great city
when the pale sun sinks below the dull gliding edge
of dark blue hanging smoke—
no lights have been turned on yet. In coal blue July evening
Berlin hides.
A horse lies dead on the street, a white and gray skeleton.
Completely deafening
minute after minute
like a clap of thunder
train on the elevated:

Hallesches Thor

Every evening when I wander home
I go here.

But in the middle of the confused roar,
over the scream and din
it can happen sometimes
that a holy silence
falls over my soul:
a picture appears.

In the summer first
it is a morning—
here lay small quiet houses
behind garden plots and hedges and trees
going back a hundred years.
Two figures approach, catch a glimpse of each other,
and the soul itself lifts, blessedly enlarged,
an infinite space
trembling with
light
shaking with tenderness.

Out in the sunny space
they step quietly—
and now—silent . . .
     stay,
two hands
bend over
the book,
cheeks meet
softly radiating
warmth to each other,
caressing arms
lay themselves
on young smooth shoulders,
eyes darken
with faithfulness,
glance up and
meet in radiant
embrace of love.

From the dust and noise
into the dimness of the trees along the quay I wander
where homeless ones sleep

on the benches—
heads sunk in their hands
children cry softly in the darkness . . .

SYMPOSIUM

Yes, you are our beautiful land,
the spirit in living blood;
yes, you bear in your figure's liveliness,
in your fine limbs' noble construction,
in your cheeks' flushed sheen,
in the strength of your deeply glancing eyes
all the light of this beautiful land.

But of your forehead's purity:

music
of clear gentle verse.

Yes, a song to you should bear
in words newly minted,
words warmly beaming
words of fragrance and fine air
all the beauty of our land:

clear land, southerly,
caressed by mild light
and the reflecting sea's softly shimmering blue veil:

land where laurels bloom,
the soft plantains endure the winter
and Zeus's beautiful tree
on strong, lifted trunk
light embracing powerful
lifts the arching of the noble crown
and Hyacinthus, lily above lilies,
bears in purpureal sign
the lament of the God.

OCTOBER

When will I see you again,
dear one?

The last time:
evening dark with autumn rain.
Then you came there in the pale lantern light
beneath the large spacious leaves of the walnut trees—
soon soon my heart said to me . . .

Around your mouth,
precociously serious,
playfully subdued jesting,
yet to me you hardly seemed happy
your arm on the neck of your friend,
and your hand fell
with its fine, tired fingers
over his shoulder.
So you walked away.
Ah your walk,
where shall I find
words soaring
words light enough
for your knees' soft bending,
slight round thighs,
light submissive line of your delicate calves?

NOTHING, NOTHING ELSE IN THE WORLD. . .

Nothing, nothing else in the world can warm my soul now
except to write poems about you.
I want to search out words that cool and burn like the
     caress of your skin,

CALAMUS

words with the shimmer of your blood's smooth light
and the luster of your eyes' deep, hard glance,
shining there under the marble whiteness of your forehead.
I want to seize the stride and stretch of your limbs,
the languid smoothness of your movements,
in verses of consuming voluptuousness.

—Translated by Sam Charters

ROBERT MUSIL

YOUNG TÖRLESS

There came two public holidays; and since they fell on a Monday and Tuesday, the headmaster gave the boys Saturday off as well, so that they had four days free. For Törless this was still too short a time to make the long journey home worth while; and he had therefore hoped that at any rate his parents would come and see him. However, his father was kept by urgent affairs at his government office, and his mother did not feel well enough to face the strain of travelling alone.

But when Törless received his parents' letter, in which they told him they could not come and added many affectionate words of comfort, he suddenly realised that this actually suited him very well. He knew now that it would have been almost an interruption—at least it would have embarrassed him considerably—if he had had to face his parents just at this stage.

Many of the boys had invitations to estates in the district. Dschjusch, whose parents owned a fine property at the distance of a day's drive from the little town, was one of those who went away, and with him went Beineberg, Reiting, and Hofmeier. Basini had also been asked, but Reiting had bidden him refuse. Törless excused himself on the grounds that he did not know for certain whether his parents might not come after all; he felt totally disinclined for innocent, cheerful frolics and amusements.

By noon on Saturday the great building was silent and almost quite deserted.

When Törless walked through the empty corridors, they echoed from end to end. There was nobody to bother about him, for most of the masters had also gone away for a few days' shooting or the like. It was only at meals, which were now served in a small room next to the deserted refectory, that the few remaining boys saw each other. When they left the table they once more took their separate ways through the many corridors and class-rooms; it was as if the silence of the building had swallowed them up, and whatever life they led in these intervals seemed to be of no more interest to anyone than that of the spiders and centipedes in the cellars and attics.

Of Törless's class the only two left were himself and Basini, with the exception of a few boys in the sick-bay. When leaving, Reiting had exchanged a few words in private with Törless in the matter of Basini, for he was afraid that Basini might make use of the opportunity to seek protection from one of the masters; he had therefore impressed it on Törless to keep a sharp eye on him.

However, there was no need of that to concentrate Törless's attention on Basini.

Scarcely had the uproar faded away—the carriages driving to the door, the servants carrying valises, the boys joking and shouting good-bye to each other—when the consciousness of being alone with Basini took complete possession of Törless's mind.

It was after the first midday meal. Basini sat in his place in front, writing a letter. Törless had gone to a corner right at the back of the room and was trying to read.

It was for the first time again the volume of Kant, and the situation was just as he had pictured it: in front there sat Basini, at the back himself, holding Basini with his gaze, boring holes into him with his eyes. And it was like this that

60

he wanted to read: penetrating deeper into Basini at the end of every page. That was how it must be; in this way he must find the truth without losing grip on life, living, complicated, ambiguous life....

But it would not work. This was what always happened when he had thought something out all too carefully in advance. It was too unspontaneous, and his mood swiftly lapsed into a dense, gluey boredom, which stuck odiously to every one of his all too deliberate attempts to get on with his reading.

In a fury, Törless threw the book on the floor. Basini looked round with a start, but at once turned away again and hurriedly went on writing.

So the hours crept on towards dusk. Törless sat there in a stupor. The only thing that struck clearly into his awareness —out of a muffled, buzzing, whirring state of generalised sensation—was the ticking of his pocket-watch. It was like a little tail wagging on the sluggish body of the creeping hours. The room became blurred . . . Surely Basini could no longer be writing . . . 'Aha, he probably doesn't dare to light a lamp,' Törless thought to himself. But was he still sitting over there in his place at all? Törless had been gazing out into the bleak, twilit landscape and now had to accustom his eyes again to the darkness of the room. Oh yes, there he was. There, that motionless shadow, that would be Basini all right. And now he even heaved a sigh—once, twice. He hadn't gone to sleep, had he?

A servant came in and lit the lamps. Basini started up and rubbed his eyes. Then he took a book out of his desk and began to apply himself to it.

Törless could hardly prevent himself from speaking to him, and in order to avoid that he hurried out of the room.

In the night Törless was not far from falling upon Basini, such a murderous lust had awakened in him after the anguish of that senseless, stupefying day. By good fortune sleep overtook him just in time.

The next day passed. It brought nothing but the same bleak

and barren quietness. The silence and suspense worked on Törless's overwrought nerves; the ceaseless strain on his attention consumed all his mental powers, so that he was incapable of framing any thought at all.

Disappointed, dissatisfied with himself to the point of the most extreme doubt, he felt utterly mangled. He went to bed early.

He had for a long time been lying in an uneasy, feverishly hot half-sleep when he heard Basini coming.

Lying motionless, with his eyes he followed the dark figure walking past the end of his bed. He heard the other undressing, and then the rustling of the blankets being pulled over the body.

He held his breath, but he could not manage to hear any more. Nevertheless he did not lose the feeling that Basini was not asleep either, but was straining to hear through the darkness, just like himself.

So the quarter-hours passed . . . hours passed. Only now and then the stillness was broken by the faint sound of the bodies stirring, each in its bed.

Törless was in a queer state that kept him awake. Yesterday it had been sensual pictures in his imagination that had made him feverish. Only right at the end had they taken a turn towards Basini, as it were rearing up under the inexorable hand of sleep, which then blotted them out; and it was precisely of this that he had the vaguest and most shadowy memory. But tonight it had from the very beginning been nothing other than an impelling urge to get up and go over to Basini. So long as he had had the feeling that Basini was awake and listening for whatever sounds he might make, it had been scarcely endurable; and now that Basini was apparently asleep, it was even worse, for there was a cruel excitement in the thought of falling upon the sleeper as upon a prey.

Törless could already feel the movements of rising up and getting out of bed twitching in all his muscles. But still he could not yet shake off his immobility.

'And what am I going to do, anyway, if I do go over to him?' he wondered, in his panic almost speaking the words aloud. And he had to admit to himself that the cruelty and lust in him had no real object. He would have been at a loss if he had now really set upon Basini. Surely he did not want to beat him? God forbid! Well then, in what way was his wild sensual excitement to get fulfillment from Basini? Instinctively he revolted at the thought of the various little vices that boys went in for. Expose himself to another person like that? Never!

But in the same measure as this revulsion grew the urge to go over to Basini also became stronger. Finally Törless was completely penetrated with the sense of how absurd such an act was, and yet a positively physical compulsion seemed to be drawing him out of bed as on a rope. And while his mind grew blank and he merely kept on telling himself, over and over again, that it would be best to go to sleep now if he could, he was mechanically rising up in the bed. Very slowly—and he could feel how the emotional urge was gaining, inch by inch, over the resistance in him—he began to sit up. First one arm moved . . . then he propped himself on one elbow, then pushed one knee out from under the bed-clothes . . . and then . . . suddenly he was racing, barefoot, on tip-toe, over to Basini, and sat down on the edge of Basini's bed.

Basini was asleep.

He looked as if he were having pleasant dreams.

Törless was still not in control of his actions. For a moment he sat still, staring into the sleeper's face. Through his brain there jerked those short, ragged thoughts which do no more, it seems, than record what a situation is, those flashes of thought one has when losing one's balance, or falling from a height, or when some object is torn from one's grasp. And without knowing what he was doing he gripped Basini by the shoulder and shook him out of his sleep.

Basini stretched indolently a few times. Then he started up and gazed at Törless with sleepy, stupefied eyes.

A shock went through Törless. He was utterly confused; now all at once he realised what he had done, and he did not know what he was to do next. He was frightfully ashamed. His heart thudded loudly. Words of explanation and excuse hovered on the tip of his tongue. He would ask Basini if he had any matches, if he could tell him the time . . .

Basini was still goggling at him with uncomprehending eyes.

Now, without having uttered a word, Törless withdrew his arm, now he slid off the bed and was about to creep back soundlessly into his own bed—and at this moment Basini seemed to grasp the situation and sat bolt upright.

Törless stopped irresolutely at the foot of the bed.

Basini glanced at him once more, questioningly, searchingly, and then got out of bed, slipped into coat and slippers and went padding off towards the door. And in a flash Törless became sure of what he had long suspected: that his had happened to Basini many times before.

In passing his bed, Törless took the key to the cubby-hole, which he had been keeping hidden under his pillow.

Basini walked straight on ahead of him, up to the attics. He seemed in the meantime to have become thoroughly familiar with the way that had once been kept so secret from him. He steadied the crate while Törless stepped down on to it, he cleared the scenery to one side, carefully, with gingerly movements, like a well-trained flunkey.

Törless unlocked the door, and they went in. With his back to Basini, he lit the little lamp.

When he turned round, Basini was standing there naked.

Involuntarily Törless fell back a step. The sudden sight of this naked snow-white body, with the red of the walls dark as blood behind it, dazzled and bewildered him. Basini was beautifully built; his body, lacking almost any sign of male development, was of a chaste, slender willowyness, like that of a young girl. And Törless felt this nakedness lighting up in his nerves, like hot white flames. He could not shake off the spell of this beauty. He had never known before what beauty was. For what was art to him at his age, what—after all—did he know of that? Up to a certain age, if one has grown up in the open air, art is simply unintelligible, a bore!

And here now it had come to him on the paths of sexuality . . . secretly, ambushing him . . . There was an infatuating warm exhalation coming from the bare skin, a soft, lecherous cajolery. And yet there was something about it that was so solemn and compelling as to make one almost clasp one's hands in awe.

But after the first shock Törless was as ashamed of the one reaction as of the other. 'It's a man, damn it!' The thought enraged him, and yet it seemed to him as though a girl could not be different.

In his shame he spoke hectoringly to Basini: "What on earth d'you think you're doing? Get back into your things this minute!"

Now it was Basini who seemed taken aback. Hesitantly, and without shifting his gaze from Törless, he picked up his coat from the floor.

"Sit down—there!" Törless ordered. Basini obeyed. Törless leaned against the wall, with his arms crossed behind his back.

"Why did you undress? What did you want of me?"

"Well, I thought . . ."

He paused hesitantly.

"What did you think?"

"The others . . ."

"What about the others?"

"Beineberg and Reiting . . ."

"What about Beineberg and Reiting? What did they do? You've got to tell me everything! That's what I want. See? Although I've heard about it from them, of course." At this clumsy lie Törless blushed.

Basini bit his lips.

"Well? Get on with it!"

"No, don't make me tell! Please don't make me! I'll do anything you want me to. But don't make me tell about it. . . . Oh, you have such a special way of tormenting me . . . !" Hatred, fear, and an imploring plea for mercy were all mingled in Basini's gaze.

Törless involuntarily modified his attitude. "I don't want to torment you at all. I only mean to make you tell the whole truth yourself. Perhaps for your own good."

"But, look, I haven't done anything specially worth telling about."

"Oh, haven't you? So why did you undress, then?"

"That's what they wanted."

"And why did you do what they wanted? So you're a coward, eh? A miserable coward?"

"No, I'm not a coward! Don't say that!"

"Shut up! If you're afraid of being beaten by them, you might find being beaten by me was something to remember!"

"But it's not the beatings they give me that I'm afraid of!"

"Oh? What is it then?"

By now Törless was speaking calmly again. He was already annoyed at his crude threat. But it had escaped him involuntarily, solely because it seemed to him that Basini stood up to him more than to the others.

"Well, if you're not afraid. as you say, what's the matter with you?"

"They say if I do whatever they tell me to, after some time I shall be forgiven everything."

"By the two of them?"

"No, altogether."

"How can they promise that? *I* have to be considered too!"

"They say they'll manage that all right."

This gave Törless a shock. Beineberg's words about Reiting's dealing with him, if he got the chance, in exactly the same way as with Basini now came back to him. And if it really came to a plot against him, how was he to cope with it? He was no match for the two of them in that sort of thing. How far would they go? The same as with Basini? . . . Everything in him revolted at the perfidious idea.

Minutes passed between him and Basini. He knew that he lacked the daring and endurance necessary for such intrigues, though of course only because he was too little interested in that sort of thing, only because he never felt his whole personality involved. He had always had more to lose than to gain there. But if it should ever happen to be the other way, there would, he felt, be quite a different kind of toughness and courage in him. Only one must know when it was time to stake everything.

"Did they say anything more about it—how they think they can do it? I mean, that about me."

"More? No. They only said they'd see to it all right."

And yet . . . there was danger now . . . somewhere lying in wait . . . lying in ambush for Törless . . . every step could run him into a gin-trap, every night might be the last before the fight. There was tremendous insecurity in this thought. Here was no more idle drifting along, no more toying with enigmatic visions—this had hard corners and was tangible reality.

Törless spoke again.

"And what do they do with you?"

Basini was silent.

"If you're serious about reforming, you have to tell me everything."

"They make me undress."

"Yes, yes, I see that for myself . . . And then?"

A little time passed, and then suddenly Basini said: "Various things." He said it with an effeminate, coy expression.

"So you're their—mi—mistress?"

"Oh no, I'm their friend!"

"How can you have the nerve to say that!"

"They say so themselves."

"What!"

"Yes, Reiting does."

"Oh, Reiting does?"

"Yes, he's very nice to me. Mostly I have to undress and read him something out of history-books—about Rome and the emperors, or the Borgias, or Timur Khan . . . oh well, you know, all that sort of big, bloody stuff. Then he's even affectionate to me. . . . And then afterwards he generally beats me."

"After what? Oh, I see!"

"Yes. He says, if he didn't beat me, he wouldn't be able to help thinking I was a man, and then he couldn't let himself be so soft and affectionate to me. But like that, he says, I'm his chattel, and so then he doesn't mind."

"And Beineberg?"

"Oh, Beineberg's beastly. Don't you think too his breath smells bad?"

"Shut up! What I think is no business of yours! Tell me what Beineberg does with you!"

"Well, the same as Reiting, only . . . But you mustn't go yelling at me again. . . ."

"Get on with it."

"Only . . . he goes about it differently. First of all he gives me long talks about my soul. He says I've sullied it, but so to speak only the outermost forecourt of it. In relation to the innermost, he says, this is something that doesn't matter at all, it's only external. But one must kill it. In that way many people have stopped being sinners and become saints. So from a higher point of view sin isn't so bad, only one must carry it to the extreme, so that it breaks off of its own accord, he says. He makes me sit and stare into a prism. . . ."

"He hypnotises you?"

"No, he says it's just that he must make all the things floating about on the surface of my soul go to sleep and become powerless. It's only then he can have intercourse with my soul itself."

"And how, may I ask, does he have intercourse with it?"

"That's an experiment he hasn't ever brought off yet. He sits there, and I have to get quite dull and drowsy from staring into the glass. Then suddenly he orders me to bark. He tells me exactly how to do it—quietly, more whimpering—the way a dog whines in its sleep."

"What's that good for?"

"Nobody knows what it's good for. And he also makes me grunt like a pig and keeps on and on telling me there's something of a pig about me, in me. But he doesn't mean it offensively, he just keeps on repeating it quite softly and nicely, in order—this is what he says—in order to imprint it firmly on my nerves. You see, he says it's possible one of my former lives was that of a pig and it must be lured out so as to render it harmless."

"And you believe all that stuff?"

"Good lord, no! I don't think he believes it himself. And then in the end he's always quite different, anyway. How on earth should I believe such things? Who believes in a soul these days anyway? And as for transmigration of souls———! I know quite well I slipped. But I've always hoped I'd be able to make up for it again. There isn't any hocus-pocus needed for that. Not that I spend any time racking my brains about how I ever came to go wrong. A thing like that comes on you so quickly, all by itself. It's only afterwards you notice that you've done something silly. But if he gets his fun out of looking for something supernatural behind it, let him, for all I care. For the present, after all, I've got to do what he wants. Only I wish he'd leave off sticking pins in me. . . ."

"What?"

"Pricking me with a pin—not hard, you know, only just to see how I react—to see if something doesn't manifest itself at some point or other on the body. But it does *hurt*. The fact is, he says the doctors don't understand anything about it. I don't remember now how he proves all this, all I remember is he talks a lot about fakirs and how when they see their souls they're supposed to be insensitive to physical pain."

"Oh yes, I know those ideas. But you yourself say that's not all."

"No, it certainly isn't all. But I also said I think this is just a way of going about it. Afterwards there are always long times—as much as a quarter of an hour—when he doesn't say anything and I don't know what's going on in him. But after that he suddenly breaks out and demands services from me— as if he were possessed—much worse than Reiting."

"And you do everything that's demanded of you?"

"What else can I do? I want to become a decent person again and be left in peace."

"But whatever happens in the meantime won't matter to you at all?"

"Well, I can't help it, can I?"

"Now pay attention to me and answer my questions. How could you steal?"

"How? Look, it's like this, I needed money urgently. I was in debt to the tuck-shop man, and he wouldn't wait any longer. Then I really did believe there was money coming for me just at that time. None of the other fellows would lend me any. Some of them hadn't got any themselves, and the saving ones are always just glad if someone who isn't like that gets short towards the end of the month. Honestly, I didn't want to cheat anyone. I only wanted to borrow it secretly. . . ."

"That's not what I mean," Törless said impatiently, interrupting this story, which it was obviously a relief for Basini to tell. "What I'm asking is *how*—how were you able to do it, what did you feel like? What went on in you at that moment?"

"Oh well—nothing, really. After all, it was only a moment, I didn't feel anything, I didn't think about anything, simply it had suddenly happened."

"But the first time with Reiting? The first time he demanded those things of you? You know what I mean. . . ."

"Oh, I didn't like it, of course. Because it had to be done just like that, being ordered to. Otherwise—well, just how many of the fellows do such things of their own accord, for the fun of it, without the others knowing anything? I dare say it's not so bad then."

"But you did it on being ordered to. You debased yourself. Just as if you had crawled into the muck because someone else wanted you to."

"Oh, I grant that. But I had to."

"No, you didn't have to." -

"They would have beaten me and reported me. Think how I would have got into disgrace."

"All right then, let's leave that. There's something else I want to know. Listen. I know you've spent a lot of money with Božena. You've boasted to her and thrown your weight about and made out what a man you are. So you want to be a man? Not just boasting and pretending to be—but with your whole soul? Now look, then suddenly someone demands such a humiliating service from you, and in the same moment you feel you're too cowardly to say no—doesn't it make a split go through your whole being? A horror—something you can't describe—as though something unutterable had happened inside you?"

"Lord! I don't know what you mean. I don't know what you're getting at. I can't tell you anything—anything at all—about that."

"Now attend. I'm going to order you to get undressed again."

Basini smiled.

"And to lie down flat on the floor there in front of me. Don't

70

laugh! I'm really ordering you to! D'you *hear* me? If you don't obey instantly, you'll see what you're in for when Reiting comes back! . . . That's right. So now you're lying naked on the ground in front of me. You're trembling, too. Are you cold? I could spit on your naked body now if I wanted to. Just press your head right on to the floor. Doesn't the dust on the boards look queer? Like a landscape full of clouds and lumps of rock as big as houses? I could stick pins into you. There are still some over there in the corner, by the lamp. D'you feel them in your skin even now? . . . But I don't mean to do that. I could make you bark, the way Beineberg does, and make you eat dust like a pig. I could make you do movements—oh, you know—and at the same time you would have to sigh: 'Oh, my dear Moth————!'" But Törless broke off abruptly in the midst of this sacrilege. "But I don't mean to—don't mean to—do you understand?"

Basini wept. "You're tormenting me . . ."

"Yes, I'm tormenting you. But that's not what I'm after. There's just one thing I want to know: when I drive all that into you like knives, what goes on in you? What happens inside you? Does something burst in you? Tell me! Does it smash like a glass that suddenly flies into thousands of splinters before there's been even a little crack in it? Doesn't the picture you've made of yourself go out like a candle? Doesn't something else leap into its place, the way the pictures in the magic-lantern leap out of the darkness? Don't you *understand* what I mean? I can't explain it for you any better. You must tell me yourself . . .!"

Basini wept without stopping. His girlish shoulders jerked. All he could get out was to the same effect: "I don't know what you're after, I can't explain anything to you, it happens just in a moment, and then nothing different can happen, you'd do just the same as me."

Törless was silent. He remained leaning against the wall, exhausted, motionless, blankly staring straight in front of him.

'If you were in my situation, you would do just the same,' Basini had said. Seen thus, what had happened appeared a simple necessity, straightforward and uncomplicated.

Törless's self-awareness rebelled in blazing contempt

against the mere suggestion. And yet this rebellion on the part of his whole being seemed to offer him no satisfactory guarantee . . . '. . . yes, *I* should have more character than he has, *I* shouldn't put up with such outrageous demands—but does it really matter? Does it matter that I should act differently, from firmness, from decency, from—oh, for all sorts of reasons that at the moment don't interest me in the least? No, what counts is not how I should act, but the fact that if I were ever really to act as Basini has done, I should have just as little sense of anything extraordinary about it as he has. This is the heart of the matter: my feeling about myself would be exactly as simple and clear of ambiguity as his feeling about himself . . .'

This thought—flashing through his mind in half-coherent snatches of sentences that ran over into each other and kept beginning all over again—added to his contempt for Basini a very private, quiet pain that touched his inmost balance at a much deeper point than any moral consideration could. It came from his awareness of a sensation he had briefly had before and which he could not get rid of. The fact was that when Basini's words revealed to him the danger potentially menacing him from Reiting and Beineberg, he had simply been startled. He had been startled as by a sudden assault, and without stopping to think had in a flash looked round for cover and a way of parrying the attack. That had been in the moment of a real danger; and the sensation it had caused him —those swift, unthinking impulses—exasperated and stimulated him. He tried, all in vain, to set them off again. But he knew they had immediately deprived the danger of all its peculiarity and ambiguity.

And yet it had been the same danger that he had had a foreboding of only some weeks previously, in this same place— that time when he had felt so oddly startled by the lair itself, which was like some forgotten scrap of the Middle Ages lying remote from the warm, bright-lit life of the class-rooms, and by Beineberg and Reiting, because they seemed to have changed from the people they were down there, suddenly turning into something else, something sinister, blood-thirsty, figures in some quite different sort of life. That had been a transformation, a leap for Törless, as though the picture of his surroundings had suddenly loomed up before other eyes— eyes just awakened out of a hundred years of sleep.

And yet it had been the same danger. . . . He kept on repeating this to himself. And ever and again he tried to compare the memories of the two different sensations. . . .

Meanwhile Basini had got up. Observing his companion's blank, absent gaze, he quietly took his clothes and slipped away.

Törless saw it happening—as though through a mist—but he uttered no word and let it go at that.

His attention was wholly concentrated on this straining to rediscover the point in himself where the change of inner perspective had suddenly occurred.

But every time he came anywhere near it the same thing happened to him as happens to someone trying to compare the close-at-hand with the remote: he could never seize the memory images of the two feelings together. For each time something came in between. It was like a faint click in the mind, corresponding more or less to something that occurs in the physical realm—that scarcely perceptible muscular sensation which is associated with the focusing of the gaze. And each time, precisely in the decisive moment, this would claim all his attention: the activity of making the comparison thrust itself before the objects to be compared, there was an almost unnoticeable jerk—and everything stopped.

So Törless kept on beginning all over again.

This mechanically regular operation lulled him into a rigid, waking, ice-cold sleep, holding him transfixed where he was— and for an indefinite period.

Then an idea wakened him like the light touch of a warm hand. It was an idea apparently so obvious and natural that he marvelled at its not having occurred to him long ago.

It was an idea that did nothing at all beyond generalising the experience he had just had: what in the distance seems so great and mysterious comes up to us always as something plain and undistorted, in natural, everyday proportions. It is as if there were an invisible frontier round every man . . . What originates outside and approaches from a long way off is like a misty sea full of gigantic, ever-changing forms; what comes right up to any man, and becomes action, and collides with his life, is clear and small, human in its dimensions and human in its outlines. And between the life one lives and the life one feels, the life one only has inklings and glimpses of, seeing it only from afar, there lies that invisible frontier, and in it the narrow gateway where all that ever happens, the images of things, must throng together and shrink so that they can enter into a man . . .

And yet, closely though this corresponded to his experience, Törless let his head sink, deep in thought.

It seemed a queer idea . . .

At last he was back in bed. He was not thinking of anything at all any more, for thinking came so hard and was so futile. What he had discovered about the secret contrivings of his friends did, it was true, go through his mind, but now as indifferently and lifelessly as an item of foreign news read in a newspaper.

There was nothing more to be hoped from Basini. Oh, there was still his problem! But that was so dubious, and he was so tired and mangled. An illusion perhaps—the whole thing.

Only the vision of Basini, of his bare, glimmering skin, left a fragrance, as of lilac, in that twilight of the sensations which comes just before sleep. Even the moral revulsion faded away. And at last Törless fell asleep.

No dream disturbed him. There was only an infinitely pleasant warmth spreading soft carpets under his body. After a while he woke out of it. And then he almost screamed. There, sitting on his bed, was Basini! And in the next instant, with crazy speed, Basini had flung off his night-clothes and slid under the blankets and was pressing his naked, trembling body against Törless.

As soon as Törless recovered from the shock, he pushed Basini away from him.

"What do you think you're doing———?"

But Basini pleaded. "Oh, don't start being like that again! Nobody's the way you are! They don't despise me the way you do. They only pretend they do, so as to be different then afterwards. But you—you of all people! You're even younger than me, even if you are stronger. We're both younger than the others. You don't boast and bully the way they do . . . You're gentle . . . I love you . . ."

"Here, I say! I don't know what you're talking about! I don't know what you want! Go away! Oh, go *away*!" And in anguish Törless pushed his arm against Basini's shoulder, holding him off. But the hot proximity of the soft skin, this other person's skin, haunted him, enclosing him, suffocating him. And Basini kept on whispering: "Oh yes . . . oh yes . . . please . . . oh, I should so gladly do whatever you want!"

Törless could find nothing to say to this. While Basini went on whispering and he himself was lost in doubt and consideration, something had sunk over his senses again like a deep green sea. Only Basini's flickering words shone out in it like the glint of little silvery fishes.

He was still holding Basini off with his arms. But something made them heavy, like a moist, torpid warmth; the muscles in them were slackening . . . he forgot them. . . . Only when another of those darting words touched him did he start awake again, all at once feeling—like something fearful and incomprehensible—that this very instant, as in a dream, his hands had drawn Basini closer.

Then he wanted to shake himself into wakefulness, wanted to shout at himself: Basini's tricking you, he's just trying to drag you down to where he is, so that you can't despise him any more! But the cry was never uttered, nor was there any sound anywhere in the whole huge building; throughout the corridors the dark tides of silence seemed to lie motionless in sleep.

He struggled to get back to himself. But those tides were like black sentinels at all the doors.

Then Törless abandoned his search for words. Lust, which had been slowly seeping into him, emanating from every single moment of desperation, had now grown to its full stature. It lay naked at his side and covered his head with its soft black cloak. And into his ear it whispered sweet words of resignation, while its warm fingers thrust all questionings and obligations aside as futile. And it whispered: In solitude you can do what you will.

Only in the moment when he was swept away he woke fleetingly, frantically clutching at the one thought: This is not myself! It's not me! . . . But tomorrow it will be me again! . . . Tomorrow . . .

—*Translated by*
Eithne Wilkins and
Ernst Kaiser

MIKHAIL KUZMIN

AUNT SONYA'S SOFA

I dedicate this true story to my sister

It's so long that I've been standing in the storeroom, surrounded by all kinds of junk, that I have only the dimmest recollections of my young days, when the Turk with a pipe and the shepherdess with a little dog scratching itself for fleas, hind leg raised, all of them embroidered on my spine, gleamed in bright hues—yellow, pink and sky-blue—as yet unfaded and undimmed by dust; and so what occupies my thoughts now more than anything else are the events to which I was witness before once more being consigned to oblivion, this time, I fear, for ever. They had me covered in a wine-colored silken material, stood me in the passageway and threw over my arm a shawl with a pattern of bright roses, as if some beauty from the days of my youth, disturbed at a tender tryst, had left it behind in her flight. I should add that this shawl was always carefully draped in exactly the same way, and if the General, or his sister, Aunt Pavla, happened to disturb it, Kostya, who had arranged this part of the house to his own taste, would restore the folds of the soft, gaily-colored stuff to their former exquisite casualness. Aunt Pavla protested against my disin-

77

terment from the storeroom, saying that poor Sophie had died
on me, that someone or other's wedding had been upset
because of me, that I brought the family misfortune; however,
not only was I defended by Kostya, his student friends and
the other young people, but even the General himself said:

"That's all prejudice, Pavla Petrovnal! If that old mon-
strosity ever had any magic power in it, sixty years in the
storeroom should have taken care of that; besides, it's standing in the passageway—no one's likely to die or propose on it
there!"

Although I wasn't very flattered to be called a "monstros-
ity," and the General proved to be less than a prophet, I did
at any rate establish myself as part of the passageway with
the greenish wallpaper, where I stood faced by a china cabi-
net, over which hung an old round mirror, dimly reflecting my
occasional visitors. There lived in General Gambakov's house,
in addition to his sister Pavla and his son, Kostya, his daughter Nastya, a student at the institute for young ladies.

The next room had a westerly outlook, and so admitted into
my passageway the long rays of the evening sun; they would
strike the rose-patterned shawl, making it glint and shimmer
more enchantingly than ever. At this moment, these rays were
falling across the face and dress of Nastya, who was sitting on
me; she seemed so fragile that I almost thought it strange that
the ruddy light did not pass through her body, which hardly
seemed a sufficient obstacle to it, and fall on her companion.
She was talking to her brother about the Christmas theatricals, as part of which they were planning to put on an act from
"Esther"; it seemed, however, that the girl's thoughts were
far from the subject of the conversation. Kostya remarked:

"I think we could use Seryozha too—his accent is pretty
good."

"Are you suggesting that Sergey Pavlovich should play a
young Israelite girl—one of my handmaidens?"

"Why that? I can't bear *travesti* roles—not that he wouldn't
look good in a woman's costume."

"Well, what other part is there for him to play?"

I knew at once that they were talking about Sergey Pavlo-

vich Pavilikin, young Gambakov's friend. To me he had always
seemed an insignificant boy, in spite of his striking good looks.
His close-cropped dark hair emphasized the fullness of his
round, strangely bloodless face; he had a pleasing mouth and
large, pale-gray eyes. His height enabled him to carry off an
inclination to plumpness, but he was certainly very heavy,
always collapsing onto me and scattering me with ash from
the *papirosy* with very long mouthpieces which he smoked one
after another; and nothing could have been more empty-
headed than his conversation. He came to the house almost
every day, notwithstanding the displeasure of Pavla Petrovna,
who could not abide him.

After a silence the young lady began hesitantly:

"Do you know Pavilikin well, Kostya?"

"What a question! He's my best friend!"

"Is he . . . But you haven't been friends all that long, have
you?"

"Ever since I began attending university this year. But
what difference does that make?"

"None, of course. I just asked because I wanted to know. . . ."

"Why do you find our friendship so interesting?"

"I would like to know whether one can trust him. . . . I'd like
to. . . ."

Kostya's laughter interrupted her.

"It depends what with! In monetary affairs I wouldn't
advise it! . . . All the same, he's a good friend, and no skinflint
when he's in funds—but you know he's poor. . . ."

Nastya said after a pause:

"No, I didn't mean that at all—I meant in matters of feeling, affection."

"What nonsense! What on earth do they put into your
heads at those institutes? How should I know?! . . . Have you
fallen for Seryozha or something?"

The young lady continued without answering:

"I want you to do something for me. Will you?"

"Is it to do with Sergey Pavlovich?"

"Perhaps."

"Well, all right—though you'd better not forget that he's
not much of a one for wasting time on young ladies."

"No, Kostya, you have to promise me!..."

"I've said I'll do it, haven't I? Well?"

"I'll tell you this evening," announced Nastya solemnly, looking into her brother's uneasily shifting eyes, eyes which, like hers, were hazel flecked with gold.

"Whenever you like—now, this evening," said the young man unconcernedly, as he got up and readjusted the rose-patterned shawl which the girl had released as she too rose.

But no ray of the evening sun gleamed on the tender roses because Nastya had gone into the next room and taken up a position at the window, as impenetrable to the ruddy light as before; she stood there gazing at the snow-covered street until the electric lights were lit.

Today I simply haven't had a moment's quiet—such comings and goings all day, and all through my passageway! And what's the point of all these amateur theatricals—that's what I'd like to know. A swarm of young misses and young men— lord knows who they all are—bustling about, yelling, running, calling for some peasants or other to saw through something or other, dragging about furniture, cushions, lengths of cloth; it's a mercy they didn't start taking things from the passage —why, they might even have carried off my shawl! At last things quieted down and a piano began to play somewhere far off. The General and Pavla Petrovna emerged cautiously and sat down beside each other; the old maid was saying:

"If she falls in love with him, it will be a family misfortune. Just think of it—a mere boy, and worse than that—with no name, no fortune, absolutely nothing to offer!..."

"It seems to me you're very much exaggerating all this—I haven't noticed anything...."

"When did men ever notice such things? But I, for one, will fight against it to the bitter end."

"I shouldn't think things will ever reach the point where you have to be for or against."

"And he has absolutely no morals at all: do you know what they say about him? I'm convinced that he's corrupting Kostya too. Nastya's a child, she doesn't understand anything," fulminated the old lady.

"Well, my dear, and whom don't they talk about? You should hear the gossip about Kostya! And it wouldn't surprise me if some of these fairy tales didn't have a grain of truth in them. Only age can protect you from gossip—as the two of us ought to know!..."

Pavla Petrovna blushed crimson and said curtly:

"You do as you wish; at least I've warned you. And *I* shall certainly be on my guard—Nastya is my blood too, you know!"

At this moment Nastya herself entered, already dressed in her costume for the play—pale blue with yellow stripes, with a yellow turban.

"Papa," she began breathlessly, turning to the General, "why aren't you watching the rehearsals?"—and without waiting for a reply she rushed on, "What about lending our emperor your ring? It has such a huge emerald!"

"You mean this one?" asked the old man in surprise, showing an antique ring of rare workmanship, set with a dark emerald the size of a large gooseberry.

"Yes, that one!" answered the young lady, not at all disconcerted.

"Nastya, you don't know what you're asking!" her aunt intervened. "A family heirloom which Maksim never parts with, and you want him to let you take it to that madhouse of yours where you'll lose it in no time? You know your father never takes it off his finger!"

"Well, it's only once or twice, and even if someone does drop it, it's sure to be somewhere in the room...."

"No, Maskim, I absolutely forbid you to take it off!"

"You see, Aunt Pavla won't let me!" said the old General with an embarrassed laugh.

Nastya stalked out crossly without the ring, and Pavla Petrovna set about comforting her brother, who was upset to see his daughter disappointed.

And again there was hubbub, rushing about, changing of clothes, leavetaking.

Mr. Pavilikin remained in the house a long time. When he and Kostya came into my passageway it was nearly four o'clock in the morning. Coming to a standstill, they kissed each other good-bye. Sergey Pavlovich said in an embarrassed voice:

"You don't know how happy I am, Kostya! But I feel so uncomfortable that this should have happened today of all days, after you had let me have that money! Lord knows what awful things you might think...."

Kostya, pale, his eyes shining with happiness, his hair rumpled, again kissed his friend, and said:

"I won't think anything at all, you idiot! It's simply coincidence, chance—something that could happen to anyone."

"Yes, but I feel awkward, so awkward...."

"Don't say another word about it, please—you can let me have it back in the spring...."

"It was just that I needed those six hundred roubles desperately...."

Kostya made no rejoinder. After a little while he said:

"Good-bye, then. Don't forget you're going to 'Manon' with me tomorrow."

"Yes, of course!..."

"And not with Petya Klimov?"

"O, *tempi passati!* Good-bye!"

"Close the door gently, and tread softly when you go past Aunt Pavla's bedroom: she didn't see you come back, and you know she doesn't much care for you. Good-bye!"

The young men embraced once more; as I said before, it was nearly four o'clock in the morning.

Without taking off her rose-trimmed fur hat after the ride, Nastya sat down on the edge of the chair, while her escort kept pacing up and down the room, his cheeks faintly pink from the frost. The girl was chattering gaily away, but underneath the bird-like twitter there lurked a certain unease.

"Wasn't that a glorious ride! Frost and sunshine—that's so nice! I adore the embankment!..."

"Yes."

"I love to go horseriding—in the summer I disappear for days on end. You've never visited our place at Svyataya Krucha, have you?"

"No. I prefer to ride in a car."

"You do have bad taste. . . . You know, don't you, that Svyataya Krucha, Alekseyevskoye and Lgovka are all my personal property—I'm a very good match. And then Auntie Pavla Petrovna is going to leave me everything. You see—I'm advising you to think things over."

"The likes of us mustn't be getting ideas above our station!"

"Where do you pick up these germs of shop-assistants' wisdom?"

Seryozha shrugged and continued his steady pacing back and forth. The young lady made one or two more attempts to start up her twittering, but each time more halfheartedly, like a broken toy, until she at last fell silent; when she spoke again, it was in a sad, gentle voice. Without taking off her hat, she sank back in the chair; as she spoke in the darkened room, she seemed to be addressing a plaint to herself:

"How long it's been since we put on our play! Do you remember? Your entrance. . . . What a lot has changed since then! You've changed too—I have, everyone has. . . . I didn't really know you then. You've no idea how much better I understand you than Kostya does! You don't believe it? Why do you pretend to be so slow on the uptake? Would it give you pleasure if I came out and said what is considered humiliating for a woman to say first? You're tormenting me, Sergey Pavlovich!"

"How dreadfully you exaggerate everything, Nastasya Maksimovna—my dimness of wit, my pride, and even, perhaps, your feelings for me. . . ."

She stood up and said almost soundlessly:

"Do I? Perhaps. . . ."

"Are you going?"—he was suddenly alert.

"Yes, I have to change for dinner. You're not dining with us?"

"No, I'm invited somewhere."

"With Kostya?"

"No. Why do you ask that?"

She was standing by the table with the magazines, reluctant to leave the room.

"Are you going to him now?"

"No, I'm leaving straight away."

"Are you? Good-bye, then! And I love you—there!" she added suddenly, turning away. No word came from him in the darkness which hid his face from her, and she threw in laughingly (or that was the effect she intended), "Well, are you satisfied now?"

"Surely you don't think that's the word I would choose?" he said, bending over her hand.

"Good-bye. Go now,"—the words came from her as she left the room.

Seryozha turned on the light and began walking in the direction of Kostya's room, whistling cheerfully.

The General was pacing about holding a newspaper; he seemed very upset about something. Pavla Petrovna was following him about the room in a rustle of black silk.

"You mustn't let it upset you, Maksim! It happens so often these days that you almost get used to it. Of course, it's dreadful, but what can we do about it? It's no good kicking against the pricks, as they say."

"It's no good, Pavla, I just can't reconcile myself to the thought of it: all that was left was his cap and a mess of blood and brains on the wall. Poor Lev Ivanovich!"

"Don't think about it, brother! Tomorrow we'll have a funeral mass said for him at Udely. Put it out of your mind, think of your own well-being—you have a son and daughter of your own to worry about."

The General, red in the face, sank down onto me, letting fall his newspaper; the old lady, nimbly picking it up and placing it out of her brother's reach, made haste to change the subject:

"Well, did you find the ring?"

The General again displayed signs of uneasiness:

"No, no, I haven't. That's another thing I'm terribly worried about."

"When do you last remember having it?"

"I showed it to Sergey Pavlovich this morning on this very sofa; he seemed most interested. . . . Then I dozed off—when I woke up it had gone, I remember that. . . ."

"Did you take it off?"

"Yes...."

"That was ill-advised of you. Quite apart from its cash value, as a family heirloom it's priceless."

"I'm sure it means some misfortune is in store for us."

"Let's hope that Lev Ivanovich's death is misfortune enough for the time being."

The General heaved a deep sigh. Pavla Petrovna pressed on relentlessly:

"Did Pavilikin take it with him, I wonder. That's just the sort of thing I'd expect of him."

"Why should he have? He had such a good look at it—and he asked how much a dealer would give for it and all that."

"Well, perhaps he just took it."

"Stole it—is that what you're trying to say?"

Pavla Petrovna had no chance to reply: the conversation was interrupted by Nastya, who came rushing excitedly into the room.

"Papa!" she cried, "Sergey Pavlovich has proposed to me; I hope you're not opposed to the idea?"

"Not now, not now!"—the General waved her away.

"And why not? Why put it off? You know him pretty well by now," said Nastya, reddening.

Pavla Petrovna rose to her feet:

"I have a voice in this matter too, and I am opposed to the match under any circumstances; at the very least I demand that we postpone this discussion until Maksim's ring is found."

"What has papa's ring to do with my fiancé?" asked the girl haughtily.

"We think Sergey Pavlovich has the ring."

"You think he has committed a theft?"

"You could put it like that."

Nastya turned to the General without answering her aunt, and said:

"And do you believe this fairy tale?"

Her father said nothing, redder in the face than ever.

The girl again turned to Pavla:

"Why are you standing between us? You hate Seryozha—

Sergey Pavlovich—and you invent all sorts of nonsense! And you're trying to set father against Kostya too. What is it you want from us?"

"Nastya, don't you dare, I forbid you! . . ." said her father, gasping for breath.

Nastya paid him no attention.

"What are you getting in such a rage about? Why can't you wait until the matter is cleared up? Can't you see that it's a matter of principle?"

"I can see that where my fiancé is concerned no one should dare even to suspect such a thing!" shouted Nastya. The General sat in silence, turning redder and redder.

"You're afraid—that's the truth isn't it?"

"There can only be one truth, and I know what it is. And I advise you not to oppose our marriage—or it'll be the worse for you!"

"You think so?"

"I know!"

Pavla gave her a searching look.

"Is there any reason for this hurry?"

"What a nasty mind you have! Kostya!"—Nastya threw herself toward her brother, who had just entered, "Kostya darling, you be the judge! Sergey Pavlovich has proposed to me, and father—Aunt Pavla has him completely under her thumb—won't give his consent until we clear up this business about his ring."

"What the devil is all this?! Do you mean to tell me you're accusing Pavilikin of theft?"

"Yes!" hissed the old lady. "Of course you'll stand up for him, you'll even redeem the ring. There are a few things I could tell about you too! I can hear the doors squeaking from my room when your friend leaves and what you say to each other. Be grateful for my silence!"

Never in all my life have I heard such an uproar, such a scandal, such a torrent of abuse. Kostya banged with his fist and shouted; Pavla appealed for respect to be shown to years; Nastya screamed hysterically. . . . But all at once everyone fell silent: all the voices, the noise and the shouting, were pierced by the strange animal-like sound emitted by the General, who, silent to this moment, had suddenly risen to his feet. Then he sank back heavily, his face between red and blue, and began to wheeze. Pavla threw herself toward him:

"What's the matter? Maksim, Maksim?"

The General only wheezed and rolled the whites of his eyes, now completely blue in the face.

"Water! Water! He's dying—it's a stroke!" whispered the aunt, but Nastya pushed her aside with the words:

"Let me see to him—I'll undo his collar!" and sank down on her knees before me.

Even the passageway was not free of the pervasive smell of incense from the old General's funeral mass; the sound of chanting too could be faintly heard. More than once I had the feeling that they were singing a farewell to me. Ah, how close I was to the truth!

The young men came in, deep in conversation; Pavilikin was saying:

"And then today I received the following note from Pavla Petrovna"—and taking a letter from his pocket, he read it aloud:

"Dear Sir, for reasons which I trust there is no need to go into here, I find your visits at this time, a time so painful to our family, to be undesirable, and I hope that you will not refuse to comport yourself in accordance with our general wish. The future will show whether former relations can be resumed, but in the meantime, I can assure you that Anastasia Maksimovna, my niece, is fully in agreement with me on this matter. Yours, etc."

He looked inquiringly at Kostya, who remarked:

"You know, from her point of view my aunt is right, and I really don't know what my sister will have to say to you."

"But, I mean to say, all because of such a little thing! . . ."

"Is that what you call papa's death?"

"But it wasn't my fault!"

"Of course it wasn't. . . . You know, not long ago I read a story in the 'Thousand and One Nights': a man is throwing date stones—a perfectly harmless occupation—and happens to hit a Genii's son in the eye, thus bringing down on his head a whole series of misfortunes. Who can predict the results of our most trivial actions?"

"But the two of us will still see each other, won't we?"

"Oh certainly! I shan't be living with the family any more, and I'm always delighted to see you. What's between us is a bit more permanent than a schoolgirl crush."

"And doesn't have to be afraid of date stones?"

"Precisely...."

Seryozha put his arm round young Gambakov, and they went out of the room together. I was never to see Pavilikin again, as I was to see little of any of the people I had grown familiar with during my final period of grace.

Early next morning some peasants came tramping in; "This one here?" they asked Pavla Petrovna, and set about lifting me. The oldest of them lingered, trying to find out if there was anything else to be sold, but on being assured that there wasn't, he went out after the others.

When they turned me on my side to get me through the doorway, something struck the floor (the carpets having already been taken up in anticipation of summer). One of my bearers picked up the fallen object and handed it to the old lady, saying:

"Now there's a fine ring for you, ma'am. Someone must have dropped it on this here couch, and it must have gone and rolled down inside the covers."

"Good. I'm very much obliged to you!" said Aunt Pavla, turning pale; hastily dropping into her reticule a ring with an emerald like a large gooseberry, she left the room.

JUNE, 1907

—*Translated by*
Neil Granoien and
Michael Green

CONSTANTIN CAVAFY

GRAY

Looking at a half-gray opal
I remembered two beautiful gray eyes
I had seen; it must have been twenty years ago . . .

For a month we loved each other.
Then he went away, I believe to Smyrna,
to work there, and we never saw each other after that.

The gray eyes—if he is alive—must have grown ugly;
the handsome face must have spoiled.

Dear Memory, preserve them as they used to be.
And, Memory, bring back to me tonight all that you can,
of this love of mine, all that you can.

THE TOBACCO-SHOP WINDOW

They stood among many others
near a lighted tobacco-shop window.

CALAMUS

Their glances chanced to meet,
and they timidly, haltingly expressed
the deviate desire of their flesh.
Then, a few steps uneasily taken on the sidewalk—
until they smiled, and gently nodded.

And after that the closed carriage . . .
the carnal closeness of their bodies;
the clasped hands, the met lips.

BODY, REMEMBER . . .

Body, remember not only how much you were loved,
not only the beds on which you lay,
but also those desires for you
that glowed plainly in the eyes,
and trembled in the voice—and some
chance obstacle made futile.
Now that all of them belong to the past,
it almost seems as if you had yielded
to those desires—how they glowed,
remember, in the eyes gazing at you;
how they trembled in the voice, for you, remember, body.

THE NEXT TABLE

He must be scarcely twenty-two years old.
And yet I am certain that nearly as many
years ago, I enjoyed the very same body.

It isn't at all infatuation of love.
I entered the casino only a little while ago;
I didn't even have time to drink much.
I have enjoyed the same body.

If I can't recall where—one lapse of memory means nothing.

90

Ah see, now that he is sitting down at the next table
I know every movement he makes—and beneath his clothes,
once more I see the beloved bare limbs.

THEIR BEGINNING

The fulfillment of their deviate, sensual delight
is done. They rise from the mattress,
and they dress hurriedly without speaking.
They leave the house separately, furtively; and as
they walk somewhat uneasily on the street, it seems
as if they suspect that something about them betrays
into what kind of bed they fell a little while back.

But how the life of the artist has gained.
Tomorrow, the next day, years later, the vigorous verses
will be composed that had their beginning here.

IN AN OLD BOOK

In an old book—about a hundred years old—
forgotten among its pages,
I found a water color unsigned.
It must have been the work of a very able artist.
It had as its title, "A Presentation of Love."

But more fitting would have been, "Of Utter Sensual Love."

For it was evident when you looked at the work
(the artist's idea was easily understood)
that the young man in the painting was not destined
to be one of those who loves more or less healthily,
remaining within the limits of the more or less
permissible—with chestnut, deep-coloured eyes;
with the exquisite beauty of his face,
the beauty of deviate attractions;

91

with his ideal lips that offer
sensual delight to a beloved body;
with his ideal limbs created for beds which
current morality brands as shameless.

BEFORE TIME CHANGES THEM

They were both deeply grieved   at their separation.
They did not desire it;   it was circumstances.
The needs of a living   obliged one of them
to go to a distant place—   New York or Canada.
Their love certainly   was not what it had been before;
for the attraction   had gradually waned,
for love's attraction   had considerably waned.
But they did not desire   to be separated.
It was circumstances.—   Or perhaps Destiny
had appeared as an artist   separating them now
before their feeling should fade,   before Time had changed
    them;
so each for the other will   remain forever as he had been,
a handsome young man   of twenty-four years.

—Translated by Rae Dalven

SHERWOOD ANDERSON

HANDS

Upon the half decayed veranda of a small frame house that stood near the edge of a ravine near the town of Winesburg, Ohio, a fat little old man walked nervously up and down. Across a long field that had been seeded for clover but that had produced only a dense crop of yellow mustard weeds, he could see the public highway along which went a wagon filled with berry pickers returning from the fields. The berry pickers, youths and maidens, laughed and shouted boisterously. A boy clad in a blue shirt leaped from the wagon and attempted to drag after him one of the maidens who screamed and protested shrilly. The feet of the boy in the road kicked up a cloud of dust that floated across the face of the departing sun. Over the long field came a thin girlish voice. "Oh, you Wing Biddlebaum, comb your hair, it's falling into your eyes," commanded the voice to the man, who was bald and whose nervous little hands fiddled about the bare white forehead as though arranging a mass of tangled locks.

Wing Biddlebaum, forever frightened and beset by a ghostly band of doubts, did not think of himself as in any way a part of the life of the town where he had lived for twenty years. Among all the people of Winesburg but one had come close to him. With George Willard, son of Tom Willard, the proprietor of the new Willard House, he had formed something like a friendship. George Willard was the reporter on the *Winesburg Eagle* and sometimes in the evenings he walked out along the highway to Wing Biddlebaum's house. Now as the old man walked up and down on the veranda, his hands moving nervously about, he was hoping that George Willard would come and spend the evening with him. After the wagon containing the berry pickers had passed, he went across the field through the tall mustard weeds and climbing a rail fence peered anxiously along the road to the town. For a moment he stood thus, rubbing his hands together and looking up and down the road, and then, fear overcoming him, ran back to walk again upon the porch on his own house.

In the presence of George Willard, Wing Biddlebaum, who for twenty years had been the town mystery, lost something of his timidity, and his shadowy personality, submerged in a sea of doubts, came forth to look at the world. With the young reporter at his side, he ventured in the light of day into Main Street or strode up and down on the rickety front porch of his own house, talking excitedly. The voice that had been low and trembling became shrill and loud. The bent figure straightened. With a kind of wriggle, like a fish returned to the brook by the fisherman, Biddlebaum the silent began to talk, striving to put into words the ideas that had been accumulated by his mind during long years of silence.

Wing Biddlebaum talked much with his hands. The slender expressive fingers, forever active, forever striving to conceal themselves in his pockets or behind his back, came forth and became the piston rods of his machinery of expression.

The story of Wing Biddlebaum is a story of hands. Their restless activity, like unto the beating of the wings of an imprisoned bird, had given him his name. Some obscure poet of the town had thought of it. The hands alarmed their owner. He wanted to keep them hidden away and looked with amazement at the quiet inexpressive hands of other men who worked beside him in the fields, or passed driving sleepy teams on country roads.

When he talked to George Willard, Wing Biddlebaum closed his fists and beat with them upon a table or on the walls of his house. The action made him more comfortable. If the desire to talk came to him when the two were walking in the fields, he sought out a stump or the top board of a fence and with his hands pounding busily talked with renewed ease.

The story of Wing Biddlebaum's hands is worth a book in itself. Sympathetically set forth it would tap many strange, beautiful qualities in obscure men. It is a job for a poet. In Winesburg the hands had attracted attention merely because of their activity. With them Wing Biddlebaum had picked as high as a hundred and forty quarts of strawberries in a day. They became his distinguishing feature, the source of his fame. Also they made more grotesque an already grotesque and elusive individuality. Winesburg was proud of the hands of Wing Biddlebaum in the same spirit in which it was proud of Banker White's new stone house and Wesley Moyer's bay stallion, Tony Tip, that had won the two-fifteen trot at the fall races in Cleveland.

As for George Willard, he had many times wanted to ask about the hands. At times an almost overwhelming curiosity had taken hold of him. He felt that there must be a reason for their strange activity and their inclination to keep hidden away and only a growing respect for Wing Biddlebaum kept him from blurting out the questions that were often in his mind.

Once he had been on the point of asking. The two were walking in the fields on a summer afternoon and had stopped to sit upon a grassy bank. All afternoon Wing Biddlebaum had talked as one inspired. By a fence he had stopped and beating like a giant woodpecker upon the top board had shouted at George Willard, condemning his tendency to be too much influenced by the people about him. "You are destroying yourself," he cried. "You have the inclination to be alone and to dream and you are afraid of dreams. You want to be like others in town here. You hear them talk and you try to imitate them."

On the grassy bank Wing Biddlebaum had tried again to

drive his point home. His voice became soft and reminiscent, and with a sigh of contentment he launched into a long rambling talk, speaking as one lost in a dream.

Out of the dream Wing Biddlebaum made a picture for George Willard. In the picture men lived again in a kind of pastoral golden age. Across a green open country came clean-limbed young men, some afoot, some mounted upon horses. In crowds the young men came to gather about the feet of an old man who sat beneath a tree in a tiny garden and who talked to them.

Wing Biddlebaum became wholly inspired. For once he forgot the hands. Slowly they stole forth and lay upon George Willard's shoulders. Something new and bold came into the voice that talked. "You must try to forget all you have learned," said the old man. "You must begin to dream. From this time on you must shut your ears to the roaring of the voices."

Pausing in his speech, Wing Biddlebaum looked long and earnestly at George Willard. His eyes glowed. Again he raised the hands to caress the boy and then a look of horror swept over his face.

With a convulsive movement of his body, Wing Biddlebaum sprang to his feet and thrust his hands deep into his trousers pockets. Tears came to his eyes. "I must be getting along home. I can talk no more with you," he said nervously.

Without looking back, the old man had hurried down the hillside and across a meadow, leaving George Willard perplexed and frightened upon the grassy slope. With a shiver of dread the boy arose and went along the road toward town. "I'll not ask him about his hands," he thought, touched by the memory of the terror he had seen in the man's eyes. "There's something wrong, but I don't want to know what it is. His hands have something to do with his fear of me and of everyone."

And George Willard was right. Let us look briefly into the story of the hands. Perhaps our talking of them will arouse the poet who will tell the hidden wonder story of the influence for which the hands were but fluttering pennants of promise.

In his youth Wing Biddlebaum had been a school teacher in

a town in Pennsylvania. He was not then known as Wing Biddlebaum, but went by the less euphonic name of Adolph Myers. As Adolph Myers he was much loved by the boys of his school.

Adolph Myers was meant by nature to be a teacher of youth. He was one of those rare, little-understood men who rule by a power so gentle that it passes as a lovable weakness. In their feeling for the boys under their charge such men are not unlike the finer sort of women in their love of men.

And yet that is but crudely stated. It needs the poet there. With the boys of his school, Adolph Myers had walked in the evening or had sat talking until dusk upon the schoolhouse steps lost in a kind of dream. Here and there went his hands, caressing the shoulders of the boys, playing about the tousled heads. As he talked his voice became soft and musical. There was a caress in that also. In a way the voice and the hands, the stroking of the shoulders and the touching of the hair was a part of the schoolmaster's effort to carry a dream into the young minds. By the caress that was in his fingers he expressed himself. He was one of those men in whom the force that creates life is diffused, not centralized. Under the caress of his hands doubt and disbelief went out of the minds of the boys and they began also to dream.

And then the tragedy. A half-witted boy of the school became enamored of the young master. In his bed at night he imagined unspeakable things and in the morning went forth to tell his dreams as facts. Strange, hideous accusations fell from his loose-hung lips. Through the Pennsylvania town went a shiver. Hidden, shadowy doubts that had been in men's minds concerning Adolph Myers were galvanized into beliefs.

The tragedy did not linger. Trembling lads were jerked out of bed and questioned. "He put his arms about me," said one. "His fingers were always playing in my hair," said another.

One afternoon a man of the town, Henry Bradford, who kept a saloon, came to the schoolhouse door. Calling Adolph Myers into the school yard he began to beat him with his fists. As his hard knuckles beat down into the frightened face of the schoolmaster, his wrath became more and more terrible. Screaming with dismay, the children ran here and there like disturbed insects. "I'll teach you to put your hands on my boy, you beast," roared the saloon keeper, who, tired of beating the master, had begun to kick him about the yard.

Adolph Myers was driven from the Pennsylvania town in the night. With lanterns in their hands a dozen men came to the door of the house where he lived alone and commanded that he dress and come forth. It was raining and one of the men had a rope in his hands. They had intended to hang the schoolmaster, but something in his figure, so small, white, and pitiful, touched their hearts and they let him escape. As he ran away into the darkness they repented of their weakness and ran after him, swearing and throwing sticks and great balls of soft mud at the figure that screamed and ran faster and faster into the darkness.

For twenty years Adolph Myers had lived alone in Winesburg. He was but forty but looked sixty-five. The name of Biddlebaum he got from a box of goods seen at a freight station as he hurried through an eastern Ohio town. He had an aunt in Winesburg, a black-toothed old woman who raised chickens, and with her he lived until she died. He had been ill for a year after the experience in Pennsylvania, and after his recovery worked as a day laborer in the fields, going timidly about and striving to conceal his hands. Although he did not understand what had happened he felt that the hands must be to blame. Again and again the fathers of the boys had talked of the hands. "Keep your hands to yourself," the saloon keeper had roared, dancing with fury in the schoolhouse yard.

Upon the veranda of his house by the ravine, Wing Biddlebaum continued to walk up and down until the sun had disappeared and the road beyond the field was lost in the grey shadows. Going into his house he cut slices of bread and spread honey upon them. When the rumble of the evening train that took away the express cars loaded with the day's harvest of berries had passed and restored the silence of the summer night, he went again to walk upon the veranda. In the darkness he could not see the hands and they became quiet. Although he still hungered for the presence of the boy, who was the medium through which he expressed his love of man, the hunger became again a part of his loneliness and his waiting. Lighting a lamp, Wing Biddlebaum washed the few dishes soiled by his simple meal and, setting up a folding cot by the screen door that led to the porch, prepared to undress for the night. A few stray white bread crumbs lay on the cleanly washed floor by the table; putting the lamp upon a low stool he began to pick up the crumbs, carrying them to his mouth one by one with unbelievable rapidity. In the dense blotch of light beneath the table, the kneeling figure looked like a priest engaged in some service of his church. The nervous expressive fingers, flashing in and out of the light, might well have been mistaken for the fingers of the devotee going swiftly through decade after decade of his rosary.

MATEI CARAGIALE

REMEMBER

This is a dreadful incident.
—Memoirs of the Bal-Mabille

There are dreams which we imagine ourselves to have lived through somehow, somewhere, just as there are actual experiences of which we ask ourselves whether they were not in fact dreams. I was thinking of this the other evening as I browsed through my papers to see which of them could be burned—paper is such a bother!—and thereby came across a letter which awakened in me the memory of an extraordinary incident, one so strange that were it not seven years since it occurred, doubts would beset me, and I should believe myself in reality only to have dreamed it, or a long time before to have read or heard of it.

It was in the year 1907. Having withstood a severe illness in Bucharest, I had returned to Berlin. My convalescence made slow progress and required careful nursing. Before my departure the doctor enjoined me to avoid the slightest emotional shock. The poor dear! Smiling, I shrugged my shoulders and told him he need trouble himself no further.

After a two-year banishment I saw Berlin once more. For

100

Berlin I have such a great weakness that even the saddest circumstances could not alter my pleasure in returning. I found the city just as I had left it: wherever once glanced, there were cascades of flowers. But it had never appeared to me as beautiful as in those first days of June.

Still, it was no longer possible to roam, to wander through the city as before. I tired rapidly, and exhaustion could easily have led to a relapse of my illness. I thus surrendered to the necessity of remaining at home for a time—a sacrifice partially compensated by the lovely baroque music sounding through the house from morning until night. Drifting in this sweet narcosis, billowed by miraculous harmonies, I let my dream freely ascend and then melt away, while with half-closed eyes I watched rainbows flutter through the fine mist of the fountain in the broad, gardenlike square. The gentle breath of sunset swayed the purpled clusters of rambling roses that twined about the front terrace of the house, drifting their scent toward me. As evening lent the shadows life, a shudder glided mysteriously across the mirror. This was the hour I awaited in order to delight in the loveliest corner of the garden, a little wooded area that had remained untouched in the middle of the city—a few ancient, dark trees with dense foliage that were worthy of serving as models to the most celebrated masters of the painterly arts.

And indeed I encountered them again in the Kaiser-Friedrich Museum, in a painting by Ruysdael: the same bushy crowns shadowed a ruined castle beside a waterfall. Never was I able to pass it without pausing a while. As I gazed at the painting, my thoughts were irresistibly drawn to a small section of blue-gray sky. I was born with the dregs of ancient superstition, a heathenish-pious love for old trees. To them I owe noble and earnest impulses, for I scarcely believe that in the entire world there is a human voice or an artful melody which could move me more deeply than the mysterious rustling the evening wind awakens in their leaves. And yet the painted tree enchanted me even more than the real ones, for this little melancholy landscape seemed a reflection of my soul.

I used to go to the museum quite frequently. However

deeply engaged I might be in viewing the pictures, the other visitors, often so interesting, by no means escaped notice, and among them a young man drew my particular attention; he never failed to appear or to catch people's eyes, for one could well think that with the aid of a magician he had stepped out of one of the antique frames. Could there be anything more delightful for someone who partakes devoutly in the mystery of the past than to encounter an image from the past in actual flesh and blood? Two years before, in the French gallery of the museum, I had seen a lady in the process of copying Mignard's portrait of Maria Mancini, and she so conspicuously resembled the model one could have thought she painted her own face while gazing into a mirror, to which she merely added the appropriate coiffure.

Just so did the young man resemble some of those youthful lords whose glances, hands and smiles have been made immortal by Van Dyck and, after him, by Van der Faes—"some" of those lords, I say, because they are almost all alike. In times past each epoch stamped with the same bearing if not precisely the same appearance those who were so closely and multiply related, dwelling side by side in crowded castles, wearing the same clothing, and practicing the same customs. But it also happens, in turn, that where one least expects it, beings appear whose true resemblance one must seek elsewhere, in other countries, among other peoples, in other centuries, without conjecturing the slightest kinship with those from whom they are so separated by the chasms of time and ancestry.

Every surmise about the young man's origin was thus futile; nonetheless, I made all sorts of reflections about his person, which in manner was truly extraordinary, peculiar, so that it invited particular attention. I was intrigued by his cool, haughty bearing; handsome as a god, he moved solitarily through life, imperturbable, his head held proudly. From the beginning I took him to be one of those exceptional creatures, one of those oddities of nature, which have always attracted me. And I saw him almost daily, for the museum was not the only place I encountered him. During my strolls through the town, which I had taken up again, I used to rest for a while in a certain tavern, in order not to become fatigued; and there one could sample the finest wares of an old Dutch distillery. After Ruysdael, then, a little Van Brouwer and Van der Hooch. Nowhere else did I recuperate better than in that narrow, rather dark room, which would have done honor to any bourgeois household, richly clad with fumed oak half-way up the wall, where the projecting panels formed a continuous shelf on which Delft pots and pitchers stood. What marvelous moments have I passed there!

Beside me, on the sole bench in this inviting but by day rather lonely tavern, the youth with the face that seemed cut from an old portrait calmly sipped the sweetest and most aromatic drinks; they resembled liquified jewels, and through their pungent spices from Java or the Antilles conjured up exotic dream images, awakened wanderlust. There, so I fancied, we were no longer strangers; and remarkably, after we had become acquainted, we admitted to each other that it seemed to us both as though we had sat together in a room similar to this long before.

It would not have seemed plausible to me that we should precisely befriend each other, for I felt I was not unjustified in assigning him to a thoroughly different world than my own. It sprang to one's eyes: the difference between a simple wild-flower and an exotic greenhouse blossom. Whether it had taken centuries for a noble race, before its final decline, to produce such a radiant flowering, in some proud, blue-blooded revival of the ideal type, or whether it was only a happy accident—more could not in any case have been achieved. Granted, it also required certain daily exertions for this ornament of mankind to present himself in utmost beauty, for I had not had the privilege of seeing so much make-up even on a woman. Should I therefore have taken him for one of those buffoons with unnatural preferences whose numbers seem everywhere to have increased of late in such deplorable proportions? No, that I could not believe, for even as a disturbing smile flitted across the lips of this painted doll, the eyes under their severe, penciled brows had that innocent clarity which gleams only beneath the lids of children and heroes.

He was also very young—twenty years old at most. What doesn't one close his eyes to at this age—particularly among the rich? The fact that it need not provide for the dawning day alters the human mind, since the feeling of responsibility is crippled; wealth makes soft and brings about a continuous state of pleasant delirium that insists on extraordinary pleasures and new, stimulating experiences. To this sort of passionless and blasé mortal, free of petty prejudice, belonged my new acquaintance, who doubtlessly had quite sufficient means at his disposal. Yet he seemed to live apart from the social whirl—indeed, completely outside society. There were yet more individuals like him in Berlin, but one rarely caught sight of them—by chance, perhaps, on a gallop through the morning mist, or in the evening as they hurried to their glittering amusements. I could only imagine him to be a resident of one of the stately avenues to the west, bordering on the royal Tiergarten and lined with magnificent villas, where money has succeeded to a notable degree in re-creating paradise on earth. So I imagined him, leafing with slender fingers through luxuriously bound books, in the voluptuous solitude of chambers with heavy mirrors and a wilting profusion of exotic flowers. Did not the very vision of such decor recall the stimulating fragrance that he used to diffuse about himself, so intoxicating that even while awake one glided into a dream?

Aubrey de Vere. When I think of him . . . One day we conversed with each other as though we were old acquaintances. His Norman name—to this day I do not know if it was the real one—did not seem strange to me, as it was the family title of the dissolute Earls of Oxford, which after they died out was assumed by the Stuarts of collateral descent, the Dukes of Saint-Albans, and joined to that of Beauclerk. Should he be descended from such ancestors, they could not have done him more honor than he to them. Though English to the marrow of his bones, in conversation he availed himself of French, and a French so perfect as has seldom been granted me to hear. His clear, supple voice with its rich *timbre* permitted the French language to become more than a means of communication; it was an accessory of seduction. When I heard who he was, I understood him at once in all matters. The bearing to which Beau Brummel had given the stamp of his name lived on in

Aubrey de Vere in full splendor. Even the fact that he found such pleasure in painting his face could now be explained. Were not the first inhabitants of Albion, as history records, painted blue from head to foot? This color was particularly dear to my new friend, who wore it in his very body, in his eyes and under the transparent skin of his hands, on which seven rings glittered, as alike as brothers—seven Ceylon sapphires. Together with an ornate bracelet and that unforgettable perfume with the fragrance of red carnations, these were the sole things to which he remained constant; otherwise, so far as his clothing was concerned, I hardly know if I saw him in the same suit twice. But this entire meticulous outfit was in his case only part of a whole of utmost perfection and noblest harmony. Aubrey de Vere possessed a wonderfully organized mind and a scintillating spirit; he would have done honor to the most exclusive club and would not have felt ill at ease in the company of scholars, for when he admitted having his linen washed in London, he appended that in the Eighteenth Century the young noblemen of Paris dispatched theirs to Flanders to be washed, and those of Bordeaux to Curaçao. He chatted in this way about everything, with analogies from the past, with allusions and enchanting details, and it often happened that he related his voyages in the ancient landscapes of the East, or to the lost islands of the Pacific Ocean, where spring reigns eternally. This much I could ascertain about his life: that in traveling continents and oceans he had seen much, that he had read even more—if not perhaps too much for his age, for it was entirely possible that he mingled what he had witnessed with what he had read, or that he regarded what he had truly seen through the distorting lenses of his books; this, combined with his wealth, had turned his head, although by nature his judgment seemed clear and cool. Thus, for example, I believed him to be occupied with daring occult researches, for which quite apart from a unique congenital inclination, he was also qualified through the most astonishing training. He seemed to have had even more connection with the spirits than with the living, for in his discourses human beings were never mentioned.

The occasions and the circumstances of undertaking such

wonderful journeys at such an early age were never explained, no more than who or what he was, where he came from, whether he had parents, relatives or friends, where he lived, at least—nothing, absolutely nothing. What self-control for a young man, to withhold everything in this manner without ever betraying himself! Since he revealed nothing, I inquired even less, and I assumed that precisely this was the reason for our forming a friendship. And even if we had continued to meet for an eternity, sooner would a remark have escaped from him than a question from me. Basically it was not important to me to learn anything. What concern was it of mine? By chance I saw him once—without his becoming aware of me— choosing flowers for four- or five-hundred marks, carnations and rare orchids; it seemed to me a dreadful extravagance. As I knew the saleswoman, it would only have been necessary to step in after he had left and purchase a *boutonnière* in order to ascertain where he had sent them, and in such a way, following the track, to make further inquiries. But to what purpose? It might well have been that the single-minded insistence with which he screened his brief past and his daily life served a particular purpose. There was (and I repeat it) such pride in his eyes; indifferent to everything that occurred on this earth, lost in the depths of a dream world, they would have dispersed the faintest shadows of mistrust or accusation. Still, it did not escape me that he was sometimes about to add something, but instantly thought better of it and swallowed his words. Did he then actually blush under his make-up, did his eyes become wreathed in sadness, as it appeared to me then, when he seemed for a brief instant to reveal some concealed misery? I cannot swear to it; however, what I know is that while he talked his deepening glance fixed itself long and wistfully on the ever-present rings, as though the jewels enclosed the secret of his life and mirrored in their clear blue ice all his thoughts and all his memories.

After some time, without our friendly relations taking intimate shape, we saw each other more frequently—sometimes in the morning, most often in the afternoon, never at night— never. Because it was hot, we had given up the Dutch tavern, and met in the Gruenwald on the terrace of a café near a little pine grove; it was an idyllic terrace, overgrown with roses of all sorts and colors, whose petals whirled into our glasses with the merest breath of wind. He always arrived without haste and without delay. Once, however, I awaited him without avail until five o'clock. When I returned home I found a letter in which he briefly excused himself for his absence, and which was signed *Sir* Aubrey de Vere. I carefully examined the commanding handwriting with its bold letters, as well as the blue seal: it showed a reclining sphinx in the center of a sash like that which adorns the British coat of arms. On the sash I read the word *Remember*.

As heraldist I was not satisfied; I had expected a proper coat of arms, not a simple emblem. After this letter Sir Aubrey gave no further sign of life. This was not to be wondered at: steaming, humid air pressed upon the city, making it seem a vast spawning-ground of indignity and baseness. One could only go out in the evening, when Sir Aubrey was unaccustomed to show himself. And yet the nights were so lovely that I could only with difficulty make the decision to return home. It was my custom to wander the city until quite late in the evening, and on one such occasion, around midnight, I had a remarkable encounter in a lonely *allée* of the Tiergarten.

Past me there moved a stately woman in a slim black sequined dress, with red hair cascading from beneath her feathered hat—a slender, bony woman with narrow hips and flat bosom. She strode along stiff as a corpse commanded by some strange power alien to its own will and driven or drawn to a mysterious nocturnal rendezvous. I scarcely know why, but from the very beginning I did not believe this to be a woman like every other, even before I seemed to recognize something familiar in her great, staring eyes, that gazed so intensely inward, and in the features of her heavily painted face. But still I had doubts. Could it be mere imagination that led me to see seven Ceylon sapphires smirking on the long-fingered hand? Stunned, I remained there, overpowered by an unclear feeling in which astonishment, disgust and fear played equal roles; then, drinking in the familiar perfume, the scent of red carnations, I resolved to follow. But it was too late; I had lost her. At the end of the *allée* hansom cabs waited; apparently the figure had entered one of them and departed.

As an old Berliner it would have been childish to permit myself to be overwhelmed by astonishment. After all, I had seen everything already! On the other hand, a vulgar curiosity drove me to lie in wait for several evenings. To no purpose. Meanwhile, the heat became ever more unbearable. On the day before the evening of which I shall now speak, people dropped in the street like flies.

It was a velvety and leaden night in which the sluggish breath of a hot wind unavailingly sought to disperse the clouds of steam that thickened the air. On the horizon flashed brief summer lightning, the woods and the joyless gardens kept silence as though an evil magic had caused them to petrify; it stank of the clandestine, of sin and despair. I proceeded only with great difficulty into the darkness which had stuffed the *allées* as with cotton-wadding, for again and again, overwhelmed by faintness, I had to halt. At the intersection where Berlin's Fountain of Roland is situated, in the glaring light that blinded me as I emerged from the darkness, I suddenly stood before Sir Aubrey—a fact which, as I observed him more closely, did not entirely give me pleasure.

Not so much because this time he had overstepped all bounds. One may think as he pleases: a man does not leave the house adorned in such a manner. The powder with which he had veneered his face was blue, the lips and the holes in his nose were tinted violet, his hair powdered with gold dust, and broad, blue-black circles were drawn around his eyes, giving him the appearance of a *chanteuse* or a dance-hall girl. Otherwise, he was faultlessly dressed, wearing a blue frock-coat under a light summer cape and with an orchid in his buttonhole; neither the bracelet nor the rings on his fingers were missing. But he seemed changed, appeared just as agitated and restless as I was sluggish and fatigued. Contrary to custom, he spoke precipitantly and insecurely, entreating me to remain with him—he, who belonged to those people who, despite their politeness, let it be understood that it requires immense sacrifice to bring themselves to be together with someone. Further still, he actually took my arm and demanded I reverse my steps. I felt his entire body trembling as in a chill and saw that his eyes, glassy as those of the red-haired woman, either stared vacantly into space or watered with exhaustion and desperation. Just as unbelievable as it had seemed to me that the passing apparition was a woman, so now I was incapable of believing that this creature dragging me into the darkness was a man. We walked silently along the edge of the wood, I depressed and concerned not to look peevish, he with a smile on his lips, gazing in the dim light at his blue jewels, to which, perhaps, clandestine memories were coupled, and to which he seemed to dedicate his final thoughts, passionately and yearningly. We moved along in silence until we reached the bridge over the canal where the Kurfürstendamm begins. There he stopped and detached himself from my arm.

Now I had quite another person facing me, one completely different than before. Could it be that his gems possessed secret powers? Slowly he had come to himself once more, had straightened his shoulders, held his head high again, and stood there stiff, cold and proud—very, very proud. The features of his elongated face now seemed pointed, the delicate blue of his eyes were transformed with the hard, sparkling glints of steel, and the smile on his narrow lips had become ghastly. With his chalky pallor and golden hair Sir Aubrey at that moment no longer looked earthly, more closely resembling a seraph or an archangel than a human being. He remained there a while as if turned to stone and his eyes bored inquisitively into the darkness, through which he suddenly slashed with his white gloves as though he wished to drive away a ghost.

"Such a strange night," he said earnestly. "Such nights are more to be feared than drunkenness; the warm wind permits dangerous fevers to spread. Stendhal writes that when a certain wind blows in Trastevere, murders occur in Rome.

"You too must feel exhausted by this humidity," he continued. "You will hopefully do me the pleasure of having something to eat with me, a trout or two and a bottle of Rhine wine, so that we may regain a little of our strength. However, you must permit that I leave you for a short while alone . . ." And he drew out his watch, a platinum blossom sprinkled with a dew of minute blue gems. "You will wait for me, won't you? It may take a little while, perhaps longer than a quarter of an hour, certainly less than half. Meanwhile, have a bit of a stroll, we shall meet here at the bridge, and whoever comes first will wait for the other." He extended me his hand, which was ice-cold, tipped his hat and turned away. I did as I was told and moved again in the direction of the woods; nearby stand the most beautiful trees one can imagine, giants from the age of the Druids, so tall and densely foliaged that at first glance one might think he were in another world. After the passage of a quarter-hour and before a half-hour had passed, I returned to the bridge but did not find my companion there. Since a delay, like all deficiencies, initially seemed unbearable, I dawdled again along the embankment, without distancing myself too far from our meeting place.

The embankment was empty of people, the houses blind. Everywhere the windows were black, yet some stood open so that inside one made out a somber glint of quicksilver leering through the darkness from the faces of mirrors. A sole upper window was illuminated as though by a mesh of faint beams, the window of a gorgeously ostentatious room in which a lamp glowed on the corner of an armoire—a lamp whose shade of green enamel permitted only a dim and poisonous light to shimmer through, the sort of light that, according to ancient accounts of witches, is favorable to the evil spirits that haunt at midnight.

I remained standing there, and my gaze remained fixed for a long while on this window. Oh, the magic of lighted windows by night. Who would dare seek to express this mystery after having read the novellas of Barbey d'Aurevilly! But in his immortal story *Le rideau cramoisi* it is a carmine-red drapery, in other, later, and so quickly forgotten works it is windows of I no longer know which colors; at my window there were neither draperies nor panes of glass, and yet through the greenish haze one could make out nothing but exquisite ornaments and mirrors that seemed hung with black crepe.

Whether some connection existed between that window which—I need only close my eyes—appears to me exactly as it was then, and what occurred on that evening, I can only surmise, not know. I returned to the bridge with as little success as the first time: of my friend, not a trace. Prepared for a longer wait than before, I leaned against the cast-iron railing close to the bank, removed the hat from my aching head, and surrendered totally to the wondrous beauty of the night.

I shall never forget it. And I must say that I have never experienced one lovelier—I who appreciate the night as no other, and who have loved it as one cannot love the day, with ardor and inexorable desire. My timid spirit, victim of an undefined discord, typically appears to be dozing off, trembling, and does not awaken to full life before the last flames of the departing day are extinguished; as the veils of night gather more and more thickly, I feel myself newborn, feel more deeply my own being, belong more to myself. Had my pecuniary means permitted me to fashion my living conditions differently, I would possibly not have caught sight of the sunlight for years. Oh, had it not been night, I would not have waited for Sir Aubrey—no! Basically it was of no consequence to me to see him ever again. I remained because I should not in any case have returned home, because I would have lingered there, roving about in the shadows under the tall, rustling trees, where one can imagine solitude to be boundless. Yet I could not forgive Sir Aubrey for keeping me awaiting, that I should wait for him while he partook of who knows what pleasures in this warm, stimulating night—perhaps, even, by that hazy greenish light, in the arms of some woman whose beauty might have seemed to him the counterpart to his own. Also, I entertained another suspicion: perhaps he had gone in order to prepare for a later hour the meeting of some occult circle, and had thereby forgotten the world of the living. However it might have been, I need not aggravate myself. With elbows propped against the railing, head cradled in my hands, I gave myself over to my meditations. Beneath me glided the broad, oily planes of the sluggish water, above which vapors mingled together like transparent gauze. The canal was somber. What a difference! By day this district presents a most charming appearance: the branches of the trees lean their crowns together in sisterly affection across the canal, which mirrors the delicate, fresh green of the light and restless foliage. Along this course glide the corpses of the drowned. I recall that on a brilliant April morning in the year 1905, the water bore a bride in her wedding dress. Moreover, in Berlin one sings a jolly song that begins, "A corpse is swimming in the Landwehr canal."

A fresh breeze cooled my forehead and awakened me from my daze. How much time had passed since I had been standing there I could not judge—I had, all undisturbed, dozed off— and could not remember having heard the Kaiser Wilhelm Memorial Church sound the time, and yet it must have sounded more than once. As I lifted my head from my hands, drunk with sleep, and rubbed my eyes, the row of houses took shape against the sky, which had become ash gray. The wind blew chilly, and the trees had commenced to sigh. I put on my hat, which I found lying on the pavement where it had fallen from my head, and again took a few steps along the embankment, in order to view once more the mysterious light. But it was extinguished. At last I determined to return home, for large drops of rain had begun to fall, and the day was dawning.

As a true night-owl I hate the dawn. Without considering that a chill could be harmful to me, I hurried through the empty streets without seeking shelter, pursued by the diffuse light that, weaving together with the rain, trickled from the gloomy sky, while from time to time a grim north wind assailed me. When I reached home, soaked to the skin, I was terribly angry, but that did not hinder my sleeping dreamlessly until noon.

Outside, the rainy weather had set in with a vengeance, and persisted for an entire week, only now and then pausing briefly in order to stream down with renewed force. Somehow I passed the time, and my thoughts often reverted to the events of that curious night. Whenever the postman came, I rushed out to see if he had anything for me. Obviously, I awaited a few lines from Sir Aubrey—which would have been only proper on his part, and I found no explanation for the fact that neither his commanding handwriting nor the seal with the sphinx was to be seen on the dampened envelopes.

On the eve of a holiday the bad weather decided to make peace. Not entirely trusting it, I began my promenade somewhat later. The diffuse light on the horizon signaled more rain. That sweet, mild evening was flooded with blue—such a deep, liquid blue that one might have imagined the city to be sunk in the mysterious depths of the sea. The streets teemed with people. The zest for life, the enchanting awareness of being able to relish the fruits of existence, was mirrored in every face, beamed from the lively, excited eyes, and lent the beauty of the women a particular gloss. The fantasy transported me to the most distant past, and I sought to picture how it might have been on such evenings in the great cities of antiquity, in Babylon, Palmyra, Alexandria, Byzantium. Thus, mingling dream and reality, I was carried along by the stream of people to the bridge over the canal where I had awaited Sir Aubrey for so many hours.

The charm of the place seemed heightened and perfected by the snow-white feathering of swans which, as though purposely, sailed the water in this blue hour. I did not cross the bridge, but entered a beer-garden nearby. As I waited for my food, my glance fell on a newspaper, and thus I learned only then what the whole town had been talking about for two full days.

In Charlottenburg, where the waters churn together as the River Spree reclaims the canal, a corpse had been fished out tightly buttoned up in a coat; it was that of a blond, slender, elegantly dressed young man in evening clothes with all the customary accessories, including gloves on his hands, but barefooted.

The young man had been murdered only a short time before. He bore a deep wound on the left side of his chest. The blow was delivered with such force that the weapon—a thin, flexible blade—had broken off and a piece remained lodged in the wound.

A small fortune in bank notes and gold had been found on the victim, separate and apart from the value of his jewelry, which he wore in wild profusion, each piece richly inlaid with Ceylon sapphires—exclusively with Ceylon sapphires. Other-

113

wise, nothing printed or written which could have thrown light on the murder victim—nothing, absolutely nothing. The label with the tailor's name had been torn out of the suit and the lid of the pocketwatch with the goldsmith's monogram had been removed. The face of the corpse was no longer recognizable, for it had been drenched with acid, which had eaten the flesh away to the very bone.

Such was the end to which Sir Aubrey was destined. It should have been a better or at least a later end, one that occurred after my departure, for I am really not certain which one of us in that moment was the more pitiable. What I endured from the moment I grasped the identity of the corpse, what I suffered—that I hardly need say. And yet it was nothing in comparison to that which might have happened to me. *Remember?*—yes, I believe so. One says that fear is blue; I have experienced it in all colors, have passed through hell; have descended into its bottomless depths, have scaled its jagged heights, the peaks of horror lost in the clouds of madness, and it is a miracle that I did not succumb completely to insanity. I was the sole being in whose company Sir Aubrey had let himself be seen by the light of day; in the Dutch tavern, on the Grunewald terrace, we must have passed for inseparable friends; to be sure, no one would have believed that I—poor I —who seemed so attached to the young man, was the one who knew least of all—indeed, less than nothing. Must this not have aroused the suspicion that I was involved in the violent death of the unknown man? I perceived how the tightly woven net of the rigorous police closed secretly around me, saw myself seized, innocently indicted, hopelessly lost like the pitiable Joseph Lesurques, paying the penalty for another's crime. In the end, I held myself for guilty—and was I not really so, since I had made friends with a person like Sir Aubrey? At that moment it became absolutely clear to me how difficult life is in a strange country, among strangers. Thus, my first thought was to leave Berlin at once and flee to my native land. At night I could not close my eyes, the darkness now depressed me, and I greeted the dawn like a redemption. When it became light, calm and confidence returned. I cast away thoughts of departure, unpacked my things, packed them again in the evening, and swore to myself by all means to depart on the following morning—and in this manner passed many days, black days, and whenever I think back on them, even now, the distant reflection of the hideous fear of that time flares up in brief shudders, and then at the slightest provocation my heart begins to flutter like a wounded bird. But like all human feelings—with the exception of hatred—fear pales and evaporates with time. At this point I should mention that my deep agitation could not be observed externally; my everyday life had altered in no respect, and I sensed no desire to take anyone into my confidence about these consuming agonies, just as I held it to be inappropriate to report to the responsible authorities what I knew of Sir Aubrey or, better, what I did not know. Later I visited the Dutch tavern, and no one inquired after my former companion, no more than at the Grunewald terrace. Everywhere the same reticence. I read each and every newspaper and became almost annoyed—not a single line in which the grisly discovery was mentioned. Apparently nothing had been ascertained. The secret was preserved intact by the sphinx.

Otherwise, from my point of view Sir Aubrey's gruesome end bore no more significance than an everyday occurrence. What would have been the point of pressing my respectful regret so far that I mourned the unknown friend like a Marcellus? Because he was young and handsome? Perhaps he was not so young as he appeared. There are people whose appearance deceives with respect to age, and so far as beauty is concerned, a special explanation does not seem superfluous. I had not found Sir Aubrey's appearance in itself so beautiful as his resemblance to figures long since buried in the dust of centuries; I found him handsome because an image of bygone times found life again in him, because the cherished past was resurrected for me—the forever vanished past. Therefore, I also resisted the temptation to visit the morgue and view under glass that which had been Aubrey de Vere; since the appearance death lends frequently extinguishes that of life, it would have been a pity to permit the image of my memory to be destroyed—that which, animated, seemed cut from an old picture frame. It was important to me that he remain as I had known him, so much resembling those handsome lords at Whitehall Palace who indulged in the wildest pleasures with Killigrew and Rochester, with Barbara Villiers and Nell Gwynn, and who, enveloped in velvet and silk, adorned with lace and ribbons, clutching roses or stroking noble hounds, smiling and striking a proud pose, were captured on canvas by Sir Lely. Still, even more than his outer appearance I treasured irrepressibly certain inner impulses and ideas that suddenly flashed in his conversation, the equal of which I have never witnessed from others or ever found in writing. On his distant voyages this unique creature had developed the capacity to perceive the coming of a storm at sea through the shuddering of the leaves of the date palm; he was able to progress into unexplored distances, which were reflected in his clear, sapphire-colored eyes; he could unriddle mysteries that were revealed only to the chosen, and never penetrated by those who out of mere vocation vainly dedicate their lives, their eye-sight and their minds to dead letters. And all that—youth, beauty and intelligence—must end in the murky waters of a canal.

At last came the day of my departure. Autumn had begun, but not the russet autumn of the south, like a Bacchus draped with a leopard-skin, grapes and fruit in his coppery hair, but the pallid autumn of the lands of rye and beer, with faded sky and a low-hanging sun that drags itself feebly to the horizon. Recently I had cocooned myself in the house; I read voraciously, I read because music was no longer being played and because there was nothing more to see through the window, though it remained open until late in the evening. The fountain no longer flung crystal sprays into the air, the roses on the terrace before the house had lost their petals, and the pretty grove of old trees that might have been painted by Ruysdael had fallen to the axe.

Seven years have passed since then. As if it were yesterday, as if it had never been at all. As if it were yesterday because I have a good memory; as if it had never been, because I make no cult of my memories. I have often thought back on the hideous drama whose blind and invisible witness I may have been on that night of terror and agitation. What actually happened; what really took place there, I have never inquired, for it was no longer important to know—quite the contrary. And the proof of that: recently, when I could have learned the truth, I refused.

Bad weather had caught me in a nightclub in Bucharest, and an acquaintance from my schooldays joined my table; I had also had a distant glimpse of him in Berlin, where apparently he had been studying something or other. Endlessly garrulous, with his droll manner he set my head spinning with all kinds of trivialities, stories from the newspapers, anecdotes about landladies' daughters and chambermaids—all quite elevating themes. What a difference between the way in which I experienced Berlin and the way it had been seen by this man who sat facing me and who took not a little pride in his cheap vulgarity. But for what reason did there awaken on this evening, vivid as never before, the memory of Sir Aubrey, why did the features of Berlin nights with their strange encounters rise so persistently before me? Were the bitter vapors of schnapps to blame, which came from that old and celebrated distillery? No, it was something other. More intoxicating than the drink was the spicy scent of carnations which drifted toward me from the woman at the adjoining table. The same scent that had wafted from the young man with the blue jewels, the scent that once had trailed behind a red-haired woman in a lonely *allée* of the Tiergarten. And I saw her and him and the window with the diffused light once more before me, everything magically vivid. And I surrendered to a hitherto unconscious urge to relate the story of Sir Aubrey de Vere.

I was listened to attentively. I only noted how, from time to time, a slight smile played over the lips of my acquaintance. When I closed with the finding of the corpse, he asked me whether this was the entire story. I nodded. "Then I will tell you the sequel," he went on, "there was a great fuss, the whole matter was immediately covered up, but one could not prevent the truth leaking out. You'll hear the most unbelievable things, just listen . . ."

I cut him off: "I want to know nothing, nothing." And while

he looked at me in astonishment, scarcely knowing what to think, I gave the last word particular emphasis by repeating it several times. "It may seem strange to you," I explained, "but to my mind the beauty of a story consists only in that which remains mysterious; when this is revealed, I find it deprived of all its magic. Circumstances desired that I encounter in my life the fragment of a novel that satisfied my yearning for an endless mystery. Why should I let you spoil that?"

Expressing myself in such a way, I was not precisely lying; and yet behind this method of regarding things—somewhat frivolous, rather literary—something higher was concealed, a noble thought that determined me to silence my acquaintance, and I doubt whether, if I had divulged the same to him, he would have been capable of grasping it. Just as I had not desired to destroy for myself the fair image of his outer appearance by viewing the disfigured face of the poor young man, so I also wished to learn nothing about him, out of fear there might be something that could affect the memory of his rare spiritual essence. May this too remain beautiful, unblemished by the shadows of secrecy and arrogance; may Sir Aubrey de Vere in all things so remain as it pleased me to see him, just so—what concern is it of mine how he really was? The sole proof that I actually knew him has now been destroyed; I burned the letter on whose seal the smiling sphinx was encircled by the word *Remember*. Remember?— yes, of course, I shall not forget; but since the years dim certain old memories and permit them to float on the boundary between reality and fancy, if I should reach an advanced age, it may later seem that this entire occurrence was merely a dream, or a story I read somewhere, or that someone told me a long while ago.

—*Translated by*
David Galloway and
Christian Sabisch

WILLEM de MERODE

GANYMEDE

His beauty had reached its fullest bloom.
One more day and the timidity of youth
Would grow into the dark daring of the man,
His taut limbs on fire with yearning.
But not yet: a quivering glow
Now silver, then a tint of gold,
Then clear and pure, then deep and purple-red,
When he turned and walked, or danced or lay,
Matched the rhythmic quiver of his breathing,
Flowing softly or drawn in quickened gasps,
When hot desire with painful throb made audible
His trembling heart's vibration and with its pulse
His seething blood was swelled to soothing sleep.
And all the tenderness of awaking youth,
Shy and fleeting as the morning dew
Destroyed by the sun in adoration,
Shone dazzlingly in Zeus's brilliant light.
The gods hold dear that class of mortal boys;
Their splendor loves to pair with such dark nakedness.
So Zeus—He saw the sweet secrecy
With which the boy each day, body and soul,

CALAMUS

Offered sacrifice, as he swept from his clear brow
The dark overflow of hair, as his eye
Lingered dreamily on the sky's blue brightness,
Or (the evening mist veiling his light limbs)
He, become flesh, desirous, quite alone,
Walked through the sadness of a shimmering field.

—Translated by
Ross McGregor

H. H. von W.

THE MARQUIS
de SAINT-BRISSAC

One of the most remarkable phenomena that I was shown on
Capri was a male personage of indeterminate age who each
day precisely at noon ascended all alone the street from the
Hotel Quisisana to the piazza, crossed the square with its
gleaming white facades, and mounted the great terrace that
faces out to sea. Totally muffled up, regardless of the weather,
and never without slouch hat and ascot, the singular man
stared intensely into the distance through blue-tinted glasses,
as though seeking a sailing ship, perhaps a steamer, or a
long-awaited fishing bark that was reluctant to show itself.
The stranger (for no native could have such an appearance)
had something stiff in his bearing, if not to say something lifeless, corpse-like. The glimpse of a grey face that one caught as
he moved past resembled the porous stone often used by artists to fake the weathered texture of antique busts. I asked my
English friends the name of this extraordinary gentleman and
learned to my astonishment that it was the Marquis de Saint-
Brissac, a close acquaintance of mine from years before, whom
I had lost sight of as a result of an appalling incident. Noting
this astonishment, my friends hastened to remark that the
Marquis had been resident on the island since the death of his

spouse. With this remark their anglo-saxon features hardened somewhat; I knew such was their manner of cutting the conversation short whenever unwelcome questions threatened. I was not to inquire further. As diversion I turned the conversation to the blue spectacles the stranger wore. I surmised that the Marquis had ruined his eyesight in the glaring sunshine. "One says," my friends replied, "he wears glasses in order that no one see that his eyes are almost always filled with tears." Deeply touched, I turned away. I divined the pain of a human being for whom the years signify only an agonizing test—not of his love, but of his patience to bear this existence further.

In the evening, before falling asleep, I recalled that moment of the past which linked me to the Marquis de Saint-Brissac. For the first time, now that the death of the Marquise was actuality, I dared set things to rights whose tragic secret had obliged me to silence. Once more I saw the Marquise in her pale silk robe, as she appeared at one of the last receptions of the late Madame de Vaugirard. I gazed into her wide, gentian-blue eyes, so reminiscent of drawings by Fidus, thickly fringed by delicate lashes. One could only adore and marvel at this exquisite, slender, dark-haired creature who bore the ancient name of Marquise de Saint-Brissac. Her conspicuous reserve only added to her charm; the Marquis was everywhere envied for this treasure. It was rumored that no other woman could approach her for marital virtue and devotion—none, at least, with such spirit and taste. To be sure, it was said that the Marquise derived from humble bourgeois origins, that she came from Alsace. However, she did not precisely live in the world of high society. She frequently accompanied her husband on extended voyages, or assisted him in his scholarly pursuits. A renowned composer and misogynist confessed on his deathbed that she was the only woman he had ever loved, and bequeathed her a priceless collection of original scores by the most famous masters.

I myself was then scarcely more than a boy. Paris seemed to me the radiant center of the European world, and Maria de Saint-Brissac dominated, reigned over this center like an enchantress. Her madonna-like name seemed significant; must

she not be mother to all of us, though childless herself? But to
an even greater degree she was a comrade; she had an incomparable manner of placing herself at our level, we were smitten by her androgynous appearance, which joined the delicacy
of classic beauty (in the sense of the art of the last century)
with that almost boyish matter-of-factness common to modern
women and to adolescents of both sexes. Now I comprehend
her deportment with greater knowledge: I recognize it as the
necessary expression of a clandestine arrangement hidden
from us all. At the same time, I see in it the tragic prerequis-
ite to the calamitous event in which I was destined to play a
part.

We found ourselves at the charming country estate of the
Saint-Brissacs, the little Château Monjoie near Reims. The
company was not particularly numerous, for the buildings
could accommodate only a few guests. The roses blossomed, the
grain deepened in color as it ripened. We admired in the distance the Gothic ornamentation that twined about the beautiful
towers of the cathedral; these towers ushered in the tranquility of evening, as they sent the rich greeting of their bells
resounding through the landscape. Then we normally strolled
a little beyond the gate, to breathe deeply the spicy odors of
meadow and field. Crickets chirped, the trumpet flowers had
already cautiously closed their white and rosy-red blossoms,
and the path was bordered with wild sage. The last fleeting
farewell of the departing day threw a blush across cloud and
sky. The sun had long disappeared. At such an hour I was
accustomed to stroll beside Frau von Ebersheide. I was much
taken by this young German woman with the noble head of a
chevalier, an Italian heart and a Russian temperament. It is
not as though I loved her as one perhaps could love a young
and tender woman. But her spirit charmed me, her grace
enraptured me, her personality enchanted me beyond the possibility of mere physical desire. She was fulfilled by a great
friendship, and this friendship had led her here. In her heart
she bore a glowing, almost irrepressible attachment to Maria
de Saint-Brissac. Such is not a rare occurrence with young
maidens, and one also encounters it from time to time among
more mature women. The Marquise shrank from the intensity

of such feelings, or so it appeared. Her husband could only with difficulty persuade her to extend an invitation to Frau von Ebersheide; it would not have happened at all were it not for certain commercial considerations which were owed Herr von Ebersheide, an influential banker. Under such circumstances it was not surprising that the Marquise shunned the unwanted guest. Who knows but that perhaps she had a subconscious apprehension of the horrors that were to come from this woman.

During the evening stroll my companion often dallied a little behind and confided in me her thoughts, her hopes and wishes. We frequently spoke of the Marquise, and I exhausted myself with advice about how Maria de Saint-Brissac might be converted to friendship. The more Frau von Ebersheide encountered rejection, the more indomitable became her desire to be near her beloved creature, to envelop her in affection. One evening, as the disc of the moon already hung over the dewy fields, my companion told me she had the irresistible urge to see Maria sleeping. "Just think, simply imagine," she said, "Maria's face without eye-shadow, it would be a completely new look—the closed lids framed by curving brows, the dark tresses of hair against her white skin, shifting with each slight movement of her head. It must be an absolute festival when she sleeps!" I tried to talk Frau von Ebersheide out of such ideas, for I found her plan incompatible with the laws of social deportment; but she was not to be influenced and remained firm by her intention. Even my reference to the fact that the Marquise was in the habit of locking her room (often enough had I heard the sound of the key), even this made no impression. "Ah, well, we shall see what fortune brings me," Frau von Ebersheide countered.

A few hours later I sat across from the Marquis at a green baize table in the library. We were both bent over our books and paid no heed to the time. It might have been midnight as we suddenly heard such frightful, desperate screaming that we both blanched and with the greatest haste climbed to the first floor to determine the cause. In the yellow salon adjoining the bed-chamber of the Marquise, we found Frau von Ebersheide lying on the floor in a dreadful state, her body distorted, flinging her hands and feet about and, as it appeared, the victim of nervous hysteria. One of the guests, a medical student at the Sorbonne, was giving her attention, while other members of our small group stood about perplexed, beside themselves; their fantastic nightgowns, the forgotten chignons, dentures and spectacles transformed them into truly fantastic apparitions. Only the Marquise was missing; her door, as we all observed, remained shut, and she might well be lying in a deep sleep. There were numerous conjectures about the condition of the sick woman; it was said that she might be epileptic. Some spoke of hysteria and somnambulation, but no one could say anything more precise about the source of the attack. Before one had the chance to discuss the alarming event properly, the Marquis sent the guests back to their rooms with a few polite but firm words. Nor could I exclude myself therefrom, and thus had to leave Frau von Ebersheide to the medical student and to her fate. Naturally, I pondered over this bizarre incident; my supposition grew increasingly strong that there was some connection between the intended visit of my friend to the Marquise and her inexplicable seizure.

The following day was to confirm this. Frau von Ebersheide kept to her room, the lady of the house remained invisible, and the guests roamed bewilderedly about the park. The Marquis sent for me. I shall never forget his eyes, how they gazed at me in that tragic hour as I entered through the lacquered folding doors into his study. Those eyes disclosed the most indescribable pain, a passionate despair which his bearing sought to conceal. He gestured to a Louis XVI chair (how I still see it, this chair!), we both took our seats and he began: "I have sent for you because I need your assistance. I can, of course, rely on your discretion?" I wordlessly extended him my hand. During the following exchange he endeavored to suppress the trembling in his voice by continuously clearing his throat. "I presume," he said, "that I have your word of honor." I nodded. "Then," he continued, "you shall come to know my secret, and . . ." he hesitated a moment, "the riddle of the preceding night. Frau von Ebersheide is in love with the Marquise, but my wife has always had an aversion to her. Yesterday, if you can imagine such a thing, the lady forces her way into Maria's bed-chamber and there . . ." Here his voice broke, the blood shot to his head. Pearls of sweat stood out on his forehead, and I feared an attack of apoplexy. He gasped for breath, arching out of his chair. I had arisen, stood close beside him, attempted to support him. "Don't trouble yourself," said the Marquis, "it must be said. Oh," and with this he raised his clenched hands, "render me your assistance in this dark hour. You shall learn something which I had sworn would never cross my lips. Frau von Ebersheide looked on Maria, and on such a summer night she was lying naked on her divan, unclothed, only her body . . ."

He fixed me with burning eyes; I was agitated by these remarks but did not grasp their true meaning. In fact, it seemed to me the modesty and decorum of his own feelings had led him to exaggerate. I was about to speak up in order to utter some word of comfort, but a lordly gesture forbade it. "Say nothing," insisted the Marquis, "until you know all! Frau von Ebersheide, the wretch, looked upon that miraculous creature known to the world as the Marquise de Saint-Brissac. She saw that body,"—the Marquis righted himself with the strength, the courage of a wounded general on the field of battle—"that body which is the body of a youth, and not that of a woman." He sank back. Unconsciously, I had raised my hands to ward off the sudden shock. "Do not judge me," said the Marquis, and his voice had lost all melody. "Perhaps you would be right. But I cannot repent. I have loved, and I shall never love again. I owe you the explanation that this young man was named Eugen Maria Krancz, that I made his acquaintance in Germany and that after some initial reluctance he determined to live at my side under the ideal disguise of a *grande dame*—not as a companion, not as a friend, but as a lover. There dwelled in him the soul of a woman, and this soul could have fulfilled itself in no other guise. We were very happy. You know it and the whole world knows it. But now," —his voice broke into sobs—"now Eugen Maria has fled, in order to die. He left a letter for me. 'Poor friend,' he wrote, 'I must fulfill my destiny, as you yours. Now that my secret is broken, I can no longer remain by your side; but without your love I would scarcely know how and where I should live. I choose death, for it is the most dignified course, and a death which will totally obliterate my body and permit no investigation.' In this way Eugen Maria wanted to save me from the venom of evil tongues, and he wanted to spare the name Saint-Brissac this disgrace. Frau Ebersheide will and must remain silent—that is the most important thing—but then, but then," and the Marquis stretched his arms toward me in anguish, "how do we overtake Eugen Maria, how deter him, what can we do? You know the Foreign Minister . . . couldn't you through diplomatic channels . . . he has certainly fled abroad . . ."

I interrupted his agitated outpouring. "Such a course is not possible. It would lead to nothing."

"But you will speak with Frau von Ebersheide?" I promised to do so. We considered many a plan for rescuing Eugen Maria; not one seemed suitable. I was nonetheless so fortunate as to be able to persuade Frau von Ebersheide that the beautiful, naked, boyish form she had seen was merely an hallucination produced by nervous illness. The broken and desperate Marquis was unspeakably grateful to me. We let it be known that the Marquise had suddenly been taken seriously ill; the guests departed the house within hours. Furthermore, almost no one appeared for the unavoidable comedy of a burial without a corpse, for all feared the hideously contagious sickness which had apparently spirited its victim away so speedily. These circumstances, combined with the genuine grief of the chatelain, prevented discovery. The family doctor had been taken somewhat into confidence, without really telling him anything beyond the fact that the Marquise had departed this life in the most ghastly manner. In the interest of the family, as little attention as possible must be drawn, and the funeral had to take place without the untraceable corpse. Immediately after the last rites I left Monjoie. Circumstances in my own family required my presence in Russia, and I saw the Marquis no more. Years later I heard in Paris that he had departed France.

Now in the tranquility of this evening hour on Capri, by the glow of a friendly lamp, I felt deeply shaken that the lonely, broken man staring out to sea each day waits still for his loved one. His weary spirit cannot believe that the exquisite, peerless body is no more, that at best the beloved soul wanders somewhere, somehow in the unknown; his own sick being dreams only of the return of the past.

As I dressed on the following morning, haggard and depressed, it almost seemed a duty to seek out the Marquis de Saint-Brissac and to assure him of my sympathy. But I quickly put the thought aside. For such deep grief human contact itself is almost a sacrilege; for mourning of this kind words are desecration. The world knew of a great love whose commemoration had robbed this singular man of his senses, but none could surmise the dimension and the secret of this love. Eugen Maria Krancz has no more become an object of hateful jokes than the Marquise de Saint-Brissac was. When Krancz terminated his narrow life in the provinces, his flight was the gateway to a life of love and beauty. When the Marquise ceased to belong to the world, she passed through a similar gateway, and once more through flight, but this time a flight into death.

Before I sailed from Capri, I selected the finest rose that I could find and through one of those dark-skinned idlers lolling about everywhere, I sent the deep red blossom to the Marquis' residence. "A greeting," I wrote in accompaniment, "in memory of Maria."

—*Translated by*
David Galloway and
Christian Sabisch

ERNEST HEMINGWAY

A SIMPLE ENQUIRY

Outside, the snow was higher than the window. The sunlight came in through the window and shone on a map on the pineboard wall of the hut. The sun was high and the light came in over the top of the snow. A trench had been cut along the open side of the hut, and each clear day the sun, shining on the wall, reflected heat against the snow and widened the trench. It was late March. The major sat at a table against the wall. His adjutant sat at another table.

Around the major's eyes were two white circles where his snow glasses had protected his face from the sun on the snow. The rest of his face had been burned and then tanned and then burned through the tan. His nose was swollen and there were edges of loose skin where blisters had been. While he worked at the papers he put the fingers of his left hand into a saucer of oil and then spread the oil over his face, touching it very gently with the tips of his fingers. He was very careful to drain his fingers on the edge of the saucer so there was only a film of oil on them, and after he had stroked his forehead and his cheeks, he stroked his nose very delicately between his fingers. When he had finished he stood up, took the saucer of oil and went into the small room of the hut where he slept.

129

"I'm going to take a little sleep," he said to the adjutant. In that army an adjutant is not a commissioned officer. "You'll finish up."

"Yes, signore maggiore," the adjutant answered. He leaned back in his chair and yawned. He took a paper-covered book out of the pocket of his coat and opened it; then laid it down on the table and lit his pipe. He leaned forward on the table to read and puffed at his pipe. Then he closed the book and put it back in his pocket. He had too much paper work to get through. He could not enjoy reading until it was done. Outside, the sun went behind a mountain and there was no more light on the wall of the hut. A soldier came in and put some pine branches, chopped into irregular lengths, into the stove. "Be soft, Pinin," the adjutant said to him. "The major is sleeping."

Pinin was the major's orderly. He was a dark-faced boy, and he fixed the stove, putting the pine wood in carefully, shut the door, and went into the back of the hut again. The adjutant went on with his papers.

"Tonani," the major called.

"Signor maggiore?"

"Send Pinin in to me."

"Pinin!" the adjutant called. Pinin came into the room. "The major wants you," the adjutant said.

Pinin walked across the main room of the hut towards the major's door. He knocked on the half-opened door. "Signor maggiore?"

"Come in," the adjutant heard the major say, "and shut the door."

Inside the room the major lay on his bunk. Pinin stood beside the bunk. The major lay with his head on the rucksack that he had stuffed with spare clothing to make a pillow. His long, burned, oiled face looked at Pinin. His hands lay on the blankets.

"You are nineteen?" he asked.

"Yes, signor maggiore."

"You have ever been in love?"

"How do you mean, signor maggiore?"

"In love—with a girl?"

"I have been with girls."

"I did not ask that. I asked if you had been in love—with a girl."

"Yes, signor maggiore."

"You are in love with this girl now? You don't write her. I read all your letters."

"I am in love with her," Pinin said, "but I do not write her."

"You are sure of this?"

"I am sure."

"Tonani," the major said in the same tone of voice, "can you hear me talking?"

There was no answer from the next room.

"He cannot hear," the major said. "And you are quite sure that you love a girl?"

"I am sure."

"And," the major looked at him quickly, "that you are not corrupt?"

"I don't know what you mean, corrupt."

"All right," the major said. "You needn't be superior."

Pinin looked at the floor. The major looked at his brown face, down and up him, and at his hands. Then he went on, not smiling. "And you don't really want—" the major paused. Pinin looked at the floor. "That your great desire isn't really —" Pinin looked at the floor. The major leaned his head back on the rucksack and smiled. He was really relieved: life in the army was too complicated. "You're a good boy," he said. "You're a good boy, Pinin. But don't be superior and be careful someone else doesn't come along and take you."

Pinin stood still beside the bunk.

"Don't be afraid," the major said. His hands were folded on the blanket. "I won't touch you. You can go back to your platoon if you like. But you had better stay on as my servant. You've less chance of being killed."

"Do you want anything of me, signor maggiore?"

"No," the major said. "Go on and get on with whatever you were doing. Leave the door open when you go out."

Pinin went out, leaving the door open. The adjutant looked up at him as he walked awkwardly across the room and out of the door. Pinin was flushed and moved differently than he had moved when he brought in the wood for the fire. The adjutant looked after him and smiled. Pinin came in with more wood for the stove. The major, lying on his bunk, looking at his cloth-covered helmet and his snow glasses that hung from a nail on the wall, heard him walk across the floor. The little devil, he thought, I wonder if he lied to me.

JEAN COCTEAU

THE WHITE PAPER

As long ago as I can remember, and even looking all the way back to that age when the senses have still to come under the influence of the mind, I find traces of my love for boys.

I have always loved the stronger sex, the one I consider it legitimate to call the fairer sex. The misfortunes I have had at the hands of a society which views the unusual as the fit object of condemnation and obliges us, if they be rare, to reform our natural inclinations.

I recall three critical, three decisive incidents. My father lived in a little château near S***. Attached to that château was a park. At the further limit of the park, beyond where the château property stopped, were a farm and a watering-place. In return for some daily milk and butter and eggs, my father enabled the farmer to avoid the cost of fencing his animals off our land.

One August morning, I was prowling about the park with a toy rifle that fired caps and, playing at hunting, using a hedge for a blind, I was waiting for some animal to pass, when from

133

my hiding-place I spied a young farm-boy leading a draft horse down to water. Wishing to ride out into the pond and knowing that people never ventured to the far end of the park, he peeled off his clothes, sprang upon the horse and guided it into the water a few yards from where, concealed, I was watching. The sunburn on his face, on his neck, his arms, his feet, contrasting with the whiteness of the rest of his skin, made me think of chestnuts bursting out of their husks; but those were not the only dark patches on his body. My gaze was drawn to another, from whose midst an enigma and every one of its details rose into the plainest view.

My ears rang. The blood rushed to my head, my face turned scarlet. The strength drained out of my legs. My heart beat like the heart of a murderer preparing to kill. Without realizing what was happening, I stood up, reeled, and fainted dead away, and it was only after a four-hour search that they found me. When I'd recovered my wits and was on my feet again, I took instinctive care not to disclose what had caused my weakness and at the risk of sounding ridiculous, I declared that I'd been frightened by a hare that had bolted from a thicket.

The second incident occurred the following year. My father had given some gypsies permission to camp in that same remote spot in the park where I had lost consciousness. I was taking a walk with my maid. All of a sudden, letting out a great shriek, she grabbed my hand and began to drag me after her, ordering me under no circumstances to look back. The weather was sparkling clear and hot. Two young gypsy lads had undressed and were climbing in a tree. A spectacle rendered unforgettable by my maid's shock and as though permanently framed by my disobedience: even if I live to be a hundred, thanks to that shriek and that mad dash I shall always see a covered wagon, a woman rocking a new-born infant, a smoking fire, a white horse grazing and, climbing a tree, two bronzed bodies each thrice-spotted with patches of black.

The third time it had to do with a young hired man whose name, if I'm not mistaken, was Gustave, who waited on the table. Aware of my glances, it would be all he could do to keep a straight face while serving. From returning again and again to dwell upon those memories of the farm-boy and of the gypsies, I'd come to have the keenest wish to touch my hand to what my eye had seen.

My scheme was wonderfully naive. I'd make a drawing of a woman, I'd take the picture and show it to Gustave, I'd make him laugh, once I'd encouraged him I'd ask him to let me touch the mystery which, seated at the dining table, I'd been trying to visualize behind the prominent bulge in his trousers. Now, the only woman I had ever seen wearing a shift was my nursemaid; I supposed that artists invented the firm breasts they put on women, and that in reality all women had flabby ones. My sketch was realistic. Gustave burst out laughing, asked who my model was; taking advantage of a new fit of mirth, with breathtaking courage I had proceeded halfway to the mark when he turned very red, batted my hand aside, pinched my ear, by way of excuse saying he was ticklish and, deathly afraid of losing his job, conducted me to the door.

Several days later Gustave stole some wine. My father dismissed him. I interceded, I wept, I tried everything, and failed. I accompanied Gustave to the railroad station, carrying the checker set and checkerboard I'd given him as a present for his little boy whose photograph he had often showed me.

My mother died in giving birth to me and I had always lived alone with my father, a sad and charming man. His sadness preceded the loss of his wife. Even when contented he had been sad and that is why, in an effort to understand his sadness, I sought beyond his bereavement for its deeper-lying roots.

The homosexual recognizes the homosexual as infallibly as the Jew recognizes the Jew. He detects him behind whatever the mask, and I guarantee my ability to detect him between the lines of the most innocent books. This passion is less simple than moralists are wont to maintain. For just as homosexual women exist, women with the outward aspect of Lesbians but who seek after men in the special way men seek after women, so homosexual men exist who do not know what they are and who live out the whole of their lives in a restlessness, in an uneasiness they ascribe to some lack of vitality, or to a sickly or retiring nature.

It has always seemed to me that my father and I too closely

resembled each other not to have this essential feature in common. He was probably unaware of his true bent; at any rate, instead of pursuing it, he struggled along another path without knowing what it was that made the way so dreary and life to hang so heavy upon him. Had he discovered the tastes he never had the chance to cultivate and which his phrases, his gestures, certain of his movements, a thousand details about his person revealed to me, he would have been thunderstruck. In his day, a man would kill himself for slighter cause. But no; he lived, living in ignorance of himself, and he accepted his burden.

To this exceeding blindness it may be that I owe the fact that I was brought into the world. Well, I deplore it, for it would have been to the benefit of us both had my father known the delights which would have spared me so much sorrow.

I entered the Lycée Condorcet in the third form. There the boys' senses awakened and, uncontrolled, grew like a baneful weed. It was nothing but holes poked in pockets and soiled handkerchiefs. Drawingboards on their laps, the pupils went particularly wild in art class. Sometimes, during an ordinary class, an ironical teacher would suddenly call upon a pupil on the verge of orgasm. The pupil, his cheeks aflame, would slouch to his feet and stammering whatever came to his head, endeavor to transform his dictionary into a fig-leaf. Our hilarity would increase his embarrassment.

The classroom smelled of gas, chalk, sperm. That mixture turned my stomach. I must say this: that which was a vice in the eyes of all my classmates, not being one in mine or, to be more exact, being the base parody of a form of love my instinct was to respect, I was the only one who appeared to disapprove of the situation. The result was perpetual sarcasm and assaults upon what the others took to be my prudery.

But Condorcet was a day-school. These practices never led as far as love affairs; they seldom got beyond the confines of a routine, clandestine sport.

One of the pupils, whose name was Dargelos, enjoyed a great prestige because of a virility considerably in advance of his years. He exhibited himself cynically and made a business of putting on a show which he even presented to pupils in other forms in exchange for rare stamps and tobacco. The seats surrounding his desk were at a premium. I still have an image of his brown skin. By the extremely short trousers he wore and the socks dragging around his ankles one could tell that he was proud of his legs. We all wore short pants, but thanks to his man's legs, only Dargelos was *barelegged*. Unbuttoned at the throat, his open shirt revealed a strong neck. A thick lock of hair hung over his forehead. That face—with its somewhat heavy lips, its somewhat slitted eyes, its somewhat snub nose—had every last one of the features of the type that was to be my undoing. Oh, it is cunning, the fatality that disguises itself, and gives us the illusion of being free and, when all is said and done, each time lures us straight into the same trap.

Dargelos's presence drove me out of my mind. I avoided him. I lay in wait for him. I dreamt of some miracle which would bring his attention to bear on me, disencumber him of his vainglory, reveal to him the real meaning of my attitude which, as things stood, he had necessarily to view as some sort of preposterous prudishness and which was nothing short of an insane desire to please him.

My sentiments were vague. I could not manage to specify them. They caused me either extreme discomfort or extreme delight. The only thing I was sure of was that they were in no way comparable to those my comrades experienced.

One day, unable to bear it any longer, I declared my problem to a pupil whose parents knew my father, and whom I saw on and off outside of school hours.

"But you're a complete idiot," said he, "there's nothing to it. Invite Dargelos to your place some Sunday, get him out there in the park, and the trick's done. It's automatic."

What trick? I'd not been plotting any trick. I mumbled something about this not having any connection with the sort of pleasure anyone could take right there in class and, unsuccessfully, I endeavored to clad my dream in the form of words. My friend shrugged his shoulders. "Why go looking for difficulties where there aren't any?" he asked. "Dargelos is bigger than we are"—he employed other terms—"but all you have to do is flatter him and you've got him wrapped around your little finger. If you like him, all you need to do is let him pitch it at you."

The crudeness of this recommendation stunned me. I realized that it was impossible to make myself understood. Supposing that Dargelos agreed to a rendezvous, what, I wondered, would I say to him, what would I do? I was not interested in fiddling around for five minutes, what I wanted was to live with him for the rest of my life. In short, I adored him, and resigned myself to suffer in silence, for, without giving my malady the name of love, I fully sensed that a whole world lay between it and our classroom exercises and that, in the class, it would evoke no response.

This adventure had no beginning but it did have an end. Urged on by the pupil in whom I had confided, I asked Dargelos to meet me in a vacant classroom after the five o'clock study hall. He turned up. I'd counted on some godsent inspiration that would dictate to me what to do. Face to face with him, I lost my bearings completely. All I saw were his sturdy legs and his scraped knees blazoned with scabs, mud and ink.

"What do you want?" he asked me, smiling cruelly. I surmised what he was imagining and that, insofar as he was concerned, my request could have no other meaning. I tried to invent some answer.

"I wanted to tell you," I mumbled, "to look out for the vice-principal, he's got it in for you."

The lie was absurd, for Dargelos's charm and bewitched our masters too. The privileges of beauty are immense. It gains its way even with those who seem the least responsive to it.

Dargelos leaned his head a little to one side and grinned. "The vice-principal?"

"Yes," I persevered, from my terror deriving the strength to continue, "the vice-principal. 'I'm watching Dargelos. He's going just a bit too far. I've got my eye on him'—I heard him say that to the headmaster."

"Ah. So I'm going just a bit too far, am I," he replied. "Well, old man, I'll give him an eyeful. And as for you, if all you want is to worry me with crap like that, I can warn you right now that the next time you do I'll plant a foot in your ass."

He disappeared.

For the space of a week I complained of cramps so as not to have to go to school and endure a glance from Dargelos. When I returned I learned that he was sick in bed. I didn't dare ask how he was getting on. There were rumors. He was a Boy Scout. They referred to an unwise dip in the mid-winter Seine, mentioned pneumonia. One afternoon during the geography lesson we were informed of his death. My tears forced me to leave the room. Youth is not the age of compassion. For a good number of pupils, this announcement, which the teacher rose to his feet to make, was simply a tacit authorization to do nothing for the rest of the day. And on the next day the renewed practice of their habits closed over their mourning.

Nevertheless, the *coup de grâce* had just been delivered to eroticism. Too many little pleasures were spoiled by the troubling phantom of the superb animal of delights whose figure had moved even death itself.

Summer vacation over, and now, having advanced into the second form, a radical change seemed to have occurred in my classmates. Their voices were different, they were smoking. They were shaving a hint of beard, they went out bareheaded, were wearing knickers or long trousers. Onanism yielded to braggadocio. Dirty post cards were circulating. *En masse,* all these lads were turning towards women as plants turn towards the sun. It was then that, in order to keep in step with the rest, I began to play out of tune with my nature, and to warp it.

Rushing headlong towards their own truth, they swirled me towards falsehood. What interested them repelled me; I blamed that upon my ignorance. I admired their dash, their composure, their unselfconsciousness. I forced myself to follow their example and to share their enthusiasms. I had continually to vanquish my disgust and my shame. This discipline finally bore fruit and made the task fairly easy. When things were at their worst, I'd tell myself that debauchery was rough going for everyone, but that the others faced up to the job with a better grace than I.

On Sunday, if the weather was fair, the whole band of us would set off with our rackets, giving it out as our intention that we were off for an afternoon of tennis at Auteuil. The rackets were stowed along the way with the concierge of one of the boys whose family lived in Marseille, and from there we hastened in the direction of the brothels in the rue de Provence. Halting before the leather drape at the entrance, the timidity proper to our youth would reassert itself. We'd pace to and fro, up and down, deliberating whether to enter that doorway as bathers hesitate about plunging into cold water. We'd toss coins to decide who was to lead the way. I'd be in a panic over the possibility that fate might designate me. Whoever was chosen to go first finally sneaked along the wall, slunk inside, the rest of us on his heels and in single file.

Nothing has a greater power to intimidate than children and whores. Too many things go into composing the gap dividing us from them. One doesn't know how to break the silence and attune one's outlook to theirs. In the rue de Provence, the only terrain of mutual understanding was the bed upon which I would lie down with the whore and the jointly accomplished act which gave neither of us the slightest pleasure.

Those visits emboldened us, we accosted streetwalkers and thus made the acquaintance of a little individual who was known as Alice de Pilbrac. She lived on the rue La Bruyère in a modest apartment which smelled of coffee. If I remember rightly, Alice de Pilbrac while she did receive us, allowed us to do no more than admire her in a sordid dressing-gown and with her thin drab hair hanging down her back. This regimen made my comrades pine or fidget, but it suited me handsomely. In the end, they grew tired of waiting and took off on a new tack. This time it was to pool our money, rent the front row for the Sunday matinee at the Eldorado, throw bouquets of violets at the vocalists and then go to the stagedoor and wait for them in the savage cold.

If I recount these trifling episodes it is to indicate the appalling fatigue and stricken feeling of utter hollowness with which our Sunday outings would reward us, and my amazement to witness my comrades feast the whole week long on the details of the miserable nothings we accomplished.

One of my friends knew the actress Berthe, through whom I met Jeanne. They were in the theatre. I took a liking to Jeanne; I asked Berthe to do me the favor of finding out if she would be willing to become my mistress. Berthe brought back word that I had been turned down and suggested that I deceive my comrade by sleeping with her. Shortly afterward, learning from him that Jeanne was disappointed at not having heard anything from me, I went to see her. We discovered that my message had never been transmitted and decided to take our revenge by reserving for Berthe the surprise of our happiness.

That adventure left such an imprint upon my sixteenth, seventeenth and eighteenth years that today, whenever I see Jeanne's name in a newspaper or her picture on a billboard, I still experience a shock. And for all that, it is still possible to say nothing at all in relating this banal affair which measured itself out in long waits in dress-shops and in playing a pretty disagreeable dual role, for the Armenian who kept Jeanne thought highly of me and made me his confidant.

It was in the second year that the scenes began. After the most lively one, which transpired at five in the afternoon on the place de la Concorde, I abandoned Jeanne on a traffic island and fled home. I was not halfway through dinner, and was already planning a telephone call, when I was told that a lady was waiting downstairs in a taxi.

It was Jeanne.

"I'm not hurt," she said, "on account of having been left stranded in the middle of the place de la Concorde, but you haven't got the guts to play the game all the way through to the end. Two months ago you'd have crossed the whole square. Don't let yourself think you proved yourself able to act like a man. All you proved is that your love is as weak as soda pop."

This poignant analysis enlightened me: it advised me that I was no longer enslaved.

In order that my love revive, I had to discover that Jeanne was unfaithful to me. She was, with Berthe. Today, this element in the story lays bare the basis of my love for her. Jeanne was a boy; she was fond of women, and I loved her with what my nature contained of the feminine. I came upon them in bed tangled up like an octopus. Administer a beating, that was what the situation called for; and instead I pleaded. They laughed at me, consoled me, and that was the bedraggled conclusion to an affair which, although it died of its own accord, nevertheless wreaked sufficient havoc upon me to alarm my father and force him to emerge from the reserve he always maintained in regard to me.

As I was returning to my father's house one evening at a later than usual hour, a woman approached me in the place de la Madeleine. She had a gentle voice. I peered at her, found her lovely, young, fresh as a rose. She said her name was Rose, she liked to talk and we strolled hither and yon until that time of night when the market-gardeners, asleep over the vegetables in their cart, drop the reins and permit their horses to wend their way through a deserted Paris.

I was to leave the next day for Switzerland. I gave Rose my name and address. She sent me letters written on lined paper and enclosed stamps for the reply postage. Back again in Paris, happier than Thomas de Quincey, I found Rose at the very same spot where we'd met the first time. She invited me to come to her hotel in Pigalle.

The Hotel M*** was lugubrious. The stairway stank of ether, which provides consolation for whores who come home without having bagged a client. The room was the prototype of rooms that are never tidied. Rose smoked in bed. I complimented her on how well she looked.

"That's because I'm made up. You should see me when I'm not," she said. "I haven't got any eyelashes. I look like a jack-rabbit."

I became her lover. She would take nothing from me, not even the smallest gift. Ah, yes, she did accept a dress since, as she claimed, it was of absolutely no commercial value to her, was too elegant for the business, and would go into the closet to be preserved as a souvenir.

One Sunday there came a knock on the door. I jumped up.

Rose told me to take it easy and get back into bed. "It's just my brother. He'll be delighted to see you."

This brother resembled the farm-boy and the Gustave of my childhood. He was nineteen and blessed with the worst sort of style. His name was Alfred or Alfredo and he talked a queer kind of French, but I was indifferent to the question of his nationality; he struck me as belonging to the country of prostitution which has its own patriotism and this language of his may have been its idiom.

If I had to wage a somewhat uphill struggle to keep my interest in the sister alive, one may imagine how precipitous was the slope down which I was carried by a tremendous interest in the brother. He, as his countrymen put it, dug me perfectly, and we were soon employing all the craft and stealth of a pair of Apaches to contrive get-togethers and to prevent Rose from finding out about them.

Alfred's body was more the body my dreams had possessed than the powerfully outfitted body of some adolescent or other. A faultless body, rigged with muscles like a schooner with ropes, whose limbs seemed to radiate out like the rays of a star from a nuclear fleece whence would rear the one thing in a man that is incapable of lying and which is absent in women, who are constructed for feigning.

I realized I'd started off on the wrong road. I swore to myself never to go astray again, and now that I was on the right one, to follow it instead of getting sidetracked into the ways of others, and to pay much more attention to what my senses demanded than to what morality advised.

Alfred reciprocated my caresses. He confessed that he wasn't Rose's brother. He was her business manager.

Rose continued to play her role and we ours. Alfred would wink at me, give me the high sign and sometimes go off into gales of wild laughter. Puzzled, Rose would frown uncomprehendingly, never suspecting that we were in a conspiracy and that between us existed ties which guile consolidated.

The hotel porter came in one day and found us wallowing to right and left of Rose. "There you are, Jules," she exclaimed, "my brother on one side of me and my sweetie-pie on the other. They're all I love in the world."

The lies began to tire the lazy Alfred. He declared that he couldn't go on living this way, working one side of the street while Rose worked the other, tramping up and down this open-air market where the vendors are the merchandise. In other words, he was asking me to get him out of there.

I assured him that nothing would give me greater pleasure. We decided that I'd reserve a room in a place des Ternes hotel where Alfred would install himself permanently, that after dinner I'd join him there for the night, that with Rose I'd pretend to think he'd disappeared and say that I was starting out to search for him, which would leave me free and net us plenty of good times.

I arranged for the room, settled Alfred in it, and dined at my father's. The meal over, I rushed to the hotel. No Alfred. I waited from nine until one in the morning. Still no Alfred; and so I went home, my heart as heavy as lead.

The next morning towards eleven I went back to the place des Ternes to see what was what; Alfred was in his room, asleep. He woke up, whimpered, whined and told me it wasn't any use trying, he didn't have the necessary self-control to break his old habits, he couldn't ever possibly do without Rose. He'd hunted for her all night long, first at her hotel at which she'd checked out, then on sidewalk after sidewalk, in every brasserie in Montmartre and in all the rue de Lappe dance halls.

"Sure," I told him, "Rose is crazy. So what? She's got a fever. She's staying with a friend of hers who lives on the rue de Budapest."

He begged me to take him there without a moment's delay.

Rose's former room at the Hotel M**** was a little palace next to this one belonging to her friend. We had to fight to keep afloat in a practically paste-like atmosphere of odors, clothing and doubtful sentiments. The women were in their slips. Alfred was on the floor, moaning and hugging Rose's knees. I was pale. Rose turned a face smeared with cosmetics and tears in my direction, she stretched her arms towards me: "Oh," she cried, "let's all go back to Pigalle and live together for ever and ever. I'm sure that's what Alfred wants. It is, isn't it, Alfred?" she added, yanking his hair. He remained silent.

I had to accompany my father to Toulon for the wedding of my cousin, the daughter of Vice-Admiral G***-F***. The future looked enormously unsure, bleak. I announced this family trip to Rose, left them—Rose and the still mute Alfred —at the Pigalle hotel, and promised I'd visit them as soon as I got back.

At Toulon I noticed that Alfred hadn't returned a little gold chain of mine. It was my fetish. I'd looped it around his wrist, forgotten about it, and he'd not remembered to remind me.

Home again in Paris, I went to the hotel and when I entered the room, Rose welcomed me with a big kiss. There wasn't much light to see by. I didn't recognize Alfred at first. What was there unrecognizable about him?

The police were scouring Montmartre. Alfred and Rose were worried sick because of their questionable nationality. They'd fixed themselves up with a set of false passports, were ready to take off at the drop of a hat, and Alfred, full of the lore he'd picked up at the movies, had dyed his hair. It was with an anthropometric precision that his little blond face contradicted the jet-black mop surmounting it. I asked him for my chain. He denied having it. Rose declared he did indeed have it. He said it wasn't true, swore it wasn't. She fished it out from under the pillow, he swore he hadn't put it there, threatened her, threatened me and pulled a pistol out of his pocket.

I made it into the hallway in one leap and went down the stairs four at a time, Alfred hot on my trail.

Outside, I hailed a taxi. I shouted my address, jumped in, and as the taxi started off, I turned and peered through the rear window.

Alfred was standing motionless outside the door of the hotel. Great tears were flowing down his cheeks. He extended his arms imploringly; he called to me. Under his badly dyed hair he was heartbreakingly pale.

I wanted to rap on the glass partition, to tell the driver to stop. I could not simply turn my back upon that solitary distress and run off like a coward to take sanctuary in family comfort; but, on the other hand, there was the chain to consider, the pistol, I thought of the false passports and of this flight in which Rose would certainly ask me to join them. And now, whenever I ride in one of those old red Paris taxis, I have only to close my eyes to conjure up the little silhouette of Alfred, and to see the tears streaming down his face under that Chicago racketeer's hairdo.

The Admiral being ill and my cousin off on her honeymoon, I had to return to Toulon. It would be tedious to describe that charming Sodom smitten by wrathful heavenly fires in the form of a caressing sun. In the evening a still sweeter indulgence inundates the city and, as in Naples, as in Venice, a holiday-making crowd saunters in slow circles through the squares where fountains play, where there are trinket and tinsel stalls, waffle-sellers, and street hawkers. From the four corners of the earth men whose hearts go out to masculine beauty come to admire the sailors who hang about singly or drift in groups, smile in reply to longing's stare, and never refuse the offer of love. Some salt or nocturnal potion transforms the most uncouth ex-convict, the toughest Breton, the wildest Corsican into these tall, flower-decked girls with their low-necked jumpers, their swaying hips, their pompoms, these lithely graceful, colorful whores who like to dance and who, without the least sign of awkwardness, lead their partners into the obscure little hotels down by the port.

One of the cafés where you can dance is owned by a former café-concert singer who has the voice of a girl and who used to do a strip-tease, starting it off as a woman. These days he wears a turtle-neck sweater and rings on his fingers. Flanked by the seafaring giants who idolize him and whose devotion he repays with mistreatment. In a large, childish hand and with his tongue stuck out he jots down the prices of the drinks his wife announces to him in a tone of naive asperity.

One evening, pushing open the door to the place run by that astonishing creature who ever basks in the midst of the respect and deferential gestures of a wife and several husbands, I stopped abruptly, rooted to the spot. I'd just caught sight, caught a profile view, of Dargelos's ghost. Leaning one elbow upon the mechanical piano, it was Dargelos in a sailor-suit.

Of the original Dargelos this facsimile had above all the barefaced arrogance, the insolent and casual manner. *Tapageuse* was spelled out in letters of gold on the flat hat tilted over his left eyebrow, his tie was knotted up over his Adam's apple and he was wearing those amply bell-bottomed pants which sailors used once upon a time to roll to the thigh and which nowadays the regulations find some moral excuse or other for outlawing.

In another place I'd never have dared put myself within range of that lofty stare. But Toulon is Toulon; dancing eliminates uncomfortable preambles, it throws strangers into each other's arms and sets the stage for love.

They were playing dipsy-doodly music full of sauciness and winning smiles; we danced a waltz. The arched bodies are riveted together at the groin; grave profiles cast thoughtful downward glances, turn less quickly than the tripping and now and then plodding feet. Free hands assume the gracious attitudes affected by common folk when they take a cup of tea or piss it out again. A springtime exhilaration transports the bodies. Those bodies bud, push forth shoots, branches, hard members bump, squeeze, sweats commingle, and there's another couple heading for one of the rooms with the globe lights overhead and the eiderdowns on the bed.

Despoiled of the accessories which intimidate civilians and of the manner sailors adopt to screw up their courage, *Tapageuse* became a meek animal. He had got his nose broken by a syphon-bottle in the course of a brawl. Without that crooked nose his face might well have been uninteresting. A syphon-bottle had put the finishing touch to a masterpiece.

Upon his naked torso, this lad, who represented pure luck to me, had *Lousy Luck* tattooed in blue capital letters. He told me his story. It was brief. That afflicting tattoo condensed it in a nutshell. He'd emerged from the brig. After the *Ernest-Renan* mutiny there'd been the inquest; they'd confused him with a colleague; that was why his hair was only half an inch long; he deplored a tonsure which wonderfully became him.

"I've never had anything but lousy luck," he repeated, shaking that bald little head reminiscent of a classical bust, "and it ain't never going to change."

I slipped my fetish-chain around his neck. "I'm not giving it to you," I explained, "it's a charm, but not much of one, I guess, for it hasn't done much for me and won't for you either. Just wear it tonight."

Then I uncapped my fountain pen and crossed out the ominous tattoo. I drew a star and a heart above it. He smiled. He understood, more with his skin than with the rest, that he was in safe hands, that our encounter wasn't like the ones he'd grown accustomed to: hasty encounters in which selfishness satisfies itself.

Lousy luck! Incredible—with that mouth, those teeth, those eyes, that belly, those shoulders and cast-iron muscles, those legs, how was it possible? Lousy luck, with that fabulous little undersea plant, forlorn, inert, shipwrecked on the frothy fleece, which then stirs, unwrinkles, develops, rouses itself and hurls its sap afar when once it is restored to its element of love. Lousy luck? I couldn't believe it; and to resolve the problem I drowned myself in a vigilant sleep.

Lousy Luck remained very still beside me. Little by little, I felt him undertaking the delicate maneuver of extricating his arm from under my elbow. I didn't for a single instant think he was meditating a dirty trick. It would have been to demonstrate my ignorance of the code of the fleet. "Gentlemanliness," "semper fidelis" and the strict up-and-up embellish the mariners' vocabulary.

I watched him out of the corner of one eye. First, several times, he fingered the chain, seemed to be weighing it, kissed it, rubbed it against his tattoo. Then, with the dreadful deliberation of a player in the act of cheating, he tested to see if I was asleep, coughed, touched me, listened to my breathing, approached his face to my open right hand lying by my face and gently pressed his cheek to my palm.

Indiscreet witness of this attempt by an unlucky child who, in the midst of the sea's wilderness, felt a life-saver coming within reach, I had to make a major effort not to lose my wits, feign a sudden awakening and demolish my life.

Day had scarcely dawned when I left him. My eyes avoided his, which were laden with all the great expectations surging up in him and the hopes to which he couldn't give expression. He returned my chain. I kissed him, I edged past him and switched off the lamp by the bed.

Downstairs, I had to write the hour—5:00—when sailors are to be waked. On a slate opposite the room numbers were quantities of similar instructions. As I picked up the chalk I noticed I'd forgotten my gloves. I went back up. A sliver of light showed under the door. The lamp by the bed must have been turned on again. I was unable to resist peeping through the keyhole. It supplied the baroque frame to a little head upon which sprouted about half an inch of hair.

Lousy Luck, his face buried in my gloves, was weeping bitterly.

Ten long minutes I hesitated before that door. I was about to knock when Alfred's visage superimposed itself in the most exact manner upon *Lousy Luck's.* I stole on tiptoe down the stairs, pushed the button opening the door and slammed the door behind me. In the center of an empty square a fountain was pronouncing a solemn soliloquy.

"No," I thought to myself, "we aren't of the same species. It's wonderful—it's enough—to move a flower, a tree, a beast. But you can't live with one."

Now the sun had risen. Cocks crowed out over the sea. The sea lay cool and dark. A man came around a corner with a shotgun on his shoulder. Hauling an enormous weight, I trudged towards my hotel.

Fed up with sentimental adventures, incapable of responding to them, I limped about, weary in body and soul. I looked for some underworld atmosphere. I found it in a public bath. The place recalled the *Satyricon,* with its little cubicles, the central inner court, the low-ceilinged room where, seated on Turkish hassocks, young men were playing cards. When the owner gave the signal they stood and lined up against the wall. He then fingered their biceps, palpated their thighs, brought their less visible and most intimate charms into view and passed them out like tickets.

The clientele knew exactly what it was after, wasted few words and less time getting down to brass tacks. I must have been a mystery to those young men who were used to clear-cut requirements and to fulfilling them speedily. They gave me the blankest of bewildered looks; for I preferred conversation to action.

In me, heart and senses are so inextricably combined that I don't know quite how to involve the one without committing the others too. It's this that leads me to overstep the limits of friendship and makes me fear a summary contact from which I run the danger of catching the germ of love. I finally came to envy those who, not suffering vaguely in the presence of beauty, knowing what they want, have everything tabbed and filed, specialize in a vice, perfect it, pay and satisfy it.

One of them issued instructions that he be insulted, another that he be draped in chains. To reach his crisis, still another (a moralist) needed the spectacle of a young Hercules slaying a rat with a red-hot needle.

I saw them come and go, it was one long procession of those sage individuals who know the exact recipe for their pleasure and for whom it's all smooth sailing because, no nonsense about it, they pay punctually and the marked price to have a respectable bourgeois complication treated. The majority were wealthy industrialists who came down from the North to exercise their penchants and then went home to their wives and children.

After a while I began to space out my visits, for my almost continual presence was beginning to arouse suspicions. In France you're apt to run into difficulties if the role you're enacting isn't all of one piece. The miser had better be miserly all the time, the jealous man always jealous. That accounts for Molière's success. The proprietor thought me in league with the police. He gave me to understand that you are either a client or merchandise. And that you can't combine the two.

This warning shook me out of my lethargy and obliged me to abandon my unworthy habits. I took to the great outdoors again, where I saw the remembrance of Alfred floating on the faces of a thousand young apprentice bakers, butchers, cyclists, errand-boys, zouaves, sailors, acrobats and other professional travesties.

One of my few regrets was the transparent mirror. You get into a dark booth and pull aside a curtain. Now you are looking through a fine metallic screen, your view commands a small bathroom. On the other side, the screen was a mirror so highly polished and so smooth that no one could possibly suspect that it was honeycombed with spyholes.

When my budget could afford it, I'd pass entire Sundays at my post. There were twelve bathrooms, and of the twelve mirrors there was only one of this kind. It had cost a lot of money, and the proprietor had had to import it from Germany. His personnel didn't know about the observatory. Young members of the working class provided the show.

They all followed the same program. They undressed and carefully hung up their new suits. Rid of their finery, charming vocational deformations allowed you to guess the sort of work they were employed in. Standing in the tub, they would gaze at their reflection (at me) pensively and start with a Parisian grin which exposes the gums. Next, they'd scratch a shoulder, pick up the soap and, handling it slowly, make it bubble into a lather. Then they'd soap themselves. The soaping would gradually turn into a caress. All of a sudden their eyes would wander out of this world, their heads would tilt back and their bodies would spit like furious animals.

Some, exhausted, would subside into the steaming bathwater, others would box a second round; the youngest distinguished themselves by climbing out of the tub and, off in a corner, wiping the tiles clean of the sap their careless stems had hurled blindly towards love.

Once, a Narcissus who was pleasuring himself brought his mouth to the mirror, pressed his lips to it and pressed his adventure with himself all the way through to the end. Invisible like the Greek gods, I put my lips to his and imitated his gestures. Never was he to know that instead of reflecting him, the mirror had acted, had lived and loved him.

Fortune steered me towards a new life. I emerged from a

bad dream. I had sunk into an unwholesome indolence which is to the love of men what assignation houses and sidewalk pick-ups are to the love of women.

I knew and admired the Right Reverend Father X***. His deftness, his light-heartedness bordered on the miraculous. Wherever he went, like some magician he alleviated burdens, lightened whatever was heavy. He knew nothing of my intimate life, he simply sensed that I was unhappy. He spoke to me, comforted me and put me in touch with high Catholic intelligences.

I have always been a believer. My belief was confused. Thanks to frequenting an unsullied company, to reading so much peace in so many serene brows, to understanding the foolishness of unbelievers, I advanced along the path towards God. To be sure, dogma consorted ill with my decision to give a free rein to my impulses, but this recent period had left me with a bitterness, with a satiety which I was in a great hurry to interpret as evidence that I'd been pursuing the wrong course. After so much imbibing of wicked brews, all this water, all this milk revealed to me a future of limpid excellence and pureness of heart. If scruples assailed me, I beat off the attack by thinking of Jeanne and Rose. I'm not barred from having normal affairs, I told myself. Nothing prevents me from founding a family and resuming honest ways. I have, in a word, been ceding to my bent through fear of making an effort. Without an effort nothing good or fine exists. I'll pit myself against the devil and I'll be victorious.

A divine period! The Church cradled me in her arms. I felt myself the adopted son of a divine family. Holy communion, yes, the sanctified bread turns all to new-driven snow, and sets the tranquil soul deliciously aglow. I soared heavenward like a little balloon. At mass when the star of sacrifice dominates the altar and all the heads are bowed, I would pray ardently to the Virgin, beseeching her to take me under her holy protection: "I greet You, Mary," I'd murmur, "gladly I welcome You unto my heart, for are You not purity itself? What to You can be our ephemeral fancies, our humble follies? 'Tis all mere chaff, is it not? Can You be swayed by an exposed bosom? That which mortals behold as indecent, in Your sanctity must You not regard all this as we regard the amorous commerce between pistil and stamen, amongst the atoms? I shall obey the directives of Your Son's ministers upon earth, but I know very well that His goodness extends further than the chicanery of a Father Sinistrarius and the stringencies of an antiquated criminal code. So be it and Amen."

Following a fit of religiosity, the soul cools down again. That's the crucial instant. Man's unsupple and angular frame is not as easily rid as the gartersnake of this fragile sheath caught in the rose-briars. It's first of all love at first sight like a bolt out of the blue, betrothal to the Beloved, marriage and austere dedication.

At the outset, everything transpires in a sort of ecstasy. A wondrous zeal lays hold of the neophyte. Later, in cold blood, he steels himself to get up from a warm bed and go to church. Fasts, prayers, orisons monopolize him. The devil, who'd been banished out of the door, comes back in by the window, disguised as a ray of sunshine.

One's salvation cannot possibly be achieved in Paris; the soul is too distracted. I decided to go to the seaside. There, I'd divide my life between church and a rowboat. Far from all distractions, I'd pray upon the waves.

I took my old hotel room at T***.

From the very first day at T*** the heat's injunctions were to undress and enjoy myself. In order to get to the church one had to take evil-smelling streets and climb steps. This church was deserted. The fishermen never entered it. I admired God's unsuccess; masterpieces ought never to be popular. Which does not however prevent them from being illustrious and awe-inspiring.

Alas! I reasoned in vain, that emptiness exerted its influence upon me. I preferred my rowboat. I rowed as far out as possible, then I dropped the oars, removed my trousers and my undershorts, and sprawled out, limbs in disorder.

The sun is a veteran lover who knows his job. He starts by laying firm hands all over you. He attacks simultaneously from every angle. There's no getting away, he has a potent grip, he pins you and before you know it, you discover, as always happens to me, that your belly is covered with liquid drops resembling mistletoe berries.

Things weren't taking at all the right direction. I contracted a low opinion of myself. I sought to turn over a new leaf and try again. Finally, my prayers were reduced to succinct requests for God's forgiveness: "My God, You pardon me, for You understand me. You understand everything. For haven't You willed everything, created everything: bodies, sexes, waves, the blue heaven and the bright sun which, enamored of Hyacinth, metamorphosed him into a flower."

I'd located an isolated little beach for my sun-bathing. I would pull my boat up onto the shingle and dry myself in the kelp. On that beach one morning I came upon a young man who was swimming without a suit and who asked me if I minded. My reply was sufficiently frank to enlighten him as to my tastes. We were soon stretched out side by side. I learned that he lived in the neighboring village and was here for his health, he was convalescing from a faint threat of tuberculosis.

The sun accelerates the growth of sentiments. We cut a good number of corners and, thanks to a series of meetings in a state of nature and removed from the objects which divert the heart from prompt action, we arrived at the stage of being in love without ever having mentioned the word. H*** left his inn and set himself up in my hotel. He wrote. He believed in God, but displayed a puerile indifference towards dogma. The Church, that amiable heretic would declare, demands of us a moral prosody equivalent to the prosody of Alexander Pope. To want to stand with one foot planted alongside the Church on the reputedly unmovable rock of Saint Peter, and with the other foot mired in modern life, is to want to live the drawn-and-quartered existence of Saint Hippolytus. They ask for passive obedience from you, he said, and I give them active obedience. God loves love. In loving one another we demonstrate to Christ that we know how to read between the lines of a lawmaker's unavoidable severity. When you address the masses you're obliged not to allude to what distinguishes the common from the extraordinary.

He scoffed at my misgivings, at my pangs of conscience, he

called them weakness. He reprobated my doubts. "I love you," said he, "and I congratulate myself upon loving you."

Our dream might perhaps have been able to last under a sky where we lived half on land, half in the water, like mythological divinities; but his mother was calling him back to Paris, and we made up our minds to go there together.

That mother lived in Versailles, and as I was staying at my father's place, we rented a hotel room where we saw each other every day. He had a good many female acquaintances. They didn't particularly alarm me, for I'd often observed the great delight inverts take in the company of women, whilst women-loving men tend to scorn them and, apart from what is incidental to making use of women, prefer to pass the time with men.

One morning when he telephoned me from Versailles I noticed that this instrument, such a fine vehicle for falsehoods, was bringing me a voice I'd not heard hitherto. I asked him if he was really calling from Versailles. He stammered, talked faster, proposed we meet at the hotel at four that same afternoon, and hung up. Chilled to the marrow, gnawed by a frightful desire to know the truth, I gave the operator his mother's number. She told me that he'd not been home for several days and that, because of extra work which was keeping him till late every day in the city, he was sleeping at the home of a friend.

Passing the time until four o'clock amounted to an ordeal. A thousand circumstances only awaiting the signal to issue forth from shadow became instruments of torture and fastened their teeth upon me. The truth rose and smote my eyes. Madame V***, whom I'd taken for his friend, was in actuality his mistress. He returned to her in the evening and spent the night with her. This certitude pierced my breast like an executioner's bullet, it raked me like a tiger's claw. But despite my having realized the truth and despite the suffering it caused me, I still hoped he'd find an excuse and manage to furnish proof of his innocence.

At four he confessed that in the past he'd loved women and that, helpless before an insuperable force, he was resuming old ways and habits; this, he went on, ought not to distress me; it had nothing to do with us, was something quite different; he loved me, was disgusted with himself, couldn't do anything about it; every sanatorium was filled with similar cases. Credit for this ambivalence should be ascribed to tuberculosis.

I invited him to choose between women and me. I thought he was going to choose me and that he'd strive to renounce them. I was in error. "I risk making a promise," he replied, "and not keeping it. That would pain you. I don't want you to be in pain. Breaking off would hurt you less than false promises and lies."

I was leaning against the door and I was so pale that he was frightened. "Good bye," I murmured in a dead voice, "good bye. You gave my existence a meaning and an orientation and I had nothing else to do but lead it with you. What's to become of me? Where am I to go now? How shall I ever endure waiting for night to fall and after it has fallen, for day to come, and tomorrow, and the tomorrow after that? How shall I pass the weeks?" I saw nothing but a room swimming on the other side of my tears, and I was counting on my fingers like an idiot.

Suddenly he came to himself, waking as though from an hypnotic spell. He sprang from the bed upon which he'd been biting his nails, he clasped me in his arms, begged me to forgive him and swore he'd send women to the devil.

He wrote a letter to Madame V***, informing her that it was all over. She feigned suicide by absorbing the contents of a tube of sleeping pills, and we lived for three weeks in the country, having given no one our address. Two months went by, and I was happy.

It was the eve of an important religious holiday. Before repairing to the Holy Repast my custom was to go to have my confession heard by Father X***. He was virtually expecting my arrival. Crossing the threshold, I warned him that I'd come not to confess but to relate; and that, alas! I knew in advance what his verdict was going to be.

"Reverend Father," I enquired of him, "do you love me?"

"I love you."

"Would you be happy to hear that I find myself happy at last?"

"I'd be delighted."

"Well then, rejoice, for I am happy, but my happiness is of a variety the Church and society disapprove, for it is friendship that causes my happiness and, with me, friendship knows neither boundary nor restraint."

Father X*** interrupted me. "I believe," said he, "that you are the victim of scruples."

"Reverend Father," I rejoined, "I'd not insult the Church by supposing that she negotiates compromises or omits to cross the t's and dot the i's. I am familiar with the doctrine of *excessive friendships*. Whom can I deceive? God sees me. Why reckon the distance in fractions of an inch? I am on the downgrade. Sin lies ahead of me."

"My dear child," Father X*** told me in the vestibule, "were it but a question of jeopardizing my situation in heaven, the danger would be slight, for I believe that the goodness and mercy of God exceed all that we can imagine. But there is also the question of my situation here on earth. The Jesuits watch me very closely."

We embraced. Walking home beside the walls over which poured the scent of gardens, I considered God's economy and deemed it admirable. According to the divine scheme, love is granted when to one love is lacking and, to avoid a pleonasm of the heart, denied to those who possess it.

I received a telegram one morning: "Don't be alarmed. Off on a trip with Marcel. Will wire the date of our return."

This message left me stupified. There'd been no hint of a trip the evening before. Marcel was a friend from whom I had nothing underhanded to fear, but whom I knew to be wild enough to head for the moon on the spur of the moment, and never once to take into account the fact that his travelling companion's frail health might well buckle under an impromptu lark.

I was about to go to where Marcel lived to obtain further information from his servant when the doorbell rang and the next moment Mlle R*** appeared, disheveled, haggard and out of breath. "Marcel has robbed us!" she cried. "Marcel has taken him away from us! Something's got to be done!

Quick, let's get going! What are you doing, standing there like a blockhead? Act! Hurry! Avenge us! The wretch!" She waved her arms, was striding up and down the room, blowing her nose, tucking stray wisps of hair in place, knocking against furniture, catching her skirt on drawer-pulls, tearing her dress to ribbons.

My worry lest my father overhear the commotion and enter prevented me from understanding right away. Then the truth hove through the clouds and, concealing my distress, I herded the madwoman towards the entry, explaining to her that for my part I'd not been robbed of anything, that H*** was simply my friend, that I knew nothing whatsoever of the liaison she'd just got through sketching so clamorously.

"What!" she continued at the top of her lungs, "what! You are unaware that that child worships me and spends most of every night in my arms? He comes in from Versailles and returns there before dawn! I've had horrible operations! My stomach is one mass of scars! Well, there's something you ought to know about those scars. He kisses them and lays his cheek upon them in order to go to sleep."

It goes without saying that this visit plunged me into an ocean of dread. I received telegrams: "Hurrah for Marseille!" and "Leaving for Tunis."

The return was terrible. H*** thought he was in for the kind of scolding a child gets after playing a prank. I requested Marcel to leave us alone. Then I threw Mlle R*** in his face. He laughed it off. I told him it wasn't funny. He denied everything. I persisted. He denied. I bullied him, he admitted everything, and I cut loose. My pain maddened me. I lashed out like a brute. I grabbed him by the ears and beat his head against the wall. Blood trickled from the corner of his mouth. In a flash I recovered my senses. Tears streaming down my face, I tried to kiss that poor mauled face. But I encountered nothing but a flash of light blue eyes over which lids closed dolorously.

I fell upon my knees in one corner of the room. A scene like that taxes one's profoundest resources. One breaks down like a puppet whose strings have been snipped.

All of a sudden I felt a hand on my shoulder. I raised my head and saw my victim gaze at me, sink to the floor, kiss my fingers, my knees, choke, sputter, groan: "Forgive me, forgive me. I am your slave. Do what you like with me."

There was a month of truce. A weary truce, a blessed calm after the storm. We resembled those water-logged dahlias which hang their heads after a heavy rain. H*** didn't look well. He was wan, drawn, and often remained at Versailles.

Whereas I feel no awkwardness in talking about sexual relations, some modesty checks me whenever I think to describe the torments I am capable of experiencing. I'll devote a few lines to them and be done with it. Love ravages me. Even when calm, I tremble lest this calm cease, and the trembling anxiety is great enough to prevent me from tasting any sweetness in calm. The least setback wrecks everything. Impossible not to have constantly to foresee the worst, to have to cope with its latent threat. One *faux pas* and I inevitably wind up in a heap on the ground. Waiting is a torture, so is possessing by dint of dreading having taken away from me what I have been given.

Doubt made me pass sleepless nights in pacing the floor, in lying down on the floor, in wishing the floor would collapse and go on collapsing forever. I made myself the promise not to betray my fears. Immediately I was face to face with H***, I'd start plying him with questions. He kept still. That silence would either touch off my rage or my tears. I accused him of hating me, of wanting to destroy me. He knew only too well that there was no use answering and that, in spite of anything he could say, I'd start in again the next day.

That was all in September. But the 12th of November is the date I'll never forget as long as I live. We were to meet at the hotel at six. As I entered, the hotel manager stopped me and, visibly embarrassed by what he had to tell me, said that the police had been there and that H***, along with a bulky suitcase, had been taken to headquarters in a car containing the chief of the vice squad and some plainclothesmen.

"The police!" I cried. "What for?" I telephoned to influential people. They made enquiries and I found out the truth which, a little before eight that evening, a woebegone H***, released after his interrogation, confirmed to me.

He had been sleeping with a Russian woman who drugged him. Tipped off that a raid was likely, she'd asked him to remove her smoking equipment and supplies to the hotel. Some tough character he'd taken up with and confided in hadn't wasted much time in betraying him. It was a professional stool-pigeon. Thus, at one fell swoop, I discovered he'd deceived me not once again but twice. He'd tried to bluff it at the police station and, assuring them all that he was used to it, had sat down cross-legged on the floor and smoked during the questioning, much to the amazement of the onlookers. By now he was done for. I couldn't reproach him. I begged him to give up drugs. He told me he'd like to, but that he was addicted, done for, that it was too late.

I received a call the following day from Versailles. He'd spat blood and been rushed to the rue B*** hospital.

He was in Room 55 on the third floor. When I entered he had scarcely enough strength to look around to see who it was. His nose had become slightly thinner, pinched. His dull eyes rested on his waxen hands.

When the nurse left and we were by ourselves, he said: "I'm going to tell you my secret. In me there was a woman and there was a man. The woman was yours, and submissive; the man used to rebel against that submissiveness. Women displeased me, but I went after them to give myself a change and to show myself that I was free. The conceited, stupid man in me was the enemy of our love. I am sorry about that. I miss that love. I don't love anyone but you. When I'm all well again, I'll be different. I'll obey you willingly, without rebelling, and I'll do everything I can to make up for the way I've wronged you."

I couldn't sleep that night either. Towards morning, I dozed off for a few minutes and had a dream. I was at the circus with H***. The circus became a restaurant divided into two little rooms. In one of them, at the piano, a singer announced he was going to sing a new song. Its title was the name of a woman who had been extremely fashionable in 1900. After his opening remarks this title was an insolence in 1926. Here is the song:

> *The lettuces of Paris*
> *Go walking in Paris.*
> *There's even an endive*
>   *And who'd ever believe*
>   *They've got endive,*
> *In Paris?*

The magnifying quality of the dream inflated this absurd song into something celestial and extraordinarily funny.

I woke up. I was still laughing. That laughter seemed to augur well. I'd not have had so ridiculous a dream, I said to myself, if the situation were grave. I'd forgot that the weariness caused by pain somethimes gives rise to ridiculous dreams.

At the rue B*** hospital I was about to open the door to the room when a nurse came up and, in a cool voice, advised me that "Fifty-five isn't in his room anymore. He's in the chapel."

Where did I find the strength necessary to turn on my heels and walk down the stairs? In the chapel a woman was praying by a casket. In it was the corpse of my friend.

How serene it was, the dear face I'd struck! But what difference now could the memory of blows and caresses make to him? He no longer loved his mother, or women, or me, or anyone. For the only thing that interests the dead is death.

Horribly alone, I rejected all notions of returning to the Church; it would be too easy to employ the Host like an aspirin tablet or to fill up on negative vitamins at the Holy Table, too simple to turn towards heaven every time I become disenchanted with things on earth.

Marriage remained as a last resort. But had I not hoped to marry out of love, I'd have thought it dishonest to dupe a girl. At the Sorbonne I'd known a Mademoiselle de S*** whose boyishness had caught my fancy and I'd often told myself that if I were to have to take a wife someday, I'd prefer her to any other. I renewed our acquaintance, frequented the house in Auteuil where she lived with her mother, and we gradually came round to considering marriage a possibility. She liked me. Her mother feared seeing her daughter become a spinster. Our engagement was effortless.

She had a younger brother whom I didn't know, for he was finishing his studies at a Jesuit college in London. He came home. How had I failed to anticipate this newest wickedness on the part of a fate which yet persecutes me and which, donning all sorts of guises, masks nothing but an unalterable destiny? What had attracted me to the sister shone like a beacon in the brother. At the very first glance I beheld the drama in its entirety and understood that a mild and peaceful existence would be denied me. It was not long before I learned that, on his side, this brother, a good product of the English school, had fallen head over heels in love with me the moment we'd met. That young man adored himself. In loving me he cuckolded himself. We met in secrecy and matters progressed relentlessly to the fatal stage.

The atmosphere in the house was charged with an evil electricity. We skillfully camouflaged our crime, but my fiancée's nerves were set on edge by what she scented in the air, and all the more so because she had no suspicion of what was causing the tension. In the end, her brother's love for me moved into an intense passion. Could this passion have hidden a secret destructive impulse or need? Maybe so. He hated his sister. He pleaded with me to break our engagement, to take back my plighted word. I did all I could to slow things down. I tried to obtain a relative calm, and succeeded, succeeded simply in delaying the catastrophe.

One evening when I'd come to pay his sister a visit I heard sounds of weeping on the other side of the door. The poor girl was lying flat on the floor, a handkerchief in her mouth and her hair all askew. Standing over her, her brother was shouting: "He's mine! Mine! Mine! Since he's too much of a coward to tell you the truth, you can hear it from me!"

I couldn't bear this scene. His voice and his eyes were so ferociously cruel that I struck him in the face.

"Ah," he cried, "you'll always regret having done that," and he shut himself in his room.

While trying to bring our victim back to life, I heard a shot. I leapt up, dashed to the door of his room, tore it open. Too late. He lay beside a wardrobe. On its mirror, at the height of one's head, one could still make out the oily imprint of a kiss and the moist smudge left by breathing.

I could no longer live in these surroundings where misfortune and mourning dogged my footsteps. Suicide was out of the question because of my faith. This faith and the unending trouble of spirit and flesh I'd been in since quitting my religious exercises led me to the idea of a monastery.

Father X***, whom I consulted for advice, told me that one could not come to these very major decisions in haste, that the rule was very austere and that, for a start, I ought to test my strength by putting in a season of retirement at M*** Abbey. He furnished me with a letter of introduction to the Superior, setting forth the reasons why this retreat I was contemplating was something other than a dilettante's caprice.

When I reached the Abbey the temperature was hovering just above freezing. The falling snow was changing into freezing rain, the earth into mud. The gatekeeper summoned a monk at whose side I walked in silence under the arcades. I questioned him upon the schedules of the masses, and when he replied a shiver ran through me. I'd just heard one of those voices which, more surely, more amply than faces or bodies, inform me as to a young man's age and beauty.

He pushed back his cowl. His profile etched itself against the stone wall. It was the profile of Alfred, of H***, of Rose, of Jeanne, of Dargelos, of Lousy Luck, of Gustave and of the farm-boy.

I arrived limp before the door to the office of Dom Z***.

Dom Z*** greeted me cordially. He already had a letter from Father X*** on his desk. He dismissed the young monk. "Are you aware," he asked, "that our house can offer few comforts and that the rule here is very austere?"

"My Father," I replied, "I have reasons for believing that, austere as it may be, the rule here is not austere enough for me. I will confine myself to this visit and shall always preserve a fond memory of the welcome I have been shown today."

Yes, the monastery drove me away like everything else. The

only thing left was to leave, to imitate those Carmelite Fathers who consume themselves in the desert and for whom love is a pious suicide. But does God allow one to cherish Him in this manner?

Never mind, I'll leave—and behind me I'll leave this book. If anyone finds it, let him publish it. It may perhaps help to explain that, in exiling myself, I am exiling not a monster but a man society doesn't permit to live since society views as an error one of the mysterious quirks in the way the divine masterpiece operates.

Instead of taking unto itself the gospel according to Rimbaud: *Lo, we are come unto the age of assassins,* contemporary youth would have been better advised to have adopted *Love is to be reinvented* for its motto. Risky experiments—the world accepts them in the realm of art because the world does not take art seriously, but it condemns them in life.

I perfectly well understand that an anthill ideal like the Russians', aiming at the plural, condemns the singular to exist in one of the highest forms. But you cannot prevent certain flowers and certain fruits from being inhaled and eaten by the rich alone.

A social vice makes a vice of my outspokenness. I have no more to say, and so I withdraw. In France, this vice does not lead to the penitentiary, thanks to the longevity of the Code Napoléon and the morals of Cambacérès. But I am not willing merely to be tolerated. That wounds my love of love and of liberty.

JAMES T. FARRELL

A CASUAL INCIDENT

The kid stood at the edge of a small, nondescript crowd at State and Quincy Streets, listening while a sleek Greek conducted a Come-to-Jesus meeting. With appropriate showmanship, the fellow introduced presentable females who stood on a soap box and gave testimony. One of them was a mother, and after she had luridly described her sinful past and the joys and satisfactions of being washed from sin in the Blood of the Lamb, she put her seven-year-old girl on the box, because the girl had been living with Jesus inside of her for two years. The mother and the Greek tenderly instructed the girl to explain just how Jesus had come to her, as quick as a snap of the fingers, and just how nice and good and holy and happy it felt when you had kindly Jesus right inside of your breast. The child stood on the soap box, fidgeting, shyly dropping her eyes, saying nothing. The crowd laughed good-naturedly at her cute gestures. All coaxing failed, and the Greek lifted her down. He declared that anyway she loved Jesus, and loving Jesus was all that counted in this dark world of sin.

"Jesus got tongue-tied that time," the kid said to a burly Pole on his right.

"Dey all queer here," the stolid Pole answered, pursing his lips.

"Yeh, and it's funny the way Jesus got tongue-tied that time," the kid said.

"Yeh," the Pole said, smiling.

"I think it's damn funny. Here they say Jesus has been inside the kid for a couple of years, and then when they ask Him to speak, He gets tongue-tied."

The meeting concluded in song and the crowd dispersed. The kid and the Pole leaned against the window of an Owl Drug Store that was jumbled and confusedly decorated and placarded. They talked, and the kid noted that the Pole was a giant, with a heavy, planed face, and a deep bass voice. He had ox eyes, and looked very masculine.

"You know, dese religious people, dey all a little queer in de head," the Pole said.

"They're nuts. But it was funny, the way Jesus got tongue-tied," the kid said.

The Pole surveyed the kid. He was about twenty, with cleanly carved features, and he was carrying several books.

"Religious guys always like de ladies, doh," said the Pole.

"Yeh, they get themselves hooked up with a skirt every time."

"I was in Seattle one time, and dey had a big big place. It was a great big tent, and dere were crowds evry night. It was dat religion, what you callum? You know? Dat religion oh, gee, I know de name well. Dat religion, you know, where dey all roll round, all crazy in de head?"

"Holy Rollers."

"Yeh, dat's it, de Holy Rollers."

"Yeh," the kid said.

"Dey had a big big tent, and so big a place, and dey had big crowds evry night, and dey made all kindsa money, too. Well, de guy what was de preacher, he liked de wimmin . . . you know what I mean?"

The Pole smiled, and pursed his lips. He described how the preacher had seduced the choir master's wife and several girls in the congregation. He had finally eloped with the former, taking along the congregation funds. There had been a story about it on the front pages of the papers. The kid considered the account to be pointless, but listened, because he had nothing to do.

"Wimmin, dey all dangerous," the Pole said, pursing his lips.

He talked on, describing his life. At the age of twelve, he had run away from his native Polish village because of the poverty of his family. He had followed the sea, going to all parts of the world, and he had had adventures on many a waterfront.

"When a young fellow goes on his own, tings happen to him. You know . . . well, tings happen to him," the Pole said.

"I know."

"A young fellow, he goes on his own, and he don't know nottin', and well . . . tings happen to him."

"You have to take your chances, and if you can't swim, you sink. It's just your tough tiddy, then," the kid said.

"Yes, but tings happen."

The Pole recounted more of his experiences, interrupting his tales to remark:

"I got a nice place now, wid a fren. We have nice big place 'n' we bring anyone we want dere. No one to bodder us."

"That's pretty nice. You can bring your women there."

"Wimmin. . . . No, dey're dangerous," the Pole said, pursing his lips.

"Yes, I guess they can get to be a nuisance."

"Where you live? . . . At home?"

"Me, I live in an undertaking parlor."

The Pole laughed. The kid explained that he was paid three dollars a week, and received a bed for hanging around, answering telephone calls and sometimes going out on the ambulance. This was his evening off. The Pole again laughed, pursing his lips and exclaiming that it was funny.

"You bring girls dere, too?"

"Hell, no! We got six religious Irishmen there, and if I brought a girl around, sure as hell there would be a gang rape."

"Well, wimmin, dey're dangerous," the Pole said, laughing.

The kid leaned back against the window, and watched the

sleepy-eyed parade of people along State Street. He heard the traffic sounds and sudden jets of conversation.

"Wanna see my place?"

"Not tonight, thanks. I feel pretty tired," the kid answered.

The Pole seemed to become confused, and, to mask his confusion, he quickly asked the kid about the books he had under his arm. The kid casually answered that they were story books. The Pole talked about the sea, and then asked the kid if he had ever been on the road. The kid nodded, and told about how he had once gotten blind drunk in Hoboken.

"Well, as I say, tings happen to young fellows."

"Yeh," the kid yawned.

"You out now, lookin' for girls?"

"Not particularly. I feel pretty tired."

"I was just wonderin'," the Pole said, shrugging his broad shoulders; he pursed his lips.

"I don't like cat houses," the kid said.

"A young fellow, he got a have girls."

"Yeh, I guess he does," the kid said.

The kid yawned, said he was getting pretty tired, and guessed that he would be getting back to the undertaking parlor.

"Come up 'n' see my place?" the Pole said.

"No, thanks, I feel too tired."

The Pole smiled, and gave the kid his address. He told him that any time he was broke, or needed a place to sleep, to come up. He pursed his lips, and looked at the kid.

"Come up 'n' see my place," he said, his voice suddenly strained.

"I feel too tired. . . . Say, there's a saloon called Reilley's in Hoboken, right off the Fourteenth Street ferry. Ever been there?"

The Pole eyed the kid queerly as the kid went on to talk about the beer at Reilley's, fifteen cents a glass with the headache guaranteed. The Pole said he guessed he would be going home.

"And I guess I'll be blowing this town again pretty damn quick," the kid said.

"Chicago's a nice town. Lotsa girls here," the Pole said.

He pursed his lips.

"Nice girls are everywhere. They grow like apples on trees."

The Pole laughed, and said nice girls were very dangerous. The kid said anyway the idea about life was to live dangerously, on a volcano.

"Girls dat are nice, sometimes dey give you ... you know ... dose," the Pole said.

"Well, you got to take your chances," the kid said.

"But dere's a way ob not taking chances," the Pole said in a tense voice.

"What do you think of Cleveland as a town?" the kid asked.

The Pole was uninterested while the kid talked of Cleveland, comparing it with Chicago and New York.

"You got nice girl, ob your own?" asked the Pole.

"No, I don't believe in dragging nuisances around with me."

"But you like de girls?"

"Yeh, sometimes."

"Tonight?"

"No."

"You goin' back to de undertaker's and read?"

"Yes."

"Oh, gee, ain't it spooky?" the Pole asked, laughing; he pursed his lips, and he concentrated his ox eyes intensely on the kid.

"I got nice place. You come on up?"

"I'm pretty busy. I'm writing a book," the kid said.

"About de girls?"

"Not particularly."

"It must be nice to write books?"

He told the kid if he'd visit him, that he would tell him lots of things to put into the book, things about geisha girls, and Asiatic beachcombers, and sailors, and towns in all parts of the world.

"I'm pretty tired. Guess I'll blow," the kid said.

"Got my address?"

"Yes, but I'm pretty busy," the kid said.

"But ain't it spooky, out dere wid de corpses?"

"I don't mind it."

"It's funny," the Pole said, laughing hoarsely.

"Yep, I guess I'll be blowing," the kid said.

"Dat's funny, livin' at de undertaker's."

"It's better than sleeping in the parks," the kid said.

"You sure you wouldn't like to come to my place a little while?" the Pole asked, pursing his lips.

"No thanks," the kid answered, yawning.

"Sure?"

"Yes."

"But you got to be careful ob de girls. Dere dangerous."

"Yeh," the kid said yawning, again stating that he was going.

"So long," the kid said.

"So long, kid . . ."

"I'm going to the I. C. station at Van Buren Street."

"So long, kid . . . but I got a nice place."

D.H. LAWRENCE

THE PRUSSIAN OFFICER

They had marched more than thirty kilometres since dawn, along the white, hot road where occasional thickets of trees threw a moment of shade, then out into the glare again. On either hand, the valley, wide and shallow, glittered with heat; dark-green patches of rye, pale young corn, fallow and meadow and black pine woods spread in a dull, hot diagram under a glistening sky. But right in front the mountains ranged across, pale blue and very still, snow gleaming gently out of the deep atmosphere. And towards the mountains, on and on, the regiment marched between the rye-fields and the meadows, between the scraggy fruit trees set regularly on either side the high road. The burnished, dark-green rye threw off a suffocating heat, the mountains drew gradually nearer and more distinct. While the feet of the soldiers grew hotter, sweat ran through their hair under their helmets, and their knapsacks could burn no more in contact with their shoulders, but seemed instead to give off a cold, prickly sensation.

He walked on and on in silence, staring at the mountains ahead, that rose sheer out of the land, and stood fold behind fold, half earth, half heaven, the heaven, the barrier with slits of soft snow, in the pale, bluish peaks.

He could now walk almost without pain. At the start, he had determined not to limp. It had made him sick to take the first steps, and during the first mile or so, he had compressed his breath, and the cold drops of sweat had stood on his forehead. But he had walked it off. What were they after all but bruises! He had looked at them, as he was getting up: deep bruises on the backs of his thighs. And since he had made his first step in the morning, he had been conscious of them, till now he had a tight, hot place in his chest, with suppressing the pain, and holding himself in. There seemed no air when he breathed. But he walked almost lightly.

The Captain's hand had trembled at taking his coffee at dawn: his orderly saw it again. And he saw the fine figure of the Captain wheeling on horseback at the farmhouse ahead, a handsome figure in pale-blue uniform with facings of scarlet, and the metal gleaming on the black helmet and the sword-scabbard, and dark streaks of sweat coming on the silky bay horse. The orderly felt he was connected with that figure moving so suddenly on horseback: he followed it like a shadow, mute and inevitable and damned by it. And the officer was always aware of the tramp of the company behind, the march of his orderly among the men.

The Captain was a tall man of about forty, grey at the temples. He had a handsome, finely-knit figure, and was one of the best horsemen in the West. His orderly, having to rub him down, admired the amazing riding-muscles of his loins.

For the rest, the orderly scarcely noticed the officer any more than he noticed himself. It was rarely he saw his master's face: he did not look at it. The Captain had reddish-brown, stiff hair, that he wore short upon his skull. His moustache was also cut short and bristly over a full, brutal mouth. His face was rather rugged, the cheeks thin. Perhaps the man was the more handsome for the deep lines in his face, the irritable tension of his brow, which gave him the look of a man who fights with life. His fair eyebrows stood bushy over light-blue eyes that were always flashing with cold fire.

He was a Prussian aristocrat, haughty and overbearing. But his mother had been a Polish countess. Having made too many gambling debts when he was young, he had ruined his prospects in the Army, and remained an infantry captain. He had never married: his position did not allow of it, and no woman had ever moved him to it. His time he spent riding—occasionally he rode one of his own horses at the races—and at the officers' club. Now and then he took himself a mistress. But after such an event, he returned to duty with his brow still more tense, his eyes still more hostile and irritable. With the men, however, he was merely impersonal, though a devil when roused; so that, on the whole, they feared him, but had no great aversion from him. They accepted him as the inevitable.

To his orderly he was at first cold and just and indifferent: he did not fuss over trifles. So that his servant knew practically nothing about him, except just what orders he would give, and how he wanted them obeyed. That was quite simple. Then the change gradually came.

The orderly was a youth of about twenty-two, of medium height, and well built. He had strong, heavy limbs, was swarthy, with a soft, black, young moustache. There was something altogether warm and young about him. He had firmly marked eyebrows over dark, expressionless eyes, that seemed never to have thought, only to have received life direct through his senses, and acted straight from instinct.

Gradually the officer had become aware of his servant's young vigorous, unconscious presence about him. He could not get away from the sense of the youth's person, while he was in attendance. It was like a warm flame upon the older man's tense, rigid body, that had become almost unliving, fixed. There was something so free and self-contained about him, and something in the young fellow's movement, that made the officer aware of him. And this irritated the Prussian. He did not choose to be touched into life by his servant. He might easily have changed his man, but he did not. He now very rarely looked direct at his orderly, but kept his face averted, as if to avoid seeing him. And yet as the young soldier moved unthinking about the apartment, the elder watched him, and would notice the movement of his strong young shoulders under the blue cloth, the bend of his neck. And it irritated him. To see the soldier's young, brown, shapely peasant's hand grasp the loaf or the wine-bottle sent a flash of hate or of

173

anger through the elder man's blood. It was not that the youth was clumsy: it was rather the blind, instinctive sureness of movement of an unhampered young animal that irritated the officer to such a degree.

Once, when a bottle of wine had gone over, and the red gushed out on to the tablecloth, the officer had started up with an oath, and his eyes, bluey like fire, had held those of the confused youth for a moment. It was a shock for the young soldier. He felt something sink deeper, deeper into his soul, where nothing had ever gone before. It left him rather blank and wondering. Some of his natural completeness in himself was gone, a little uneasiness took its place. And from that time an undiscovered feeling had held between the two men.

Henceforward the orderly was afraid of really meeting his master. His subconsciousness remembered those steely blue eyes and the harsh brows, and did not intend to meet them again. So he always stared past his master, and avoided him. Also, in a little anxiety, he waited for the three months to have gone, when his time would be up. He began to feel a constraint in the Captain's presence, and the soldier even more than the officer wanted to be left alone, in his neutrality as servant.

He had served the Captain for more than a year, and knew his duty. This he performed easily, as if it were natural to him. The officer and his commands he took for granted, as he took the sun and the rain, and he served as a matter of course. It did not implicate him personally.

But now if he were going to be forced into a personal interchange with his master he would be like a wild thing caught, he felt he must get away.

But the influence of the young soldier's being had penetrated through the officer's stiffened discipline, and perturbed the man in him. He, however, was a gentleman, with long, fine hands and cultivated movements, and was not going to allow such a thing as the stirring of his innate self. He was a man of passionate temper, who had always kept himself suppressed. Occasionally there had been a duel, an outburst before the soldiers. He knew himself to be always on the point of breaking out. But he kept himself hard to the idea of the Service. Whereas the young soldier seemed to live out his warm, full nature, to give it off in his very movements, which had a certain zest, such as wild animals have in free movement. And this irritated the officer more and more.

In spite of himself, the Captain could not regain his neutrality of feeling towards his orderly. Nor could he leave the man alone. In spite of himself, he watched him, gave him sharp orders, tried to take up as much of his time as possible. Sometimes he flew into a rage with the young soldier, and bullied him. Then the orderly shut himself off, as it were out of earshot, and waited, with sullen, flushed face, for the end of the noise. The words never pierced to his intelligence, he made himself, protectively, impervious to the feelings of his master.

He had a scar on his left thumb, a deep seam going across the knuckle. The officer had long suffered from it, and wanted to do something to it. Still it was there, ugly and brutal on the young, brown hand. At last the Captain's reserve gave way. One day, as the orderly was smoothing out the tablecloth, the officer pinned down his thumb with a pencil, asking:

"How did you come by that?"

The young man winced and drew back at attention.

"A wood axe, Herr Hauptmann," he answered.

The officer waited for further explanation. None came. The orderly went about his duties. The elder man was sullenly angry. His servant avoided him. And the next day he had to use all his will-power to avoid seeing the scarred thumb. He wanted to get hold of it and——A hot flame ran in his blood.

He knew his servant would soon be free, and would be glad. As yet, the soldier had held himself off from the elder man. The Captain grew madly irritable. He could not rest when the soldier was away, and when he was present, he glared at him with tormented eyes. He hated those fine, black brows over the unmeaning, dark eyes, he was infuriated by the free movement of the handsome limbs, which no military discipline could make stiff. And he became harsh and cruelly bullying, using contempt and satire. The young soldier only grew more mute and expressionless.

"What cattle were you bred by, that you can't keep straight eyes? Look me in the eyes when I speak to you."

And the soldier turned his dark eyes to the other's face, but there was no sight in them: he stared with the slightest possible cast, holding back his sight, perceiving the blue of his master's eyes, but receiving no look from them. And the elder man went pale, and his reddish eyebrows twitched. He gave his order, barrenly.

Once he flung a heavy military glove into the young soldier's face. Then he had the satisfaction of seeing the black eyes flare up into his own, like a blaze when straw is thrown on a fire. And he had laughed with a little tremor and a sneer.

But there were only two months more. The youth instinctively tried to keep himself intact: he tried to serve the officer as if the latter were an abstract authority and not a man. All his instinct was to avoid personal contact, even definite hate. But in spite of himself the hate grew, responsive to the officer's passion. However, he put it in the background. When he had left the Army he could dare acknowledge it. By nature he was active, and had many friends. He thought what amazing good fellows they were. But, without knowing it, he was alone. Now this solitariness was intensified. It would carry him through his term. But the officer seemed to be going irritably insane, and the youth was deeply frightened.

The soldier had a sweetheart, a girl from the mountains, independent and primitive. The two walked together, rather silently. He went with her, not to talk, but to have his arm round her, and for the physical contact. This eased him, made it easier for him to ignore the Captain; for he could rest with her held fast against his chest. And she, in some unspoken fashion, was there for him. They loved each other.

The Captain perceived it, and was mad with irritation. He kept the young man engaged all the evenings long, and took pleasure in the dark look that came on his face. Occasionally, the eyes of the two men met, those of the younger sullen and dark, doggedly unalterable, those of the elder sneering with restless contempt.

The officer tried hard not to admit the passion that had got hold of him. He would not know that his feeling for his orderly was anything but that of a man incensed by his stupid, perverse servant. So, keeping quite justified and conventional in his consciousness, he let the other thing run on. His nerves, however, were suffering. At last he slung the end of a belt in his servant's face. When he saw the youth start back, the pain-tears in his eyes and the blood on his mouth, he had felt at once a thrill of deep pleasure and of shame.

But this, he acknowledged to himself, was a thing he had never done before. The fellow was too exasperating. His own nerves must be going to pieces. He went away for some days with a woman.

It was a mockery of pleasure. He simply did not want the woman. But he stayed on for his time. At the end of it, he came back in an agony of irritation, torment, and misery. He rode all the evening, then came straight in to supper. His orderly was out. The officer sat with his long, fine hands lying on the table, perfectly still, and all his blood seemed to be corroding.

At last his servant entered. He watched the strong, easy young figure, the fine eyebrows, the thick black hair. In a week's time the youth had got back his old well-being. The hands of the officer twitched and seemed to be full of mad flame. The young man stood at attention, unmoving, shut off.

The meal went in silence. But the orderly seemed eager. He made a clatter with the dishes.

"Are you in a hurry?" asked the officer, watching the intent, warm face of his servant. The other did not reply.

"Will you answer my question?" said the Captain.

"Yes, sir," replied the orderly, standing with his pile of deep Army plates. The Captain waited, looked at him, then asked again:

"Are you in a hurry?"

"Yes, sir," came the answer, that sent a flash through the listener.

"For what?"

"I was going out, sir."

"I want you this evening."

There was a moment's hesitation. The officer had a curious stiffness of countenance.

"Yes sir," replied the servant, in his throat.

"I want you to-morrow evening also—in fact you may consider your evenings occupied, unless I give you leave."

177

The mouth with the young moustache set close.

"Yes, sir," answered the orderly, loosening his lips for a moment.

He again turned to the door.

"And why have you a piece of pencil in your ear?"

The orderly hesitated, then continued on his way without answering. He set the plates in a pile outside the door, took the stump of pencil from his ear, and put it in his pocket. He had been copying a verse for his sweetheart's birthday card. He returned to finish clearing the table. The officer's eyes were dancing, he had a little, eager smile.

"Why have you a piece of pencil in your ear?" he asked.

The orderly took his hands full of dishes. His master was standing near the great green stove, a little smile on his face, his chin thrust forward. When the young soldier saw him his heart suddenly ran hot. He felt blind. Instead of answering, he turned dazedly to the door. As he was crouching to set down the dishes, he was pitched forward by a kick from behind. The pots went in a stream down the stairs, he clung to the pillar of the banisters. And as he was rising he was kicked heavily again and again, so that he clung sickly to the post for some moments. His master had gone swiftly into the room and closed the door. The maid-servant downstairs looked up the staircase and made a mocking face at the crockery disaster.

The officer's heart was plunging. He poured himself a glass of wine, part of which he spilled on the floor, and gulped the remainder, leaning against the cool, green stove. He heard his man collecting the dishes from the stairs. Pale, as if intoxicated, he waited. The servant entered again. The Captain's heart gave a pang, as of pleasure, seeing the young fellow bewildered and uncertain on his feet with pain.

"Schöner!" he said.

The soldier was a little slower in coming to attention.

"Yes sir!"

The youth stood before him, with pathetic young moustache, and fine eyebrows very distinct on his forehead of dark marble.

"I asked you a question."

"Yes, sir."

The officer's tone bit like acid.

"Why had you a pencil in your ear?"

Again the servant's heart ran hot, and he could not breathe. With dark, strained eyes, he looked at the officer, as if fascinated. And he stood there sturdily planted, unconscious. The withering smile came into the Captain's eyes, and he lifted his foot.

"I forgot it—sir," panted the soldier, his dark eyes fixed on the other man's dancing blue ones.

"What was it doing there?"

He saw the young man's breast heaving as he made an effort for words.

"I had been writing."

"Writing what?"

Again the soldier looked him up and down. The officer could hear him panting. The smile came into the blue eyes. The soldier worked his dry throat, but could not speak. Suddenly the smile lit like a flame on the officer's face, and a kick came heavily against the orderly's thigh. The youth moved sideways. His face went dead, with two black, staring eyes.

"Well?" said the officer.

The orderly's mouth had gone dry, and his tongue rubbed in it as on dry brown-paper. He worked his throat. The officer raised his foot. The servant went stiff.

"Some poetry, sir," came the crackling, unrecognisable sound of his voice.

"Poetry, what poetry?" asked the Captain, with a sickly smile.

Again there was the working in the throat. The Captain's heart had suddenly gone down heavily, and he stood sick and tired.

"For my girl, sir," he heard the dry, inhuman sound.

"Oh!" he said, turning away. "Clear the table."

"Click!" went the soldier's throat; then again, "click!" and then the half-articulate:

"Yes, sir."

The young soldier was gone, looking old, and walking heavily.

The officer, left alone, held himself rigid, to prevent himself

179

from thinking. His instinct warned him that he must not think. Deep inside him was the intense gratification of his passion, still working powerfully. Then there was a counteraction, a horrible breaking down of something inside him, a whole agony of reaction. He stood there for an hour motionless, a chaos of sensations, but rigid with a will to keep blank his consciousness, to prevent his mind grasping. And he held himself so until the worst of the stress had passed, when he began to drink, drank himself to an intoxication, till he slept obliterated. When he woke in the morning he was shaken to the base of his nature. But he had fought off the realisation of what he had done. He had prevented his mind from taking it in, had suppressed it along with his instincts, and the conscious man had nothing to do with it. He felt only as after a bout of intoxication, weak, but the affair itself all dim and not to be recovered. Of the drunkenness of his passion he successfully refused remembrance. And when his orderly appeared with coffee, the officer assumed the same self he had had the morning before. He refused the event of the past night—denied it had ever been—and was successful in his denial. He had not done any such thing—not he himself. Whatever there might be lay at the door of a stupid insubordinate servant.

The orderly had gone about in a stupor all the evening. He drank some beer because he was parched, but not much, the alcohol made his feeling come back, and he could not bear it. He was dulled, as if nine-tenths of the ordinary man in him were inert. He crawled about disfigured. Still, when he thought of the kicks, he went sick, and when he thought of the threat of more kicking, in the room afterwards, his heart went hot and faint, and he panted, remembering the one that had come. He had been forced to say: "For my girl." He was much too done even to want to cry. His mouth hung slightly open, like an idiot's. He felt vacant, and wasted. So, he wandered at his work, painfully, and very slowly and clumsily, fumbling blindly with the brushes, and finding it difficult, when he sat down, to summon the energy to move again. His limbs, his jaw, were slack and nerveless. But he was very tired. He got to bed at last, and slept inert, relaxed, in a sleep that was rather stupor than slumber, a dead night of stupefaction shot through with gleams of anguish.

In the morning were the manoeuvres. But he woke even before the bugle sounded. The painful ache in his chest, the dryness of his throat, the awful steady feeling of misery made his eyes come awake and dreary at once. He knew, without thinking, what had happened. And he knew that the day had come again, when he must go on with his round. The last bit of darkness was being pushed out of the room. He would have to move his inert body and go on. He was so young, and had known so little trouble, that he was bewildered. He only wished it would stay night, so that he could lie still, covered up by the darkness. And yet nothing would prevent the day from coming, nothing would save him from having to get up and saddle the Captain's horse, and make the Captain's coffee. It was there, inevitable. And then, he thought, it was impossible. Yet they would not leave him free. He must go and take the coffee to the Captain. He was too stunned to understand it. He only knew it was inevitable—inevitable, however long he lay inert.

At last, after heaving at himself, for he seemed to be a mass of inertia, he got up. But he had to force every one of his movements from behind, with his will. He felt lost, and dazed, and helpless. Then he clutched hold of the bed, the pain was so keen. And looking at his thighs he saw the darker bruises on his swarthy flesh, and he knew that if he pressed one of his fingers on one of the bruises, he should faint. But he did not want to faint—he did not want anybody to know. No one should ever know. It was between him and the Captain. There were only the two people in the world now—himself and the Captain.

Slowly, economically, he got dressed and forced himself to walk. Everything was obscure, except just what he had his hands on. But he managed to get through his work. The very pain revived his dull senses. The worst remained yet. He took the tray and went up to the Captain's room. The officer, pale and heavy, sat at the table. The orderly, as he saluted, felt himself put out of existence. He stood still for a moment submitting to his own nullification—then he gathered himself, seemed to regain himself, and then the Captain began to grow vague, unreal, and the younger soldier's heart beat up. He clung to this situation—that the Captain did not exist—so that he himself might live. But when he saw his officer's hand tremble as he took the coffee, he felt everything falling shattered. And he went away, feeling as if he himself were coming to pieces, disintegrated. And when the Captain was there on horseback, giving orders, while he himself stood, with rifle and knapsack, sick with pain, he felt as if he must shut his eyes— as if he must shut his eyes on everything. It was only the long agony of marching with a parched throat that filled him with one single, sleep-heavy intention: to save himself.

II

He was getting used even to his parched throat. That the snowy peaks were radiant among the sky, that the whity-green glacier-river twisted through its pale shoals, in the valley below, seemed almost supernatural. But he was going mad with fever and thirst. He plodded on uncomplaining. He did not want to speak, not to anybody. There were two gulls, like flakes of water and snow, over the river. The scent of green rye soaked in sunshine came like a sickness. And the march continued, monotonously, almost like a bad sleep.

At the next farmhouse, which stood low and broad near the high road, tubs of water had been put out. The soldiers clustered round to drink. They took off their helmets, and the steam mounted from their wet hair. The Captain sat on horseback, watching. He needed to see his orderly. His helmet threw a dark shadow over his light, fierce eyes, but his moustache and mouth and chin were distinct in the sunshine. The orderly must move under the presence of the figure of the horseman. It was not that he was afraid, or cowed. It was as if he was disembowelled, made empty, like an empty shell. He felt himself as nothing, a shadow creeping under the sunshine. And, thirsty as he was, he could scarcely drink, feeling the Captain near him. He would not take off his helmet to wipe his wet hair. He wanted to stay in shadow, not to be forced into consciousness. Starting, he saw the light heel of the officer prick the belly of the horse; the Captain cantered away, and he himself could relapse into vacancy.

Nothing, however, could give him back his living place in the hot, bright morning. He felt like a gap among it all. Whereas the Captain was prouder, overriding. A hot flash went through the young servant's body. The Captain was firmer and prouder with life, he himself was empty as a shadow. Again the flash went through him, dazing him out. But his heart ran a little firmer.

The company turned up the hill, to make a loop for the return. Below, from among the trees, the farm-bell clanged. He saw the labourers, mowing bare-foot at the thick grass, leave off their work and go downhill, their scythes hanging over their shoulders, like long, bright claws curving down behind them. They seemed like dream-people, as if they had no relation to himself. He felt as in a blackish dream: as if all the other things were there and had form, but he himself was only a consciousness, a gap that could think and perceive.

The soldiers were tramping silently up the glaring hill-side. Gradually his head began to revolve, slowly, rhythmically. Sometimes it was dark before his eyes, as if he saw this world through a smoked glass, frail shadows and unreal. It gave him a pain in his head to walk.

The air was too scented, it gave no breath. All the lush green-stuff seemed to be issuing its sap, till the air was deathly, sickly with the smell of greenness. There was the perfume of clover, like pure honey and bees. Then there grew a faint acrid tang—they were near the beeches; and then a queer clattering noise, and a suffocating, hideous smell; they were passing a flock of sheep, a shepherd in a black smock, holding his crook. Why should the sheep huddle together under this fierce sun? He felt that the shepherd would not see him, though he could see the shepherd.

At last there was the halt. They stacked rifles in a conical stack, put down their kit in a scattered circle around it, and dispersed a little, sitting on a small knoll high on the hill-side. The chatter began. The soldiers were steaming with heat, but were lively. He sat still, seeing the blue mountains rising upon the land, twenty kilometres away. There was a blue fold in the ranges, then out of that, at the foot, the broad, pale bed of the river, stretches of whity-green water between pinkish-gray shoals among the dark pine woods. There it was, spread out a long way off. And it seemed to come downhill, the river. There was a raft being steered, a mile away. It was a strange country. Nearer, a red-roofed, broad farm with white base and square dots of windows crouched beside the wall of beech foliage on the wood's edge. There were long strips of rye and clover and pale green corn. And just at his feet, below the knoll, was a darkish bog, where globe flowers stood breathless still on their slim stalks. And some of the pale gold bubbles were burst, and a broken fragment hung in the air. He thought he was going to sleep.

Suddenly something moved into this coloured mirage before his eyes. The Captain, a small, light-blue and scarlet figure, was trotting evenly between the strips of corn, along the level brow of the hill. And the man making flag-signals was coming on. Proud and sure moved the horseman's figure, the quick, bright thing, in which was concentrated all the light of this morning, which for the rest lay fragile, shining shadow. Submissive, apathetic, the young soldier sat and stared. But as the horse slowed to a walk, coming up the last steep path, the great flash flared over the body and soul of the orderly. He sat waiting. The back of his head felt as if it were weighted with a heavy piece of fire. He did not want to eat. His hands trembled slightly as he moved them. Meanwhile the officer on horseback was approaching slowly and proudly. The tension grew in the orderly's soul. Then again, seeing the Captain ease himself on the saddle, the flash blazed through him.

The Captain looked at the patch of light blue and scarlet, and dark head, scattered closely on the hill-side. It pleased him. The command pleased him. And he was feeling proud. His orderly was among them in common subjection. The officer rose a little on his stirrups to look. The young soldier sat with averted, dumb face. The Captain relaxed on his seat. His slim-legged, beautiful horse, brown as a beech nut, walked proudly uphill. The Captain passed into the zone of the company's atmosphere: a hot smell of men, of sweat, of leather. He knew it very well. After a word with the lieutenant, he went a few paces higher, and sat there, a dominant figure, his sweat-marked horse swishing its tail, while he looked down on his men, on his orderly, a nonentity among the crowd.

The young soldier's heart was like fire in his chest, and he breathed with difficulty. The officer, looking downhill, saw three of the young soldiers, two pails of water between them, staggering across a sunny green field. A table had been set up under a tree, and there the slim lieutenant stood, importantly busy. Then the Captain summoned himself to an act of courage. He called his orderly.

The flame leapt into the young soldier's throat as he heard the command, and he rose blindly, stifled. He saluted, standing below the officer. He did not look up. But there was the flicker in the Captain's voice.

"Go to the inn and fetch me . . ." the officer gave his commands. "Quick!" he added.

At the last word, the heart of the servant leapt with a flash, and he felt the strength come over his body. But he turned in mechanical obedience, and set off at a heavy run downhill, looking almost like a bear, his trousers bagging over his military boots. And the officer watched this blind, plunging run all the way.

But it was only the outside of the orderly's body that was obeying so humbly and mechanically. Inside had gradually accumulated a core into which all the energy of that young life was compact and concentrated. He executed his commission, and plodded quickly back uphill. There was a pain in his head as he walked that made him twist his features unknowingly. But hard there in the centre of his chest was himself, himself, firm, and not to be plucked to pieces.

The Captain had gone up into the wood. The orderly plodded through the hot, powerfully smelling zone of the company's atmosphere. He had a curious mass of energy inside him now. The Captain was less real than himself. He approached the green entrance to the wood. There, in the half-shade, he saw the horse standing, the sunshine and the flickering shadow of leaves dancing over his brown body. There was a clearing where timber had lately been felled. Here, in the gold-green shade beside the brilliant cup of sunshine, stood two figures, blue and pink, the bits of pink showing out plainly. The Captain was talking to his lieutenant.

The orderly stood on the edge of the bright clearing, where great trunks of trees, stripped and glistening, lay stretched like naked, brown-skinned bodies. Chips of wood littered the trampled floor, like splashed light, and the bases of the felled trees stood here and there, with their raw, level tops. Beyond was the brilliant, sunlit green of a beech.

"Then I will ride forward," the orderly heard his Captain say. The lieutenant saluted and strode away. He himself went forward. A hot flash passed through his belly, as he tramped towards his officer.

The Captain watched the rather heavy figure of the young soldier stumble forward, and his veins, too, ran hot. This was to be man to man between them. He yielded before the solid, stumbling figure with bent head. The orderly stooped and put the food on a level-sawn tree-base. The Captain watched the glistening, sun-inflamed, naked hands. He wanted to speak to the young soldier, but could not. The servant propped a bottle against his thigh, pressed open the cork, and poured out the beer into the mug. He kept his head bent. The Captain accepted the mug.

"Hot!" he said, as if amiably.

The flame sprang out of the orderly's heart, nearly suffocating him.

"Yes, sir," he replied, between shut teeth.

And he heard the sound of the Captain's drinking, and he clenched his fists, such a strong torment came into his wrists. Then came the faint clang of the closing of the pot-lid. He looked up. The Captain was watching him. He glanced swiftly away. Then he saw the officer stoop and take a piece of bread from the tree-base. Again the flash of flame went through the young soldier, seeing the stiff body stoop beneath him, and his hands jerked. He looked away. He could feel the officer was

nervous. The bread fell as it was being broken. The officer ate
the other piece. The two men stood tense and still, the master
laboriously chewing his bread, the servant staring with
averted face, his fist clenched.

Then the young soldier started. The officer had pressed open
the lid of the mug again. The orderly watched the lip of the
mug, and the white hand that clenched the handle, as if he
were fascinated. It was raised. The young followed it with his
eyes. And then he saw the thin, strong throat of the elder man
moving up and down as he drank, the strong jaw working.
And the instinct which had been jerking at the young man's
wrists suddenly jerked free. He jumped, feeling as if it were
rent in two by a strong flame.

The spur of the officer caught in a tree root, he went down
backwards with a crash, the middle of his back thudding sick-
eningly against a sharp-edged tree-base, the pot flying away.
And in a second the orderly, with serious, earnest young face,
and underlip between his teeth, had got his knee in the officer's
chest and was pressing the chin backward over the farther
edge of the tree-stump, pressing, with all his heart behind in a
passion of relief, the tension of his wrists exquisite with relief.
And with the base of his palms he shoved at the chin, with all
his might. And it was pleasant, too, to have that chin, that hard
jaw already slightly rough with beard, in his hands. He did
not relax one hair's breadth, but, all the force of all his blood
exulting in his thrust, he shoved back the head of the other
man, till there was a little "cluck" and a crunching sensation.
Then he felt as if his head went to vapour. Heavy convulsions
shook the body of the officer, frightening and horrifying the
young soldier. Yet it pleased him, too, to repress them. It
pleased him to keep his hands pressing back the chin, to feel
the chest of the other man yield in expiration to the weight of
his strong, young knees, to feel the hard twitchings of the
prostrate body jerking his own whole frame, which was
pressed down on it.

But it went still. He could look into the nostrils of the other
man, the eyes he could scarcely see. How curiously the mouth
was pushed out, exaggerating the full lips, and the moustache

bristling up from them. Then, with a start, he noticed the nostrils gradually filled with blood. The red brimmed, hesitated, ran over, and went in a thin trickle down the face to the eyes.

It shocked and distressed him. Slowly, he got up. The body twitched and sprawled there, inert. He stood and looked at it in silence. It was a pity *it* was broken. It represented more than the thing which had kicked and bullied him. He was afraid to look at the eyes. They were hideous now, only the whites showing, and the blood running to them. The face of the orderly was drawn with horror at the sight. Well, it was so. In his heart he was satisfied. He had hated the face of the Captain. It was extinguished now. There was a heavy relief in the orderly's soul. That was as it should be. But he could not bear to see the long, military body lying broken over the tree-base, the fine fingers crisped. He wanted to hide it away.

Quickly, busily, he gathered it up and pushed it under the felled tree trunks, which rested their beautiful, smooth length either end on the logs. The face was horrible with blood. He covered it with the helmet. Then he pushed the limbs straight and decent, and brushed the dead leaves off the fine cloth of the uniform. So, it lay quite still in the shadow under there. A little strip of sunshine ran along the breast, from a chink between the logs. The orderly sat by it for a few moments. Here his own life also ended.

Then, through his daze, he heard the lieutenant, in a loud voice, explaining to the men outside the wood, that they were to suppose the bridge on the river below was held by the enemy. Now they were to march to the attack in such and such a manner. The lieutenant had no gift of expression. The orderly, listening from habit, got muddled. And when the lieutenant began it all again he ceased to hear.

He knew he must go. He stood up. It surprised him that the leaves were glittering in the sun, and the chips of wood reflecting white from the ground. For him a change had come over the world. But for the rest it had not—all seemed the same. Only he had left it. And he could not go back. It was his duty to return with the beer-pot and the bottle. He could not. He had left all that. The lieutenant was still hoarsely explaining. He must go, or they would overtake him. And he could not bear contact with anyone now.

He drew his fingers over his eyes, trying to find out where he was. Then he turned away. He saw the horse standing in the path. He went up to it and mounted. It hurt him to sit in the saddle. The pain of keeping his seat occupied him as they cantered through the wood. He would not have minded anything, but he could not get away from the sense of being divided from the others. The path led out of the trees. On the edge of the wood he pulled up and stood watching. There in the spacious sunshine of the valley soldiers were moving in a little swarm. Every now and then, a man harrowing on a strip of fallow shouted to his oxen, at the turn. The village and the white-towered church was small in the sunshine. And he no longer belonged to it—he sat there, beyond, like a man outside in the dark. He had gone out from everyday life into the unknown and he could not, he even did not want to go back.

Turning from the sun-blazing valley, he rode deep into the wood. Tree trunks, like people standing grey and still, took no notice as he went. A doe, herself a moving bit of sunshine and shadow, went running through the flecked shade. There were bright green rents in the foliage. Then it was all pine wood, dark and cool. And he was sick with pain, and had an intolerable great pulse in his head, and he was sick. He had never been ill in his life. He felt lost, quite dazed with all this.

Trying to get down from the horse, he fell, astonished at the pain and his lack of balance. The horse shifted uneasily. He jerked its bridle and sent it cantering jerkily away. It was his last connection with the rest of things.

But he only wanted to lie down and not be disturbed. Stumbling through the trees, he came on a quiet place where beeches and pine trees grew on a slope. Immediately he had lain down and closed his eyes, his consciousness went racing on without him. A big pulse of sickness beat in him as if it throbbed through the whole earth. He was burning with dry heat. But he was too busy, too tearingly active in the incoherent race of delirium to observe.

III

He came to with a start. His mouth was dry and hard, his heart beat heavily, but he had not the energy to get up. His heart beat heavily. Where was he?—the barracks—at home? There was something knocking. And, making an effort, he looked round—trees, and litter of greenery, and reddish, bright, still pieces of sunshine on the floor. He did not believe he was himself, he did not believe what he saw. Something was knocking. He made a struggle towards consciousness, but relapsed. Then he struggled again. And gradually his surroundings fell into relationship with himself. He knew, and a great pang of fear went through his heart. Somebody was knocking. He could see the heavy, black rags of a fir tree overhead. Then everything went black. Yet he did not believe he had closed his eyes. He had not. Out of the blackness sight slowly emerged again. And someone was knocking. Quickly, he saw the blood-disfigured face of his Captain, which he hated. And he held himself still with horror. Yet, deep inside him, he knew that it was so, the Captain should be dead. But the physical delirium got hold of him. Someone was knocking. He lay perfectly still, as if dead, with fear. And he went unconscious.

When he opened his eyes again he started, seeing something creeping swiftly up a tree trunk. It was a little bird. And the bird was whistling overhead. Tap-tap-tap—it was the small, quick bird rapping the tree trunk with its beak, as if its head were a little round hammer. He watched it curiously. It shifted sharply, in its creeping fashion. Then, like a mouse, it slid down the bare trunk. Its swift creeping sent a flash of revulsion through him. He raised his head. It felt a great weight. Then, the little bird ran out of the shadow across a still patch of sunshine, its little head bobbing swiftly, its white build, so compact, with piece of white on its wings. There were several of them. They were so pretty—but they crept like swift, erratic mice, running here and there among the beech-mast.

He lay down again exhausted, and his consciousness lapsed. He had a horror of the little creeping birds. All his blood seemed to be darting and creeping in his head. And yet he could not move.

He came to with a further ache of exhaustion. There was the pain in his head, and the horrible sickness, and his inability to move. He had never been ill in his life. He did not know where he was or what he was. Probably he had got sunstroke. Or what else?—he had silenced the Captain for ever—some time ago—oh, a long time ago. There had been blood on his face, and his eyes had turned upwards. It was all right, somehow. It was peace. But now he had got beyond himself. He had never been here before. Was it life, or not life? He was by himself. They were in a big, bright place, those others, and he was outside. The town, all the country, a big bright place of light: and he was outside, here, in the darkened open beyond, where each thing existed alone. But they would all have to come there sometime, those others. Little, and left behind him, they all were. There had been father and mother and sweetheart. What did they all matter? This was the open land.

He sat up. Something scuffled. It was a little brown squirrel running in lovely undulating bounds over the floor, its red tail completing the undulation of its body—and then, as it sat up, furling and unfurling. He watched it, pleased. It ran on again, friskily, enjoying itself. It flew wildly at another squirrel, and they were chasing each other, and making little scolding, chattering noises. The soldier wanted to speak to them. But only a hoarse sound came out of his throat. The squirrels burst away —they flew up the trees. And then he saw the one peeping around at him, half-way up a tree trunk. A start of fear went through him, though in so far as he was conscious, he was amused. It still stayed, its little keen face staring at him half-way up the tree trunk, its little ears pricked up, its clawey little hands clinging to the bark, its white breast reared. He started from it in panic.

Struggling to his feet, he lurched away. He went on walking, walking, looking for something—for a drink. His brain felt hot and inflamed for want of water. He stumbled on. Then he did not know anything. He went unconscious as he walked. Yet he stumbled on, his mouth open.

When, to his dumb wonder, he opened his eyes on the world

again, he no longer tried to remember what it was. There was thick, golden light behind golden-green glitterings, and tall, grey-purple shafts, and darknesses farther off, surrounding him, growing deeper. He was conscious of a sense of arrival. He was amid the reality, on the real, dark bottom. But there was the thirst burning in his brain. He felt lighter, not so heavy. He supposed it was newness. The air was muttering with thunder. He thought he was walking wonderfully swiftly and was coming straight to relief—or was it to water?

Suddenly he stood still with fear. There was a tremendous flare of gold, immense—just a few dark trunks like bars between him and it. All the young level wheat was burnished gold glaring on its silky green. A woman, full-skirted, a black cloth on her head for head-dress, was passing like a block of shadow through the glistening, green corn, into the full glare. There was a farm, too, pale blue in shadow, and the timber black. And there was a church spire, nearly fused away in the gold. The woman moved on, away from him. He had no language with which to speak to her. She was the bright, solid unreality. She would make a noise of words that would confuse him, and her eyes would look at him without seeing him. She was crossing there to the other side. He stood against a tree.

When at last he turned, looking down the long, bare grove whose flat bed was already filling dark, he saw the mountains in a wonder-light, not far away, and radiant. Behind the soft, grey ridge of the nearest range the farther mountains stood golden and pale grey, the snow all radiant like pure, soft gold. So still, gleaming in the sky, fashioned pure out of the ore of the sky, they shone in their silence. He stood and looked at them, his face illuminated. And like the golden, lustrous gleaming of the snow he felt his own thirst bright in him. He stood and gazed, leaning against a tree. And then everything slid away into space.

During the night the lightning fluttered perpetually, making the whole sky white. He must have walked again. The world hung livid round him for moments, fields a level sheen of grey-green light, trees in dark bulk, and the range of clouds black across a white sky. Then the darkness fell like a shutter, and the night was whole. A faint flutter of a half-revealed world, that could not quite leap out of the darkness!—Then there again stood a sweep of pallor for the land, dark shapes looming, a range of clouds hanging overhead. The world was a ghostly shadow, thrown for a moment upon the pure darkness, which returned ever whole and complete.

And the mere delirium of sickness and fever went on inside him—his brain opening and shutting like the night—then sometimes convulsions of terror from something with great eyes that stared round a tree—then the long agony of the march, and the sun decomposing his blood—then the pang of hate for the Captain, followed by a pang of tenderness and ease. But everything was distorted, born of an ache and resolving into an ache.

In the morning he came definitely awake. Then his brain flamed with the sole horror of thirstiness! The sun was on his face, the dew was steaming from his wet clothes. Like one possessed, he got up. There, straight in front of him, blue and cool and tender, the mountains ranged across the pale edge of the morning sky. He wanted them—he wanted them alone—he wanted to leave himself and be identified with them. They did not move, they were still and soft, with white, gentle markings of snow. He stood still, mad with suffering, his hands crisping and clutching. Then he was twisting in a paroxysm on the grass.

He lay still, in a kind of dream of anguish. His thirst seemed to have separated itself from him, and to stand apart, a single demand. Then the pain he felt was another single self. Then there was the clog of his body, another separate thing. He was divided among all kinds of separate things. There was some strange, agonised connection between them, but they were drawing farther apart. Then they would all split. The sun, drilling down on him, was drilling through the bond. Then they would all fall, fall through the everlasting lapse of space. Then again, his consciousness reasserted itself. He roused on to his elbow and stared at the gleaming mountains. There they ranked, all still and wonderful between earth and heaven. He stared till his eyes went black, and the mountains, as they stood in their beauty, so clean and cool, seemed to have it, that which was lost in him.

IV

When the soldiers found him, three hours later, he was lying with his face over his arm, his black hair giving off heat under the sun. But he was still alive. Seeing the open, black mouth the young soldiers dropped him in horror.

He died in the hospital at night, without having seen again.

The doctors saw the bruises on his legs, behind, and were silent.

The bodies of the two men lay together, side by side, in the mortuary, the one white and slender, but laid rigidly at rest, the other looking as if every moment it must rouse into life again, so young and unused, from a slumber.

WILLIAM CARLOS WILLIAMS

THE SAILOR'S SON

As the ferry came into the slip, there was a pause, then a young fellow on a motorcycle shot out of the exit, looked right and left, sighted the hill, opened her up and took the grade at top speed. Right behind him came three others bunched and went roaring by, and behind them, a youngster travelling in fast company, his eyes fastened on the others. Behind him an older guy sitting firm and with a face on him like a piece of wood, ripped by without a quiver.

That day Manuel waited in vain for his friend to visit him on the farm where he had taken a job for the summer. It came on to rain about eleven in the morning. The cows had been put to pasture, the chickens fed, the eggs collected. It was Sunday. He had been down for the papers and had taken them up to the big house. What the hell? He might as well go up to his room and write to Margy.

Lousy weather, he said to himself cutting across the lawn uphill through the slippery, wet grass. I suppose he guessed it and didn't want to risk the bad roads. But that boy is there, all right, he certainly is there.

In his room, on the third floor of the dignified country house

195

where he was employed that year, he got out the ruled pad and a pencil and proceeded to write.

Dear Marge: Where have you been keeping yourself? I'm starting on the third month up here and you haven't been up to see me in six weeks. Why don't you come up some week-end sometime?

Then he stopped and thought a minute during which he tapped the butt of the long pencil against his closed lips, tap, tap, tap, tap, thinking; going on after a moment:

Drop me a line when to expect you. There's not much news except I'm pretty much alone here. I don't mind it though as long as I can earn something until I can get a job in the city. Not much chance for that now, I guess. I often think how good you are to me, giving me money and keeping me this spring while I was hunting for work. I'll never forget it. As soon as I can get back to New York and make what I ought to be getting, we can make our dream come true. I can just see a little apartment all neat and pretty. At first, I suppose, we'd both better work so we can save up a few dollars but after a year I like to think you'll quit that office for good. Christian didn't show up today. I suppose it's the rain. If you run into him, tell him I wanted to know why he didn't show up. I hope you can get up here sometime. I'm crazy to see you. This is a good place though, good food and all that but I've got to see my friends. So long, dearie, Yours, Manuel.

He put the letter in an envelope, addressed it and stuck it into his coat pocket. He took out his pipe and started to smoke. The rain beat down on the roof over his head with a drumming as of fingers tapping with their soft pads. He felt nervous and oppressed. He put his pipe aside, it didn't have the taste he expected of it and lay down on the bed wondering. What the hell? He felt lonesome and neglected.

But downstairs Mrs. Cuthbertson felt relieved. She liked Manuel, his work was satisfactory, he drove the car excellently and was docile and obedient. He was a real good boy. But she didn't have much use for the bozo who drove up from the city each week-end on a motorcycle for a visit to stay over till Sunday.

It's an old friend, Manuel explained to her, I've known him from the other side. I don't mind paying for his meals if that's what you mean, Mrs. Cuthbertson. Or he can ride down to the town for them.

Now, I've told you, Manuel, said Mrs. C., that I like you and I want you to stay here and help me. You are not so strong, you look twice as well as when you came up here this spring. But I don't think that young man is a good influence on you. I can't find you anywhere when he is here. I tell you if you want to stay here, you had better tell him not to come up so often. Once a month is all right but not every week-end. That is not what we hired you for. I do not like his looks. He has a fresh look in his eyes. You are not the same nice boy when he is here.

It was Mrs. Cuthbertson's habit to talk this way to the young men she hired to do the work for her in summer. She picked out boys that she liked and then looked after them. She talked their talk and most of them liked her. But this time she had not been quite frank with Manuel. She did not tell him that what she really objected to was his friend's air of proprietorship over Manuel, and the whole farm for that matter, when he was there. He drove up on his motorcycle; put the machine anywhere at all in the garage and proceeded to eat fruit, wander about the lawns and enjoy himself as if he owned the place. Manuel shared his meals with him and at night his bed. This was the point on which Mrs. C. stuck. Yet she didn't quite feel that she wanted to come out with it—just yet.

Mrs. Cuthbertson knew that Manuel was engaged to be married. Why didn't his girl come up to visit him more often if he was lonely? It would have been much better. But this young man was a nuisance. Manuel was a different person when he was there, silly, excited and worth nothing. At first she thought it would only last a few times, but every Saturday it had been the same. Mrs. C. was determined it should not continue longer.

But the following Saturday being fine, sure enough about four in the afternoon you could hear the chug chug of the motor as it took the steep hill, up the dirt road leading to the farm entrance. And there was the boy himself, the same cocky youngster who had shot out of the ferry entrance the week before. He honked his horn.

As Mrs. C. heard this, she called to Manuel to warn him. But he was already out the back door. She called to him from the kitchen window but though he must have heard her, he kept right on going at a run to meet his friend.

Hello, kid, Gees' I'm glad to see you. I almost passed out last week. Why didn't you come up? Did the rain keep you?

Sure, what the hell, he lied, don't you think I'd a been here if I could a made it? How are you, Baby? Feelin' your oats?"

You said it.

And with that, Manuel swung open the garage doors and the kid rolled his cycle into the space, standing it over against the wall, on one side.

Mrs. Cuthbertson was watching from the kitchen window, her jaw set, and a determined look in her eyes. Pretty soon she saw the men come out of the garage and after hanging around the corner of the building, talking a minute, she saw Manuel cast a quick look up at the house, then the two disappeared behind the stonework.

Mrs. C. waited a few minutes and went out. The hay barn lay directly behind the big stone garage building, its entrance concealed from view as far as the house on the hill was concerned. Mrs. Cuthbertson walked slowly along on the grass avoiding the cinder roadway and approached the barn. She saw no one about so she went further and listened. She thought she heard voices in the barn but listen as she would, she could not make out what they were saying.

With that she boldly walked up to the big doors and, being a powerful woman, she swung one of them open and walked in. The men were lying in the hay. She looked, felt her stomach rise into her throat and then she let her tongue go. The visitor she ordered off the farm at once. He laughed and walked past her out of the door without a quiver. But with Manuel it was different.

After rearranging his clothes, he sat down in the hay where he was and cried like a child. Then he got up and came to her begging her not to send him away. She felt sorry for the boy and after a few strong words ordered him up to his room to pack.

But there she was. The work had to be done. She had no one to take his place. So after an hour, she called the fellow down again and told him exactly what was on her mind. You may stay this week out, she said, until I get someone to take your place, but then you go.

He begged, he pleaded, in vain. Then he went upstairs, wrote another letter to his girl and the following morning when he had gone down with the milk he mailed it.

The next Sunday the girl, or woman rather, appeared. Why had Manuel been fired? Was he not good enough for the job? Mrs. Cuthbertson told the woman as much as she had the words for—but, to her surprise, it made no great impression.

The boy is lonesome up here, said the woman. Why do you keep his friends away? I am engaged to marry him, I don't care what he does. Why should you worry? Well, that was a hot one. Manuel begged to be kept on. He had nowhere else to go. He could not get a recommendation. What should he do? Tears came to his eyes. Finally the fiancée grew abusive and Mrs. Cuthbertson losing her temper very nearly struck her. It was a wild moment. But in the end Manuel was fired. And the woman took him back to the city with her where she told him she would pay for a room until she could find work for him elsewhere.

FEDERICO GARCÍA LORCA

ODE TO WALT WHITMAN

Along East River and the Bronx
the young men were singing, baring their waists,
with the wheel and the leather, the hammer, the oil.
Ninety thousand miners whittled silver from the rocks
and the boys traced ladders and perspectives.

But nobody slept
or wished to be: river;
none loved the big leaves
or the beach's blue tongue.

Along East River and Queensborough,
the young men were grappling with Industry.
The Jews sold the faun of the river
circumcision's rosette;
and the sky, over bridges and rooftops
emptied its buffalo herds to the push of the wind.

But nobody dawdled,
or wished to be: cloud;
none looked for the fern
or the drum's yellow wheel.

At moon-rise,
the block and the tackle will veer and startle the sky;
a zenith of needles will circle all memory in
and the coffins move off with the jobless.

Ah, filthy New York,
New York of cables and death.
What angel do you carry, concealed in your cheek?
What ineffable voice will speak the truths of the wheat?
Who, the terrible dream of your tainted anemones?

Not for one moment, Walt Whitman, comely old man,
have I ceased to envision your beard full of butterflies,
your corduroy shoulders, worn thin by the moon,
your chaste, Apollonian thighs,
your voice like a pillar of ashes;
patriarch, comely as mist,
you cried like a bird
whose sex is transfixed by a needle;
satyr's antagonist,
grapevine's antagonist,
and lover of bodies under the nap of the cloth.
Not for a moment, manly and comely one,
on mountains of railroads and coal and advertisements,
but you dreamed yourself river, and slept like a river,
with that comrade who took to your heart
the little complaint of the ignorant leopard.

Not a moment, blood-brother, Adam, and masculine,
lone man in a sea, Walt Whitman, comely old man—
for look!—on the rooftops,
or huddled in bars,
or leaping in packs from the gutters,
or held between legs of the motorist, shuddering,
or whirling on platforms of absinthe,
the perverts, Walt Whitman, all pointing you!

This one—and this one! They fall
on your decent and luminous beard,
the blond-headed northerners, the blacks from the sanddunes,
a legion of gestures and outcries,

catlike and serpentine—
perverts—the pack of them perverts, Walt Whitman—
grimy with tears, so much meat for the whiplash,
for the boot or the bite of the animal-tamers.

And this one! And this one! The taint of their fingernails
    points
to the brink of your dream
where the playfellow munches your apple
with a faint taste of gasoline,
and the sunlight sings out on the navels
of the boys at their games under bridges.

But you never went looking for the scar on the eye,
or the overcast swamp where the boys are submerged,
or the freezing saliva
or the contours, split open, like the sac of the toad,
that the perverts in taxis and terraces carry
as the moon whips them on into terrified corners.

You looked for a nude that could be like a river,
the bull and the dream that could merge, like seaweed and
    wheel,
sire of your agony, your mortality's camellia,
to cry in the flames of your secret equator.

It is fitting that no man should seek
in another day's thickets of blood for his pleasure.
Heaven has shores for our flights out of life,
and the corpse need not make itself over at dawn.

Agony, agony, dream, ferment and dream.
It is the world's way, my friend: agony, agony.
Under the town-clock the dead decompose.
War takes its course with a million gray sewer-rats, sobbing.
The well-to-do will to their darlings
little candle-lit death-beds,
and life is not noble, or wholesome, or holy.

Yet we might, if we would, lead our appetite on
through the vein of the coral or the heaven-sent nude.

Tomorrow our passion is rock, and Time,
a wind come to sleep in the branches.

Wherefore my voice is not raised
to admonish the boy who inscribes
a girl's name on his pillow, Walt Whitman, old friend;
not to shame the young man who dresses himself like a bride
in the dark of the clothes-closet,
or the stags of the dance-hall
who drink at the waters of whoredom and sicken,
or the green apparition of men
who cherish mankind and burn out their lips in the silence.
But you! against all of you, perverts of the cities,
immodest of thought and tumescent of flesh,
mothers of filthiness, harpies, sleeplessly thwarting
the Love that apportions us garlands of pleasure.

Always against you, whosoever bestow upon boys
the foul drop of death with wormwood of venom.
Against you to the end!
North American *fairies,*
Pájaros of Havana,
Jotos of Mexico,
Sarasas of Cádiz,
Apios of Seville,
Cancos of Madrid,
Floras of Alicante,
Adelaidas of Portugal.

Perverts of the world, dove-killers!
Toadies of women, dressing-room bitches,
brazen in squares in a fever of fans
or ambushed in motionless landscapes of hemlock.

No quarter! Death
oozes out of your eyes
and clusters gray flowers at the edge of a dog.
No quarter! Beware!
Let the pure, the bewildered,
the illustrious, classic, and suppliant
shut the festival doors in your face.

CALAMUS

And you, on the shores of the Hudson, handsome Walt Whitman, asleep
with your beard to the pole, open-handed.
In the delicate marl or the snow, your tongue always summon-
ing
the comrades to watch your gazelle, disembodied in air.
Sleep on; for nothing abides.

A dancing of walls rocks the meadows
and America drowns under engines and tears.
I could wish for a stirring of wind from the deepest abyss of
the night
to undo all the letters and flowers from the arch where you
drowse,
while a black boy declares to the gold-getting white
kingdom come in a tassel of corn.

—Translated by
Ben Belitt

CHRISTOPHER ISHERWOOD

ON RUEGEN ISLAND

(SUMMER 1931)

I wake early and go out to sit on the veranda in my pyjamas. The wood casts long shadows over the fields. Birds call with sudden uncanny violence, like alarm-clocks going off. The birch-trees hang down laden over the rutted, sandy earth of the country road. A soft bar of cloud is moving up from the line of trees along the lake. A man with a bicycle is watching his horse graze on a patch of grass by the path; he wants to disentangle the horse's hoof from its tether-rope. He pushes the horse with both hands, but it won't budge. And now an old woman in a shawl comes walking with a little boy. The boy wears a dark sailor suit; he is very pale and his neck is bandaged. They soon turn back. A man passes on a bicycle and shouts something to the man with the horse. His voice rings out, quite clear yet unintelligible, in the morning stillness. A cock crows. The creak of the bicycle going past. The dew on the white table and chairs in the garden arbour, and dripping from the heavy lilac. Another cock crows, much louder and nearer. And I think I can hear the sea, or very distant bells.

The village is hidden in the wood, away up to the left. It

consists almost entirely of boarding-houses, in various styles of seaside architecture—sham Moorish, old Bavarian, Taj Mahal, and the rococo doll's house, with white fretwork balconies. Behind the woods is the sea. You can reach it without going through the village, by a zig-zag path, which brings you out abruptly to the edge of some sandy cliffs, with the beach below you, and the tepid shallow Baltic lying almost at your feet. This end of the bay is quite deserted; the official bathing-beach is round the corner of the headland. The white onion-domes of the Strand Restaurant at Baabe wobble in the distance, behind fluid waves of heat, a kilometre away.

In the wood are rabbits and adders and deer. Yesterday morning I saw a roe being chased by a Borzoi dog, right across the fields and in amongst the trees. The dog couldn't catch the roe, although it seemed to be going much the faster of the two, moving in long graceful bounds, while the roe went bucketing over the earth with wild rigid jerks, like a grand piano bewitched.

There are two people staying in this house, besides myself. One of them is an Englishman, named Peter Wilkinson, about my own age. The other is a German working-class boy from Berlin, named Otto Nowak. He is sixteen or seventeen years old.

Peter—as I already call him; we got rather tight the first evening, and quickly made friends—is thin and dark and nervous. He wears horn-rimmed glasses. When he gets excited, he digs his hands down between his knees and clenches them together. Thick veins stand out at the sides of his temples. He trembles all over with suppressed, nervous laughter, until Otto, rather irritated, exclaims: '*Mensch, reg' Dich bloss nicht so auf!*'

Otto has a face like a very ripe peach. His hair is fair and thick, growing low on his forehead. He has small sparkling eyes, full of naughtiness, and a wide, disarming grin, which is much too innocent to be true. When he grins, two large dimples appear in his peach-bloom cheeks. At present, he makes up to me assiduously, flattering me, laughing at my jokes, never missing an opportunity of giving me a crafty, understanding wink. I think he looks upon me as a potential ally in his dealings with Peter.

This morning we all bathed together. Peter and Otto are busy building a large sand fort. I lay and watched Peter as he worked furiously, enjoying the glare, digging away savagely with his child's spade, like a chain-gang convict under the eyes of an armed warder. Throughout the long, hot morning, he never sat still for a moment. He and Otto swam, dug, wrestled, ran races or played with a rubber football, up and down the sands. Peter is skinny but wiry. In his games with Otto, he holds his own, it seems, only by an immense, furious effort of will. It is Peter's will against Otto's body. Otto is his whole body; Peter is only his head. Otto moves fluidly, effortlessly; his gestures have the savage, unconscious grace of a cruel, elegant animal. Peter drives himself about, lashing his stiff, ungraceful body with the whip of his merciless will.

Otto is outrageously conceited. Peter has bought him a chest-expander, and, with this, he exercises solemnly at all hours of the day. Coming into their bedroom, after lunch, to look for Peter, I found Otto wrestling with the expander like Laocoön, in front of the looking-glass, all alone: 'Look, Christoph!' he gasped. 'You see, I can do it! All five strands!' Otto certainly has a superb pair of shoulders and chest for a boy of his age—but his body is nevertheless somehow slightly ridiculous. The beautiful ripe lines of the torso taper away too suddenly to his rather absurd little buttocks and spindly, immature legs. And these struggles with the chest-expander are daily making him more and more top-heavy.

This evening Otto had a touch of sunstroke, and went to bed early, with a headache. Peter and I walked up to the village, alone. In the Bavarian café, where the band makes a noise like Hell unchained, Peter bawled into my ear the story of his life.

Peter is the youngest of a family of four. He has two sisters, both married. One of the sisters lives in the country and hunts. The other is what the newspapers call 'a popular society hostess.' Peter's elder brother is a scientist and explorer. He has been on expeditions to the Congo, the New Hebrides, and the Great Barrier Reef. He plays chess, speaks with the voice of a man of sixty, and has never, to the best of Peter's belief, performed the sexual act. The only member of the family with whom Peter is at present on speaking terms is his hunting sister, but they seldom meet, because Peter hates his brother-in-law.

Peter was delicate, as a boy. He did not go to a preparatory school but, when he was thirteen, his father sent him to a public school. His father and mother had a row about this which lasted until Peter, with his mother's encouragement, developed heart trouble and had to be removed at the end of his second term. Once escaped, Peter began to hate his mother for having petted and coddled him into a funk. She saw that he could not forgive her and so, as Peter was the only one of her children whom she cared for, she got ill herself and soon afterwards died.

It was too late to send Peter back to school again, so Mr Wilkinson engaged a tutor. The tutor was a very high-church young man who intended to become a priest. He took cold baths in winter and had crimpy hair and a Grecian jaw. Mr Wilkinson disliked him from the first, and the elder brother made satirical remarks, so Peter threw himself passionately on to the tutor's side. The two of them went for walking-tours in the Lake District and discussed the meaning of the Sacrament amidst austere moorland scenery. This kind of talk got them, inevitably, into a complicated emotional tangle which was abruptly unravelled, one evening, during a fearful row in a barn. Next morning, the tutor left, leaving a ten-page letter behind him. Peter meditated suicide. He heard later indirectly that the tutor had grown a moustache and gone out to Australia. So Peter got another tutor, and finally went up to Oxford.

Hating his father's business and his brother's science, he made music and literature into a religious cult. For the first year, he liked Oxford very much indeed. He went out to tea-parties and ventured to talk. To his pleasure and surprise, people appeared to be listening to what he said. It wasn't until he had done this often that he began to notice their air of slight embarrassment. 'Somehow or other,' said Peter, 'I always struck the wrong note.'

Meanwhile, at home, in the big Mayfair house, with its four bath-rooms and garage for three cars, where there was always too much to eat, the Wilkinson family was slowly falling to pieces, like something gone rotten. Mr Wilkinson with his diseased kidneys, his whisky, and his knowledge of 'handling men', was angry and confused and a bit pathetic. He snapped and growled at his children when they passed near him, like a surly old dog. At meals nobody ever spoke. They avoided each other's eyes, and hurried upstairs afterwards to write letters, full of hatred and satire, to their intimate friends. Only Peter had no friend to write to. He shut himself up in his tasteless, expensive bedroom and read and read.

And now it was the same at Oxford. Peter no longer went to tea-parties. He worked all day, and, just before the examinations, he had a nervous breakdown. The doctor advised a complete change of scene, other interests. Peter's father let him play at farming for six months in Devonshire, then he began to talk of the business. Mr Wilkinson had been unable to persuade any of his other children to take even a polite interest in the source of their incomes. They were all unassailable in their different worlds. One of his daughters was about to marry into the peerage, the other frequently hunted with the Prince of Wales. His elder son read papers to the Royal Geographical Society. Only Peter hadn't any justification for his existence. The other children behaved selfishly, but knew what they wanted. Peter also behaved selfishly, and didn't know.

However, at the critical moment, Peter's uncle, his mother's brother, died. This uncle lived in Canada. He had seen Peter once as a child and had taken a fancy to him, so he left him all his money, not very much, but enough to live on, comfortably.

Peter went to Paris and began studying music. His teacher told him that he would never be more than a good second-rate amateur, but he only worked all the harder. He worked merely to avoid thinking, and had another nervous breakdown, less serious than at first. At this time, he was convinced that he would soon go mad. He paid a visit to London and found only

his father at home. They had a furious quarrel on the first evening; thereafter, they hardly exchanged a word. After a week
of silence and huge meals, Peter had a mild attack of homi-
cidal mania. All through breakfast, he couldn't take his eyes
off a pimple on his father's throat. He was fingering the
bread-knife. Suddenly the left side of his face began to twitch.
It twitched and twitched, so that he had to cover his cheek
with his hand. He felt certain that his father had noticed this,
and was intentionally refusing to remark on it—was, in fact,
deliberately torturing him. At last, Peter could stand it no
longer. He jumped up and rushed out of the room, out of the
house, into the garden, where he flung himself face downwards
on the wet lawn. There he lay, too frightened to move. After a
quarter of an hour, the twitching stopped.

That evening Peter walked along Regent Street and picked
up a whore. They went back together to the girl's room, and
talked for hours. He told her the whole story of his life at
home, gave her ten pounds and left her without even kissing
her. Next morning a mysterious rash appeared on his left
thigh. The doctor seemed at a loss to explain its origin, but
prescribed some ointment. The rash became fainter, but did
not altogether disappear until last month. Soon after the
Regent Street episode, Peter also began to have trouble with
his left eye.

For some time already, he had played with the idea of con-
sulting a psycho-analyst. His final choice was an orthodox
Freudian with a sleepy, ill-tempered voice and very large feet.
Peter took an immediate dislike to him, and told him so. The
Freudian made notes on a piece of paper, but did not seem
offended. Peter later discovered that he was quite uninterested
in anything except Chinese art. They met three times a week,
and each visit cost two guineas.

After six months Peter abandoned the Freudian, and
started going to a new analyst, a Finnish lady with white hair
and a bright conversational manner. Peter found her easy to
talk to. He told her, to the best of his ability, everything he
had ever done, ever said, ever thought, or ever dreamed.
Sometimes, in moments of discouragement, he told her stories
which were absolutely untrue, or anecdotes collected from

case-books. Afterwards, he would confess to these lies, and they would discuss his motives for telling them, and agree that they were very interesting. On red-letter nights Peter would have a dream, and this gave them a topic of conversation for the next few weeks. The analysis lasted nearly two years, and was never completed.

This year Peter got bored with the Finnish lady. He heard of a good man in Berlin. Well, why not? At any rate, it would be a change. It was also an economy. The Berlin man only cost fifteen marks a visit.

'And you're still going to him?' I asked.

'No . . .' Peter smiled. 'I can't afford to, you see.'

Last month, a day or two after his arrival, Peter went out to Wannsee, to bathe. The water was still chilly, and there were not many people about. Peter had noticed a boy who was turning somersaults by himself, on the sand. Later the boy came up and asked him for a match. They got into conversation. It was Otto Nowak.

'Otto was quite horrified when I told him about the analyst. "What!" he said, "you give that man fifteen marks a day just for letting you talk to him! You give me ten marks and I'll talk to you all day, and all night as well!"' Peter began to shake all over with laughter, flushing scarlet and wringing his hands.

Curiously enough, Otto wasn't being altogether preposterous when he offered to take the analyst's place. Like many very animal people, he has considerable instinctive powers of healing—when he chooses to use them. At such times, his treatment of Peter is unerringly correct. Peter will be sitting at the table, hunched up, his downward-curving mouth lined with childhood fears: a perfect case-picture of his twisted, expensive upbringing. Then in comes Otto, grins, dimples, knocks over a chair, slaps Peter on the back, rubs his hands and exclaims fatuously: *'Ja, ja . . . so ist die Sache!'* And, in a moment, Peter is transformed. He relaxes, begins to hold himself naturally; the tightness disappears from his mouth, his eyes lose their hunted look. As long as the spell lasts, he is just like an ordinary person.

Peter tells me that, before he met Otto, he was so terrified of infection that he would wash his hands with carbolic after picking up a cat. Nowadays, he often drinks out of the same glass as Otto, uses his sponge, and will share the same plate.

Dancing has begun at the Kurhaus and the café on the lake. We saw the announcements of the first dance two days ago, while we were taking our evening walk up the main street of the village. I noticed that Otto glanced at the poster wistfully, and that Peter had seen him do this. Neither of them, however, made any comment.

Yesterday was chilly and wet. Otto suggested that we should hire a boat and go fishing on the lake: Peter was pleased with this plan, and agreed at once. But when we had waited three quarters of an hour in the drizzle for a catch, he began to get irritable. On the way back to the shore, Otto kept splashing with his oars—at first because he couldn't row properly, later merely to annoy Peter. Peter got very angry indeed, and swore at Otto, who sulked.

After supper, Otto announced that he was going to dance at the Kurhaus. Peter took this without a word, in ominous silence, the corners of his mouth beginning to drop; and Otto, either genuinely unconscious of his disapproval or deliberately overlooking it, assumed that the matter was settled.

After he had gone out, Peter and I sat upstairs in my cold room, listening to the pattering of the rain on the window.

'I thought it couldn't last,' said Peter gloomily. 'This is the beginning. You'll see.'

'Nonsense, Peter. The beginning of what? It's quite natural that Otto should want to dance sometimes. You mustn't be so possessive.'

'Oh, I know, I know. As usual, I'm being utterly unreasonable ... All the same, this is the beginning ...'

Rather to my own surprise the event proved me right. Otto arrived back from the Kurhaus before ten o'clock. He had been disappointed. There had been very few people there, and the band was poor.

'I'll never go again,' he added, with a languishing smile at me. 'From now on I'll stay every evening with you and Christoph. It's much more fun when we're all three together, isn't it?'

Yesterday morning, while we were lying in our fort on the beach, a little fair-haired man with ferrety blue eyes and a small moustache came up to us and asked us to join in a game with him. Otto, always over-enthusiastic about strangers, accepted at once, so that Peter and I had either to be rude or follow his example.

The little man, after introducing himself as a surgeon from a Berlin hospital, at once took command, assigning to us the places where we were to stand. He was very firm about this—instantly ordering me back when I attempted to edge a little nearer, so as not to have such a long distance to throw. Then it appeared that Peter was throwing in quite the wrong way: the little doctor stopped the game in order to demonstrate this. Peter was amused at first, and then rather annoyed. He retorted with considerable rudeness, but the doctor's skin wasn't pierced. 'You hold yourself so stiff,' he explained, smiling. 'That is an error. You try again, and I will keep my hand on your shoulder-blade to see whether you really relax . . . No. Again you do not!'

He seemed delighted, as if this failure of Peter's were a special triumph for his own methods of teaching. His eye met Otto's. Otto grinned understandingly.

Our meeting with the doctor put Peter in a bad temper for the rest of the day. In order to tease him, Otto pretended to like the doctor very much: 'That's the sort of chap I'd like to have for a friend,' he said with a spiteful smile. 'A real sportsman! You ought to take up sport, Peter! Then you'd have a figure like he has!'

Had Peter been in another mood, this remark would probably have made him smile. As it was, he got very angry: 'You'd better go off with your doctor now, if you like him so much!'

Otto grinned teasingly. 'He hasn't asked me to—yet!'

Yesterday evening, Otto went out to dance at the Kurhaus and didn't return till late.

* * *

There are now a good many summer visitors to the village. The bathing-beach by the pier, with its array of banners, begins to look like a medieval camp. Each family has its own enormous hooded wicker beach-chair, and each chair flies a little flag. There are the German city flags—Hamburg, Hanover, Dresden, Rostock and Berlin, as well as the National, Republic and Nazi colours. Each chair is encircled by a low sand bulwark upon which the occupants have set inscriptions in fir-cones: *Waldesruh. Familie Walter. Stahlhelm. Heil Hitler!* Many of the forts are also decorated with the Nazi swastika. The other morning I saw a child of about five years old, stark naked, marching along all by himself with a swastika flag over his shoulder and singing *'Deutschland über alles'*.

The little doctor fairly revels in this atmosphere. Nearly every morning he arrives, on a missionary visit, to our fort. 'You really ought to come round to the other beach,' he tells us. 'It's much more amusing there. I'd introduce you to some nice girls. The young people here are a magnificent lot! I, as a doctor, know how to appreciate them. The other day I was over at Hiddensee. Nothing but Jews! It's a pleasure to get back here and see real Nordic types!'

'Let's go to the other beach,' urged Otto. 'It's so dull here. There's hardly anyone about.'

'You can go if you like,' Peter retorted with angry sarcasm: 'I'm afraid I should be rather out of place. I had a grandmother who was partly Spanish.'

But the little doctor won't let us alone. Our opposition and more or less openly expressed dislike seem actually to fascinate him. Otto is always betraying us into his hands. One day, when the doctor was speaking enthusiastically about Hitler, Otto said, 'It's no good your talking like that to Christoph, Herr Doktor. He's a communist!'

This seemed positively to delight the doctor. His ferrety blue eyes gleamed with triumph. He laid his hand affectionately on my shoulder.

'But you *can't* be a communist! You *can't!*'

'Why can't I?' I asked coldly, moving away. I hate him to touch me.

'Because there isn't any such thing as communism. It's just

an hallucination. A mental disease. People only imagine that they're communists. They aren't really.'

'What are they, then?'

But he wasn't listening. He fixed me with his triumphant, ferrety smile.

'Five years ago I used to think as you do. But my work at the clinic has convinced me that communism is a mere hallucination. What people need is discipline, self-control. I can tell you this as a doctor. I know it from my own experience.'

This morning we were all together in my room, ready to start out to bathe. The atmosphere was electric, because Peter and Otto were still carrying on an obscure quarrel which they had begun before breakfast, in their own bedroom. I was turning over the pages of a book, not paying much attention to them. Suddenly Peter slapped Otto hard on both cheeks. They closed immediately and staggered grappling about the room, knocking over the chairs. I looked on, getting out of their way as well as I could. It was funny, and, at the same time, unpleasant, because rage made their faces strange and ugly. Presently Otto got Peter down on the ground and began twisting his arm: 'Have you had enough?' he kept asking. He grinned: at that moment he was really hideous, positively deformed with malice. I knew that Otto was glad to have me there, because my presence was an extra humiliation for Peter. So I laughed, as though the whole thing were a joke, and went out of the room. I walked through the woods to Baabe, and bathed from the beach beyond. I felt I didn't want to see either of them again for several hours.

If Otto wishes to humiliate Peter, Peter in his different way also wishes to humiliate Otto. He wants to force Otto into making a certain kind of submission to his will, and this submission Otto refuses instinctively to make. Otto is naturally and healthily selfish, like an animal. If there are two chairs in a room, he will take the more comfortable one without hesitation, because it never even occurs to him to consider Peter's comfort. Peter's selfishness is much less honest, more civilized, more perverse. Appealed to in the right way, he will make any sacrifice, however unreasonable and unnecessary.

215

But when Otto takes the better chair as if by right, then Peter immediately sees a challenge which he dare not refuse to accept. I suppose that—given their two natures—there is no possible escape from this situation. Peter is bound to go on fighting to win Otto's submission. When, at last, he ceases to do so, it will merely mean that he has lost interest in Otto altogether.

The really destructive feature of their relationship is its inherent quality of boredom. It is quite natural for Peter often to feel bored with Otto—they have scarcely a single interest in common—but Peter, for sentimental reasons, will never admit that this is so. When Otto, who has no such motives for pretending, says, 'It's so dull here!' I invariably see Peter wince and look pained. Yet Otto is actually far less often bored than Peter himself; he finds Peter's company genuinely amusing, and is quite glad to be with him most of the day. Often, when Otto has been chattering rubbish for an hour without stopping, I can see that Peter really longs for him to be quiet and go away. But to admit this would be, in Peter's eyes, a total defeat, so he only laughs and rubs his hands, tacitly appealing to me to support him in his pretence of finding Otto inexhaustibly delightful and funny.

On our way back through the woods, after my bathe, I saw the ferrety little blond doctor advancing to meet me. It was too late to turn back. I said 'Good morning' as politely and coldly as possible. The doctor was dressed in running-shorts and a sweater; he explained that he had been taking a *'Waldlauf'*. 'But I think I shall turn back now,' he added. 'Wouldn't you like to run with me a little?'

'I'm afraid I can't,' I said rashly. 'You see, I twisted my ankle a bit yesterday.'

I could have bitten my tongue out as I saw the gleam of triumph in his eyes. 'Ah, you've sprained your ankle? Please let me look at it!' Squirming with dislike, I had to submit to his prodding fingers. 'But it is nothing, I assure you. You have no cause for alarm.'

As we walked the doctor began to question me about Peter

and Otto, twisting his head to look up at me, as he delivered each sharp, inquisitive little thrust. He was fairly consumed with curiosity.

'My work in the clinic has taught me that it is no use trying to help this type of boy. Your friend is very generous and very well meaning, but he makes a great mistake. This type of boy always reverts. From a scientific point of view, I find him exceedingly interesting.'

As though he were about to say something specially momentous, the doctor suddenly stood still in the middle of the path, paused a moment to engage my attention, and smilingly announced:

'He has a criminal head!'

'And you think that people with criminal heads should be left to become criminals?'

'Certainly not. I believe in discipline. These boys ought to be put into labour-camps.'

'And what are you going to do with them when you've got them there? You say that they can't be altered, anyhow, so I suppose you'd keep them locked up for the rest of their lives?'

The doctor laughed delightedly, as though this were a joke against himself which he could, nevertheless, appreciate. He laid a caressing hand on my arm:

'You are an idealist! Do not imagine that I don't understand your point of view. But it is unscientific, quite unscientific. You and your friend do not understand such boys as Otto. I understand them. Every week, one or two such boys come to my clinic, and I must operate on them for adenoids, or mastoid, or poisoned tonsils. So, you see, I know them through and through!'

'I should have thought it would be more accurate to say you knew their throats and ears.'

Perhaps my German wasn't quite equal to rendering the sense of this last remark. At all events, the doctor ignored it completely. 'I know this type of boy very well,' he repeated. 'It is a bad degenerate type. You cannot make anything out of these boys. Their tonsils are almost invariably diseased.'

* * *

217

There are perpetual little rows going on between Peter and Otto, yet I cannot say that I find living with them actually unpleasant. Just now, I am very much taken up with my new novel. Thinking about it, I often go out for long walks, alone. Indeed, I find myself making more and more frequent excuses to leave them to themselves; and this is selfish, because, when I am with them, I can often choke off the beginnings of a quarrel by changing the subject or making a joke. Peter, I know, resents my desertions. 'You're quite an ascetic,' he said maliciously the other day, 'always withdrawing for your contemplations.' Once, when I was sitting in a café near the pier, listening to the band, Peter and Otto came past. 'So this is where you've been hiding!' Peter exclaimed. I saw that, for the moment, he really disliked me.

One evening, we were all walking up the main street, which was crowded with summer visitors. Otto said to Peter, with his most spiteful grin: 'Why must you always look in the same direction as I do?' This was surprisingly acute, for, whenever Otto turned his head to stare at a girl, Peter's eyes mechanically followed his glance with instinctive jealousy. We passed the photographer's window, in which, every day, the latest groups snapped by the beach camermen are displayed. Otto paused to examine one of the new pictures with great attention, as though its subject were particularly attractive. I saw Peter's lips contract. He was struggling with himself, but he couldn't resist his own jealous curiosity—he stopped too. The photograph was of a fat old man with a long beard, waving a Berlin flag. Otto, seeing that his trap had been successful, laughed maliciously.

Invariably, after supper, Otto goes dancing at the Kurhaus or the café by the lake. He no longer bothers to ask Peter's permission to do this; he has established the right to have his evenings to himself. Peter and I generally go out too, into the village. We lean over the rail of the pier for a long time without speaking, staring down at the cheap jewellery of the Kurhaus lights reflected in the black water, each busy with his own thoughts. Sometimes we go into the Bavarian café and Peter gets steadily drunk—his stern, Puritan mouth contracting slightly with distaste as he raises the glass to his lips. I say nothing. There is too much to say. Peter, I know, wants me to make some provocative remark about Otto which will give him the exquisite relief of losing his temper. I don't, and we drink —keeping up a desultory conversation about books and concerts and plays. Later, when we are returning home, Peter's footsteps will gradually quicken until, as we enter the house, he leaves me and runs upstairs to his bedroom. Often we don't get back till half past twelve or a quarter to one, but it is very seldom that we find Otto already there.

Down by the railway station, there is a holiday home for children from the Hamburg slums. Otto has got to know one of the teachers from this home, and they go out dancing together nearly every evening. Sometimes the girl, with her little troop of children, comes marching past the house. The children glance up at the windows and, if Otto happens to be looking out, indulge in precocious jokes. They nudge and pluck at their young teacher's arm to persuade her to look up, too.

On these occasions, the girl smiles coyly and shoots one glance at Otto from under her eyelashes, while Peter, watching behind the curtains, mutters through clenched teeth: 'Bitch . . . bitch . . . bitch . . .' This persecution annoys him more than the actual friendship itself. We always seem to be running across the children when we are out walking in the woods. The children sing as they march—patriotic songs about the Homeland—in voices as shrill as birds. From far off, we hear them approaching, and have to turn hastily in the opposite direction. It is, as Peter says, like Captain Hook and the Crocodile.

Peter has made a scene, and Otto has told his friend that she mustn't bring her troop past the house any more. But now they have begun bathing on our beach, not very far from the fort. The first morning this happened, Otto's glance kept turning in their direction. Peter was aware of this, of course, and remained plunged in gloomy silence.

'What's the matter with you to-day, Peter?' said Otto. 'Why are you so horrid to me?'

'Horrid to *you*?' Peter laughed savagely.

219

'Oh, very well then.' Otto jumped up. 'I see you don't want me here.' And, bounding over the rampart of our fort, he began to run along the beach towards the teacher and her children, very gracefully, displaying his figure to the best possible advantage.

Yesterday evening there was a gala dance at the Kurhaus. In a mood of unusual generosity, Otto had promised Peter not to be later than a quarter to one, so Peter sat up with a book to wait for him. I didn't feel tired, and wanted to finish a chapter, so suggested that he should come into my room and wait there.

I worked. Peter read. The hours went slowly by. Suddenly I looked at my watch and saw that it was a quarter past two. Peter had dozed off in his chair. Just as I was wondering whether I should wake him, I heard Otto coming up the stairs. His footsteps sounded drunk. Finding no one in his room, he banged open my door. Peter sat up with a start.

Otto lolled grinning against the doorpost. He made me a half-tipsy salute. 'Have you been reading all this time?' he asked Peter.

'Yes,' said Peter, very self-controlled.

'Why?' Otto smiled fatuously.

'Because I couldn't sleep.'

'Why couldn't you sleep?'

'You know quite well,' said Peter between his teeth.

Otto yawned in his most offensive manner. 'I don't know and I don't care . . . Don't make such a fuss.'

Peter rose to his feet. 'God, you little swine!' he said, smacking Otto's face hard with the flat of his hand. Otto didn't attempt to defend himself. He gave Peter an extraordinarily vindictive look out of his bright little eyes. 'Good!' He spoke rather thickly. 'To-morrow I shall go back to Berlin.' He turned unsteadily on his heel.

'Otto, come here,' said Peter. I saw that, in another moment, he would burst into tears of rage. He followed Otto out on to the landing. 'Come here,' he said again, in a sharp tone of command.

'Oh, leave me alone,' said Otto, 'I'm sick of you. I want to sleep now. To-morrow I'm going back to Berlin.'

This morning, however, peace has been restored—at a price. Otto's repentance has taken the form of a sentimental outburst over his family: 'Here I've been enjoying myself and never thinking of them ... Poor mother has to work like a dog, and her lungs are so bad ... Let's send her some money, shall we, Peter? Let's send her fifty marks . . .' Otto's generosity reminded him of his own needs. In addition to the money for Frau Nowak, Peter has been talked into ordering Otto a new suit, which will cost a hundred and eighty, as well as a pair of shoes, a dressing-gown, and a hat.

In return for this outlay, Otto has volunteered to break off his relations with the teacher. (We now discover that, in any case, she is leaving the island tomorrow.) After supper, she appeared, walking up and down outside the house.

'Just let her wait till she's tired,' said Otto. 'I'm not going down to her.'

Presently the girl, made bold by impatience, began to whistle. This sent Otto into a frenzy of glee. Throwing open the window, he danced up and down, waving his arms and making hideous faces at the teacher who, for her part, seemed struck dumb with amazement at this extraordinary exhibition.

'Get away from here!' Otto yelled. 'Get out!'

The girl turned, and walked slowly away, a rather pathetic figure, into the gathering darkness.

'I think you might have said goodbye to her,' said Peter, who could afford to be magnanimous, now that he saw his enemy routed.

But Otto wouldn't hear of it.

'What's the use of all those rotten girls, anyhow? Every night they came pestering me to dance with them ... And you know how I am, Peter—I'm so easily persuaded ... Of course, it was horrid of me to leave you alone, but what could I do? It was all their fault, really . . .'

Our life has now entered upon a new phase. Otto's resolutions were short-lived. Peter and I are alone together most of the day. The teacher has left, and with her, Otto's last induce-ment to bathe with us from the fort. He now goes off, every morning, to the bathing-beach by the pier, to flirt and play ball with his dancing-partners of the evening. The little doctor has also disappeared, and Peter and I are free to bathe and loll in the sun as unathletically as we wish.

After supper, the ritual of Otto's preparations for the dance begins. Sitting in my bedroom, I hear Peter's footsteps cross the landing, light and springy with relief—for now comes the only time of the day when Peter feels himself alto-gether excused from taking any interest in Otto's activities. When he taps on my door, I shut my book at once. I have been out already to the village to buy half-a-pound of peppermint creams. Peter says goodbye to Otto, with a vain lingering hope that, perhaps to-night, he will, after all, be punctual: 'Till half past twelve, then . . .'

'Till one,' Otto bargains.

'All right,' Peter concedes. 'Till one. But don't be late.'

'No, Peter, I won't be late.'

As we open the garden gate and cross the road into the wood, Otto waves to us from the balcony. I have to be careful to hide the peppermint creams under my coat, in case he should see them. Laughing guiltily, munching the pepper-mints, we take the woodland path to Baabe. We always spend our evenings in Baabe, nowadays. We like it better than our own village. Its single sandy street of low-roofed houses among the pine-trees has a romantic, colonial air; it is like a ramshackle, lost settlement somewhere in the backwoods, where people come to look for a non-existent gold mine and remain, stranded, for the rest of their lives.

In the little restaurant, we eat strawberries and cream, and talk to the young waiter. The waiter hates Germany and longs to go to America. *'Hier ist nichts los'*. During the season, he is allowed no free time at all, and in the winter he earns nothing. Most of the Baabe boys are Nazis. Two of them come into the restaurant sometimes and engage us in good-humoured politi-cal agruments. They tell us about their field-exercises and mil-itary games.

'You're preparing for war,' says Peter indignantly. On

these occasions—although he has really not the slightest interest in politics—he gets quite heated.

'Excuse me,' one of the boys contradicts, 'that's quite wrong. The Führer does not want war. Our programme stands for peace, with honour. All the same . . .' he adds wistfully, his face lighting up, 'war can be fine, you know! Think of the ancient Greeks!'

'The ancient Greeks,' I object, 'didn't use poison gas.'

The boys are rather scornful at this quibble. One of them answers loftily, 'That's a purely technical question.'

At half past ten we go down, with most of the other inhabitants, to the railway station, to watch the arrival of the last train. It is generally empty. It goes clanging away through the dark woods, sounding its harsh bell. At last it is late enough to start home; this time, we take the road. Across the meadows, you can see the illuminated entrance of the café by the lake, where Otto goes to dance.

'The lights of Hell are shining brightly this evening,' Peter is fond of remarking.

Peter's jealousy has turned into insomnia. He has begun taking sleeping-tablets, but admits that they seldom have any effect. They merely make him feel drowsy next morning, after breakfast. He often goes to sleep for an hour or two in our fort, on the shore.

This morning the weather was cool and dull, the sea oyster-grey. Peter and I hired a boat, rowed out beyond the pier, then let ourselves drift, gently, away from the land. Peter lit a cigarette. He said abruptly:

'I wonder how much longer this will go on . . .'

'As long as you let it, I suppose.'

'Yes . . . We seem to have got into a pretty static condition, don't we? I suppose there's no particular reason why Otto and I should ever stop behaving to each other as we do at present . . .' He paused, added: 'Unless, of course, I stop giving him money.'

'What do you think would happen then?'

Peter paddled idly in the water with his fingers. 'He'd leave me.'

The boat drifted on for several minutes. I asked: 'You don't think he cares for you, at all?'

'At the beginning he did, perhaps . . . Not now. There's nothing between us now but my cash.'

'Do you still care for him?'

'No . . . I don't know. Perhaps . . . I still hate him, sometimes—if that's a sign of caring.'

'It might be.'

There was a long pause. Peter dried his fingers on his handkerchief. His mouth twitched nervously.

'Well,' he said at last, 'what do you advise me to do?'

'What do you want to do?'

Peter's mouth gave another twitch.

'I suppose, really, I want to leave him.'

'Then you'd better leave him.'

'At once?'

'The sooner the better. Give him a nice present and send him back to Berlin this afternoon.'

Peter shook his head, smiled sadly:

'I can't.'

There was another long pause. Then Peter said: 'I'm sorry, Christopher . . . You're absolutely right, I know. If I were in your place, I'd say the same thing . . . But I can't. Things have got to go on as they are—until something happens. They can't last much longer, anyhow . . . Oh, I know I'm very weak . . .'

'You needn't apologize to me,' I smiled, to conceal a slight feeling of irritation: 'I'm not one of your analysts!'

I picked up the oars and began to row back towards the shore. As we reached the pier, Peter said:

'It seems funny to think of now—when I first met Otto, I thought we should live together for the rest of our lives.'

'Oh, my God!' The vision of a life with Otto opened before me, like a comic inferno. I laughed out loud. Peter laughed, too, wedging his locked hands between his knees. His face turned from pink to red, from red to purple. His veins bulged. We were still laughing when we got out of the boat.

In the garden the landlord was waiting for us. 'What a pity!' he exclaimed. 'The gentlemen are too late!' He pointed over the meadows, in the direction of the lake. We could see the smoke rising above the line of poplars, as the little train drew out of the station: 'Your friend was obliged to leave for Berlin, suddenly, on urgent business. I hoped the gentlemen might have been in time to see him off. What a pity!'

This time, both Peter and I ran upstairs. Peter's bedroom was in a terrible mess—all the drawers and cupboards were open. Propped up on the middle of the table was a note, in Otto's cramped, scrawling hand:

> *Dear Peter. Please forgive me I couldn't stand it any longer here so I am going home.*
>
> > *Love from Otto.*
> > *Don't be angry.*

(Otto had written it, I noticed, on a fly-leaf torn out of one of Peter's psychology books: *Beyond the Pleasure-Principle*.)

'Well . . .!' Peter's mouth began to twitch. I glanced at him nervously, expecting a violent outburst, but he seemed fairly calm. After a moment, he walked over to the cupboards and began looking through the drawers. 'He hasn't taken much,' he announced, at the end of his search. 'Only a couple of my ties, three shirts—lucky my shoes don't fit him!—and, let's see . . . about two hundred marks . . .' Peter started to laugh, rather hysterically: 'Very moderate, on the whole!'

'Do you think he decided to leave quite suddenly?' I asked, for the sake of saying something.

'Probably he did. That would be just like him . . . Now I come to think of it, I told him we were going out in that boat, this morning—and he asked me if we should be away for long . . ."

'I see . . .'

I sat down on Peter's bed—thinking, oddly enough, that Otto has at last done something which I rather respect.

Peter's hysterical high spirits kept him going for the rest of the morning; at lunch he turned gloomy, and wouldn't say a word.

'Now I must go and pack,' he told me when we had finished. 'You're off, too?'

'Of course.'

'To Berlin?'

Peter smiled. 'No, Christopher. Don't be alarmed! Only to England . . .'

'Oh . . .'

'There's a train which'll get me to Hamburg late to-night. I shall probably go straight on . . . I feel I've got to keep travelling until I'm clear of this bloody country . . .'

There was nothing to say. I helped him pack, in silence. As Peter put his shaving-mirror into the bag, he asked: 'Do you remember how Otto broke this, standing on his head?'

'Yes, I remember.'

When we had finished, Peter went out on to the balcony of his room: 'There'll be plenty of whistling outside here, to-night,' he said.

I smiled: 'I shall have to go down and console them.'

Peter laughed: 'Yes. You will!'

I went with him to the station. Luckily, the engine-driver was in a hurry. The train only waited a couple of minutes.

'What shall you do when you get to London?' I asked.

Peter's mouth curved down at the corners; he gave me a kind of inverted grin: 'Look round for another analyst, I suppose.'

'Well, mind you beat down his prices a bit!'

'I will.'

As the train moved out, he waved his hand: 'Well, good-bye, Christopher. Thank you for all your moral support!'

Peter never suggested that I should write to him, or visit him at home. I suppose he wants to forget this place, and everybody concerned with it. I can hardly blame him.

It was only this evening, turning over the pages of a book I have been reading, that I found another note from Otto, slipped between the leaves.

Please dear Christopher don't you be angry with me too because you aren't an idiot like Peter. When you are back in Berlin I shall come and see you because I know where you live; I saw the address on one of your letters and we can have a nice talk.

Your loving friend,
Otto.

I thought, somehow, that he wouldn't be got rid of quite so easily.

Actually, I am leaving for Berlin in a day or two, now. I thought I should stay on till the end of August, and perhaps finish my novel, but suddenly, the place seems so lonely. I miss Peter and Otto, and their daily quarrels, far more than I should have expected. And now even Otto's dancing-partners have stopped lingering sadly in the twilight, under my window.

EDWARD MORGAN FORSTER

THE OBELISK

Ernest was an elementary schoolmaster, and very very small; it was like marrying a doll, Hilda sometimes thought, and one with glass eyes too. She was larger herself: tall enough to make them look funny as they walked down the esplanade, but not tall enough to look dignified when she was alone. She cherished aspirations; none would have guessed it from her stumpy exterior. She yearned for a trip in a Rolls-Royce with a sheikh, but one cannot have everything or anything like it, one cannot even always be young. It is better to have a home of one's own than to always be a typist. Hilda did not talk quite as she should, and her husband had not scrupled to correct her. She had never forgotten—it was such a small thing, yet she could not forget it—she had never forgotten that night on their honeymoon when she had said something ungrammatical about the relative position of their limbs.

He was now asking her to decide whether they should sit in the shelter or walk to the obelisk. There was time to do one or the other before the bus went, but not to do both.

'Sit down will be best,' she replied. But as soon as they were in the shelter, looking at the undersized and undercoloured sea, she wished she had chosen the obelisk. 'Where is it? What's it for? Who's it to?' she asked.

'I don't know to whom it was erected—to some local worthy, one presumes. As regards its situation, it stands above the town in the direction of the landslip.'

'Would *you* like to go to it?'

'I can't honestly say that I should. My shoes are somewhat tight.'

'Yes, I suppose we're best where we are and then some tea. Do you know how far off it is?'

'I can't say that I do.'

'It may be quite near. Perhaps you could ask these people.' She lowered her voice, not to be overheard by the people in question: two sailors who were seated on the other side of the glass screen.

'I don't think I could well do that,' said Ernest timidly; a martinet at home and at school, he was terrified of anything unfamiliar.

'Why not?'

'They won't know.'

'They might.'

'There is no naval station here, Hilda, they are merely visitors like ourselves, no ships are ever stationed at a small watering-place.' He breathed on his pince-nez, and placed it between himself and the sea.

'Shall I ask them?'

'Certainly, if you wish to do so.'

Hilda opened her mouth to speak to the sailors, but no sound came out of it. 'You ask, it seems better,' she whispered.

'I don't wish to ask, I shall not ask, I have told you my reasons already, and if you are incapable of following them I really can do no more.'

'Oh, all right, dear, don't get in such a fuss, it doesn't matter, I'm sure I don't want to go to your obelisk.'

'Why, in that case, do you want to inquire how to get there? And why "my" obelisk? I was not aware that I possessed one.'

She felt cross—Ernest did tie one up so—and determined to

speak to the sailors to prove her independence. She had noticed them as she sat down, one of them particularly. 'Please excuse me,' she began. They were laughing at something, and did not hear her. 'Please could you kindly tell us—' No reply. She got up and said to her husband, 'Oh, let's go, I hate this place.'

'Certainly, certainly,' said he, and they moved off down the esplanade in an offended silence. Hilda, who had been in the wrong, soon felt ashamed of herself. What on earth had made her behave like that, she wondered; it had been almost a quarrel, and all about nothing. She determined never to mention the beastly obelisk again.

This was not to be, for it appeared on a noticeboard, 'To the Obelisk and Landslip', and an arrow pointed to a gap in the crumbly cliffs. She would have marched by, but Ernest stopped. 'I think I should—I think I *should* like to go if you don't object,' he said, in a voice that was intended to be conciliatory. 'I could talk to the class about it on Monday. I am very short of material.'

Turning back, she looked at the shelter where they had sat. She could see the long dark legs of the sailors sticking out of it; the esplanade was almost deserted otherwise. 'No, of course I shouldn't mind,' she said.

'Excellent, excellent, admirable.' He led the way. The sea, such as it was, disappeared, and they began climbing a muddly sort of gorge—not romantic, though she tried to pretend it was so. Rocks of no great size overhung them, a stream dripped through mud. The weather was stuffy and an aeroplane could be heard being sick in the distance. Hilda took a stern line with herself; whatever they did this afternoon, she wanted to be doing something else. How nice Ernest was really! How genuine! How sincere! If only his forehead wasn't quite so bulgy, and had a little more hair hanging over it, if his shoes weren't quite so small and yellow, if he had eyes like a hawk and an aquiline nose and a sinewy sunburnt throat . . . no, no, that was asking too much, she must keep within bounds, she must not hope for a sinewy throat, or for reckless arms to clasp her beyond redemption . . . That came of going to those cinemas . . .

'It's ever so lovely here, don't you think,' she exclaimed, as they rounded a corner and saw a quantity of unripe blackberries.

'I should scarcely describe it in those terms.'

'I'm ever so glad we didn't stick in that awful shelter.'

'What makes you keep on saying "ever so"?'

'Oh, I'm sorry. Did I? Ever so what oughtn't I to have said?'

'No, no, you are getting it wrong. "Ever so what" is not the question, but "ever so" itself. The phrase is never needed. I can't think why it has become so popular. It is spreading into circles where one would not expect to hear it. Curious. You try to form a sentence in which "ever so" is not redundant.'

She tried, but her thoughts went off to that disastrous night when he had pulled her up in much the same way, and had made her feel worthless, and had humiliated her, and had afterwards tried to caress her, and she couldn't stand it. That had been his fault, but it was her fault if she minded now, she wanted to be really educated, and here he was helping her. Penitent, she looked at his pink and pear-shaped face, slightly beaded with sweat and topped by too small a hat, and determined to improve her grammar and to really love him.

There was a scrambling noise behind, and the two sailors came rushing up the path like monkeys.

'What do these fellows want here? I don't like this,' cried Ernest.

Stopping dead short, they smiled, showing dazzling teeth. One of them—not the one she had noticed—said, 'We right for the Oboblisk, chum?'

Ernest was nervous. The place was deserted, the path narrow, and he wouldn't anywhere have been easy with people whose bodies were so different from his own. He replied with more than his usual primness: 'Obelisk. The notice on the esplanade says "To the Obelisk and Landslip". I fear I can tell you no more.'

'Call it the Ob and be done, eh!'

'Thank you, sir, thank you, and thank you, madam,' said the other sailor. He was a much better type—an educated voice and a gallant bearing, and when Hilda stood aside to let them stride past he saluted her. 'Excuse us, sir,' he called back, as if the path and indeed the whole gorge was Ernest's private property. 'Sorry to trouble you, but we thought we'd go a walk, make the most of our brief time on shore, sir, you know.'

'A sensible thing to do,' said Ernest, who was recovering from his alarm, and liked being called sir.

'Just a little change, anyhow. Got a fag on you, Tiny?'

The other sailor fumbled in his jumper. 'Fergot 'em again,' he replied.

'Well, of all the . . .'

'Ferget me own what d'ye call 'em next.'

'Nice person to go out with, isn't he, sir? Promised to bring along a packet, then lets us both down!'

'Have one of mine if it comes to that,' said Ernest.

'No, sir, I won't do that, but it's very good of you all the same.'

'Oh, come along, my man, take one.'

'No, sir; I don't cadge.'

'Oh!' said Ernest, rather taken aback.

'Do have one, my husband has plenty.'

'No, thank you, madam, I'd rather not.' He had pride and a will, and a throb of pleasure went through her, pleasure mixed with despair. She felt him looking at her, and turned away to inspect the blackberries. In a moment he would go on, dart up the path with his companion, and disappear as it were into heaven.

'What about you?' said Ernest to the sailor so strangely called Tiny.

Tiny had no such scruples. He thrust out his huge paw with a grin and a grunt. 'Her' sailor shook his head and looked a little disdainful. 'There's nothing Tiny wouldn't say no to, is there, Tiny?' he remarked.

'Tiny's a sensible fellow,' said Ernest. The sailors, by their civil yet cheerful demeanour, had quite reassured him. He now dominated the situation, and behaved as if he was conducting an open-air class for older boys. 'Come along, Tiny.' He stretched up a match to the expectant lips.

'Thanks ever so,' Tiny responded.

Hilda let out a cackle. It was 'ever so', the forbidden phrase.

The sailors laughed too, as did Ernest. He had become unusually genial. He astonished her by saying, 'Oh, Hilda, I'm so sorry, here I am smoking and I never asked you whether you would smoke too.' It was the first time he had invited her to smoke in public. She declined, thinking he was testing her, but he asked her again and she took one.

'I'm ever so—I'm very sorry.'

'That's quite all right, dear, might I have a match?'

'Her' sailor whipped a box out of his breast. Tiny, equally polite, blew on the tip of his cigarette and held it towards her. She felt flustered, enmeshed in blue arms, dazzled by rose-red and sunburnt flesh, intoxicated by strength, saltiness, the unknown. When she escaped it was to her husband. Her sailor still held out the lighted match which she had used. 'Sir, may I change my mind and have one of your cigarettes after all?' he said coolly.

'Of course, of course, come along all and sundry.'

He took one, used the lighted match on it, then blew the match out and placed it in his breast. The match they had shared—there it lay . . . close to him, hidden in him, safe . . . He looked at her, touched his jumper, smiled a little and looked away, puffing his cigarette. At that moment the sun blazed out and it turned into a nice afternoon.

She looked away too. There was something dangerous about the man, something of the bird of prey. He had marked her down for his fell purpose, she must be careful like any other heroine. If only he wasn't so handsome, so out-of-the-way handsome. 'Who's saying no, Stan, now?' his companion guffawed. So his name was Stan . . . Stanley perhaps. What had led such a man to join the Navy? Perhaps some trouble at home.

'Stan's sensible, don't you tease Stan,' piped Ernest. They proceeded in a safe enough formation towards the Obelisk, the two sailors in front, she behind Tiny's buttocks, from which she had nothing to fear. Gradually the order altered—Ernest's fault. He was elated with his success, and kept on pestering the men with questions about their work. Tiny fell back to deal with them, but was ill-informed. So 'Stan' joined them, and she went on ahead. It was nicer than she expected—everyone good-tempered, including her husband. But she still wished she had not come.

'It's a funny thing, a day on shore,' said the easy silky voice. He had stolen up behind her—no scrambling this time. She turned, and his eyes moved up and down her body.

'How do you mean, funny? I don't understand.'

'You hardly know what to do with yourself. You're let out of prison, as it were, the discipline stops, you find a shipmate who happens to be on leave too, you go off with him, though you have nothing in common, he wants to go to the pictures, so you go, he thinks he'd like a walk, so you go, he asks the way of strangers, with the result that you inflict yourself on them too. It's a funny life, the Navy. You're never alone, you're never independent. I don't like tacking on to people, the way that youngster I'm with does. I've told him of it before, but he turns everything into a joke.'

'Why is he called Tiny?'

'Merely because he's so large. Another joke. You know the kind of thing, and how weary one gets of it. Still, life's not a bed of roses anywhere, I suppose.'

'No, it isn't, it isn't.'

She ought not to have made such a remark, and she was glad when he ignored it and went on: 'And I've got to be called Stan although my name's really Stanhope.'

'Stanhope?'

'It was my mother's family name. We came from Cheshire. However, all that's over, and I'm Stan.' There was a tinge of melancholy in his voice which made it fatally attractive. For all his gaiety, he had suffered, suffered . . . When she threw away her cigarette he did the same and he gently touched his breast.

This frightened Hilda. She didn't want any nonsense, and she suggested that they should wait for her husband. He obeyed, and turned his profile to her as they waited. He looked even finer that way than full-face; the brow was so noble, the nose and the chin so firm, the lips so tender, the head poised so beautifully upon the sinewy neck, the colouring lovelier than imagination can depict. Here, however, was Ernest, coming round the corner like a cheerful ant. He held Tiny's cap in his hand, and was questioning him on the subject of his naval costume.

'Are we going on any further?' she called.

'I think so. Why not?'

'It seems turning out rather a climb.'

'We have plenty of time, abundance of time, before the bus goes.'

'Yes, but we must be keeping these gentlemen back, you and I walk so slowly.'

'I was not aware of walking slowly. You in a hurry, Stan?' he called familiarly.

'Not the least, not in the very least, sir, thank you.'

'You, Tiny?'

'Hurry for what?'

'Do you want to go on and leave us?'

Grateful to Hilda for calling him a gentleman, he beamed up at her and said, 'What's 'is name, please?'—pointing to Ernest as if he were some rare animal and could not answer questions.

'My husband—his name's Ernest.'

'Think his trilby'd fit me?' His hand shot out to pull it off, but he was checked by a quiet word of reproof from Stanhope. Ernest scuttled back a step. 'Chum, I won't hurt you, chum, chuck chuck, chum, chum,' as if feeding chicken.

'Certain people always go too far, they spoil things, it's a pity,' Stanhope remarked to her as they continued their walk.

How right he was—though for the moment Tiny had entertained her, also she got a wicked pleasure when Ernest's cowardice got exposed. She smiled, and felt clever herself, not realizing that Stanhope now walked behind her, which was exactly what she had not meant to happen. 'My husband and him seem getting on quite nicely,' she said.

'Tiny's always ready to play the fool, day in, day out. I'm afraid I don't understand it. Something wrong with me, I suppose.'

'One gets rather tired of anything that's always the same, I think.'

He offered no opinion, and they walked on for five minutes without saying anything. The path was well marked and not steep, and many pretty flowers, both yellow and pink, grew between the stones. Glimpses of the sea appeared, dancing blue, the aeroplane turned into a gull. The interval separating the two sailors gradually increased. 'What made you join the Navy?' she said suddenly.

He told her—it was fascinating. He was of good family— she had guessed as much!—but wanted to see the world. He had left a soft job in an office when he was eighteen. He told her the name of the office. She happened to have heard of it in her typist days, and was instantly possessed by a feeling of security. Of course she was safe with him—ridiculous. He reeled off the names of ports, known and unknown. He was not very young when you were close to him, but Hilda did not like very young men, they were not distinguished, and her dream was distinction. These well-marked features, this hair, raven-black against the snowy line of the cap, yet flecked at the temples with grey, suited her best, oh and those eyes, cruel eyes, kind eyes, kind, cruel, oh! they burnt into your shoulders, if you turned and faced them it was worse. And she so dumpy! She tried to steady herself by her modesty, which was considerable, and well-grounded. And a batch of people came downhill and passed them—it was only an extension of the esplanade. 'No, Hilda, no one like this is going to bother to seduce you,' she told herself.

'I suppose I can't persuade you,' he said. He took out of his jumper a cigarette-case, and opened it.

'But I thought you hadn't got any cigarettes,' she cried.

He snapped the case up, put it back, and said, 'Caught!'

'What do you mean? Why ever did you ask for one when you had all those?'

'I decline to answer that question,' he smiled.

'I want to know. You must answer. Tell me! Oh, go on! Do tell me.'

'No, I won't.'

'Oh, you're horrid.'

'Am I? Why?' The ravine had got wilder, almost beautiful. The path climbed above thick bushes and little trees. She knew they ought to wait again for Ernest, but her limbs drove her on. She repeated: 'You must tell me. I insist.' He drove her more rapidly before him. Then he said, 'Very well, but promise not to be angry.'

'I'm angry with you already.'

'Then I may as well tell. I pretended I'd no cigarettes on the chance of your husband offering me one.'

'But why? You said no when he did.'

'It wasn't a cigarette that I wanted. And now I suppose you're angry. I didn't want to go on, and it was my only chance of stopping. So I asked Tiny for one. I knew he'd be out of them, he always is. I wanted to—' He took the extinguished match from his pocket. 'Better throw this away now, hadn't I? Or you'll be angry again.'

'I'm not angry, but don't start being silly, please.'

'There are worse things than silliness.'

Hilda didn't speak. Her knees were trembling, her heart thumping, but she hurried on. Whether he threw the match away or not she did not know. After a pause he said in quite a different voice: 'I've done quite enough talking, you know. Now you talk.'

'I've nothing to say,' she said, her voice breaking. 'Nothing ever happens to me, nothing will, I . . . I do feel so odd.' He seemed to tug her this way and that. If only he wasn't so lovely! His hand touched her. Almost without her knowing, he guided her off the path, and got her down among the bushes.

Once there, she was lost. Under pretext of comforting he came closer. He persuaded her to sit down. She put her hand to his jersey to thrust him off, and it slid up to his throat. He was so gentle as well as so strong, that was the trouble, she did not know which way to resist him, and those eyes, appealing, devouring, appealing. He constrained her to lie down. A little slope of grass, scarcely bigger than a couch, was the scene of her inadequate resistance; beyond the dark blue of his shoulders she could see the blue of the sea, all around were thick thorny bushes covered with flowers, and she let him do what he wanted.

'Keep still,' he whispered. 'They're passing.'

From the path came the sound of feet.

'Don't talk just yet.' He continued to hold her, his chin raised, listening. 'They've gone now, but talk quietly. It's all right. He won't know. I'll fix up a story. Don't you worry. Don't you cry.'

'It's your fault, you made me . . .'

He laughed gently, not denying it. He raised her up, his arms slanting across her back unexpectedly kind. He let her say whatever she wanted to, as long as she did not say it too loud, and now and then he stroked her hair. She accused him, she exalted Ernest, repeating, 'I'm not what you think I am at all.' All he said was 'That's all right,' or 'You shan't come into any trouble, I swear it, I swear it, and you mustn't cry,' or 'I play tricks—yes. But I never let a woman down. Look at me. Do as I tell you! Look at me, Hilda.'

She obeyed. Her head fell on his shoulder, and she gave him a kiss. For the first time in her life she felt worthy. Her humiliation slipped from her, never to return. She had pleased him.

'Stanhope . . .'

'Yes, I know.'

'What do you know?'

'I'm waiting until it's absolutely safe. Yes.'

He held her against him for a time, then laid her again on the grass. She was consciously deceiving her husband, and it was heaven. She took the lead, ordered the mysterious stranger, the film-star, the sheikh, what to do, she was, for one moment, a queen, and he her slave. They came out of the depths together, confederates. He helped her up, then respectfully turned away. She hated grossness, and nothing he did jarred.

When they were back on the path, he laid his plans. 'Hilda, it's no use going on to the Obelisk,' he said, 'it's too late, they're in front of us and we shall meet them coming down. He'll want to know how they passed us without seeing us, and if you've an explanation of that I've not. No. We shall have to go back and wait for them on the esplanade.'

She patted her hair—she had good hair.

'Make up some story when they arrive. Muddle them. We shall never muddle them if we meet them face to face on this path. You leave it to me—I'll confuse them in no time.'

'But how?' she said dubiously, as they started the long descent.

'I shall see when I see them. That's how I always work.'

'Don't you think it would be better if you hid here, and I went down alone? Our bus leaves before very long, then you'll be safe.'

He shook his head, and showed his teeth, scorning her gaily. 'No, no, I'm better at telling stories than you, I don't trust you. Take your orders from me, don't ask questions, and it'll be all right. I swear it will. We shall pull through.'

Yes, he was wonderful. She would have this gallantry to look back upon, especially at night. She could think of Ernest quite kindly, she'd be able to put up with him when he made his little wrong remarks or did his other little wrong things. She'd her dream, and what people said was false and what the Pictures said was true: it was worth it, worth being clasped once in the right arms, though you never had them round you again. She had got what she longed for, and it was what she longed for, not a smack in the face, not a sell . . . She had always yearned for a lover who would be nice *afterwards*—not turn away like a satisfied brute, as handsome men are supposed to do. Stanhope was—what do you call it . . . a gentleman, a knight in armour, a real sport . . . O for words. Her eyes filled with happy tears of happiness.

Swinging ahead of her on to the esplanade, he gave her his final instructions. 'Take your line from me, remember we've done nothing we shouldn't, remember it's going to be much easier than you think, and don't lose your head. Simpler to say than to do, all the same don't do it, and if you can't think of anything else to do look surprised. Our first job is to sit down quietly on the esplanade and wait.'

But they were not to wait. As they came out of the gap in the cliffs, they saw Ernest on a bench, and Tiny leaning on the esplanade railings observing the sea. Ernest jumped up all a bunch of nerves, crying, 'Hilda, Hilda, where have you been? Why weren't you at the Obelisk? We looked and looked for you there, we hunted all the way back—'

Before she could answer, indeed before he had finished, Stanhope launched a violent counter-attack. 'What happened to you, sir? We got up to the Obelisk and waited, then we've been shouting and calling all the way back. The lady's been so worried—she thought an accident had happened. Are you all right, sir?' He bayed on, full-chested, magnificent, plausible, asking questions and allowing no time for their reply.

'Hilda, impossible, you couldn't have been, or I should have seen you.'

'There we were, sir, we had a good look at the view and waited for you, and then came down. It was not meeting you on the way back that puzzled us so.'

'Hilda, were you really . . .'

By now she had had her cue, and she heard her voice a long way off saying in fairly convincing tones, 'Oh yes, we got up to the Obelisk.'

And he believed, or three-quarters believed her. How shocking, but what a respite! It was the first lie she had ever told him, and it was unlikely she would ever tell him a worse. She felt very odd—not ashamed, but so queer, and Stanhope went on with his bluffing. The wind raised his dark forelock and his collar. He looked the very flower of the British Navy as he lied and lied. 'I can't understand it,' he repeated. 'It's a relief to know nothing's wrong, but not to run into you as we came down . . . I don't understand it, I'm what you may call stumped, well, I'm damned.'

'I'm puzzled equally, but there is nothing to be gained by a prolonged discussion. Hilda, shall we go to our bus?'

'I don't want you to go until you feel satisfied,' said she. A false step; she realized as much as soon as she had spoken.

'Not satisfied? I am perfectly satisfied. With what have I to be dissatisfied? I only fail to grasp how I failed to find you when I reached the monument.'

Hilda dared not go away with him with things as they were. She didn't know how to work out the details of the lie, it was in too much of a lump. Alarmed, she took refuge in crossness. 'You've got to grasp it some time or other, you may as well now,' she snapped. Her lover looked at her anxiously.

'Well, be that as that may be, we must go.'

'What's your explanation, Tiny?' called Stanhope, in his splendid authoritative way, to create a diversion.

Tiny cocked up one heel and replied not.

'He can scarcely solve a problem which baffles the three of us, and it is so strange that you were ahead of us on the path going up, yet a good ten minutes behind us coming down,' enunciated Ernest.

'Come along, Tiny, you've a tongue in your head, haven't you, mate? I'm asking you a question. Don't stand there like a stuck pig.'

'Ber-yutiful view,' said Tiny, turning round and extending his huge blue arms right and left along the railings of the esplanade. 'You was showing the lady the Ob, perhaps.'

'Of course we inspected the monument. You know that. You haven't answered my question.'

''Ope you showed it 'er properly while you was about it, Stan. Don't do to keep a thing like that all to yourself, you know. Ern, why they call that an ob?'

'Obelisk, obelisk,' winced Ernest, and was evidently more anxious to go.

'You said it, obblepiss.'

'I said nothing of the sort.'

'You said it, obblepiss.' The giant was grinning amiably, and seemed totally unaware that anything had gone wrong. But how different sailors are! How unattractive, in Tiny's case, was the sun-reddened throat and the line of broad shoulders against the sea! He was terribly common, really, and ought not to be answering people back. 'Anyone ever seed a bigger one?' he inquired. No one replied, and how should they to so foolish a question? 'Stands up, don't it?' he continued. No one spoke. 'No wonder they call that a needle, for wouldn't that just prick.'

'Stop that infernal talk at once,' exploded Stanhope, and he seemed needlessly vexed, but, oh, how handsome he looked, and how his dark eyes flashed; she was glad to see him angry and to have this extra memory.

'Stan, Stan, what's the matter, Stan?'

'If you speak again I'll brain you.'

'Ever seed a bigger one—a bigger obolokist, I mean. That's all I said. Because I'ave. Killopatra's Needle's bigger. Well? Well? What you all staring at me for? What you think I was going to say? Eh? Oh, look at little Ern, ain't he just blushing. Oh, look at Stan. Lady, look at 'em.'

Hilda did observe that the two older men were going most extraordinary colours, her lover purplish, her husband rose-pink. And she did not like the tone of the conversation herself, she scarcely knew why, and feared something awkward might come out if it went on much longer. 'We must go, or we shall miss that bus,' she announced. 'We shall never clear up why we never met, and it isn't of the least importance. Ernest, do come along, dear.'

Ernest muttered that he was willing, and the episode ended. Goodbyes were said, by Tiny tempestuously. Plunging across the esplanade, he seized the unfortunate schoolmaster's arm, and whirled it around like a windmill. 'Goo bye, Ern, take care of yerself, pleased to have met yer, termater face and all,' he bawled.

'Pleased to have met you both,' said Ernest with restraint.

'Ju-jitsu . . . now as yer neck snaps . . .'

Hilda and Stanhope profited by this noisy nonsense to say their farewells. They would not have dared otherwise. The touch of his hand was cool and dry, but he was nearly worn out, and it trembled. It had not been easy for him, returning her unreproached and unsuspected to her husband, fighting for her, using strategem after strategem, following hopeless hints . . . The perfect knight! The gangster lover who really cares, who knows . . . 'My darling . . . thank you for everything for ever,' she breathed. He dared not reply, but his lips moved, and he slipped his left hand into his breast. She knew what he meant: the match was there, the symbol of their love. He would never forget her. She had lived. She was saved.

What a contrast to the other—so boisterous, so common, so thoroughly unattractive! It was strange to think of them in the same uniform, strange to look down the esplanade and see them getting more and more like one another as the distance increased. The actual parting had gone off easily. Ernest had produced his cigarettes again. 'Have one more, both of you, before you repair to your boat,' he called. The powerfully made sailors stooped, the lean distinguished fingers and the battered clumsy ones helped themselves again to his bounty.

Perky, he had lit up himself, and now he was strutting away with his good little wife on his arm.

Of course the first few minutes alone with him were awful. Still, she drew strength from the fact that she had deceived him so completely. And somehow she did not despise him, she did not despise him at all. He seemed nicer than usual, and she was pleased when he started to discuss the relative advantages of gas and electricity. He said one thing, she another, while the cloud of her past swept gloriously out to sea. Home and its details had a new freshness. Even when the night came, she should feel differently and not mind.

They reached the bus-stop with several minutes to spare. There was a picture-postcard kiosk, and she had a good idea: she would buy a postcard of the Obelisk, so that if the topic came up again she would know what it looked like.

There was an excellent selection, and she soon visualized it from several points of view. Though not as tall as Cleopatra's Needle, it boasted a respectable height. One of the cards showed the inscription 'Erected in 1879 to the memory of Alfred Judge, one-time Mayor'. She memorized this, for Ernest often mentioned inscriptions, but she actually bought a card which brought in some of its surroundings. The monument was nobly placed. It stood on a tongue of rock overlooking the landslip.

'Well, you won't have seen that today! Will you?' said the woman in the kiosk as she took payment.

Hilda thought she would fall to the ground. 'Oh gracious, whatever do you mean?' she gasped.

'It's not there to be seen.'

'But that's the Obelisk. It says so.'

'It says so, but it's not there. It fell down last week. During all that rain. It's fallen right over into the landslip upside-down, the tip of it's gone in ever so far, rather laughable, though I suppose it'll be a loss to the town.'

'Ah, there it is,' said her husband, coming up and taking the postcard out of her hand. 'Yes, it gives quite a good idea of it, doesn't it? I'll have one displaying the inscription.'

Then the bus swept up and took them away. Hilda sank into a seat nearly fainting. Depth beneath depth seemed to open.

For if she couldn't have seen the Obelisk he couldn't have seen it either, if she had dawdled on the way up he must have dawdled too, if she was lying he must be lying, if she and a sailor —she stopped her thoughts, for they were becoming meaningless. She peeped at her husband, who was on the other side of the coach, studying the postcard. He looked handsomer than usual, and happier, and his lips were parted in a natural smile.

STANLEY KAUFFMANN

FULVOUS YELLOW

Mr. and Mrs. Sprague were a very nice middle-aged couple. They lived in Albany, New York, and they had managed to remain mentally alive. They read a lot of books, some of them not chosen by book clubs, owned a few nice paintings, and had quite a good collection of phonograph records, including "Scheherazade."

They were proudest, however, of their son Everett. He was an unusual and talented boy. In six months down in New York City he had done well. He was already top assistant to one of the most important dress designers in the business.

"Fashion stylists," Mrs. Sprague had corrected her husband once. "Ev says they don't call them dress designers any more."

"Fashion stylists," Mr. Sprague agreed quickly.

They were on their way down to New York now to visit Ev. They hadn't seen him in almost four months. When he had first got his New York job, he had come home every week end. Then his visits had slacked off to every two weeks. Then four months had gone by without his visiting them. But Mr. and Mrs. Sprague were not foolish or demanding parents. They understood that their son was in a new life, making new friends, finding new interests, and as long as his letters once a week told them that he was well and happy, they were reasonably content.

Now Mr. Sprague had managed to get Friday off from the office and they were going down for a long week end. They hadn't told Ev in advance; they wanted it to be a surprise. They sent a wire just before they got on the train.

"Make sure you send it to the new address," said Mrs. Sprague. "Remember, he moved last month."

"I know that as well as you do," Mr. Sprague replied testily. Ev was as much his son as hers.

They had lunch in the dining car. The steward put them at a table for four and then seated a big bald man next to Mr. Sprague. They fell into talk and the big bald man told them that he was on his way to his son's wedding in Brooklyn Heights. The Spragues agreed that that was fine and envied the bald man. Then they told him about Ev's progress in six short months.

"What's your son's work?" asked the bald man, impressed.

"He's a dress de—he's in fashion styling," Mr. Sprague said. "Always had an eye for color, and things like that."

"Always," agreed his mother. "Ever since he was a very little boy."

"Oh," said the man, with the hint of a wrinkle between his brows. "That's fine. Fine."

Mr. Sprague noticed the wrinkle. "You know," he said with a laugh, "lots of people have the wrong idea about the fashion field. It takes ability and business sense just like any other business."

"Oh, sure, I know," nodded the bald man quickly. "I saw an article about it in *Life*."

Ev wasn't at the station to meet them, but Mr. Sprague said that probably the wire hadn't given him time enough to get away. On an off chance, he called the apartment before he tried the office and was surprised to hear Ev answer.

Ev was glad to hear his father's voice. Yes, he'd received the wire but he hadn't been able to meet the train. He had some things he had to finish up for Ty. Ty was his roommate.

Also his boss. Why didn't they take a cab and come right over before they went to their hotel?

It was a remodeled private house in the East Fifties, not far from the river. The card for Apt. 3 said "Emmet" with "Sprague" written in below it. Mr. Sprague gave the bell two pokes.

Ev stood at the top of the stairs in a striped basque shirt and a pair of slacks. "Hello, Mother," he said. "Gosh, it's good to see you. What a wonderful surprise. Hello, Father."

He used to call Mr. Sprague "Dad." Mr. Sprague thought he looked a little pale. Working too hard, probably.

The apartment was eye-filling. The furniture was low and modern, pearl gray and coral red. There were good reproductions of Picasso and Matisse and Utrillo in wide natural-wood frames. And there were small white-enameled wrought-iron gates between the living room and the tiny kitchen.

Ev gave his parents each a glass of sherry and apologized for not having been up to Albany for so long. "But gosh, I've been busy," he said. He indicated the drawing board at the side of the room; there was a large colored sketch of a woman in a coat tacked on it. "We're doing some rush work on a new line of casual clothes and Ty's given me some of the tougher things. But I don't mind. It's pretty exciting."

"Do you always work at home, Ev?" his mother asked.

"When I've got something really tough, yes. Because that office is a madhouse." He laughed. It was Mr. Sprague's boy's laugh, all right. "That's one advantage of living with your boss."

"It's certainly a nice place to work," said Mr. Sprague. He cleared his throat. "Ev—er, you mind if I ask? This is all pretty expensive, isn't it? And—"

"Oh, I pay my share," Ev replied. "Of the rent, anyway. Ty had the place for years before I moved in, of course, so I got the use of the furnishings for nothing. But when he saw that hole I was boarding in on Forty-fifth Street, he insisted on my coming in with him."

"He sounds like a very nice man," said his mother.

"Ty?" laughed Ev. "You'll love him. He ought to be along

pretty soon. I phoned him when I got your wire and he said he'd come home early."

"By the way, Ev," said Mr. Sprague, "I've got regards for you. Or a bawling out, depending on how you look at it. Joanie Carson wants to be remembered, and she says she's not going to write to you again until you answer her last letter."

Ev laughed shortly. "Joanie Carson. That child."

"She still talks about you, Ev," said his mother.

"Does she?" said Ev.

Ty came in soon. He was a big man with a large, roundish face. He wore a beautiful gabardine suit and brown suède shoes. He had two boxes under his arm, and he gave one—a corsage box—to Mrs. Sprague.

"I'm so happy to meet Ev's parents" he said with a pleasant smile. "I hope you won't mind—I've brought you these, and I've taken the liberty of arranging things for this evening." He took a ticket envelope from his pocket. "There's a new musical—a smash—but a friend of mine did the costumes and he got tickets for me. 'Ice to the Eskimos.' Have you heard of it?"

"Oh, yes," said Mr. Sprague, who kept up on things. "I read the review of it. We'd love to see it. That's very nice of you, Mr. Emmet."

Mrs. Sprague opened her box. "Orchids!" she exclaimed. "How lovely! Oh, Mr. Emmet, you shouldn't have—really."

Ty bowed, almost from the waist. "Pleasure, I assure you. It's only once that I'll meet Ev's parents for the first time. Talented Ev." He put his hand briefly on Ev's shoulder. "Which reminds me—this other box." He opened it as he spoke. "I was passing Quentin's at lunch time today—" He explained to the Spragues. "Quentin's a friend of mine who keeps a shop. Men's accessories. Really unusual things." From the box he took a silk muffler, a beautiful tawny yellow. "There, Ev. What do you think of it?"

"It's stunning," said Ev. "But—"

Ty proceeded to wind it around Ev's neck and to knot it. "It'll go nicely with your chocolate-brown jacket."

Ev shook his head. "Ty, as Mother says, you shouldn't have —really."

"Nonsense." Ty hushed him grandly. "Anniversary present. You know," he said to the Spragues, "it's a wonderful coincidence, your coming down today. It's just a month today that Ev's been living here."

"Yes," said Mr. Sprague, "that's right, I guess it is. I remember Ev's letter telling us about it came right on my birthday."

"But just the same, Ty," said Ev, stroking the silken scarf around his neck, "you're much too extravagant and generous."

Ty shrugged. "When I saw it in the window, I thought of you at once. It seemed your color somehow. A kind of—" he hesitated for a word, "—fulvous yellow."

"What kind?" asked Mr. Sprague.

"Fulvous," said Ty. "Tawny. Smoky yellow."

"Oh," said Mr. Sprague. He nodded thoughtfully. Then he sighed and got up. "Well, I suppose we ought to go on to our hotel."

They agreed to meet in the hotel lobby to go out to dinner, and Ev put them in a cab. On the way to the hotel, which was not far, Mrs. Sprague held the flower box carefully and Mr. Sprague sat with his hands in his lap, one on each leg, palms down.

After a while, Mrs. Sprague said, "It's a lovely apartment, don't you think?"

"Very pretty," he replied.

She looked at him. "Mr. Emmet's a nice man, don't you think?"

The taxi stopped for a light. Then the light changed and they went on.

"Very nice," said Mr. Sprague.

That night Ty took the Spragues to a French restaurant where the headwaiter knew him quite well and where the specialty was little soufflé potatoes. At dinner Ty told them what a fine future he thought Ev had in designing. He said he felt no hesitancy in telling them, even at this early date, that he was training Ev for the time when they might operate a studio together.

249

"I think there are really great things ahead for Ev," said Ty.

Ev flushed happily and turned to his mother. "Gosh, Mother, wasn't I lucky to meet him? Some people have to struggle for years before they get a real break."

"Not the ones like you, Ev," said Ty, patting his arm. "Not the ones with real talent."

"Well, Ev," said his mother gently, "we've been bragging all over Albany about your wonderful progress."

"Yes," said his father, "we have been."

In the cab on the way to the theater Ty explained that their seats wouldn't be together; he'd had to take what he could get. But he and Ev would be sitting almost directly behind the Spragues. Mr. Sprague wanted to take the second row, but Ty insisted that his guests have the better seats.

The show was loud and fast. The audience expected it to be funny, and where the show fell short of the mark, the audience's expectation filled up the gap and they laughed anyway. There was a scene in the first act in which a girl in a tight sweater threw herself on a bashful sailor's lap and made love to him. While the audience was howling, Mr. Sprague, vaguely disinterested, glanced around at the row behind. Ev was chuckling and Ty, his arm linked with Ev's, was smiling; the smile made his face seem larger.

Later, Ty wanted to take them to a supper club for drinks, but Mr. and Mrs. Sprague asked to be excused after their long day. Ty promised to pick them up in his car next morning at ten-thirty; they would drive out to his beach club on Long Island for lunch.

The Spragues were in the lobby next morning promptly at ten-thirty. They had not wanted much breakfast, but the coffee was very good and Mr. Sprague had had a barbershop shave, complete with hot towel, which had refreshed him.

Ty came smiling through the revolving doors and behind him came Ev in his chocolate-brown jacket with the new muffler knotted about his neck. Mr. Sprague thought that Ty was right, the muffler went very well with the jacket.

"Good morning," beamed Ty. "A wonderful day. I'll get you some suits out at the club so you can take a dip."

"Goodness," laughed Mrs. Sprague, "do you think they'd have any to fit me?"

"Why, they must have," said Mr. Sprague. "Lots of fellows' mothers must come to visit them, don't they, Ev?"

"Sure, I suppose so," Ev nodded.

"It's a long time since Ev and I went swimming together," said Mr. Sprague. "Can you still do that shallow dive I taught you, Ev?"

Ty's car was a roadster and Mr. and Mrs. Sprague sat together in the little back seat. Mr. Sprague was busy most of the time keeping his hat on his head, but Ty wore a beret when he drove and Ev's hair never seemed the worse for wind. Mr. Sprague sat right behind his son and could see Ev's hair.

They got suits quickly enough at the club and Mrs. Sprague dabbled in the shallow end of the pool while the men swam. Mr. Sprague was very good for his age but he soon climbed up on the edge of the pool, puffing, and dangled his legs in the water. Ty swam over soon after and hoisted himself up next to Mr. Sprague.

"Those are nice trunks," said Mr. Sprague. Ty had Hawaiian trunks, yellow with a blue flower design.

"These?" smiled Ty. "They're Ev's idea. He picked them out for me. Said he liked them but didn't quite dare to wear them himself." Ev's trunks were a solid light blue. "Ev," he called, "let's see you dive."

Ev, swimming in toward the board, laughed and said, "Right. The professor will be happy to oblige."

"Where he did learn to dive, Mr. Sprague?" asked Ty.

"Oh, I taught him some," said Mr. Sprague, "and he was on the team at school."

Ev climbed to the board and walked to the end. He raised his arms and arched himself.

"Watch this, now," said Ty, watching.

Ev leaped into the air, then spread his arms wide in the sun and came sailing down. Just before he hit the water, he brought his hands together over his head.

Ty applauded. "Ah, perfect," he said. "That was perfect."

"Pretty good," said Mr. Sprague. "Knees might have been a little straighter."

251

They had lunch on the terrace overlooking the pool. Ty was dissatisfied with the salad dressing and asked the waiter to bring him oil and seasoning so that he could mix a dressing himself. "It seems a shame to invite you all the way out here and then just give you run-of-the-mill fare," he said to the Spragues.

"Wait till you taste this, Mother," said Ev. "You've never tasted anything like this salad dressing."

Mr. Sprague thought it was very good indeed, but he wasn't especially hungry. When he had finished lunch, he lit a pipe and said, "I thought maybe tonight we'd all have dinner and go up to the Stadium concert to hear Lily Pons. The ticket man in the hotel said he might get me tickets."

"Oh, I always love Lily Pons," said Mrs. Sprague. "So do you, Ev."

Ev glanced at Ty, then said, "Yes, Mother, I do. But I'm afraid I can't go tonight. I should have told you yesterday. I'm terribly sorry, but gosh, I didn't know that you were coming this week end."

"Oh," said Mrs. Sprague.

"It's my fault, Mrs. Sprague," Ty said. "You see, we were invited to this dinner party about a week ago and I accepted for us. Business friends, and some people from out of town. It's really rather important, but I suppose I could make excuses for you, Ev, if you wanted to go with your parents."

"Well—" said Ev.

"No, no," said Mr. Sprague, "I wouldn't want to interfere. I know how these things are, I'm a businessman myself. It's our fault for not letting you know far enough ahead. No, you go out to your party, Ev. Your mother and I will make out."

When they started back, Ty invited Mrs. Sprague to sit in front with him. Ev sat in back next to his father and they talked for a while of things in New York, then they talked a little about things in Albany. Then they just sat and enjoyed the ride.

Ty dropped them at their hotel and Ev apologized for not being able to see them again that night. They said they understood perfectly. They all agreed to have dinner next day at three so that the Spragues could catch the five-o'clock train, and Mrs. Sprague thanked Ty for the pleasant day. Then Ev got into the front seat next to Ty and they drove off.

Mr. Sprague watched them go. Mrs. Sprague said, "Well, do you want to see the man about Lily Pons?"

"Oh," said Mr. Sprague, "sure."

They went to the agency counter, but the man said he had only one seat left for that night and it wasn't a very good one. "I guess it's just as well that Ev went to his party," said Mrs. Sprague.

"Yes," replied Mr. Sprague thoughtfully. He said, "Anyway, that Stadium's awfully far uptown."

They rested for a while in their room, then went to an Italian restaurant which Ev had recommended. They couldn't understand most of the things on the menu and finally ordered meat balls and spaghetti.

"What would you like to do tonight?" asked Mrs. Sprague.

"Oh, I don't know," he answered. "I don't much care. What would you like to do?"

"Would you like to go to the Music Hall?" she asked. "You always like to go to the Music Hall."

"Well, it's probably pretty crowded," he said. "What's playing there?"

"That life-of-a-composer picture," she said. "They say it's very good."

Mr. Sprague moved his spoon over close to his knife and lined it up exactly parallel. Then he pushed the knife ahead gently until the bottom was precisely level with the spoon. "Well," he said, "I don't know. I suppose we can see it up home."

"Sure," said Mrs. Sprague. "Sure we can."

They bought some papers and magazines after dinner and went back to their room. Later, when he undressed for bed, Mr. Sprague took his wallet out of his pocket, as was his custom, to put it in a drawer. He remembered a picture of Ev and himself that he carried in his wallet and found it. It had been snapped on an Adirondacks fishing trip about six years before. The boy was wearing high-top shoes and breeches and a plaid shirt open at the throat. He was grinning and squinting into the sun. In his hands he held the string of bass and pickerel he had caught that day.

When Mrs. Sprague came out of the bathroom, she scolded her husband for reading in the dark; and he went in and brushed his teeth.

They waited in the lobby next day until half-past three before Mr. Sprague called the apartment. Ev answered sleepily. When he recognized his father's voice, he seemed to wake up. "Oh, gosh, Father," he said, "what time is it?"

Mr. Sprague told him.

"Good Lord," said Ev. "I had no idea. We were up terribly late. Gosh, I'm sorry, Father. I'm awfully sorry."

"Well," said Mr. Sprague, "those things happen."

"Are you still going to catch the five-o'clock?" Ev asked.

"I'm afraid we have to, Ev," answered Mr. Sprague.

"Then that spoils our dinner date," Ev said. "That's terrible."

"Oh, well," Mr. Sprague said, "we had a late breakfast. It doesn't matter."

"Well, at least we'll come over and take you to the train," Ev said. "We'll be right over."

Ty had dark circles under his eyes, but Ev looked all right. He had on a hound's-tooth jacket today, but he was still wearing the muffler.

Ty let go of Ev's arm to gesture apologetically. "A fine thing," he smiled ruefully, "a fine thing. And I wanted to make a good impression on you both. What ever are you going to think of me now?"

"Well," said Mr. Sprague, "as I told Ev, these things happen."

They drove to the station, and Ty and Ev put them aboard the train. Ty shook hands with both of them, said how happy he'd been to meet them, and hoped they'd forgive them for oversleeping. Then Ev kissed his mother's cheek and shook hands with his father.

"Ev," said Mr. Sprague calmly, "please. I know how busy you are. But try to come up next Friday, won't you? I'd like to have one of our old-fashioned week ends. Real old walk and talk. Try. Won't you, Ev?"

"All right, Father," nodded Ev, "I'll try. I really will. It was awfully nice to see you again."

Harlem, Hastings, Harmon. Change of engines. Mr. and Mrs. Sprague sat in the coach and didn't talk much. The train was really quite comfortably air-conditioned, but Mr. Sprague had buttoned his jacket to the top.

The waiter came through with the last call for dinner. Mrs. Sprague said, "We'd better have something, dear," and they went into the dining car. She ordered a sandwich and tea; he ordered a piece of pie and coffee.

The waiter brought their food. Mr. Sprague had been staring out the window, but he picked up his fork automatically and turned his attention to the pumpkin pie. He stared at it a minute, then he prodded the viscous, flabby filling with his fork. Then he dropped his fork sharply.

His wife looked up anxiously, and after a moment, he spoke.

"Fulvous yellow," he said.

WITOLD GOMBROWICZ

PUTO

Cursed be the distortions of mankind! Cursed be this dung-smeared pig! To hell with this filthy muckhole! And that one, the one WALKING along, with whom I WALKED, that was no bull, but only a poor cow!

The local people endow him with the name "Puto"—a man who as a man wishes not to be a man, but instead runs after men, pursues them giddily, adores—oh, loves them, is enflamed by them, desires them, lusts after them, flirts with them, dances attendance on them, fawns over them. When I first glimpsed these lips which, though masculine, bled with womanish rouge, I had not the shadow of a doubt but that destiny had blessed me with such a Puto. With him I had walked along in public view—walked like a pair forever paired.

And as we walked he told me in breathy tones everything about himself, and I listened. This man, a real *mestizo,* a Portuguese whose mother was a Persian Turk, was born in Libya and was named Gonzalo; he is very rich, gets out of bed in the morning around 11 or 12 and drinks coffee, then goes into the street and walks around, following boys and young men. When he has picked one out, he approaches forthwith and asks about some street or other; and after he has made his advances he begins to chatter about this and that, only to determine whether the young man can be talked into sin for two-and-a-half or even ten pesos. Most of the time, in fear and trembling, he dared not speak of it, they brushed him off, and he went away like a wet poodle. Hence, off again, after another young man, a youth or boy who caught his eye . . . And thus, my dear, once more questions about a street, talks either about games or about dances—coaxing, and all that in order to seduce him for five or ten pesos; but either such a young man gave him a sharp answer or spat at his feet. Then he takes to his heels, but strangely aroused. And so again on the track of a dark-haired lad or a blond, accosting, questioning. When he grows weary he goes home to rest, and then, after having recuperated somewhat on a chaise longue, back to the streets and to the quest, wandering, accosting, questioning—now a mechanic, then a laborer, a dishwasher or soldier or sailor. But most of the time, trembling with fear, scarcely having approached him, he turns away again; or, my dear, he even follows one who suddenly walks into a shop or otherwise disappears from his field of vision, and nothing comes of it. And so yet again he returns home limp and weary, though burning with desire, and after he has eaten a little and rested on the chaise longue, he dashes into the street to eye some handsome man or other, to chat him up. If he makes a catch and the two come to terms over two, five, or ten pesos, he immediately pilots him home and there, having locked the door, takes off jacket, tie, trousers, throws them to the floor, strips to his shirt and dims the light, sprays the air with perfume. And then the young man really lets him have it, empties the closet or snatches his money! Frightened out of his wits, Puto dares not cry out, permits him to take everything and endures the most agonizing blows. From these blows and cuffs he burns and flames even more with desire, and goes once more into the street, fired by passion, burning and flaming, enraptured, even though terrified and exhausted, and again on the track of young men, on the track of mechanics, laborers, soldiers or sailors; but scarcely has he approached one than he retreats, for even when the desire is great, fear is greater still. And it is already late at night and the streets more and more empty:

Puto thus returns home, strips to his shirt and stretches his tired, lonely bones out in bed, in order to arise again in the morning, drink coffee, and run after young men. And on the day after that, when he has gotten out of bed, into the streets once more to run after boys.

And so I think to myself: What does it all mean, where is it getting me, what am I doing? And I would have long since left him, but I was loathe to abandon my only companion. For he was a companion. But as he stood there with me under the trees, it was a little strange, for he was neither fish nor fowl. Although he had fine black hairs on the back of his hand, the hand was somehow a dainty, feminine hand, plump, white . . . and probably the foot as well . . . and albeit the cheek was dark with the stubble of a beard, this same cheek appeared fair and delicate, as if it were not dark but white after all . . . and also, though the foot was masculine, it behaved as if it wished to be a dainty feminine foot and played the coquette with wondrous flutters . . . and while the head of this man in the prime of life was becoming bald and grizzled at the temples, it seemed as though out of this head there emerged another that wished to be a dainty feminine head . . . It was as though he did not like himself, and as though he transformed himself in the nocturnal quiet, and one no longer knew whether this was He or She . . . and being neither the one nor the other, he has the semblance of a creature and not of a man.

He was waiting in ambush, the rogue, he stands there, says not a word, and only stares mutely at his boy. I think, what a devil and werewolf, and why then am I standing here with him when he is bringing me disgrace, and I have him to thank, as well, for my disgrace at the ambassador's reception. To hell with him, the devil take him—and yet I shall not leave him, for he walked with me, and now we walk together.

An older man with salt-and-pepper hair approached the young man; when Puto saw this, he was dreadfully insulted, began to signal to me, and said, "My curse and my misfortune! What an old fossil, what does he want from him, probably they have a rendezvous here, and the old man is going to buy himself a little fun! . . . Go and listen in on what they're saying to each other . . . get going, eavesdrop, I'm dying with jealousy . . . get going, go . . ."

His hot breath almost singed my ear. I stepped out from under the trees, drew near the youngster, who was of medium build, fair-haired, his foot, his hand middle-sized, and such eyes, such teeth, such a shock of hair, that—oh, rogue, oh, you rascal Gonzalo! . . . And what is that I hear! It is my own native tongue!

As if scalded I sprang away from the two and back to Gonzalo: "Do as you please, but I am leaving and want nothing to do with that, for they are my countrymen and probably father and son! I want nothing to do with it, and I'm going home!"

He seized my hand. "Oh," he cried, "God sent you to me, you—my friend, and you will not deny me your assistance! And if these are your countrymen, it will be child's play to make yourself acquainted with them. And then you will introduce me to them, and I will be your friend, a devoted friend forever, and give you 10, 20, 30 thousand or even more! Come, let's follow them, they're already entering the park!"

I would have liked to clobber him. But he draws near, presses himself against me: "Come, let's go, we're going together anyhow—come, come, let's go, let's go!" And still talking he went ahead, and I fell in behind him, stumbled, and we are walking, we are walking, we are walking! We trot into the park. And there: the rattle of miniature trains thundering round a boulder, here and there clowns or pyramids of empty bottles, there again carousels or swings or a trampoline, further on a round-about with wooden horses, target-shooting, an artificial grotto or distorting mirror, and thus, my dear, everything is revolving, flying, rocketing through the din of amusement, and in the midst of it all Japanese lanterns and the dazzling blossomings of Roman candles! And the people wander about in confusion: one stands staring at the swing, another at a clown, and then he drifts from the mirror to the bottle-game and gapes at this or that; but everything is a chaos, torn this way and that—here a monster, there a mesmerist. The pleasure-seeking boils and bubbles so, swings are swinging, carousels revolve, chasing their own tails, and the people walk and walk and walk and walk from swing to carousel, or from carousel to swing. The swings are swinging. And the people are WALKING. And only the mirrors entice the Japanese lanterns, and the bottles cry out with the ballyhooing pitchman's voice, and if it is not the bottles, then the miniature train comes rattling past, or it's the lake in the artificial grotto, or a clown; and through it all a glitter and buzz and the spinning of pleasure-seeking, and a drilling and flying of entertainment. But when the amusements only amuse each other, the people depart, and walk, walk! . . .

The young man and his father (for it was his father) were sitting at a small table and drinking beer; Gonzalo and I sat at a table nearby, and Gonzalo insisted that I introduce myself: "Go to them, drink with them as fellow-countrymen do, and I shall also drink, and then we will drink together, in company!"

The hall is large, with many lights, and the people stare so that I become ill at ease again, and I say, "It doesn't work that way, that would be too forward" . . . and rack my brain for some excuse or other to leave, for to me it is a disgrace to sit at a table with such an individual. He pleads with me. I resist. We are drinking wine, and the music is playing, and dancing couples twirl about the floor. Again Gonzalo insists I should go over to them, and as though intoxicated he stares at his chosen one and, wishing to please him and to catch his eye, he winks broadly, flutters his hands, giggles and frisks about on his chair . . . and then with a nudge in the side he asks the waiter for wine and rolls little balls out of bread and flicks them into the air, accompanying his prank with shrill peals of laughter. I feel more and more ashamed, for people are staring; and so I say that I must excuse myself and go to the toilet, but really with the intention to get out of his sight and do a vanishing act. I go to the toilet, go . . . But someone in the crowd seizes me by the arm, and who is it? . . . Pitzkal! And behind Pitzkal the Baron, and beside him Ciumkala! I am baffled. How did they get here? And I wonder if they're not looking for a fight, for perhaps that's the reason they came after me, and wanted to avenge themselves for that disgrace they had to swallow at the ambassador's reception . . . But no!

"My dear Mr. Witold, my dear sir! And so we meet again! Come, let's have something to drink! Let's have a drink together! Just one! Come, it's my treat!"

"No, it's my treat."

"No, no, it's mine."

Pitzkal at once roared, "What do you mean it's your treat, you clown! Are you the ones who spotted him?! The drinks are on me!"

But the Baron takes my arm, leads me aside, and buzzes fiercely as a bee, "Don't listen to them; my ears are already ringing with their boorishness; the two of us, we'll have a drink together, please, please, old man!"

Then Pitzkal grabs me by the sleeve and drags me away and whispers in my ear, "What does this ridiculous French lapdog mean by boring you to death with his idiotic, cretinous snobbery? Come with me, we'll have a drink together and without all this pretense!"

And I reply, "God be praised, God be praised, there could be no greater honor for me than to have a drink with these gentlemen, my friends, but I am here with a companion."

As I say it, they nudge each other with their elbows, one after the other, and blink their eyes, nod their heads: "Companion, companion! Ah yes, with a companion! To be sure, as it appears, with Gonzalo—you devil, you! You've made friends with Gonzalo, you go around with him, and the whole world sees you! The man is worth millions! You're really not as crazy as people say. Come on, let's have one—let's have one! Let's have a drink! It's my treat!"

"No, no, it's on me!"

Ever more heartily, more chummily, they urge me, and since they dare not poke me with their elbows, they nudge each other in the ribs, showing off to each other, and one says to the next, "Let's go, let's have a drink!" I realize they pretend as though this is all happening only among themselves, but it is all directed toward me . . . And they begin to embrace and kiss each other (for with me they wouldn't have such audacity), and: "Let's go, let's get going, it's my treat, no, no, it's on me!" Pitzkal shakes his portmonnaie, the Baron his, Ciumkala takes out a banknote, each shows the other his money and holds it under his nose. And Pitzkal cries out, "Why do you want to treat me, I shall treat, and perhaps I shall give you another 100 pesos, if I so desire!"

The Baron shouts, "I'll give you 200!"

And Ciumkala: "I've got 300 here, 300 is what I've got, and another 15 in change!"

I see that, although they're so generous with each other, invite each other and show each other their money, they basically want to treat me and show me their money. But they don't dare . . . And already they suspect me of some kind of romance with the filthy-rich Puto, and for that reason they would promise me mountains of gold, and scarcely know how to regale me, how to entice me! After such a grievous offence and this insult, that they apparently take me for Puto's sweetheart, I would have liked to take a swing at them; but I only shouted that they shouldn't turn my head, for I had no time! . . . And so I quickly turned, entered the restroom, and they with me. There was a man spending a penny in a urinal. I to a urinal, they to urinals. But when the man who had already spent his penny had left, the horde pounced on me, and the Baron shouted to Pitzkal, "Here are 500 pesos for you," and Ciumkala to the Baron: "Here are 600 for you," and Pitzkal to Ciumkala: "Here are 700, 700, take it when I give it to you!" They pull their money out, wave it around under each others' noses and under mine, shove it into each others' hands. They must be insane!

I realize that, although they were giving each other money, they would much rather give it to me in order to buy my goodwill, except that it was embarrassing to them and they didn't have the courage. And so I say, "Don't get so heated-up, gentlemen, take it easy, easy." But they were only looking for a way to force the money on me, and finally the Baron clapped his hand on his head: "Oh, I have a hole in my pocket! I'd better give you the money or I might lose it!" And began to stuff the money into my pockets, and the others, seeing this, stuffed theirs in too: "Take mine as well, and mine too, because I've also got a hole in my pocket." I say, "For God's sake, gentlemen, why give it to me?" But at this instant some-one else enters to make water, so they return to the urinals, unbutton their pants, whistle nonchalantly, as if nothing was up, as if they had to spend a penny ... As soon as the one who had entered had made his departure, they sidled up to me again, and having more courage—they were off and running, stuffing the money in my pockets and crying, "Take it, take it!"—I say, "For heaven's sake, gentlemen, why are you giving me this, what should I do with your money?" In that instant someone entered to take a leak, and they returned to the urinals, whistling nonchalantly, but hardly were we alone together than they sprang at me again, and Pitzkal shouted, "Take it, take it, when somone gives, you have to take it, take it, for he has 300 or 400 million!"—"Don't take it from Pitz-kal, take it from me," screamed the Baron, droning and buzz-ing like a wasp, "from me you should take it. God knows, he's got 400 or even 500 million!"

Ciumkala, however, wheezed and groaned, sighing, "I beg your mercy, and maybe it's even 600 million, do take my small change, most venerable gentleman!" Fired-up, flushed, they squeezed against me, waving their money, thrusting and stuff-ing it in my pockets, two at a time and then a third, one reach-ing over the other, then over the third, and so all together, all at once, until I didn't have the heart to resist any longer and gave in, let them stuff the money into my pockets. All of them dashed to the urinals, for someone had entered. With the money I ran to the door, out of the restroom and into the hall; and there the music is playing, the couples revolving. I remain standing there with the money and observe that my Gonzalo is still larking about and showing off.

Now he flutters his hand, then he darts a glance, then he flicks a bread-ball, now tinkles a melody on his glass, then crooks his little finger, and thus at the center of his own little comedy, he is like a turkey among sparrows, and greets his own jokes with peals of soprano laughter! Those sitting close to him actually think he's a little tipsy, but I know what kind of wine has intoxicated him, and to whom his larking is directed. Although, disgusted as I was, I would have liked to go home, run away and be rid of the whole lot, this instant pierced me like a dagger (and there he is, stretching his foot in the air), and he was after all my companion (and here he fluttered his handkerchief in my direction), my devotee (he claps his hands, flings his knees apart), with whom I walked (his fingers dance lightly on the air), and I simply cannot permit that he cut such capers for me before all these people (he is tooting on a paper trumpet). And thus I returned to the table.

As he caught sight of me he began to wave and nod his head playfully. Only when I had drawn near did he cry: "Ha, ha, sit down, sit down, and let's amuse ourselves! High-ho! Sweetheart, lovebird!

> *Hansel is a lovely lad,*
> *But Jan's physique is not so bad!"*

And he flicks a bread-ball at my nose, blows his paper trumpet, and says softly, "Traitor, where have you been, what have you done, my little campaign bores you!" And he immediately clinks his glass of wine against mine, flings shreds of paper in the air and then fills my glass with wine. "Let's drink! Let's drink!

> *Mama says I may not dance,*
> *But I waltz at every chance!*

Hey-ho, let us amuse ourselves, let's have a ball!" He pours more wine for me. It is hard to refuse when he makes his request so forcefully. We drink. But nearby, at another table, the Baron, Pitzkal, Ciumkala have taken their seats and are calling for wine. The devil take them! One could tell by looking at them that after having given me money they were feeling bolder, and as soon as Gonzalo drinks they grab their glasses, clinking them together, drink, draining them to the dregs, shout hoorah, heigh-ho, and let come what may! Not having sufficient courage to drink to us, they drank to each other. We, Gonzalo and I, also drank to each other.

> *"Little eye, why do you gleam?*
> *Hansel comes, that's why you beam!"*

And softly he said to me, "Go over to the old guy and ask them to join us. We'll get acquainted."

I say, "It doesn't work that way."

Under the table he shoves something into my hand and urges, "Take it, take it, hold onto it." And it was money. "Take it," he insists, "you need it, look on me as a friend, an admirer, you were my friend already, and I'll be a friend to you!" I don't want to take it, but he pushes it at me violently, forces it on me. I would have liked to throw the money at his feet; but as I already had the money from the others, and now this added to it, I didn't know what to do; for all in all it probably amounted to at least four thousand. Meanwhile, the Baron and his chums were drinking to each other, but they also began to drink to me. With their money in my pocket I couldn't do anything else but drink to them as well; they in turn to me; Gonzalo as well to me; I to Gonzalo; they to Gonzalo; Gonzalo to them! We all drink to each other. What fun!

And at last I get up and, approaching the old gentleman, I utter these words: "Excuse this intrusion, but I recognize my own native language, and thus would like to greet a fellow-countryman."

Immediately rising with the utmost civility, he introduced himself as Thomas Kobrzycki, a former major, now retired, and he also presented his son Ignaz. Then he requested that I take a seat. I sit, he offers beer, but one could tell that my company was not to his taste, and this because of the company I myself had kept. And above all, because there they are—shouting, guzzling, and kicking up a row! Realizing that he is an extraordinarily upright, correct kind of gentleman, I express myself in these words: "I am with a group, but they seem to be a little tipsy; and you will certainly appreciate that no one can seek his own company in such a place as this; sometimes it would be better if one's acquaintances were transformed into strangers."

And they are still roistering about. But he says, "I understand your quandary, and if you permit, please join us in our quieter amusement." So we continue with our conversation.

The man was exceptionally upright and proper, with dry, even features, salt-and-pepper hair, light grey eyes with bushy brows, a gaunt but hairy face, a hawk-nose that sprouted wooly hair, and ears that were also overgrown with bushy tufts of old grey hair. From close-up the son seemed to me quite well developed and pleasing, and had such hands, such feet, such even teeth and such a shock of hair that—oh, you rogue Gonzalo, you rogue! . . . And there the others were, screaming and shouting! The old man tells me that he is preparing his son for the military, and if he doesn't succeed in getting back to his own country, then he will register in England or in France, in order to combat the enemy. And he explains, "We went to this park so that my Ignaz could have a little diversion before his departure, and I wanted to show him the common folk amusing themselves." He speaks, and across the way they are drinking. What was remarkable about this man was the extraordinary circumspection and deliberation of his speech, his whole precise manner of behavior, and he was so circumspect and cautious in words and actions that he might have been an astronomer continuously examining the skies of his inmost self, listening and questioning. He was also extremely polite. In view of such cultivation, such circumspection, an ever greater sense of shame seized me because of my cronies and my situation and my petty intentions. But I didn't want to confess my concerns, and instead only said, "I wish you the greatest success with your splendid objective, and beg to be allowed to drink—also with your son—to the consummation of these noble, capital intentions." And so we clinked our glasses together. But as I touched glasses with the son, Gonzalo drank to me—and also the Baron, Pitzkal and Ciumkala. "Hip-hip, let's drink, let's have fun!"—I had to drink to them; and they returned the toast.

The old man says, "I see that they are drinking."

"To be sure, they are drinking."

"They are drinking to you, as well."

"They drink to me because they are acquaintances."

He was sunk in thought, inwardly agitated . . . and finally in an undertone: "Oh, it is really not the proper time for such amusements . . . not the time . . ."

I felt ashamed! Then, leaning toward him, I whispered into his ear, "For Christ's sake, get your son out of here, and I say that to you out of friendship, for they are indeed drinking to someone, but they are not drinking to me!" The old gentleman's face seemed to darken: "And to whom are they drinking then?" I reply, "They are drinking to that foreigner there, my chum, but he is drinking neither to them nor to me, but to your son."

He flared up and stiffened. "He is drinking to my little Ignaz? Whatever for?"

"Yes, he is drinking to Ignaz, and you must leave with your Ignaz, for that one over there is after him. Go on, get going, I say!"

And at this moment they all make a great uproar, draining their glasses, trumpeting and rioting continuously, emptyig glasses, mugs and tumblers. And hip, hip, tralala! A row, a racket like a country fair! The old gentleman became red as a tomato: "I have also observed him glancing at my son, but I didn't know why."

"Get out, get out of here with your son, you're only making yourself ridiculous in front of these men."

"I with Ignaz" (and still we whispered in each other's ears), "I will not take to my heels with Ignaz, for my son is no maiden! For God's sake, don't mix Ignaz up in this thing, say nothing to Ignaz! I will settle the matter myself with that man."

In the meantime the Baron and Pitzkal were vigorously toasting Gonzalo, and Gonzalo waves to us with his handkerchief and drains his glass—oh, what a fine time we are having, oh, how we are enjoying it all.

The old gentleman seized his glass as if he wanted to drink to Gonzalo, and suddenly he slammed the table with the glass and sprang to his feet! Gonzalo leapt up as well! Instantly the others began to get up, for they could see there was going to be a brawl. Only the son did not move, but he was apparently not feeling well, for he realized what was up, and the poor thing turned the color of a boiled lobster.

And so the old man stands there; and Gonzalo also stands there. The latter, in spite of his girlishness, was a portly man;

however, since the smell of a brawl was in the air, he had become very feeble; and thus Puto is afraid, and the old man merely stands there. And this continued for quite some time. Gonzalo moved the fingers of his left hand delicately and playfully, as if he were wagging his tail and imploring that the whole thing be turned into a joke, a *jeu d'esprit*. But the old man just stands there, and in shock and fear and uncertainty Gonzalo raised to his mouth the glass he held in his other hand, and drank to him. That was his misfortune! He had apparently forgotten that with just such a toast he had thrown the first stone!

One heard the old man asking, "To whom are you drinking?!"

But to whom was he drinking? He was drinking to no one. He drank out of fear, and doesn't take the glass away from his mouth, since if he were to set it down, he would have to answer! He drinks, then, only to be drinking. And there's the hitch—devil, devil—that just as he had surreptitiously drunk to the son before, the drinking is once more aimed at the son (the son sits at the table and makes not a move), and so he only stands there, this rogue, and drinks—ah, only a very, very little—to the son! Puto was becoming aware of this, and fearing the wrath of doubting Thomas, he became limp as a rag, and still he drinks out of sheer fear, only more and more he delivers himself with this drinking to the wrath of Thomas ... And fearing ever more and more this wrath, he drinks and drinks!

Thomas bellows, "Ah, you are drinking to me!"

Puto wasn't drinking to him at all, but to the son. However, Thomas had apparently bellowed so intentionally in order to deflect this drinking away from his son. At that point Pitzkal, the Baron and Ciumkala roared with laughter! Gonzalo fixes one eye on the old man and drinks—even though he has drained the glass, drinks and drinks ... But now he is pointedly drinking to the youngster, and through his drinking he transforms himself into a dame, seeks protection from Thomas' wrath. For, after all, he is no longer a man! He is already a woman!

Then Thomas screams, anger making him as red as a monstrous tomato, "I forbid you, sir, to drink to me, I forbid absolutely that a stranger drink to me!"

But what kind of "sir" is that? No sir, but a lady! And she is not drinking to him but to the son. Thus he drinks and drinks, and though the glass is empty, he drinks and drinks and prolongs his drinking to infinity and defends himself with his drinking, with his drinking he drinks everything away and doesn't stop drinking. Until finally, since he cannot drink any more, he lowers the glass from his mouth and flings it at the old man.

That made a racket! The glass shattered over old Thomas's eye in a thousand splinters!

Thomas didn't budge an inch, but stood there.

The son leapt to his feet, but Thomas roared, "Don't get involved in this, Ignaz!"

And then nothing: he stands there, simply stands there. And he is bleeding, and a big drop runs along his cheek. Now it is clear there will be a punch-up, that they're going to smash each others' heads in . . . Pitzkal, the Baron, Ciumkala sprang from the table and grabbed whatever they could grab, the one a beer mug, the other a bottle, the third a stake or a stool. Thomas, however, doesn't budge, but is simply standing there. They fume so that it seems to grow dark. Those who were some distance away draw closer, and Pitzkal and the Baron, who don't dare begin a scrap with anyone else, commence to slug it out with each other, smashing heads, biting ears . . . and everything seems to go dark—a buzz, a fog, for I too had been drinking. But Thomas stands there. And a second drop of blood oozes out and follows the trail of the first . . .

I see: but nothing; only Thomas is standing there, and Gonzalo is standing as well. A third drop flows slowly from Thomas and follows the trail of the first two, then drips onto his jacket. By God's most gracious majesty, what is this, why doesn't Thomas move? But he only stands there. And a new drop, a fourth one, wells out of him. From these quiet drops it grows quiet in the hall, and Thomas looks at us, and we at Thomas; and now a fifth drop ebbs forth.

CALAMUS

It drips, drips. We all stand there. Gonzalo doesn't stir. And then he returns to his table, takes his hat, and walks slowly away, until his back disappears from view. Then, when Gonzalo had departed, each turned, took his hat, went home, and so we all dispersed—everything . . . everything was dispersed.

—Translated by
David Galloway and
Christian Sabisch

WILLIAM INGE

THE BOY IN THE BASEMENT

SCENE ONE

The setting is an old Victorian house of fussy dignity, kept in the most excellent tidiness and repair. It is in a small mining town close to Pittsburgh. Outside the house, pinned into the ground, is a small, neatly painted sign, "Rest in peace with Scranton. Mortuary." SPENCER SCRANTON, *a man nearing fifty, lives in this house with his father and mother, using the house as a funeral parlor as well as a home. Most of the action of the play takes place in the kitchen of the house— a big, clean, white room, with a table in the center. One gets the feeling that the family lives a great deal of its life here, using it as a kind of sitting room, too. At the right end of the room is a stairway leading to the second floor. At the back of the room, a doorway leading to the outside and the garage. At the left of the room, a big bay window and a door leading to the steps into the basement. A small, dark room at the left indicates the basement. It is in darkness until the action moves there. It is then dimly lighted. When the play opens,* MR. SCRANTON, SPENCER'S *invalid father, is alone onstage, sitting in a big overstuffed chair in the bay window, looking out of*

271

the window through his thick-lensed glasses that blur our vision of his eyes and give him an almost inanimate appearance. He is an ancient man, close to eighty, whose life for several years now has been confined to this chair, where he sits like a discarded bridegroom, his only activity looking out of the bay window onto the little bit of world before him. After a few moments, SPENCER *comes up from the basement, where he has been at work. There is a troubled look on his face that one feels is there most of the time; it is the expression of a man trying to solve some problem that lies too deeply in his subconscious for him ever to see very clearly. He is a big man with long, hairy arms and big hands, yet with a kind of reluctance about him, as though his very size is an embarrassment to him. His sleeves are rolled up above his wrist, and he looks weary. He goes to the stove, finds a pot of coffee there and pours himself a cup. Then he brings his cup to his father, showing it to him. This is his way of asking his father if he wants some. His father shakes his head slowly, and* SPENCER *takes his coffee to the table at center and sits wearily, lighting a cigarette. Now* MRS. SCRANTON *comes down the stairway from above. She is a regal-looking woman in her early seventies, still very alert and active. This is a lovely spring afternoon, and she is dressed to go out. She looks very dignified with her white hair in a neat bun at the back of her head and wearing a simple navy-blue print dress and a small, queenly hat. She is putting on her white gloves as she comes into the kitchen and speaks to* SPENCER.

MRS. SCRANTON   Have you finished with poor old Mrs. Herndon?

SPENCER . . Yes.

MRS. SCRANTON   Were the burns real bad?

SPENCER   One whole side of her, raw and purple.

MRS. SCRANTON   (*Makes an ugly face*)   Poor old lady. Did you fix her up to look all right?

SPENCER   Yah. Covered her face with grease paint. She looks like a chorus girl now.

MRS. SCRANTON Son! You mustn't talk disrespectful of the dead.

SPENCER Well, they all get to lookin' pretty much alike. One dead body after another. That's all life gets to be.

MRS. SCRANTON The good Lord doesn't like us to complain. Well, I'm sure you've done a nice job on her. You always do. You're a regular artist in your work. Imagine—burned to death, a poor old critter like her, when her henhouse caught fire. We all have to go sometime, but I pray to the good Lord I won't have to go that way. Her family wants the most expensive funeral, you know.

SPENCER Well, they'll get it.

MRS. SCRANTON Is the organ tuned?

SPENCER Yes.

MRS. SCRANTON Elsie Featheringill is going to sing. I've got to find out what her numbers are. I hope she picks something I won't have to practice. Can the family pay?

SPENCER I guess so.

MRS. SCRANTON I hope so. You're going to need the money, aren't you?

SPENCER What do ya mean by that, exactly?

MRS. SCRANTON After last weekend in Pittsburgh. Turned out to be pretty expensive, didn't it?

SPENCER I told you, I...

MRS. SCRANTON Calling me here in the middle of the night, telling me you have to have two hundred dollars wired to you that very minute. What in God's name were you doing that you had to have two hundred dollars that very minute?

SPENCER I told you, I... I had a little trouble with the car...

MRS. SCRANTON You said it was something wrong with the power brakes, but they act just the same now as they did before. Besides, why did the man have to have the money

273

that very minute? Any dependable garage would wait till morning, surely. And besides, you sounded like you'd been drinking.

SPENCER I . . . I'd had a beer. That's all. Just one glass of beer.

MRS. SCRANTON I still don't see what you were doing, out until three o'clock in the morning. I certainly wonder at times what goes on those weekends you spend in the city.

SPENCER What goes on when I leave this house is *my* business.

MRS. SCRANTON Were you with a woman?

SPENCER No!

MRS. SCRANTON No, you never took to women the way your brother did. Well, maybe he taught you a lesson. You see where he's ended up, don't you? A mental hospital for the rest of his life. And what sent him there? Whiskey and women. Whiskey and women.

SPENCER (*As though it were too painful for him to think about*) Stop it, Mom.

MRS. SCRANTON (*With a nod at* MR. SCRANTON) It's a wonder he didn't end up the same way, but a stroke got him instead. Something was bound to get him some day.

SPENCER A-men!

MRS. SCRANTON Well, I've done everything I can for the men in my family. Everything I can. If they choose to go on in their own godless ways, I can't help it. I don't know why you have to keep running into the city every weekend, but I'm not going to plague you about it any more.

SPENCER I just gotta have a change once in a while.

MRS. SCRANTON Lotta good the change does you. You've been jumpy and nervous ever since you got back from that last trip. Something happened there, I guess I'll never know about. Maybe the good Lord is keeping it from me, just to spare me. God knows, I've had enough to put up with in my life. Well ... (*With a long resentful look at* MR. SCRANTON) I guess my boys didnt come by their ways from any stranger.

SPENCER Don't pick on the Old Man any more, Mom.

MRS. SCRANTON Who says I "pick" on him?

SPENCER You *do*.

MRS. SCRANTON If I hadn't picked on him once in a while, where'd we be now, I'd like to know? Did he have any ambition? No. It was me that made him go to work and earn enough money to send you to school. If it hadn't been for me, we'd be living now in a pigsty. That's the truth. You've got to admit it. (SPENCER *lowers his head in recognition of the probable truth*) Well, I'm going to my meeting now.

SPENCER Have a good time.

MRS. SCRANTON We ladies don't have these meetings to have a good time. We meet to accomplish things. To try to keep some semblance of order in this godless little mining town.

SPENCER What's the meeting about this afternoon?

MRS. SCRANTON Some of us ladies disapprove of some of the movies they've been showing down at the theater. Movies that are too insinuating for our young people to see today. We're going to see to it that these movies are not to be shown any more. We've got the churches behind us, and we're getting the businessmen behind us, too. It's no wonder our young people are making so much trouble today, if that's the kind of thing they see.

SPENCER When'll you be back?

MRS. SCRANTON In time to get your dinner. Good-bye, Son.

SPENCER Good-bye, Mom.

MRS. SCRANTON I'm going to take the Buick.

SPENCER O.K.

(*She goes to her husband's chair to speak to him*)

MRS. SCRANTON (*In a loud voice, for he is hard of hearing*) I'm going now.

MRS. SCRANTON (*He cannot speak, but only makes guttural sounds*) Uh?

MRS. SCRANTON I said I'm going to my meeting now.

MR. SCRANTON Uh?

MRS. SCRANTON Well, never mind.
(*She goes out the back door.* SPENCER *continues sitting by the table, finishes his coffee, then gets up and stretches.* MR. SCRANTON *makes a series of guttural sounds which draw* SPENCER *to his side. Apparently* SPENCER *understands him*)

SPENCER I'm sorry, Pop. There isn't any beer. Her Royal Highness won't let us keep it. (MR. SCRANTON *makes a sound of annoyance*) I'm sorry, Pop. If I bring home beer, she takes it right out of the ice box and pours it down the sink. She just won't have it lying around. (MR. SCRANTON *makes another series of sounds*) Yah. I'm sorry, too, Pop.
(*Now* JOKER EVANS *bursts in through the back door. He is a delivery boy for the supermarket. He carries a large sack of groceries under his arm and sets it on the kitchen table. He is a boy of about eighteen, handsome, husky, full of quick life and humor. There seems to be a spirit of real camaraderie between him and* SPENCER. SPENCER'S *face brightens immediately upon* JOKER'S *sudden entrance*)

JOKER (*In a voice that even stirs* MR. SCRANTON) Supermarket!

SPENCER Well, hello, Joker, ya li'l bastard!

JOKER Hi, Spence! Man, it's a great day outside. It's quit raining now, and its really spring. Man, it's great to be alive, a day like this.

SPENCER (*Laconically*) Yah! Sure!

JOKER A bunch of us cats are taking dates down to the river tonight. A wienie roast. Why don't you get a date, Spence, and join us?

SPENCER (*Chuckles warmly at the foolishness of the invita-*

tion)   Me? Go on a wienie roast with a bunch of you young punks?

(*They begin boxing with each other, slapping at each other good-naturedly*)

JOKER   Sure. Why not? You can be our chaperon. We'd promise not to do anything you wouldn't do. How's that?

SPENCER   How do you know what I'd do and what I wouldn't do?

JOKER   Jeepers! You tie one on in Pittsburgh almost every weekend, don't you? Yah, you may act respectable around here during the week, but I'll bet you really throw a ball when you get to the city.

SPENCER   Mind your business, you!

JOKER   Why don't you take me with you sometime, Spence? Huh? How 'bout it? Show me the city, too.

SPENCER   You no-good li'l bastard, I wouldn't take you to a dog fight.

JOKER   Yah? You're scared I'd steal all your women away from you, aren't ya?

SPENCER   Why, you li'l bastard, you couldn't get to first base with the women I see.

JOKER   (*With a total lack of self-consciousness or conceit*)   Bet I could. Girls like me. (*Spencer makes a disparaging noise*) No fool, Spence! They *do*. They really like me. Ya know why? They can't boss me. Yah! I'm real independent with 'em. I just take the attitude . . . (*He strikes a pose of boyish boastfulness*) Ho-hum, girls! Here I am. If you like me, I'll see what I can do to make you happy. Now I can't keep 'em off me.

SPENCER   You stuck-up little bastard!

JOKER   I'm *not* stuck-up. I just hold my own, that's all. And man, if you don't learn to hold your own with a girl, she can give you real misery.

SPENCER You got yourself a girl now?

JOKER *Do* I? Sue Carmody. Best-lookin' girl in the whole school. Jeepers, I never knew I could fall so hard. We've been goin' together about three months now. She's the greatest. A real good sport, too. Know what I mean?

SPENCER You going to marry her?

JOKER I sure wish I could. She wants to get married, but I just gotta get to college if I ever wanta get outa this town. If I married her now, I'd have to stay here and maybe go to work in the mines. I wouldn't like that, and in a few years we'd both be miserable. Sue was trying to hold me at first, but I had a long talk with her and helped her see things my way. She understands how it is now.

SPENCER She going to wait for you?

JOKER We talked all that over, too. I don't know if it's fair. By the time I get outa college, I may be in love with some-one else. She may be, too. You can't tell about those things. We finally agreed that after I go to college we no longer have any strings on each other, except when I come home for vacations. And while I'm gone, if either of us finds someone we like better, then . . . Well, we'll try to under-stand.

SPENCER You talked all this over together?

JOKER Yah. It was tough to have to face it all. But I decided we'd better be grown-up about things. I didn't wanta go around feeling someone had any strings on me. Know what I mean?

SPENCER Yah. I know what you mean.

JOKER And she shouldn't feel I have any strings on her, either.

SPENCER When did you decide to go to college for sure?

JOKER Oh, the scholarship came through.

SPENCER That's swell, Joker.

JOKER (*A little ruefully*) Yah, but it means I'll have to play football, and that's kind of a pain. I wanted to quit that jazz after I got outa high school, and really settle down and do some work. But if that's the only way I can get to college, O.K. I'll play football.

SPENCER What're ya gonna study?

JOKER Gee, I wanta go into medicine, but I don't know if I'll be able to make it. I think I can make the grades O.K. I'm pretty smart, did ya know it? Yah. I'm graduating this spring in the top five percent of the class. But I don't know if I'll have the dough. It takes about three years longer to get through medical school, and I won't be able to play football then. I'll have to manage on my own. The folks can't help me much. I might be able to get another scholarship, though. Oh well, I won't have to worry about that for a few years anyway. If I can't make it through medical school, I'll get myself a job coaching some high school football team, maybe.

SPENCER (*Deeply serious*) Gee, kid, I hope you can make it. It'd be great, you getting to be a doctor.

JOKER We'd fix us up a system, Spence. I'd kill off all my patients and send 'em to you.
(*Now they laugh again,* SPENCER *slapping* JOKER *on the shoulder with rough good nature*)

SPENCER No thanks. I got more patients now than I want.

JOKER (*Sobering up*) I sure don't envy you your job. I'd think it'd get kinda depressing being around dead people all the time.

SPENCER (*Melancholy again*) Yah. One dead body after another. That's all my life is.

JOKER How come you never got married, Spence?

SPENCER (*Wishing he could dodge the question*) Oh, I . . . I just never got around to it, Joker.

JOKER You know what? I bet in some ways you never grew

up, Spence. No fool! I can have as much fun talkin' with you as with any guy my own age. And I bet you have more fun talkin' with me than you do with all the squares you meet at the Rotary Club . . .

SPENCER   That's the God's truth.

JOKER   In some ways, Spence, you're like a kid, too. Know it?

SPENCER   (*Reflectively*)   I suppose.

JOKER   (*Looking at the clock on the wall*)   Gee, I gotta beat it. I gotta finish my deliveries.
(*He starts for the door as* SPENCER *thinks of something*)

SPENCER   Oh, just a minute, kid, before you go off in such a hurry.
(*He digs a wallet out of his pocket*)

JOKER   What is it, Spence?

SPENCER   I still owe you for washing the hearse for me last Sunday.

JOKER   Oh . . . yah. Gee, I'm glad you remembered.

SPENCER   (*Handing him a bill*)   Here!

JOKER   (*Looks at the bill and whistles*)   You mean . . . all this, Spence?

SPENCER   Sure.

JOKER   Ten bucks? For washing the carcass wagon?

SPENCER   Sure. It was a hard job, all covered with mud.

JOKER   Gee, Spence, you coulda got it done anywhere in town for three or four bucks.

SPENCER   Shut up, ya li'l bastard. If I say it's worth ten bucks, don't bicker with me.

JOKER   (*Deeply touched*)   Sure. Thanks a lot, Spence.

SPENCER   Forget it.

JOKER   I . . . I'll *never* forget it, Spence. Gee, you've always been swell to me.

SPENCER   Get outa here now before I throw you out.

JOKER   Gee, Spence, if there's anything I can ever do for you, anything at all, just let me know, huh?

SPENCER   Sure. Sure. Beat it now.

JOKER   So long, Spence.

(*He runs out the back door now as* SPENCER *begins putting away the groceries—into the refrigerator, the bread box, and the cupboard. He turns on the kitchen radio, too, and gets a lilting, romantic Viennese waltz that starts him whistling,* MR. SCRANTON *utters a new series of unintelligible sounds*)

SPENCER   What's that, Pop? (MR. SCRANTON *repeats the sounds*) Her Royal Highness is bound to find out. (MR. SCRANTON *makes new noises, somewhat angrily*) Well, I guess it wouldn't hurt either of us to have a short one.
(SPENCER *opens the basement door and brings out a large bottle of embalming fluid, which he opens; he pours a small snifter full, which he gives to his father. Then he pours one for himself. For a moment, the atmosphere is quite merry. The old man begins nodding his head in rhythm with the waltz, and* SPENCER *takes a dustmop from the cupboard, drapes an apron around it and uses it as a dancing partner. He is waltzing about the room when he hears the Buick drive into the garage. Then he returns the mop to the cupboard hurriedly, and puts the bottle of embalming fluid back behind the basement door*)

SPENCER   Her Royal Highness. She's back.
(*The old man sobers up and* SPENCER *returns to the table, lighting a cigarette and looking very solemn when she comes in. The second we see her, we know she is somehow stricken. It is as though a flash of lightning had parted the skies for a moment and given her a glimpse into some far truth she had never before quite realized, and now she is dumbfounded and horror stricken. She grasps the doorway for support.* SPENCER *looks at her wonderingly*)

SPENCER   Mom, you back already?

MRS. SCRANTON   (*In a hoarse and halting voice*)   I came back as soon as I could ... after I heard ... certain things.

SPENCER   (*Frightened by her tone and demeanor*)   Wh ... what'd you hear, Mom?

MRS. SCRANTON   I heard my dearest friends ... some of the finest ladies in this town ... talk about certain things that went on in the city ... that made my blood chill ... and made me understand things I never understood before ...

SPENCER   (*Terrified but trying to conceal it*)   Wh ... what do you mean, Mom?

MRS. SCRANTON   I was presiding over the meeting, too, and I had to beg them to pardon me. I said I had one of my migraine headaches and had to go home that instant. But I just couldn't sit there and face them any longer. I ... I don't know how I'll ever keep my head high again, when I walk down the streets of this town.

SPENCER   (*Very flustered*)   Mom, I ... d-don't know wh-what you're talking about.

MRS. SCRANTON   And to think ... I raised my son, praying he'd become a great man. I raised both my sons to be great men. No one can say I didn't do my part. And *look* how destiny laughs in my face.

SPENCER   Mom, t-tell me.

MRS. SCRANTON   (*Spying the book of matches on the kitchen table which Spencer has been using to light cigarettes. She grabs them and forces them in his face*)   Where did you get these matches?
(*Her very tone is like a condemnation to hell*)

SPENCER   I ... uh ... I don't remember, Mom. I g-guess I just picked them up some place.

MRS. SCRANTON   The Hi Ho Bar ... in Pittsburgh. That's where they came from.

SPENCER   Yah. I see, Mom. I ... I don't know *where* I got 'em.

MRS. SCRANTON   You got them when you went there last Saturday night, and the place was raided, and you called me for two hundred dollars to pay the policeman to keep him from putting you in jail and to keep your name out of the paper. (*Her detective work has thoroughly shattered* SPENCER's *nerves. He can no longer look at her. He cannot even speak. His incoherent grunts give him a moment's resemblance to his father's mumbling inarticulateness*)

MRS. SCRANTON   And the police raided the place because it's a meeting place for degenerates. (SPENCER *collapses over the table, his head in his arms.* MRS. SCRANTON *now has the bearing of a tragic victor*) Dear God, my own son! My own flesh and blood! Corrupting himself in low degeneracy. Going to some disgusting saloon, where men meet other men and join together in . . . in some form of unnatural vice, in some form of . . . of lewd depravity. (*With this,* SPENCER *runs upstairs in panic.* MRS. SCRANTON *now drops to the floor, on her knees, leaning on the table in anguished prayer*) O God, why do you make me suffer so? Why do you thrust every kind of sorrow and humiliation on me to endure? Haven't I always tried to live in your holy light? And haven't I always fought to keep my family there? My loved ones? Why do you continue to punish me, O Lord? I've loved my son since the day he was born and kept him to my breast with loving care. I think I even loved him more than I loved my own husband, for my son's infant love was innocent and pure, and demanded no fleshly act to satisfy its need. O God, will you punish me forever? *I,* who have fought so hard for the *right!* Have fought so hard to keep my mind and heart and body *pure* and free from all physical craving. All my life, I've been a God-fearing woman. Maybe you punish me for sins I don't know anything about. Are you, O Lord? Are you punishing me for sins I know not of? Then tell me, so I can atone for them and be forgiven. I don't want to suffer all my life long. When was the day I did wrong? Dear God, when was the day I did wrong? (SPENCER *comes hurrying down the stairs now, wearing the jacket to his conservative blue suit, a white shirt, a dark tie and a gray hat. He carries a topcoat over one arm and a suitcase. He has made up his mind what he has to do. He heads straight for the back door,* MRS. SCRANTON *slowly rousing herself to the fact of his leaving*) Son! Where you going?

SPENCER   I don't know. I'm just goin'.

MRS. SCRANTON   (*Getting up, running to him and grasping his arm*)   Son!

SPENCER   I should have left here a long time ago, but I didn't. I just stayed on, and on, and on. But I'm going now. Never you fear. And it'll be a cold day in hell before I ever come back.

MRS. SCRANTON   Son! Listen to me. Now don't do anything crazy...

SPENCER   I suppose it's something crazy if I wanta be my own boss. Forty-six years old. And I stay around here and listen to your yapping. I don't have to do it. See? I'm as free as the next one. I can get a job like that. (*Snaps his fingers*) And live the way I wanta live. And to hell with you!

MRS. SCRANTON   (*Breathlessly*)   I'm your mother, Son. I'm your mother. You can't leave your old home. Now think a minute...

SPENCER   (*Loosening her hands on his arm*)   It's no use, Mom. I'm goin.' By God, I'm goin'.
(*He tears out the door*)

MRS. SCRANTON   (*Crying desperately*)   Son! Son! Don't do anything foolish. Come back here, Son. You'll be sorry you left this way. Now come back here and be reasonable. (*But she only hears the sound of the Buick pull out of the garage and drive away. She utters one last futile cry*) Son! (*But he is gone. She drags herself back into the kitchen and drops into the chair by the table*) Oh God, give me peace! Give me peace!
(*She sobs.* MR. SCRANTON *has not moved throughout the scene but has continued staring out the window like a piece of patient wreckage*)
Curtain

284

SCENE TWO

It is early the next morning. The sun is just beginning to show and bring a soft light to the interior of the house. MRS. SCRANTON *is alone onstage, sitting in her husband's chair, looking out of the window but seeing nothing. She is dressed in a long night dress and loose robe, her long, white hair down her back. Her face is stricken with emptiness and grief. She is absolutely immobile for several moments. Then she hears the Buick drive into the driveway, into the garage. A wave of relief comes over her that makes us think for a moment she might faint. But she has never fainted in her life, and she doesn't now. In a few moments* SPENCER *comes in carrying his suitcase, tossing his hat on the post at the bottom of the stairway. He is defeated and knows it. And his bearing tells us he accepts the fact, although sadly. He sets the suitcase down at the bottom of the stairs and stands there, not knowing what to say, hoping his mother will take over the situation. But she doesn't. There is something almost shy about the woman now, and her eyes are full and her chin trembles. Finally,* SPENCER *speaks.*

SPENCER   That you, Mom?

MRS. SCRANTON   (*Jumps up from her chair and runs to him*) My boy! My boy! My boy!
(*All the fears and resentments they have fought inside themselves during the past several hours are purged now in a fast embrace. Their need, their desperate dependence on each other, their deep love bring them together like lovers*)

SPENCER   Mom!
(*They share a fast embrace. Undoubtedly, this is the only person* SPENCER *truly loves*)

MRS. SCRANTON   Oh, my son! Thank God you're back. If you hadn't come back, I'd have been ready for the basement myself.

SPENCER   Yah. I came back.

MRS. SCRANTON   You won't ever leave me again, will you, Son?

SPENCER   No, Mom.

MRS. SCRANTON   Because it's like we'd made a pact together, a long time ago. If one of us breaks it, we're both destroyed.

SPENCER   I know it, Mom.

MRS. SCRANTON   I've just been sitting here all night. I got your father to bed and then came down here and just sat, staring out the window. It's morning now, isn't it? Where have you been, Son?

SPENCER   I just drove all over, one town to another. Not stopping any place. Just driving. I'm not sure I know now where I've been.

MRS. SCRANTON   Well, you're back now. That's the important thing. And we're going to try to treat each other nicer now, aren't we? To speak to each other with a little more consideration.

SPENCER   Sure, Mom.

MRS. SCRANTON   It's just all wrong for us to get so impatient with each other.

SPENCER   Sure, Mom.

MRS. SCRANTON   (*Sighing deeply*)   Oh God, I'm still heaving with relief. (*Upstairs now,* MR. SCRANTON *makes some guttural noises that demand their attention*) Your father's up. You go help him downstairs and I'll get your breakfast. (*Now there is a knocking at the back door*) Oh, it's the body. I took a call for you while you were gone. Some young boy got drowned in the river last night. They said they'd bring the body over first thing this morning. I was too distracted to get the details.

SPENCER   One dead body after another. That's all my life is.

MRS. SCRANTON   Now, Son, let's not complain.

SPENCER   How'd you know I'd be back?

MRS. SCRANTON   (*A little hesitantly, with just an edge of guilt*)
I . . . I thought . . . you would be. (SPENCER *accepts the
minor debasement and her self-confidence, and goes wearily
upstairs as* MRS. SCRANTON *opens the back door, admitting
two men, dressed as miners, carrying a body on a stretcher,
the body covered with a blanket*) Right this way, gentlemen.
Over here to the basement door. (*The two silent men carry
the body through the kitchen to the basement door, then
down the stairs, as* SPENCER *brings his father down the stairs
from the second floor, the old man hanging onto* SPENCER
*with infant dependence, having to feel his way cautiously
every step he takes. Down in the basement, the two men put
the body on a long white slab, something like a kitchen side-
board, that drains into a big sink. They keep their heads
down in heavy grief.* MRS. SCRANTON *is talking with them in
a low voice that comes over to the audience as just a mum-
ble. Their answers to her are monosyllables. She is a business woman now.* SPENCER *is just getting his father into the
big chair as* MRS. SCRANTON *leads the two men up from the
basement*) Yes, we'll take care of the dear boy. My son does
the best work in town. You can ask anyone. I know what a
grief it is to you, sudden death always is. But he'll have the
boy looking like he could sit up and speak to you. He'll have
a fine Christian burial. You may depend on that. (*She lets
the two men out the back door now, and turns to* SPENCER)
It's the Evans boy. (SPENCER *gasps*) Delivered groceries here
for the supermarket. The one that washed your hearse for
you sometimes.

SPENCER   (*As though to himself*)   No . . . No . . .

MRS. SCRANTON   (*Busying herself at the stove, getting breakfast*)   The little fool, he and a bunch of kids decided to go
swimming last night in the river. Boys and girls together,
going in swimming *naked*. Oh! That's what they do. Those
high school kids have no shame. What are things coming to?
And after all these spring rains. They might have known

what to expect. Oh, that old devil river gets someone every year.

SPENCER (*Runs down the basement stairs*) Joker! Joker! (*He tears the blanket off the young, naked body and stares at it, unable to believe what has happened. Then he returns slowly back up the stairs to the kitchen*) Mom! It's Joker! It's Joker!

MRS. SCRANTON I know. That's what I was trying to tell you. The little fool went in swimming after all these spring rains we've been having. Should have known better. Oh, that old devil river gets someone every year.

SPENCER (*Can only mutter to himself with a feeling of mysterious loss*) Joker! Joker!

MRS. SCRANTON I'm afraid you'll have to get right to work on him. They want the funeral tomorrow. They just want the cheap funeral, too, so don't go to any extra pains. Remember, you've got old Mrs. Herndon's funeral this afternoon at two-thirty. I've got to practice some of Elsie Featheringill's numbers, too. (*Dazed,* SPENCER *returns to the basement and stands beside the body, just staring at it.* MRS. SCRANTON *goes over to her husband's chair and delivers an ultimatum*) There'll be no more whiskey drinking.

MR. SCRANTON Uh?

MRS. SCRANTON (*Louder*) I said there'll be no more whiskey drinking. I found where you were hiding it, in the bottle of embalming fluid.

MR. SCRANTON Uh?

MRS. SCRANTON Nothing! How do you want your eggs?

MR. SCRANTON Uh?

MRS. SCRANTON I said, how do you want your eggs?

MR. SCRANTON Uh?

MRS. SCRANTON (*Giving up*) Well, I'll poach them. They're easier on the digestion.

MR. SCRANTON Uh?

MRS. SCRANTON (*Shouting*) Nothing! (*To herself now, returning to stove*) You don't *want* to hear me. You never did want to hear me. I could holler my lungs out and you still wouldn't hear me.
(*She is busy getting breakfast.* MR. SCRANTON *looks out of his window on a sunny morning, birds twittering now in the trees.* MRS. SCRANTON, *contented as a new bride, sings "Rock of Ages" as she gets breakfast. Down in the basement,* SPENCER *finally moves from his frozen stance at* JOKER's *side to rub one soft hand warmly over the boy's chest, as though it were precious metal*)

SPENCER (*In a tone of reverence and awe*) Joker, you little bastard! I never expected to see you down here. Why couldn't you have been more careful, boy? You were alive. Didn't you appreciate it? Most of us are just pretending, and it don't matter when we end up down here. But you were alive. You were alive. Jesus! And I wanted you to stay that way.
(MRS. SCRANTON, *a little curious as to what is going on, sticks her head in the basement door and calls down*)

MRS. SCRANTON (*Suspiciously*) What are you doing down there?

SPENCER You'd be suspicious if I was in the same room with a stuffed owl.

MRS. SCRANTON Don't be sassy. (SPENCER *has no retort*) You can eat your breakfast while he's draining, can't you?

SPENCER (*In a firm voice*) I won't want any breakfast.

MRS. SCRANTON Oh, well you'll want coffee. It's ready. Do you want me to help you down there?

SPENCER (*Most definitely*) I do *not*.

MRS. SCRANTON Well, you don't have to bite my head off.
(*She slams the door and goes back to her work.* SPENCER *now picks up one of the boy's hands and kisses it warmly*)

289

SPENCER   Jesus Christ, Joker, I wanted you to live.
(*Now he takes his scalpel. It is the hardest thing he ever
had to do in his life, and he has to steel himself to do it, but
he severs the main arteries, feeling the pain of doing it to
himself, and then drops to a chair, his perspiring face in his
hands*)

Curtain

JEAN GENET

RITON

Let us continue the account of the events on the rooftops. Anxiety prevented the sergeant from sleeping. He got up during the night and made the rounds of the apartment. In the bedroom, the three soldiers were sleeping on the bed in a tangle that the most indulgent of men would have regarded as scandalous, but it was fatigue alone that thus entangled the soldiers at the edge of the grave. He entered the dining room, carefully directing the beam of his flashlight. At his feet he saw the sight I have depicted. Riton was sleeing with his arm out and his hand almost entirely buried in the trousers of the sleeping Erik.

At daybreak, when they were awakened, caution obliged the soldiers to remain sitting where they were lest their walking make a sound that would worry the tenants on the floor below. Nevertheless, they would have liked to explore the conquered rooms that were still warm with the life of the occupants who had fled. Apartments offer themselves to the burglar with painful immodesty. Without looking for them, we find the very personal habits of the bourgeois, and I can say for a fact that I have opened drawers in which there were underpants with shit stains, and hard, dried, crumpled socks that emitted their sad fragrance when spread out. I have even found abandoned fragments of shit in the drawers of elegant commodes. For a long time I thought that women are the dirtier, but actually men are. As for the imagination of both, it's on a par with that of the police. If they have hidden the hundred francs in a fold of the window curtain, under a pile of sheets, or behind a frame, their mind is at rest. At rest, except for the mortal anxiety that is the very stuff of their life when they are more than fifty feet away from the hoard. But who am I to talk, since I piss in the sink, I forget turds that I leave in old newspapers in the wardrobes of hotel rooms, and I don't have the guts to leave my money in my room for an hour. I walk with it, I steal with it, I sleep with it.

The soldiers did not wash themselves. Nothing came out of the taps. The lack of water made them panicky. There was hardly any left in their canteens. The sergeant allowed them to talk in an undertone, for the noises of day drowned out their murmuring. Their blond hair was in their eyes, and at the corner of their eyelids were bits of white mucus. It was a miserable awakening. The apartment seemed the domain of death to the soldiers. It was as disturbing to be there as in certain regions where the land is mined, where snakes bulge their delicate throats, where rose-laurels grow. We were afraid. Not of the danger but of the accumulation of fateful signs. At each window the sergeant posted a man who could fire on the insurgents. Then he divided the day's food into eight equal parts. Although he did not want to talk about it, he twice made smiling remarks about Riton to Erik, which showed that he knew what had happened. Erik smiled and, in the presence of his joking comrades, admitted the night's adventure. There was no scandal. They laughed a little and were silently amused as they looked at the kid whose beauty was suddenly revealed to them. He was squatting on the bed and eating bread with chocolate. Riton bit into the chocolate and took a canteen in order to drink, but Erik snatched it from his hands. The child's astonished eyes looked into his. Erik murmured with a gentle laugh as he handed the canteen back to him without having drunk:

"I'm German."

Riton smiled back. Erik pointed a finger at him:

"You're French," and he laughed a little more loudly.

And I can understand polygamy when I realize how quickly the charms of a boy-girl are exhausted and how much more slowly those of a boy-male disappear. Erik tried to act as if he were joking about that pretension, but the fact that it was already stated, even though in an ironic tone, indicated sufficiently that it was at the basis of his relations with Riton. The pride which he sensed, instead of saddening Riton, afforded him a kind of repose. Five Germans were in the room. Erik was standing behind the bed. His comment distracted the attention of the soldiers, who spoke about something else, but a soldier smilingly stroked Riton's tousled hair as he walked by him. The kid was filled with surprise and then anxiety. He tossed his head to shake off the hand, but he didn't dare make a gesture or scowl, not even frown. And immediately he realized, from the soldiers' looks and laughter, that they knew. He thought they were mocking contemptuously. He blushed. Not having been able to wash, his face shined and the blush seemed sparkling, then warm. One of the soldiers saw him in the mirror, and, without showing the kid that he had noticed the blush, revealed it smilingly to Erik, who gently went up behind Riton, took him by the neck, pulled him back a little, and kissed him very sweetly on the hair, in the presence of his comrades and the sergeant. Nobody commented on the gesture, which was natural and charming. Riton smiled, for, though he pretended not to care, he was so in love with Erik, whose sovereign person had just compelled everyone's recognition by that quiet kiss, that he was willing to announce his marriage.

Then Riton suddenly felt he was falling over a precipice. Did Erik really love him? He would have liked to tell him that at the hour of their death in each other's arms, the most human thing was to grant each other the greatest happiness. But that was hard to say. He did not know German. He felt like crying. For a moment they all looked at one another gravely, in silence. The soldiers who had been posted at the half-open windows with instructions to shoot were lying flat on their stomachs on the rug so as not to be seen from the houses opposite. When they assumed that position, the sun was hardly up. The light was gray, though the weather promised to be fine. They saw nothing on the boulevard, which was slightly blurred by a light mist. They were watching listlessly. Erik cleaned his revolver and Riton his machine gun. The others dozed off. An hour later, the sun had driven off the mist, and when Riton went to the window, behind a tulle curtain with lace designs, after a moment of amazement the strangest emotion took hold of his mind and body, twisted him, and left him in tatters. He did not cry. The whole boulevard was decked with two rows of French flags. He solemnly bade France farewell. The flags were out for his treason. He was being thrown out of his country, and upon awakening, every Frenchman waved at his window the flag of freedom regained, of purity recaptured. He was going to the realm of the dead that day, and it was a fête on earth, in the sun, in the blue air. He was in the realm of the dead. He did not cry. But he realized that he loved his country. Just as it was on the day Jean died that I knew I loved him, so it was on losing France that he knew he loved her. The English and American flags were at the windows along with the French. A tri-colored shit and spew was dripping from everywhere. Riton realized the meaning of the house's silent activity. All night long the whole city had been spinning yards of red, white, and blue cotton fabric. And that morning, the *Marseillaise*, weary of flying over Paris, had dropped to the streets, torn and exhausted. That miracle had taken place on the day of his death. For a second Riton thought he could still go down the stairs without the Boches' knowing it (the Boches—the word clearly shows that grief invents a whole symbolism whereby one hopes to act mystically: I hesitated to write the word Boche with a capital B, out of contempt, in order to make it a *common* noun—the Boches and the Militiamen killed Jean, whom I revere, and as I see it this is the finest story of Boche and Militiaman, which I offer up to his memory. Erik has my favor). Or spring from the balcony to the street. He would not hurt himself, for this was the day when to wish for a miracle sufficed for it to take place. The Fritzes would no doubt shoot, and he then thought very seriously of running the risk of death from a German bullet. A feeling of purification, of redemption, was involved in the idea, bringing to his eyelids a tear that did not flow. He had betrayed France, but he would be dying for her. He very nearly performed a heroic act, a tailspin among the three colors.

"What the hell do I care about France? They're all jerks. Fuck 'em all on foot and on horseback."

He was bound to think that. But he was still too young for his face to remain serene, and the corners of his puffy little mouth drooped painfully at the thought of what France was doing to him, at the thought of the joy he was losing, and also because, despite its force, the bitterness of losing the things of the world always accompanies the gravest joy of marvelous expeditions in forbidden lands. He made a face. It did not occur to him that he had gambled and lost and that he was paying. What he felt was not comparable to the pain caused by turning up the wrong card. It was due mainly to the decision taken by France, his friends, his family: to expel him from joy, from play, from pleasures, and to display the flags in honor of that exile. His mouth was still pasty after the bread and chocolate. It was dark in the room where the Germans were sleeping. He was not combed. Hairs from combs and brushes were strewn all over the bedroom. An untidy soldier whose belt was unbuckled and whose shirt was half out of his trousers, playing the role of a bare-headed girl getting out of bed, went from the bedroom to the living room. Riton sniffled. A drop of snot had just started dripping from his nose. He would never again wash his face. He tried to clean the corner of his somewhat rheumy eyes with his fingernail. A slight breeze stirred all the flags.

It's bright and gay!
Good morning, swallows, it's bright and gay!

He whistled a measure of the tune between his teeth. The first car that passed in the street was white and had a red cross on the roof. There were more wounded Frenchmen. He had fired. A slight pride at the thought of it cheered him. He had killed young men on the barricades. He had wounded others with the machine gun. With Mademoiselle. Girls were looking after the wounded, were kissing them. France would make speeches. France. France, France, forever. He had Erik. Then and there that love did not fill him enough. There was a place for regret in him. The Germans suddenly—for a great sorrow gives you extraordinary lucidity, things which do not go together dovetail, and others that appeared to be decked in splendid clothes look scraggy in their bony nakedness—the Germans seemed to him to be what they were: monsters. It was not because they shot Frenchmen. Riton did not regret those they had killed. He regretted not being able to be near those who sniveled for them. The Germans did their job. Everything about them was monstrous, that is, was opposed to the joy of the French. The Germans were dismal, black, but the others were green. In that room they had the gravity of people whose destiny is only pain. Riton was not good at thinking; nevertheless he ventured the following reflection to himself:

"Who are my pals now, my com-rades? It's them, it ain't my Paris pals. I'm washed up, and that's no shit, I'm washed up, Riton my boy."

The soldiers were snoring. A subterranean soul animated that exceptional tomb which had been raised to the top of a giant building from which Riton, his heart overflowing with peace, could watch the naive joy of the inhabitants of the earth. He stood stock-still, his face still ravaged. His grief lasted five to six minutes, long enough to prepare him for what follows. He squatted with his back to the window and looked at the loose-leaf calendar on the wall, the block calendar that showed August 15, Assumption Day, and he loosened his belt a bit. The sergeant was rereading his letters. Erik was gazing sadly at his harmonica, he was waiting for a screaming of sirens to be able to play a little, if only in a muted tone. Three shots shook the apartment. The soldier in the bedroom had fired at some fellows crossing the boulevard. The question of shooting had been discussed. They had decided to fire only when it was essential so as to husband ammunition, and particularly so as not to give away their hideout. The house was certainly not abandoned. They were to shoot mainly to help German comrades who were grappling in the street with insurgents. The sergeant seemed frightened by the sniper's firing. They no doubt had a plan of escape over the rooftops, but they could not have gone very far since the block of houses was only a steep rock cut out among four streets. If they were found, it was sure death. After the shots the silence became crueler. Anxiety made its way into the apartment in the form of signs revealed by the objects. It seemed impossible that a radio would be there or that the frame of a photo would be turned or that a spot on the wall would be visible if they were not to die that day, if they were not to be blasted. The seven males and the kid, who were all tired from the struggle, which had lasted perhaps a quarter of an hour, were caught in the pose in which the burst of gunfire had stopped them. An anguish had been floating in the apartment since morning, an anguish so painful that it made the air in the rooms and the look of the faces almost black. Every angle, every sharp point of a motionless gesture, a badly wrinkled fold of cloth, a hole, a finger, instantly emitted distress signals. They were extremely nervous. The anguish with which the rooms were mined increased a hundredfold in two seconds. The sergeant muttered reproaches to the sniper, who answered in a scarcely higher tone with another mutter whose meaning was conveyed chiefly by the lips. The sergeant mastered his desire to scream an order, but the impossibility of expressing his rage exasperated him. He made the unfortunate gesture of pushing the soldier away from his weapon and giving it to a comrade whom he posted in his place. The sniper's little mug, buffeted by locks of hair, contracted, the look on his face hardened. Under constraint, the anger grew. This rapid and necessarily silent scene was prolonged as the men waited anxiously. The soldier had half sprung up, with one knee barely touching the floor and his hands empty, one of them hanging at his side, the other clutching his hair, but quivering with an uncompleted movement, somewhat like that of the runner set to go waiting impatiently to continue—and already continuing by the quivering of his body—with a run or a leap. Anger contorted his mouth, turned his face pale, the accompanying hatred brought his knitted eyebrows together into a mass of darkness from which lightning flashed at regular intervals to strike the sergeant and destroy Germany. Cowed by the necessity of being submissive even at such a moment, the soldier remained in that position, stupefied and motionless. But anxiety had made its way into the apartment. Sitting at the foot of the bed, on the edge, Erik, without realizing it, kept his dry lips on the bee's nest of his harmonica. He didn't give a damn. They waited. The sergeant, who, after his short-tempered gesture, had remained still for a moment, hesitated a second and went into the living room. As he walked out, his body discovered Riton, who was crouching, gaping, as the sniper stared at him. It was nighttime. Unless it was continually day. I even think there was neither night nor day at the top of the tall building. In broad daylight they were sometimes in utter darkness, that is, every moment revealed a nighttime activity. They went through space so gently, the movement of the Earth was so slow, that the soldiers' gestures were all gentleness. A body was asleep with its head on a heap of rope. Or a boy was whispering. A boy was dreaming. The maneuver was muted. Riton got up. Suddenly he was concerned with what day it was. He went to the wall to tear off the pages of the calendar. This gesture drew him out of the tragic a little and then put him back into it more deeply.

"It's ass-headed, but I've got to see what day it is."

As he stood up, his trousers, which had no belt loops, slid completely out from under the belt, and the shirt bunched up against his chest and back. He was hardly aware of it, yet he made the gesture of pulling up his pants with his hand. In order to go to the wall, he had to push aside or disturb the sniper, who had not moved and whose eyes, which had been hostile since the sergeant had left the room, weighed on Riton. When the kid neared him, the soldier, on seeing the sloppiness of his attire, finally found an excuse for releasing his anger. He roughly grabbed the belt and pulled the kid, whose torso was delicate despite its hardness. It was also flexible, and it bent back, as if to regain its balance, or to escape, but the soldier prevented it by putting his left hand even more angrily around his waist. Riton thought he was being playful and, though he had seldom fooled around with that soldier, supported himself with both hands on the curly head which the swiftness of the whole rather brusque movement had knocked against him. Now, the soldier, despite his anger, was unable, on feeling the irony, to keep from being (in, to be sure, a very imprecise way) under the charm of the noblest posture of respect and faith. A kind of confusion ruffled his soul and made him slightly dizzy. The child, who saw in the mirror over the fireplace that Erik was watching him from behind, tried to get away. The soldier felt it and tightened his embrace, and Riton, clutching the Fritz's hair, pressed the head harder against himself. The forehead rested on his belly, in the space between the belt and the trousrs, while the mouth was crushed on the stiff blue cloth of the fly. The significance of the posture was changing. The German seemed to be clinging to the kid by the belt, as to a lifebuoy. The wounded male, who was in a rage, was on his knees before a sixteen-year-old Frenchman who seemed to be his protector and to be indulgently crowning his head with two strong clasped hands. Everyone in the room waited in silence. The soldier refused to let go of the kid, holding him firmly with his muscular arms, furious and humiliated at the fact that his face was lost in the shadow of the trousers, whose smell he breathed in with his open mouth. He tried to raise his head, but the buckle of the belt scraped his forehead. Pain made him finally make the gesture toward the performing of which everything was converging, the gesture after which the day was later named: with wild fury, the German, whose arms were tensed and whose torso had suddenly come to life on his thighs, which were buttressed by his rising motion, bent the kid under him. Ritons eyes became those of a hunted animal. He wanted to flee, but he was trapped, and his head banged against the wooden bed. The three other soldiers were silently watching his almost motionless *corps à corps*. Their attention and silence were part of the action itself. They made it perfect by making it public and publicly accepted. Their attention—their presence, at three points in the room—enveloped the action. Two men and a soldier were on guard at the sixth-floor windows of a mined building, which was menaced by a hundred rifles, so that a black pirate could bugger a young traitor at bay. Fear is a kind of element in which gestures are made without their being recognized. It could play the role of the ether. It even lightens acts that are not conditioned by what caused it. It quickens one's knowledge of them. It weighs down and blurs others. This fear that the nest would be spotted, that the house would explode, that they would be drilled, did not seem to preoccupy them. Rather, it made a kind of emptiness inside them, in which there was room only for that extraordinary fact, which was really unexpected at the hour of death. Since they were at the edge of the world, at the top of that rock posted at the outermost point of Finis Terrae, they could watch with their minds at ease, could give themselves utterly to the perfect execution of the act. Since they could view it only in its closed form, which was cut off from the future, it was the ultimate one. After it, nothing else. They had to make it as intense as possible, that is, each of them had to be as acutely conscious of it as he could be so as to concentrate as much life as possible in it. Let their moments be brief, but charged with consciousness. A faint smile played over their lips. Erik's hand, which was lying on the bed, was still holding his harmonica. He was smiling with the same smile as the others. When Riton's head banged against the wooden bed, there was a dull but weak thud, and he uttered a very faint moan of pain. The three witnesses of the struggle, who felt no pity but were very angry with the one who threatened to botch everything, made the same gestures of the arms and silently articulated, opening their mouths wide, the same threats whose meaning the kid understood from the hardness of their features and expressions. Instead of cursing the torturer, their hatred was directed toward the child who was capable of depriving them of the joy of his tortures. Finally sure that the thud would be without danger, the hatred subsided when silence was restored. The subtle smile flowered on their mouths again, but the kid, who had been knocked out by the blow on the chin, from which blood was flowing, was already lying on the bed, with his pants down, his face against the sheets, his body pounded by the husky body of the soldier, who had the self-possession to lay down his burden delicately so as not to make the spring of the mattress groan. There was only the barest creaking. For Riton it had happened. . . . Unable to imagine how far that fury would go, he nevertheless made the movements that might help calm the soldier. The militiaman on the mattress placed his legs, which had been dangling down to the floor, next to Erik, who had remained seated, with his harmonica in his fist. The other soldiers looked on.

"Good thing I cleaned my hole a little."

The sergeant, who was at the door, was also watching. Annoyed at having been too rough with a soldier who was fighting and who would probably die that day, he dared not interfere. Besides, he was under the sway of a feeling that I shall speak about presently. In the silence of the city, which was at times disturbed by the sound of a Red Cross car carrying arms, there entered through the half-open window, from a thin, cracked voice, purer for being cracked—a broken toy— the following song, composed of the tenacity of the weak, which rose up from the pavement and, passing through the foliage of the trees, reached the ear of Riton, to whom the melody seemed radiant:

They have broken my violin . . .

Riton, who had been knocked senseless by the Fritz, bit the bolster so as not to scream. The brute stopped and panted a little, letting his cheek rest against the back of Riton's neck. He snorted. A short rest, a lull in the fellow's fury, enabled the kid to make out the end of the stanza, which the fragile voice was repeating:

For its soul was French.
It fearlessly made the echoes
Sing the Marseillaise.

Riton dared not stir. He first wondered anxiously whether he should clean himself or simply suck the jissom in. And what could he clean himself with if there was not water? He could only wipe himself. With his handkerchief. The soldier, whose bearded chin Riton felt on the back of his neck, gave a shove, which made the kid groan.

. . . Sing the Marseillaise . . .

Erik had not stirred. He had to watch the kid who had been drowned by force get sawed in half.

Riton wanted the rape to be over with, and he feared the end of it.

Surely they would all take a crack at him. Erik's presence, which he still felt at the edge of the bed, kept him from moving his rump to make the soldier come more quickly.

... made the echoes ...

Finally the warmth of the liquid escaped in slower and slower throbs, like the blood of a cut artery. The fellow from the North was discharging into his bronze eye. . . . When he raised himself up, gently so as not to make any noise, the soldier was calm. He was smiling. He remained standing beside the bed for a moment. He looked defiantly at his smiling cronies, then, slowly, smiling more broadly and tossing back his blond hair with a flick of his head, he adjusted his trousers and little black tank driver's jacket and rebuckled his belt. He said to the soldiers:

"What are you waiting for?"

He looked Erik in the eye. Riton, relieved of the bruiser but still outstretched, had pulled up his pants and tucked in his shirttails. Turning his head, he waited with a feeble smile on his lips. One of the soldiers who was sitting in the armchair was about to follow up, but he changed his mind and, turning to the door, laughingly invited the sergeant to enjoy himself first. The sergeant looked at Erik and signaled to him. Erik whispered a word, and they all went out. Nothing happened. They had to flee by the rooftops.

The German soldiers and Riton had gone back to the roof. They felt they were being pursued less by the tenants of the building than by fear. They were fleeing from it. Slowly, in broad daylight, following the least exposed slopes of the roof, they got to a corner formed by three chimneys. The hiding place was narrow. It could hardly contain them, though they squatted together in a kind of cluster from which the notion of the individual disappeared. No thought was born of that armed mass, but rather a somnolence, a dream whose chief and mingled themes were a feeling of dizziness, the act of falling, and nostalgia for the Vaterland. No longer worried about being heard, they spoke aloud. Riton was caught in Erik's legs. They crouched against each other, and they spent the day that way, crushed by the five soldiers who at times overflowed onto the sky. There were potshots all around them, but they could see nothing, not a single patch of street, or a single window of an apartment. The heat was overpowering. Toward evening, the mass of males was loosened by a little elasticity. Numbed limbs came to life again. Erik and Riton awoke. Beneath the shelter of the chimneys, the sergeant divided the remaining food and they ate their last meal. The general idea was to get down under cover of darkness and make their way to the Bois de Vincennes. There was much less shooting. Evening was imposing its calm. There was nothing visible on the rooftops; yet they felt that every windowsill, every balcony, concealed a danger, the side of every chimney was capable of being a soldier's shield and the other side that of his enemy. The sergeant and the men crawled off to explore. Two Germans remained in the hideout with the weapons and water. They were to shoot only in case of emergency. Erik and Riton went around the chimney and sat down at the foot of that cliff, with the machine gun between Riton's legs. Erik was weary. His springy blond beard softened his face, which was hollowed by fatigue. Neither of them spoke. They were coming out of their tangled sleep. Their eyes were dim, their mouths slack. The visibility was a little better from their observatory and they could see a few housefronts and windows. Opposite them, about two hundred yards away, one of the windows lit up with a faint, shifting light. A man's silhouette stood out in the rectangle. Riton aimed and then fired a burst. The silhouette moved back into the shadow. Erik's firm, imperious hand came down on Riton's.

"Don't."

Riton pulled away impatiently and his nervous finger let loose a second burst.

"Don't," Erik repeated hoarsely in a scolding but low tone. "Don't."

Erik uttered the word more calmly, more gently, he seemed

303

to be roaring from a deeper, more mysterious part of the forest. His hand remained, preventing Riton from continuing to shoot.

"Not . . . (Erik hesitated, trying to find the word) not . . . now."

Riton's hand lost its will power and Erik's became more friendly. Gently, with the other hand, the German took the machine gun and put it down at his side. He had not let go of Riton, in fact he made his hug more affectionate. He drew the kid's head to him. He kissed him.

"Up. . . ."

This single word had the curtness of an order, but Riton was already used to Erik's ways. He stood up. Leaning back against the brick monument, facing a Paris that was watching and waiting, Erik buggered Riton. Their trousers were lowered over their heels where the belt buckles clinked at each movement. The group was strengthened by leaning against the wall, by being backed up, protected by it. If the two standing males had looked at each other, the quality of the pleasure would not have been the same. Mouth to mouth, chest to chest, with their knees tangled, they would have been entwined in a rapture that would have confined them in a kind of oval that excluded all light, but the bodies in the figurehead which they formed looked into the darkness, as one looks into the future, the weak sheltered by the stronger, the four eyes staring in front of them. They were projecting the frightful ray of their love to infinity. That sharp relief of darkness against the brick surface was the griffin of a coat of arms, the sacred image on a shield behind which two other German soldiers were on the lookout. Erik and Riton were not loving one in the other, they were escaping from themselves over the world, in full view of the world, in a gesture of victory. It was thus that, from his room in Berlin or Berchtesgaden, Hitler, taking a firm stand, with his stomach striking their backs and his knees in the hollows of theirs, emitted his transfigured adolescents over the humiliated world. But Erik's fatigue was already, and more obstinately, drawing him back. He was reentering himself, was recapturing his youth, his first marriage with the executioner in the shrubbery when each of his hands, which were equally skillful in wielding the ax, unbuttoned a fly, pushed aside a shirt, took out a prick, and Erik raised his frightened eyes to those of the brute and said to him sweetly:

"Don't be angry with me if I don't do it well, but it's the first time."

Standing against a tree, the executioner made Erik face him, and he put his member between the kid's thighs. Riton's arms grabbed Erik's disheveled head and pressed the strong, famous neck, which bent forward, Erik's head finally touched the pale face, which was an utter appeal, a dying concert. Riton's arms quivered around the captured neck and enclosed it in a basket of tenderness and roses, of children's frills, of lace, and the kid's voice murmured against the ear of the half-naked warrior:

"All right now. Come in, it's time."

In passing through all his flesh, the memory of the executioner obliged Erik to greater humility toward the child. All his excitement receded. The executioner's hideous but hard face and sovereign build and stature, which he could see in his mind's eye, must be feeling freer, either the thought of them gave him greater pride in buggering Riton and caused him to beat and torture him so as to be surer of his freedom and his own strength and then take revenge for having been weak, or else he had remained humiliated by past shame and finished his job with greater movements and reached the goal in a state of brotherly anguish. Riton, surprised at the respite of love, wanted to murmur a few very mild words of reproach, but the vigor of the movements gave him the full awareness that great voluptuaries always retain in love. He said, almost sobbingly: "You won't have me! No, you won't have me!" and at the same time impaled himself with a leap.

"*Einmal.* . . ."

The whole member entered in, and Riton's behind touched Erik's warm belly. The joy of both of them was great, as was their confusion, since that joy had been attained. In the kind of swing which is in the form of a closed cage, the kind you see at county fairs, two kids pool their efforts. The cage goes up. Each oscillation acquires greater amplitude, and when the cage reaches the zenith after describing a semi-circle, it hesitates before falling in order to complete its perfect curve. For two seconds it is motionless. During that moment the kids are upside down. It is then that their faces come together and their mouths kiss and their knees get entangled. Beneath them the crowd, whose heads are inverted, looks on. Riton became even more tender. He murmured as one prays:

"Say, listen, see if you can't get it all in!"

For Erik this sentence was only a graceful song. He answered with an equally lovely sentence and in an equally hoarse tongue. And Riton:

"You're right, try."

Then suddenly Erik's body arches a little.

Only white roses could emerge from Erik's member to enter the bronze eye. They flowed out slowly with each quick but regular pulsation of the prick, as round and heavy as cigar smoke rings from pursed lips. Riton felt them rising within him by a path swifter than that of the intestines all the way up to his chest, where their fragrance spread in layers, though surprisingly it did not perfume his mouth. Now that Riton is dead, killed by a Frenchman, if one perhaps opened his chest would one find, caught in the trellis of the thorax, a few of those slightly dried roses?

Erik covered the sweating face with kisses. The perforating tool so hurt the child that he longed for an increase of pain so as to be lost in it.

"*Ich....*"

Erik's mouth was speaking, breathing on the kid's shoulder. And his back kept thrusting. His eyes, which he had kept closed, opened on those of Riton. It's banal to say: "Those eyes have beheld death." Yet such eyes do exist, and after the ghastly encounter, the gaze of the men who possess them retains an unwonted hardness and brilliance.

Erik's eyes: Erik had known the snows of Russia, the cruelty of hand-to-hand fighting, the bewilderment of being the only survivor of a company; death was familiar to his eyes. When he opened them, Riton saw their brilliance despite the darkness. Remembering all of Erik's campaigns, he also thought very quickly: "He's been face to face with death."

Erik had stopped work. His eyes kept staring; his mouth was still pressed against Riton's.

Riton murmured: "I now have the impression that I love you more than before." Erik did not understand.

No tenderness could have been expressed, for as their love was not recognized by the world, they could not feel its natural effects. Only language could have informed them that they actually loved each other. We know how they spoke to each other at the beginning. Seeing that neither understood the other and that all their phrases were useless, they finally contented themselves with grunts. This evening, for the first time in ten days, they are going to speak and to envelop their language in the most shameless passion. A happiness that was too intense made the soldier groan. With both hands clinging, one to the ear, the other to the hair, he wrenched the kid's head from the steel axis that was getting even harder.

"Stop."

Then he drew to him the mouth that pressed eagerly to his in the darkness. Riton's lips were still parted, retaining the shape and caliber of Erik's prick. The mouths crushed against each other, linked as by a hyphen, by the rod of emptiness, a rootless member that lived alone and went from one palate to the other. The evening was marvelous. The stars were calm. One imagined that the trees were alive, that France was awakening, and more intensely in the distance, above, that the Reich was watching. Riton woke up. Erik was sad. He was already thinking of faraway Germany, of the fact that his life was in danger, of how to save his skin. Riton buttoned his fly in a corner, then quietly picked up the machine gun. He fired a shot. Erik collapsed, rolled down the slope of the roof, and fell flat. The soldiers in the hideout neither heard the fall nor noticed the oddness of the shot. For ten seconds, a joyous madness was mistress of Riton. For ten seconds, he stamped on his friend's corpse. Motionless, with his back against the chimney and his eyes staring, he saw himself dancing, screaming, jumping about the body and on it and crushing it beneath his hobnailed heels. Then he quietly came to his senses and slowly made his way to other rooftops. All night long, all the morning of August 20, abandoned by his friends, by his parents, by his love, by France, by Germany, by the whole world, he fired away until he fell exhausted, not because of his wounds but with fatigue, as sweat glued desperate locks of hair to his temples. For a moment, he was so afraid of being killed that he thought of suicide. The Japanese, according to the papers, advised their soldiers to fight on even after death so that their souls could sustain and direct the living. . . . The beauty of that objurgation (which shows me a heaven bursting with a *potential* activity and full of dead men eager to shoot) impels me to make Riton utter the following words:

"Help me die."

—Translated by
Bernard Frechtmann

FRANK O'HARA

GRAND CENTRAL

The wheels are inside me thundering.
They do not churn me, they are inside.
They were not oiled, they burn
with friction and out of my eyes
comes smoke. Then the enormous bullets
streak towards me with their black tracers
and bury themselves deep in my muscles.
They won't be taken out. I can still
move. Now I am going to lie down
like an expanse of marble floor
covered with commuters and information:
it is my vocation, you believe that,
don't you? I don't have an American
body, I have an anonymous body, though
you can get to love it, if you love
the corpses of the Renaissance; I am
reconstructed from a model of poetry,
you see, and this might be a horseless
carriage, it might be but it is not,

it is riddled with bullets, am I.
And if they are not thundering into me
they are thundering across me, on
the way to some devastated island
where they will eat waffles with the
other Americans of American persuasion.
On rainy days I ache as if a train
were about to arrive, I switch my tracks.
During the noon-hour rush a friend
of mine took a letter carrier across
the catwalk underneath the dome
behind the enormous (wheels! wheels!)
windows which are the roof of the sun
and knelt inside my cathedral, mine
through pain! and the thundering went on.
He unzipped the messenger's trousers
and relieved him of his missile, hands
on the messenger's dirty buttocks,
the smoking muzzle in his soft blue mouth.
That is one way of dominating the terminal,
but I have not done that. It will be
my blood, I think, that dominates the trains.

LARRY

Watching the muddy light attack
some resemblances, you took
my letters from your drawers and said
"You were careful to me." Some look.

Outside in white trousers the night
works. A bus signals into oblivion
and is already at the boundary. If
we lower ourselves by rope down

in front over the marquee we won't
get burned by the neon and it'll be

sheer agony. The mountain kind. I wished
already some bar chirruping, aknee

with painters' molls hep to genius.
So we're great friends constant and true
to not being sure of your being sure
of my being sure of your being sure of you.

LEBANON

Perhaps he will press his warm lips
to mine in a phrase exceptionally historic,
which seemed to have lived on lips
in Galilee now that I have already felt

its sting. The sweet fetid dust
of his breath will linger upon my lips
as if my understanding were affected and a soul
of passion and arrogant surmise had my lips

for a moment and then passed through my lips
into the rendering azure of the temple.
It was coolly dawning and his lips
opened, ''I'll go with you to the other country,

no matter that my all is here,
my childhood on the plains' grapelike lips,
my father's handkerchief, my mother's tomb,
my memory of games; they go up like lips

in a stadium; all that comes from my white lips
and shall ease you on the unnecessary journey.''
And thus the day did blanch upon his lips
despite the dirty windowpanes and cold air.

He did go to the mountains and perhaps I
shall be daily upon those wooded sloping lips,
so that as he is fleetly hunting goats
my breath will find its altar in those lips.

CALAMUS

my will relaxes with the fresh green reeds
which spring arrogantly though they're not sown.
Indeed, they want no wind. They are a lake,
and bend when they wish and do not invite
the sun. They flay the air and do not break;
indifferently they disappear at night,
   and just as calmly earth's of them bereft.
   They found earth mute and passionless, and left.

HOMOSEXUALITY

So we are taking off our masks, are we, and keeping
our mouths shut? as if we'd been pierced by a glance!

The song of an old cow is not more full of judgment
than the vapors which escape one's soul when one is sick;

so I pull the shadows around me like a puff
and crinkle my eyes as if at the most exquisite moment

of a very long opera, and then we are off!
without reproach and without hope that our delicate feet

will touch the earth again, let alone "very soon."
It is the law of my own voice I shall investigate.

I start like ice, my finger to my ear, my ear
to my heart, that proud cur at the garbage can

in the rain. It's wonderful to admire oneself
with complete candor, tallying up the merits of each

of the latrines. 14th Street is drunken and credulous,
53rd tries to tremble but is too at rest. The good

love a park and the inept a railway station,
and there are the divine ones who drag themselves up

and down the lengthening shadow of an Abyssinian head
in the dust, trailing their long elegant heels of hot air

crying to confuse the brave "It's a summer day,
and I want to be wanted more than anything else in the
   world."

A WHITMAN'S
BIRTHDAY BROADCAST WITH STATIC

Pas la jeunesse à moi,
ni delicacy, ich kann nicht, ich kann nicht, keines
    Vorsprechen!
Ugly on the patio, silly on the floor, unkempt,
dans le vieux parc je m'asseois, et je ne vois pas
    à droite ni à gauche.
Personne! mais des bruits, des vagues particulières,
    und ich habe Kummer, es könnte ihm ein Schaden
    zustossen, lacht der Kundschafter.
And then someone comes along who's sick and I say
    "Tiens, ça! c'est las de l'amour, c'est okay!"
    and fall.
Da, ich bin der Komponist, und ich bin komponiert.

██

LONNIE COLEMAN

THE THEBAN WARRIORS

██

The night Montgomery came aboard we were in Norfolk, Virginia, about to sail for North Africa. Starboard watch had liberty. I was port, so I was sitting around third division quarters with some of the other guys chewing the fat. There were four or five of us, and I don't remember what we were talking about. Whatever it was, we forgot it when Montgomery showed up. He clattered down the ladder with his sea bag, shouting, "Where are third division bunks?" We looked around at him. He was a big, good-looking boy with his hat pushed back on his head.

I answered. "This is third division."

He looked at me and smiled. "Thank you. Now, would you be a dear and help me with my bag? Your mother's all tired out. Such a time I had finding the ship, I thought I'd never—" I helped him get the sea bag to the deck.

"What you got in here, Mac? It's like lead."

"You're not far wrong. I take a few things around with me to keep in trim. One mustn't let down. Such a temptation in wartime, don't you think? Is there an empty bunk?"

I pointed to the only one reluctantly, for it was above mine.

"Thank you. Will we be neighbors?"

314

I nodded. He looked around at the others. "Cat got your tongues? All of you in third division? We'd better get acquainted. My name is William Montgomery, and I'm a bosun second."

"I'm Barney Casper," I said, and we shook hands. He had a strong grip, and he didn't seem to be putting it on.

I told him the names of the others, who were still too surprised to say anything, and they shook hands all around. They looked relieved after shaking hands. Whether his grip relieved their minds or whether just touching him made them believe he was real, I don't know, but everybody relaxed some.

Montgomery smiled. "Good, now we all know one another. It's so important to start off right. Mother says a first impression is seldom erased. Or maybe she says never. She talks such a lot, I can't always quote her precisely. Like a canary bird, chatter, chatter, chatter. I tell her it's no wonder four husbands left her, but she says never mind, it's easy to get another when you're in the theater. And didn't she ever laugh when I told her I had been assigned to the *Nellie Crocker*. She said, 'Monty, my dear, don't you ever in future let me hear you say the Navy doesn't know what it's doing!' Such a wit, mother. Now I don't suppose any of you has a bit of gin in his locker?" He sailed his hat onto his bunk, sat down beside me and unfastened his pea jacket. "That's just coffee in those?" He referred to the mugs we held in our hands. "How cosy you all look sitting there with your thick hands around those thick mugs—what fun we'll have! I can see it now—sitting around in the evenings drinking joe, or do you call it java here? Telling tales of dare-and-do, chanting sea chanties. What a lot I shall have to remember in my old age. Tell me, do any of you dance?" Noting the startled looks on our faces he went on with a laugh. "I don't mean together, of course. Unless you do. If you do, speak right up and say so; I always think it's best to be frank with one another. Surprise can be so disturbing. I meant dancing like in a show. I wondered if there were any entertainment on board, if we might get up a little show now and then to amuse ourselves. I don't do anything much. I sing a bit, though I'll never be professional, mother says. I don't care in the least, for that isn't the life for little old me. I prefer something more rugged. Powder and rouge are all very well in their place, but I mean, they make you feel like such a belle, don't you agree?"

The young freckled sailor named Walters stared at Montgomery with his mouth open.

Montgomery sighed. "Sports are more my field. I love to box. Anybody box aboard? Isn't that funny, alliterative you know, *b-b-b*, to say nothing of the *d's*."

"When we're at sea or in foreign ports," I said, "we have boxing matches every Sunday."

"Thank you. You seem to be the spokesman for the group. Do you yourself box?"

"No."

"I'll teach you if you like. You ought to be good. You're big. You look like you've got the muscle. What's the matter, are you slow on your feet?"

"I can't think quick enough to know what the other fellow's going to do next."

"Oh, it isn't a matter of thinking. Look at the professionals. Oafs. Couldn't box a hedge if it took brains, not a one of them. Let me teach you."

"We'll see."

Sellers had been quiet all this time, but he seemed finally to have made up his mind how things stood. He said with a fishy smile and in a mincing voice, "You can teach me how to box, Monty-dear!"

Montgomery placed his hands on his thighs and leaned forward, shaking his head. "This moment always comes when I meet new people," he said to me, or anyway in my direction. Then looking at Sellers: "We'd better get this straight right off. I don't like ugly little men who snicker. You are ugly and little, and you snicker. God knows, I would be loath to touch you even in punishment, but I warn you, I make the jokes about myself. I hope you understand. Now perhaps you'd like to rephrase your request?"

Sellers flushed and looked at me. I simply looked back at him, neither supporting nor deserting. He looked at the others who, one by one, decided to play it cautious.

"Good," Montgomery said after a pause. "That's all settled. Now tell me about things. What's the captain like?"

"He's a good guy," Walters, the youngest sailor, said. "He's strict, but only about things that count. He ain't chicken."

Montgomery looked pleased. "Charming."

"The exec's the tough one," Walters went on.

"So often the case," Montgomery said. "What about the division officer? What's his name?"

"Ensign Mason," I said.

"First name?"

"Wes. Wesley, I think."

"Wesley Mason," he repeated. "He sounds terribly earnest. Is he?"

"He's the best division officer on the ship," Walters said. "All the fellows like him."

"Is he terribly butch?" Montgomery asked, and when he was again met with blank looks, expanded: "You know, rough, rugged—oh hell, where have you been all your lives? Don't people talk where you come from? I can see I'll have to teach a language course around here, so I won't have to translate every remark I make. Now let's see what we have. A good captain, a tough executive officer—both in the grand tradition. And a division officer who is popular with his men. What a spot to be in. Now the really important question. How's the chief?"

"He makes you work," I said.

"Good. I don't approve of slackness in a chief. How does he make you work? Does he curse, is he mean, or does he just tell you what to do and leave you to do it?"

"He tells you what to do," I said, "and he leaves you to do it, but if he comes back and finds you haven't done it, he's likely to curse a little, and he's been known to get mean."

"You know," he said, "you're not only nice, but you have wit and intelligence too. Are you married?"

"Look—"

"Are you?"

"No, but—"

317

"You've got a girl."

"Sure."

"The way you say it, I don't believe you. At least not an important one, I'll bet. You sound more and more intelligent." He slid out of his bunk. "Where's the head? I want to take a shower. Is the water on?"

"Water's almost always on, and the head's aft and star-board."

He began to undress, and we watched him silently. I'd seen a lot of guys undress in my time and never noticed them, but somehow the way Montgomery did it, he made you curious so that you had to notice. He was showing himself off like one of those women who strip in night clubs. Not that obvious maybe, but as though it were some kind of act. He was conscious of himself, never relaxed. He didn't look uncomfortable, I don't mean that. In fact, he smiled, as though at himself and us too. He was well built, with a flat belly, big muscular thighs, and a good back and good arms. The black hair started at the bottom of his neck and went down to his toenails. While he was undressing, we didn't say much. He had been talking such a streak himself that when he stopped, nobody seemed to find anything on his mind. And the way I said, we couldn't help looking at Montgomery. As he reached into his sea bag for a towel, he said with a laugh, "I don't know when I've had such a good audience. Thank you, lads. You've made me feel right at home." He slung the towel over his shoulder and went off humming.

Contrary to what all of us expected, Montgomery got along fine. Everybody in the division heard about him right off, and within a day everybody on the ship must have known about him. He seemed to enjoy causing a stir, and didn't change his way of talking much, no matter where he was. If people froze, he just kept talking, but made out like it was a joke and that he was innocent of the impression he caused. We'd come up to muster every morning after we got to sea, with nothing facing us but a long day's work and a night with a watch in it somewhere, and there Montgomery would be with his hands on his hips. "What shall it be today, girls? Let's get out the car-riage and horses, put on our red dresses and high-heeled shoes, carry our sauciest parasols, and drive right by the Methodist Church like we're good as anybody!"

The thing was, Montgomery looked too much a man for anybody to take offense out loud. Some of the boys talked to one another privately, and some made fun of him behind his back, which he knew and which I don't think bothered him, but nobody came right out and said anything to his face. It got to where he was pretty well liked, or anyway, people were glad he made some kind of joke they could laugh at. I think the fact that he never tried anything made everybody believe his talk was all put on. Even the chief smiled now and then, and only once in a while, when he had something big on his mind, he'd say, "Hell, Montgomery, knock it off, so I can think."

Montgomery never shirked when there was work to be done, and sometimes his joking made the work seem easier. When a working party was called at night, he'd slide out of his bunk without a whimper, saying one time, "La, dears, I feel like a call girl."

Every afternoon after work he had a sun bath and some exercise. He did this in the gun tubs aft, out of sight of the midships house. We weren't supposed to be on deck with any of our clothes off when we were at sea, because of the possibility of attack. Montgomery worked out in regular boxer's trunks, and he had a set of dumbbells he varied the weights on. He invited me to work out with him several times, but I never took him up on it, although some of the others were eager enough. He never asked them though. They'd stand around looking at him, counting off for him. He'd smile at them once in a while or maybe say something funny, but most of the time he acted like he was off by himself.

The first Sunday we were at sea, he boxed. There had been considerable speculation up to this time about whether he just happened to be built well or whether he actually had any strength behind him. Well, we found out. He took on our best boxer for three rounds, and when he got in the ring, he didn't kid. I think it was the first time any of us had seen him without a smile on his face. Kelly, the man he was fighting, was heavier than he was and had the backing of the whole ship. You could tell that from the way the men yelled and carried on. It took Montgomery about one minute to learn everything about Kelly though: where he was weak, where he was strong, how good his breath was going to be, how quick his fists and his feet were. Montgomery fought with a serious look on his face, so most of the boys watching thought he was scared. One or two of them got brave and called out, "Kill the fairy, Kelly!" By that time Kelly probably knew he wasn't going to do anything worth watching, so he tried to make himself look good. He acted like he was mad and tried a few hard punches that looked all right and raised the boys' spirits some but didn't much more than touch Montgomery. Montgomery looked solemn for the whole first round, like he didn't even hear what the boys were yelling. When he came out for the second round, he went after Kelly. He knocked him to the mat for a slow count of seven in the first thirty seconds, and the crowd got quiet. Then he let up until just before the bell ending the second round, when he knocked him to the mat again. Kelly stayed there even after the bell rang. In the third and last round Kelly was too groggy to care what he was doing, knowing that Montgomery could have taken him any time he wanted to. The crowd didn't know anything about boxing, but they could have learned from watching Montgomery. It was as pretty a demonstration match as you'd want to see. He didn't hurt Kelly. He just made him look like a damn fool.

That stupid crowd, when they finally saw what was happening, started yelling for Kelly's hide, like they'd been rooting for Montgomery all along. Montgomery didn't pay any attention to them at all until the bout was over. Then, when the referee held up one of his hands, he cupped his crotch with the other hand and smiled at them like he knew they were crud.

After the match a lot of the guys crowded around him and followed him down to the compartment, where he started to undress to take a shower. They yelled the usual things and slapped him on the back, those who could get close enough to touch him. People always want to touch athletes after they've won, as if doing so gives them luck or lets them share in the victory. But Montgomery just went about his business. I'm a boxing fan, and I was excited about how good he was, so I stuck around when the others drifted away. He looked at me as he toweled himself down. "What do you say, Barney, was I all right?"

"You were four-o," I said, meaning perfect.

He wrinkled his face. "I was showing off. I shouldn't have. Now nobody will want to box me, and I won't have any fun."

"You'll have fun all right," I said, remembering how he had looked and how cool he had kept in the ring. "All the guys would like to work out with you; you can get a sparring mate any time you want to. That is, if you promise not to hurt them."

He blinked. "That isn't the question. The little dirty-drawers idiots can always be had for the nudging. I'm more particular." He smiled again. "I'm saving myself. I always get what I want, too."

"Good. Swell," I said uncertainly, thinking for the first time he might be talking about something else.

He looked at me steadily, draping the towel over his shoulders. "You know what I mean. Don't play dumb."

"I don't get you," I said honestly.

"I'm dead serious. I may joke, because unless I do it's all too tedious—"

"I don't know what you mean," I said, beginning to understand.

He saw my understanding. "I mean I've got my eye on you, and I'll get you sooner or later."

"Sure," I said, trying to make a joke of it. "You'll get me. Right flat on my ass on the mat, like you did Kelly today." Suddenly we were both blushing.

"Tell me about yourself, Barney. Where did you come from?"

"My old man's a cop in Baltimore. I worked on a Coca-Cola truck a couple of years after I finished high school. Then the call to the colors."

He shrugged. "It doesn't explain anything, does it? It seldom does. You know the score in all kinds of ways, but nothing in your background points to why. You could have got every bit of education you have from a cereal-box top."

"Now wait a minute," I laughed, glad to be on a safe topic.

"I studied civics and hygiene and American history. I learned to scan *Lady of the Lake* and memorized speeches from *Julius Caesar* just like everybody else."

"That isn't how you got your charm."

"You know," I said finally, "I've busted guys for saying less than you've said to me."

"Why don't you try busting me?"

"You're bigger than I am," I laughed.

"That isn't the reason." I started to go. He put his hand on my arm, not holding me, but making me pause. "I have to laugh when I hear you straight guys talk about beating up fairies. You'd be surprised how few get beat up. It's usually the plain janes no self-respecting faggot would look at twice who're always talking about what they'd do if anybody tried to lay a hand on them. Let's face it, Barney, the world of straight men is a fraud. They can all be had if anybody wants them enough to work things the right way. And wait his chance. Like I'm waiting my chance with you."

I shook his hand away. "Don't wait too long, Monty."

He laughed. "You see, you like me. You're calling me Monty already."

"I'm calling you Monty because in spite of pretending to be queer as a three-dollar bill, you're a nice guy basically."

"You don't know how nice I can be."

"Oh, hell, you're impossible."

"I'm the most possible thing you ever met up with."

"Look, Montgomery, don't make me mad. It's all right to kid the others but—"

"I kid them because they bore me, and because it's an easy way to insult them."

"So kid me too if you like, the way you've just been doing. But if I thought for a minute—"

He wasn't smiling at all. "There's no hurry. I can wait. When I get you, it's going to be for good, and nobody's going to pretend afterwards that nothing happened. When it happens, we'll both want it to happen. Understand?"

"Why me?"

"The ones I've liked come in all shapes and sizes, blonde and brunette and redhead, skinny and strong. But there's one thing they have in common that makes them stand out from everybody else around. They're men, not babies.''

"Thanks," I said as sarcastically as I could manage. "What a crazy bastard you are, Montgomery!"

He scratched his thigh absently and smiled. I was suddenly aware of his nakedness, even though he had taken off his boxing trunks a long time ago and had used the towel for nothing more than to dry himself. "When you want to hear some more of my crazy talk, let me know!"

My embarrassment made me lose my temper again. "Any time you say, Monty old boy, because I want you to know one thing—I'm not afraid of you!"

"Tonight at ten-thirty by the incinerator on the fantail," he said quickly.

I walked away calling over my shoulder, "Go take a cold shower."

The trouble was, I couldn't forget the things he said. The more I thought about them, the madder I got, and I wondered why I hadn't told him to go to hell. One reason, I guess he was impossible to tell to go to hell. He could talk as well as he could box. When somebody's doing something you don't like, you can beat hell out of them, outtalk them, or walk away. I stood no chance of beating Montgomery. I couldn't outtalk him. And I hadn't walked away. I thought of things I should have said. I realized I should have told him all about my girl back in Baltimore. She's a pretty thing, and smart too. Sometimes I think she's smarter than I am, though no better educated. We both finished high school and went to work right afterwards. She doesn't let anyone outsmart her, whether in talk or deeds. Next time he got going, I'd tell him about Doris. Just thinking about her made me feel better. We were going to get married in a year or two, as soon as we'd saved something and it began to look like I might live through the war. Or maybe the war would be over.

Since it was Sunday, I didn't have much to do until midnight. Then I was to have the bosun watch on the bridge. I kept away from Monty. I was careful not to eat at the same table with him or sit near him later when they showed the movie. The movie was over before ten o'clock, and I went back to the compartment to write a letter to Doris. I got out her last one, the one I'd had just before we left Norfolk, and read it over. It was all about this girl friend of hers that worked in the blanket department of the same big store, Price and Sons, that Doris worked in. Doris was in kitchenware. This girl was getting married to a marine, and the other girls had given her a big shower. Doris wrote about the shower and all the presents, and what they'd served. She said she'd almost got tipsy. I had to smile reading that again, because Doris never drank more than a couple of beers, or one drink of regular liquor, or a little wine maybe over an entire evening, so I knew she was kidding.

Reading her letter made me feel good, but all of a sudden Montgomery was on my mind. I thought: I'll show the bastard I'm not nervous about him. I looked around the compartment. He wasn't there. "What time is it?" I asked Sellers, who was sitting on an upturned bucket on the deck writing a letter to somebody.

"Nearly ten-thirty. You got the midwatch?"

"Yes." I dropped my writing board, swung out of my bunk, and went topside.

Sure enough, he was leaning on the rail by the incinerator. I felt damn good about coming out to meet him, because I felt stronger than him, and in my mind I was daring him to say anything wise. He didn't seem surprised at seeing me at all, not surprised nor glad nor sorry.

He said, "Hello, Barney."

I didn't know what to say. I mumbled something about its being hot below deck.

He said, "Well, we're getting a little farther south every hour."

"Yeah."

I leaned on the rail alongside him. I kept expecting him to say something so I'd know what he was thinking, but damned if he didn't just look down at the water and the foam made by the propellers and not say a word for a long time.

I was about to make a crack like, "Well, here I am, you smart bastard, what are you going to do about it? You see I'm not scared of seeing you by yourself," when he said, "It's such a nice night. I almost wish I had a watch."

"Oh yeah?" Somehow that made me mad. "Well, I got one at midnight, and if you're so keen to stay up and watch the stars and the sea floating by, you can take mine," I said. "If you want to. Don't let me deprive you of any pleasures."

His head jerked around. "What's the matter, Barney?"

"Nothing's the matter," I said. "I just said if you want to stay up the whole god damn night, then you might as well take my watch and do so, that's all I said."

"You want me to take your watch?" he asked slowly.

"No! I didn't say that. I just said that if—"

"I'll take your watch if you're tired, and you can take one of mine some time. I don't mind."

I don't know why, but I got more excited. "I'm not asking you to do a god damn thing for me, not a *god damn* thing. If I had—oh hell, you're all tired out from your big boxing match. You're lucky not to have a watch."

"Barney, something's the matter," he said, innocent as you please. "Have I done anything wrong? Has anybody else done something or said something to hurt you?"

"I never asked you any favors, did I?" I shouted. "Did I?" He shook his head. "If anybody asked you did I ask you any favors, you'd say no, wouldn't you, isn't that right?"

"Barney, what the hell—"

I backed away from him. "Just keep away from me. Keep away from me, understand?"

I went below and crawled into my bunk to try to rest until time to go on watch. I didn't feel like writing a letter to Doris, but I thought about her. Usually when I thought about her I remembered the times we talked or danced, or the plans we had, the way her face looked, and her hair and eyes. Sometimes about kissing her, but we'd never gone much further than that. Now I thought of her naked, and I was shocked at myself and excited. I thought of her breasts, but I didn't know what they looked like, so I just thought about breasts. Doris used to let me feel them, but only in the dark, and I'd never seen them. Now I tried to think what they would look like, and what her body would look like. It was very important to know. I was horny for her for the first time I'd known her.

It seemed no time at all before somebody touched my shoulder and said, "It's time to go on watch, Barney." It was Montgomery, and he was looking at me seriously.

"You feel all right?"

I swung out of the bunk. "You got the messenger watch, haven't you, Walters?" I said. He nodded. "Come on, let's get up there."

All during watch I felt horny as a bull, and I made up my mind that first liberty in Algiers I was heading straight for the Sphinx Club. When the watch was over and I crawled in my bunk to go to sleep, Montgomery's arm had slipped over the side of his bunk while he was sleeping.

Next day after I'd had noon chow I was in the gun tub aft taking a sun bath. I kept my dungarees on but had my shirt off and was lying on deck face down when I heard somebody flop down beside me. I didn't turn my head or open my eyes, but I knew it was Montgomery, and I was glad. "That you, Montgomery?" I said, calm and easy.

He seemed to be himself again. "You're getting a nice tan on your upper body," he said, "but you ought to get it all over. You never know who'll see you all over."

"Yes, I do," I answered, still easy and calm.

His "Who?" was surprised and expectant, I thought.

"Rina," I said.

"Rina? Such a name, like a burlesque queen."

"Rina's a well-stacked piece in the Sphinx Club in Algiers, and that's where I'm heading the first liberty I get."

"All right, I'll go with you."

My eyes snapped open, and I raised up to look at him. He was the one who was calm and easy now, lying on his back with sun glasses on and his boxing trunks pulled tight to his body. "You don't understand, Monty old fellow," I said. "This isn't your kind of thing at all. This Sphinx Club is a house where they keep a lot of little pussy cats."

"I know what it is," he said, "and I'm coming with you."

"I don't want you to."

"Afraid?"

"Come on, I don't give a damn. I just don't see why."

"I like to keep posted on what the competition has to offer," he said. "But that isn't the real reason I'm coming. I want to be there when you change your mind. I know those cold little bitches with their ooh-la-las and pretense of passion. They couldn't fool a gorilla. If you think that's going to satisfy you, you've got something to learn. I want to be there when you learn, Barney."

"I know what it's like, and it's damn good, don't try to tell me! They make me feel like a man, not like a—"

"What, Barney?" he said, and I could feel him looking at me through the dark glasses. The sun had reddened the tips of dark hair on his chest.

We were in different watches, but Montgomery fixed things so we left the ship together on the first liberty when we hit Algiers. It was hot as hell, and we didn't talk much as we headed for the Casbah. I saw some leather pocketbooks and thought about getting one for Doris, then decided I couldn't take it with me where I was going. There was a bar with tables on the sidewalk facing the park just where the Casbah begins, and we stopped for a couple of vermouths. "You're really going through with it," I said.

"Varieties of religious experience." He finished off his wine. "Let's go."

We knocked at the door at the end of the little alley and were let in by a quiet, hard-faced old woman. Montgomery smiled. "Enchanting. The perfect porter for the house of sin." He pushed his cap back on his head. The old woman led us through the entrance room with its copy of the Sphinx that gave the place its name. It had the face of a young girl and big, tinted breasts. The next room had a lot of chairs and sofas in it. There were a couple of sailors sitting there with girls on their laps. They looked around at us. The girls smiled, and one of them called something over her shoulder in French. This was the part of coming to the place I hated, the preliminaries. I looked at Montgomery, who was taking in the room with a smile on his face that wasn't exactly a smile, though he seemed relaxed enough.

"It's a lovely place," he said. "Puts you right in the mood

for love, even if you weren't already, don't you agree? That darling sofa, a bit worn and not too clean, but who cares? Those nice muddy-rose walls, how divinely appropriate, the telling feminine touch. And over all the aura, the essence, the very smell of sin. They'd better bring out the girls before I attack you."

A door opened behind us and two girls entered. One was blonde, and the other was brunette. They wore short dresses with nothing underneath, and they had on a lot of rouge and lipstick and eye make-up. The blonde was Rina, and she remembered me. She came over with her arms open and a big smile on her face that made her look older. "*Chéri,* you have come back!"

"Hello, Rina," I said. "Yes, I'm back, and I brought a friend along this time." I hugged her and avoided her lips. She smelled a little like the disinfectant in a men's room.

Rina drew away from me to look at Montgomery. "He is very nice, your friend. Handsome," she said mockingly. "My lucky friend!" She pulled the brunette forward. "Marjane," she introduced.

Montgomery stepped toward her, smiling. "William. Willy."

"Willi!" the brunette squealed. She patted his chest. "Nice! Handsome! Rich! The Virgin smiles on me today!"

"There's nothing like being smiled on by a virgin," Montgomery laughed, putting his arms around Marjane, pulling her to him hard and kissing her full on the lips.

Rina looked at me swiftly and laughed. "He is—hot!" She nodded her head rapidly, raising her black penciled eyebrows. I sat on the sofa and pulled her down on my lap. She squealed as I unbuttoned the top of her dress. Montgomery had raised Marjane's dress until it was gathered about her waist, leaving her naked from there down. He had his hands on her behind, and she was giggling and slapping his hands.

Rina said, "Don't look at them, look at me, *chéri*! I excite you, *chéri*!"

The two girls had adjoining rooms upstairs, and we all rode together on the small slow elevator with the wrinkled old woman who had let us in. When the elevator stopped, the girls went ahead of us while we paid the old woman, who explained what I already knew, that we were to pay the girls the same we paid her, or more if we desired.

"Willi!" Marjane called.

"Barney!" Rina called.

"Isn't it all too thrilling?" Montgomery said to me as we went toward them. "The real thing, no counterfeit here."

Marjane grabbed Montgomery by the hand, bit his thumb, and pulled him into her room. I followed Rina.

After a while she drew away from me. "First time today for me," she bragged. "What is wrong, you don't want love?"

"Love?" I said.

"Love, this is love!" she exclaimed. "I am love, *chéri!*" She smiled patiently. "Tell Rina what is wrong."

"Nothing's wrong."

"You listen to them all the time you lie with me. They laugh. Come! We have good time like Willi—" She took my head in her hands to kiss me. I was about to kiss her when I heard Montgomery laugh again. I drew away. Rina shrugged and relaxed on the bed. I got up, found a cigarette in my jumper and lit it. In the next room I could hear Marjane grunting like a hog. Rina looked at the wall and began to laugh.

"Shut up," I said.

"Give me a cigarette."

I threw the pack on the bed beside her. She fished one out and put it between her lips. She was staring at me as I held the match for her. "*Chéri,* you love this Willi?"

I went cold all over. I put out my cigarette on the floor, took hers out of her mouth and put it out too. Then I jumped at her.

I waited for Montgomery on the sidewalk in front of the house. When he came out, he didn't smile, he didn't frown. He just looked at me like he knew everything there was to know about me. He lit a cigarette, cupping his hand around the match out of habit, although there was no wind in the alley. When he blew the match out, he watched it until it stopped smoking before he dropped it. He said, "Where would you like to go, *chéri?*"

I turned away and walked quickly down the alley. He came after me whistling, caught up and walked in step with me, not saying anything. I wouldn't look at him. I walked across the street into the park and down one of the paths. When I sat down on a bench, he sat down beside me. He was still whistling. Finally I looked at him. His face was relaxed. I studied his face and then his neck, and then I let my eyes follow all the way down his body. I knew just what he looked like under the white jumper and white pants, I remember thinking that. I said, "You certainly stayed with her a long time!" He turned and looked at me. He looked at my face the way I had looked at his, and then his eyes followed down my body. "Why don't you say something? What are you thinking?"

"I am thinking," he said slowly, "what an ugly thing a woman's body is, and what a beautiful thing a man's is."

"That's funny," I said. "That certainly is funny, considering the way you were going on with that French whore."

"I was being kind," he said. "She knows she's ugly, and I thought it would be nice to make her feel for a little while that she wasn't."

"Big-hearted Monty."

He shrugged.

"How many times were you kind to her?"

"Just once," he said softly.

"I guess you talked to her afterwards."

"A little."

I lit a cigarette very carefully because my hands were shaking. When it was going I said, "Did you talk to Rina too?"

"She knocked on the door when she heard us talking, and Marjane let her in. It's a friendly, informal place."

"What did she say about me?" I demanded.

After a slight hesitation he said evenly, "She and Marjane made fun of you. She told Marjane that you had been listening to us and that you couldn't do anything until you got mad. She said she thought you were queer for me."

"She's a god damn—"

"I told them, although I don't know why it should matter to you what they think, I told them you were straight as dye. I told them it was I who wanted you."

My laugh sounded ugly. "What did they say to that?"

"They didn't believe me."

"I guess the three of you had a good laugh about it. Did you kiss Rina too?"

"Oh hell, Barney."

"Well, did you?"

He didn't say anything for a long time, and when he did, it wasn't an answer to my question. "Are you ready, Barney?"

"Ready?"

"I think you are. I have to know, though. I have to be certain. Don't you understand yet what I was doing? I was showing you how empty that is, showing you it isn't what you want. I know what's in you, and I know it isn't going to be satisfied with a whore shrieking ooh-la-la. You want somebody to touch you with love. If things had happened differently, it might have been your Doris. But they didn't happen that way. She's there, I'm here, and I'm going to have you. When the war's over, you can go back to her if you want to. But I don't think you'll want to. Why didn't she let you make love to her when you were with her? Don't you know that most women hate men and use their sex to insult them and dominate them? I'm offering you something better than that, you damned fool. I'm offering you myself, and I'm promising you that I'll take you and hold you and keep you as long as—such promises last. I love you, Barney."

It was that that made me cry. My mouth was open, and I was biting my knuckles, and I couldn't see for the tears.

"Barney, this is what we're going to do. I found out about a place a few blocks from here. It's a sort of hotel where we can rent a room for a few hours, and they don't ask any questions about why two sailors want to rent it. We can take a bath, get clean again, and then we can be together until it's time to go back to the ship. Wouldn't you like that?"

It was a long time before I could answer. "I guess I'd like a bath."

He stood up.

"Are you sure this place is safe?" I said.

"Come on."

GIORGIO BASSANI

DR. FADIGATI

That summer, like the one before it, we went on holiday to Riccione, on the nearby Adriatic coast. Every year we did the same. My father had tried vainly to drag us up into the Dolomites, to places he had been to in the war, but in the end he had resigned himself to returning to Riccione, and renting the same small house beside the Grand Hotel. I remember it all very well: myself, my mother, and Fanny, my little sister, going to Riccione on August 10th, with the maid. (Ernesto, my brother, had been in England since the middle of July, living *au pair* with a family in Bath to practise the language.) As for my father, he stayed in town, and was to join us later, as soon as he could get away from his rural labours at Masi Torello.

The very day I arrived I heard at once about Fadigati and Deliliers. On the beach, which even then was crammed with families on holiday from Ferrara, people were talking of nothing but the pair of them and their scandalous "friendship".

Since the beginning of August they had been seen going from one hotel to another in various seaside towns scattered between Porto Corsini and the Punta di Pesaro. The first time they appeared was at Milano Marittima; from there they went on to the canal port of Cervia, and took a fine room at the Mare e Pineta Hotel. After a week they went on to Cesenatico, at the Britannia Hotel. And then gradually, everywhere they went arousing an enormous amount of noise and gossip, they went to Viserba, to Riccione itself, to Rimini and to Cattolica. They were making the journey by car: a red Alfa Romeo 1750 two-seater, very sporty looking.

Around August 20th they turned up unexpectedly at Riccione, staying at the Grand Hotel as they had done ten days before.

The car was brand new and its motor gave out a kind of snarl. Apart from travelling in it, the two friends went driving in it every afternoon, just at sunset when most bathers left the beach to stroll along the front. Deliliers always drove, fair and sunburnt and dazzlingly handsome in his tight shirts and cream woollen trousers (on the hands that lay negligently on the driving wheel, he wore unimaginably expensive-looking leather gloves), and obviously the car was entirely at the disposal of his every whim. Dr. Athos Fadigati, the well-known professional man from Ferrara, who for the occasion wore a flat tartan beret and a pair of mechanic's goggles, as if he was a substitute driver (goggles he never removed, even if the car had to crawl at walking pace along the road in front of the café Zanarini), merely rode up and down, stuck in the seat beside his companion.

They still slept in the same room, and ate at the same table. In the evenings, too, they sat at the same little table when the Grand Hotel orchestra, having carried its instruments from the dining-room down to the outside terrace, exposed to the sea breezes, changed abruptly from light music to jazz. The terrace soon filled up (I often went myself with new friends I had made at the seaside), and Deliliers never missed a tango or a waltz, a quickstep or a slow foxtrot. Fadigati never danced, of course. Every now and then he pressed to his lips the little stick he had taken out of his drink, and his round eyes never ceased watching, over the rim of the glass, Deliliers's perfect movements as he danced at a distance with young girls or with the smartest and most expensive-looking women. As soon as they returned from their drive, they both went punctually to put on evening dress; Fadigati's was grave and heavy and black, Deliliers wore a natty white jacket, short on the hips.

They went on the beach together too—although in the morning it was usually Fadigati who left the hotel first.

He arrived before nine o'clock, when there was still nobody about, greeted respectfully by the bathing hut assistants, whom (people said) he always tipped generously. He was dressed from head to foot in normal city clothes (only later, when it grew hotter, he left off his tie and shoes, but the white panama hat with its brim lowered over his glasses he never took off at all), and went to sit down under the solitary umbrella which he had ordered to be set farther ahead than the rest, only a few yards from the sea. Stretched out in a chaise-lounge, his hands crossed behind his neck and a detective story open on his knees, he remained for a good two hours, doing nothing and looking at the sea.

Deliliers would come along at about eleven o'clock. With his lazy, animal walk, which the slight difficulty of walking in his wooden beach shoes made even more elegant, he would cross the space of burning sand between the bathing huts and the tents unhurriedly, almost naked. The white trunks which he was still tying at his left hip, the gold chain he wore round his neck, from which a medal of the Madonna hung just above his thorax, somehow accentuated his nakedness. And although, especially during the first days, he found it something of an effort to greet even me, when he saw me there beside our tent; although, as he made his way through the spaces between the tents and umbrellas he never failed to wrinkle his forehead with annoyance; yet it was hard to believe him, for it was obvious that he felt most people there, men as well as women, in their hearts admired him, and this he enjoyed a great deal.

Everyone admired him, men and women, there was no doubt about it at all. But Fadigati had to make up for the indulgence which Deliliers was shown on the beach at Riccione by people from Ferrara.

In the tent next to us that year was Signora Lavezzoli, wife of the lawyer. Today she seems nothing but an old woman and has lost much of her old importance. But then, in the mature

splendour of her forty years, surrounded by the perpetual
deference of her three adolescent children, two boys and a girl,
and the no less perpetual deference of her worthy husband,
the distinguished expert in civil law, a university don and an
ex-deputy, well, in those days she could be considered one of
those who most authoritatively inspired public opinion in
our town.

Pointing her eyeglasses at the umbrella Deliliers made for,
Signora Lavezzoli, who was born and had grown up at Pisa,
"on the banks of the Arno", and used her quick Tuscan
speech with extraordinary dexterity, kept us continually
informed of all that was happening over there.

With the tone of voice and almost the technique of a radio
sports commentator, she would tell us how, say, the couple had
got up and were now going to the nearest raft: obviously Deliliers had expressed a wish to go bathing and the "old man",
so as not to wait "palpitating" under the umbrella, had got
permission to go with him. Or else she would describe Deliliers's gymnastics after bathing to dry himself off in the sun,
while the "beloved" stood there doing nothing with a sponge
towel in his hand, so anxious to dry him and touch him, she'd
swear.

Oh, that Deliliers—she would then comment from her tent to
ours, though addressing my mother in particular: believing
she had lowered her voice, perhaps, so as not to let the children hear, but in fact talking louder than ever—that Deliliers
was nothing but a spoilt boy, a lout that military service would
do a great deal of good. But Dr. Fadigati, no. A man of his
class, of his age, was in no way excusable. Well, so he had special tastes? He was "like that"? What of it! No one had ever
made a fuss of it before. But to come and make an exhibition
of himself here at Riccione, where of course he knew people
would know him; to come and make a spectacle of himself
here, while everywhere in Italy there were thousands of
beaches where there would be absolutely no danger of meeting
a single person from Ferrara! No, really: only someone really
filthy (and as she said this Signora Lavezzoli's big blue eyes
would shoot great flames of authentic indignation) only a
"real degenerate"—she went on—would do a thing like that.

Signora Lavezzoli went on talking, and I would have given a
great deal to shut her up once and for all. I felt she was
unjust. I didn't like Fadigati, of course, but it wasn't he who
seemed offensive. I knew Deliliers's character perfectly well.
In choosing this beach so near to Ferrara, he had shown all
his beastliness, all his lack of restraint. Fadigati had had
nothing to do with it, I was sure. My feeling was, he felt
ashamed. If he didn't greet me, if he even pretended not to
recognize me, that must be why.

Unlike Lavezzoli, who had been at the sea since the beginning of August and so like everyone else knew all about the
scandal (though while his wife held court all he did was read
Anthony Adverse in his tent; I never even heard him speak),
my father arrived at Riccione only on the morning of the 25th,
a Saturday: even later than he had expected to be, and not
knowing a thing, of course. He came by train without warning,
and not finding a soul at home, even the cook, came down to
the beach at once.

He noticed Fadigati almost at once. And before my mother
or the Lavezzolis could stop him he went gaily across to him.

"Just look who's here!" he cried, striding up to the doctor's big umbrella.

Fadigati jerked round. My father was already holding out
his hand, and Fadigati tried to pull himself up out of his
chaise-longue.

At last he managed to. After which, for at least five minutes,
we saw them standing under the big umbrella, talking with
their backs to us.

Both of them were gazing at the motionless strip of sea,
smooth, palely luminous, completely unruffled. And my father,
whose whole person expressed the joy of having "shut up
shop" (this was how he put it at Riccione when he wanted to
refer to all the unpleasant things he had left in town: business, the empty house, the heat of summer, melancholy lunches
at the *Roveraro,* mosquitoes, etc.), raised his arm and pointed
out to Fadigati the hundreds of rafts scattered at odd distances along the shore, and, a long way off, scarcely visible on
the horizon and as if suspended in mid-air, the rust-coloured
sails of small fishing boats. At last they came toward our tent,

Fadigati about a yard in front of my father with a strange expression on his face, at once imploring, disgusted, and guilty. It must have been eleven o'clock; Deliliers had not yet appeared. As I got up to meet them, I noticed the doctor glanced anxiously at the line of bathing huts, from where, at any minute, he hoped or feared to see his friend emerge.

He kissed my mother's hand.

"You do know Signor Lavezzoli, don't you?" my father said loudly, right away. Fadigati hesitated a moment. He looked at my father, and nodded; then turned, obviously on tenterhooks, towards the Lavezzolis' tent.

Lavezzoli seemed more than ever immersed in *Anthony Adverse*. The three children lay on the sand a couple of yards away, in a ring round a blue towel, browning their backs, as immobile as lizards. Their mother was embroidering a table-cloth, which hung in long folds from her knees. She looked like a Renaissance madonna on a throne of clouds.

My father, who was famous for his straightforwardness, had noticed nothing amiss in the situation until he found himself up to his neck in it.

"Just look who's here!" he cried.

Before her husband could answer, Signora Lavezzoli intervened. She looked quickly up from her tablecloth, and suddenly held out the back of her hand to Fadigati.

"Of course, of course," she warbled, and smiled invitingly, showing her fine mouthful of teeth.

Downcast, Fadigati crossed over to the sun, walking a little unsteadily as usual because of wearing shoes on the sand. When he reached the Lavezzolis' tent, he kissed Signora Lavezzoli's hand, shook hands with her husband, who meantime had risen, and shook hands too with the three children, one by one. Finally he came back to our tent, where my father had already prepared a chaise-longue for him beside my mother. He seemed much calmer than a while before: relieved as a student after a difficult exam.

As soon as he was sitting down he gave a sigh of satisfaction.

"How lovely it is here," he said. "How delightfully airy!"
He turned sideways to talk to me.

"Remember last month at Bologna, how terribly hot it
was?" he said.

Then he explained to my parents, whom I had never told
anything about our meetings on the morning train at 6.50, how
for the last three months we had been "the best of friends".
He talked casually, like a man of the world. Obviously he could
scarcely believe that he was there with us, even with the
alarming Lavezzolis, restored to what just then he regarded as
his circle, accepted again by the cultivated, well-bred society
to which he had always belonged. "Ah!" he said every now
and then, throwing out his chest for a breath of balmy sea air.
It was clear that he felt free and happy: and at the same time
filled with gratitude (a little indiscreetly, I thought) towards
everyone who allowed him to feel so.

Meantime my father had started talking about the incredible sultriness of August in Ferrara.

"You couldn't sleep at night," he said, with a grimace of
discomfort, as if the memory of the heat in the city was
enough to make him feel its oppressiveness. "Do believe me,
doctor, you couldn't sleep a wink. Some people say the modern
age began in the year when Flit was invented. I don't dispute
it. But Flit means you've got to have the windows hermeti-
cally sealed. And closed windows means sheets that stick to
your skin with sweat. I'm not joking; till yesterday I swear I
dreaded the coming of night. Those damned mosquitoes!"

"Here it's completely different," said Fadigati enthusiastically. "Even on the hottest nights you can always breathe."

And he began to dwell on the advantages of the Adriatic
compared with the whole of the rest of Italy. He was Venetian,
he admitted, he had spent his childhood and adolescence on the
Lido, so probably his judgement was not entirely unbiased.
But he did really feel the Adriatic was a great deal more rest-
ful than the Tyrrhenian.

Signora Lavezzoli pricked up her ears. Disguising her
malice with a pretence at civic pride, she began defending the
Tyrrhenian warmly. If, like him, she could have chosen

338

between a holiday at Riccione and one at Viareggio, she wouldn't have hesitated a moment, she declared.

"Look at the way it is in the evenings," she continued. "Going past the café Zanarini makes you feel you're not a single mile from Ferrara. In the summer at least, it's rather nice, quite frankly, to see new faces: just once in a way different from those you see the rest of the year. It feels like walking along the Giovecca, or along the Corsa Roma, along the arches of the caffè della Borsa, don't you think so?"

Fadigati moved uneasily on his chaise-longue. Again his eyes crept across to the bathing huts. But there was still no sign of Deliliers.

"Perhaps, perhaps," he replied with a nervous smile, and looked out to sea again.

As happened every morning between eleven and twelve, the water had quickly changed colour. It was no longer the pale oily mass it had been half an hour before. The wind from the open sea, the sun which stood almost at its zenith, had made it smooth and blue, scattered with innumerable glints of gold. The first bathers began to run across the beach. And the three Lavezzoli children, when they had asked their mother's permission, went to their bathing hut to change.

"Perhaps," repeated Fadigati. "But, dear lady, where do you find afternoons like those the sun gives us here, when it sets behind 'the blue vision of San Marino'?"

He declaimed Pascoli's line in a sing-song, slightly nasal voice, separating each syllable and accentuating the diaeresis in *vision*. An embarrassed silence followed, but the doctor went on at once.

"I know of course that the sunsets on the Levant Riviera are magnificent. All the same, you have to pay dearly for them: the price, I mean, is burning hot afternoons, with the sea turned into a kind of burning-glass, so that people have to shut themselves up at home or at best take refuge in the pine-woods. You will have noticed, too, the colour of the Adriatic after midday. It's more black than blue, it never dazzles one. The surface of the water doesn't reflect the sun's rays, it absorbs them. Or rather it does reflect them, but in the direction of . . . Yugoslavia! As for me,'' he continued, as if he had forgotten nothing, ''I always long for lunch to be over so that I can come back to the beach at once. There's no lovelier moment to enjoy our divine Amarissimo in perfect peace than two in the afternoon.''

''I imagine you come here with your . . . inseparable friend,'' said Signora Lavezzoli acidly.

Called rudely back to reality, Fadigati was silent and confused. Then, several hundred yards away, in the direction of Rimini, a crowd suddenly gathering attracted my father's attention.

''What's happening?'' he asked, putting a hand to his forehead to see better.

Shouts of hurrah and clapping came to us on the wind.

''It's the Duce going into the water,'' explained Signora Lavezzoli reproachfully.

My father made a face. ''Surely they don't cheer him even in the sea?'' he growled between his teeth.

Romantic, patriotic, politically ingenuous and inexperienced like so many other Jews of his generation, my father had joined the fascist party when he returned from the front in 1919. So he had been a fascist from the very beginning and this in his heart he had remained, in spite of his mildness and integrity. But since Mussolini, after his early quarrels, had begun to make friends with Hitler, he had grown anxious. He thought of nothing but a possible outburst of antisemitism in Italy, too, and every now and then, though suffering for it, he let fall some bitter comment on the régime.

''He's so simple, so human,'' went on Signora Lavezzoli, taking no notice of him. ''Such a good husband, too. Every Saturday morning he takes the car and dashes off, and he's quite capable of coming all the way from Rome to Riccione in one go.''

''Marvellous!'' sneered my father. ''How happy Donna Rachele must be!''

He looked meaningly at Lavezzoli, trying to get him to agree. Lavezzoli was no fascist. He had even signed Croce's famous Manifesto in 1924 and for some years, at least until

1930, he was supposed to be a liberal democrat and antifascist. It was all in vain, though. Lavezzoli's eyes had at last been torn from the closely printed pages of *Anthony Adverse*, but were insensible to my father's silent pleading. Stretching out his neck, half-closing his eyes, he was staring obstinately at the water. The children had hired a boat and were going too far into the open sea ...

"The other day," said Signora Lavezzoli, "Filippo and I were going home arm-in-arm through the Viale dei Mille. It was half-past seven or a little later. Suddenly, through the gate of a house, who d'you think I saw coming? The Duce himself, dressed in white from head to foot. Instinctively I said 'Good evening, your Excellency.' And he took off his hat and said most charmingly: 'Good evening, madam.' Isn't it true, Pippo," she went on, turning to her husband, "isn't it true he was terribly nice?" Lavezzoli nodded.

"Perhaps we should be modest enough to recognize we were mistaken," he said gravely, turning to my father. "We mustn't forget it was he who gave us our Empire."

I can remember every word spoken that far-away morning, as if everything was taken down on a tape recorder.

When he had pronounced sentence (my father's eyes opened wide as he heard it), Lavezzoli returnd to his book. But there was no stopping his wife. Encouraged by what her husband had said, and in particular by the word *Empire,* which she had probably never yet heard on her husband's austere lips, she continued to insist on the Duce's good heart and on the generous nature he had inherited from his birthplace, the Romagna.

"That reminds me," she said. "I must tell you something I saw for myself three years ago right here at Riccione. One morning the Duce was bathing with the eldest boys, Vittorio and Bruno. About one o'clock he came out of the water and what d'you think was waiting for him? A telegram had arrived a moment before with the news of the assassination of the Austrian Chancellor Dollfuss. That year our tent was very close to the Mussolinis' tent, so what I'm saying is really true. As soon as he read the telegram, the Duce came out with a tremendous swear word in dialect—oh, of course, one must realize he's a passionate man! Then he began crying, I saw the tears running down his cheeks! They were great friends, the Mussolinis and the Dollfusses. What's more, Dollfuss's wife, a tiny, thin, very pretty, unobtrusive little creature, was their guest that very summer with the children. And as he wept the Duce was obviously thinking of what he'd have to say in a few minutes to that unhappy mother, when they all got together for lunch. . . ."

Suddenly Fadigati rose to his feet. Since Signora Lavezzoli's poisonous remarks had wounded him so deeply, he had not opened his mouth. All he did was bite his lips thoughtfully. Why was Deliliers so long? What could have happened?

"Will you excuse me?" he stammered, embarrassed.

"But it's early," protested Signora Lavezzoli. "Aren't you waiting for your friend? There are still twenty minutes to go!"

Fadigati stammered something incomprehensible. He shook hands all round and then went off in the direction of his umbrella. When he reached it he leant down to pick up the detective story and the sponge towel, and then we saw him cross the beach under the midday sun, but this time going directly to the hotel.

He walked tiredly, holding his detective story under his arm and the towel over his shoulder, his face altered with sweat and with anxiety. So much so that my father, who had been told everything right away, and was following his progress with pitying eyes, murmured softly: "Poor chap."

Straight after lunch I went back to the beach alone.

I sat in our tent. Yes, at two in the afternoon the Adriatic became dark blue, almost black. That day, though, as far as you could see, the top of every wave was crested with a tuft of foam, whiter than snow. The wind was still blowing from the open sea, but now came a little sidelong. If I raised my father's military field-glasses to take in the spur of the Punta di Pesaro which closed in the arc of the bay on my right, I could see high up the tops of the pines doubled over, and their foliage flung wildly about. Pressed on by the afternoon wind from Greece the long, ink-coloured, white-crested waves came on in serried and successive ranks. From where I was, they seemed to be hurling themselves to land like an invasion force. But, as they approached, their foamy crests gradually diminished, and vanished altogether in the last few yards. Stretched out on my chaise-longue, I could hear the dull roar of each wave against the shore.

The empty sea, from which the fishermen's sails had gradually disappeared (on the following morning, which was Sunday, I would see most of them spread out on the benches of the canal gates at Rimini and Cesenatico), was like the empty beach. In a tent not far from ours someone was playing a gramophone. I couldn't say what music it was, perhaps it was jazz. For more than three hours I stayed so, my eyes fixed on an old cockleshell fisherman dragging the bottom of the sea not far from the shore, and my ears filled with that music, which was no less sad and tireless than he was. When I got up, shortly after five, the old man was still searching, the gramophone still playing. The sun was setting and the shadows of the tents and the umbrellas had lengthened. The shadow of Fadigati's umbrella now nearly touched the water.

Outside the Grand Hotel, facing the sea, was a pavilion adjoining the beach. As soon as I set foot there, I noticed Fadigati sitting on one of the cement benches in front of the outside staircase of the hotel.

He had seen me, too. Too late to avoid him!

"Good afternoon," I said, and went up to him.

He indicated the bench. "Why don't you sit down? Do, for a moment."

I obeyed. He put his hand into the inside pocket of his jacket, took out a packet of Nazionali cigarettes, and offered them to me. There were only two cigarettes in the packet. He realized I was hesitating to accept.

"They're Nazionali!" he exclaimed, a strangely fanatical gleam in his eyes.

At last he realized the reason for my hesitation and smiled.

"Oh go on, do take one!" he said. "We'll share them like good friends, one for you and one for me."

343

A car whistled on the asphalt and curved into the square. Fadigati turned to look at it, but without hope. And it wasn't his Alfa: it was a Fiat 1500, a grey Berlin.

"I think I should go," I said. All the same I took one of the two cigarettes.

He noticed my beach shoes. "I see you've come from the beach. The sea must have been wonderful today."

"Yes, but not for swimming," I said.

"Don't ever think of bathing before the right time, I do beg you!" he exclaimed. "You're a boy and of course your heart's excellent, you lucky fellow, but congestion may strike in a moment, even the strongest."

He held out the lighted match to me. "And now, have you got a date?" he asked.

I answered—and it was quite true—that at six the young Lavezzolis were expecting me. We had arranged to meet on the tennis court behind the café Zanarini. It was true it was still twenty to six. But I had to go home and change and get my racket and balls; in fact I was afraid I wouldn't be in time.

"Let's hope Fanny doesn't get it into her head to come, too!" I went on. "Mummy won't let her come without doing her pigtails, and that'll mean I'll lose another good ten minutes."

While I was talking, I saw him carry out a curious ritual. He took the Nazionali from his lips so as to light it at the opposite end, where the trade mark was. Then he threw away the empty packet. Only then did I realize that the ground around us was scattered with cigarette stubs, more than a dozen.

"Have you seen how much I smoke?" he said.

"I have."

A question was burning on my lips: "What about Deliliers?" But I couldn't bring it out.

I got up and shook hands.

"Before, if I'm not mistaken, you didn't smoke at all," I said.

"I'm trying to make my modest contribution to the spread of sore throats," he retorted wretchedly. "I thought I ought to."

I moved off a few steps.

"Did you say the tennis court near the café Zanarini?" he called after me. "Maybe later I'll come along and admire you."

Afterwards we learnt that nothing serious had happened to Deliliers. Just this: instead of bathing at Riccione, he had suddenly got it into his head to bathe at Rimini, where, high up in the Hotel Vittoria, he knew some sisters from Parma. He had taken the car and vanished without even bothering to leave a note for Fadigati, and came back about eight o'clock, Signora Lavezzoli told us, when she happened to be drinking an aperitif with her husband in the hall of the Grand Hotel. Suddenly they had seen Deliliers crossing the hall in a great hurry, looking furiously angry, with Fadigati almost in tears at his heels.

It was Deliliers who came up to me that same evening on the terrace of the Grand Hotel.

I had gone there with my parents and the Lavezzolis again, the lawyer and his wife. I was still tired from the tennis, and so not dancing, but listening in silence to Signora Lavezzoli, who, though clearly she must have known how much it would wound us, had begun talking "objectively" of Hitler's Germany—just imagine!—and its "undeniable" greatness.

"You must realize, though, that your dear Dollfuss appears to have been liquidated by Hitler," I tried to make her see.

"What does that mean?" she retorted at once, with the compassionate and patient air of a school-mistress ready to justify any amount of cheating in her brightest pupil. "That's political necessity, alas. Let's leave our personal likes or dislikes out of it: the fact is that in certain circumstances the head of a government, a statesman worthy of the name, must for the good of his own people pass over the sensibilities of ordinary people . . . little people like ourselves." And she smiled proudly, completely contradicting her last words.

Horrified, my father opened his mouth to say something. But once again Signora Lavezzoli gave him no time. As if she was changing the subject, she turned directly to him, and went on to describe an "interesting" article which had appeared in the last number of *Catholic Civilization,* signed by the well-known Father Gemelli.

The theme of the article was the so-called Jewish question. According to Father Gemelli, she said, the recurrent persecutions of the "Israelites" in every part of the world for nearly two thousand years could only be explained as a sign of God's anger. The article ended with this question: May a Christian, even if in his heart he hates the idea of violence, pass judgement on historical events through which God's will is expressed?

At that point, not very politely, I got up from my cane armchair and left.

And so I was leaning against the side of the large window that separated the dining-room from the terrace, and the orchestra, if I am not mistaken, had started *Blue Moon*.

> *But you, pale moon, why*
> *Are you so sad, what is . . .*

the usual idiotic voice was singing, when suddenly I felt two fingers tapping me hard on the shoulder.

"Hello," said Deliliers.

It was the first time he had spoken to me at Riccione. "Hello," I answered. "How are you?"

"A bit better today," he said, winking. "What about you? What are you doing?"

"Oh reading, working," I lied. "I've got a couple of exams in October."

"Oh of course!" said Deliliers, thoughtfully scratching his hair, which shone with brilliantine, with his little finger.

But he wasn't thinking about his hair. Suddenly his expression changed. In a low voice, as if letting me into an important secret, peering back over his shoulder every now and then as if he were afraid of being surprised, he quickly told me about his bathe at Rimini with the two girls from Parma.

"Why don't you come with me tomorrow morning in the car? I'm going back. Come on, do help me! I can't go with two girls all on my own. Just leave your old work!"

At the end of the room Fadigati appeared, wearing a dinner jacket, his short-sighted eyes peering round behind his spectacles.The moonlit gloom created artificially for *Blue Moon* prevented him seeing Deliliers's white jacket straight away.

"Well," I said, "I don't know if I can."

"I'll wait for you in the hotel."

"I'll try and come. What time do we leave?"

"Half-past nine. That's all right?"

"Yes, but it's not definite."

I jerked my chin in Fadigati's direction. "You're wanted."

"Well, that's fixed then?" said Deliliers, turning on his heel and going up to Fadigati who was feverishly cleaning his spectacles with his handkerchief.

And a few seconds later the unmistakable roar of the Alfa Romeo rose from the nearby square to tell the entire hotel that the "couple", perhaps to celebrate their reconciliation, had decided to make it a very special evening.

I must confess that the following morning I was tempted for a moment to go to Rimini with Deliliers.

What attracted me most was the thought of going along the sea road by car. But afterwards?—I wondered. What did Deliliers's suggestion really mean? And who really were these sisters from Parma he had told me about? Were they two ordinary girls we could take into the pine-woods, which was all too easy; or two girls of good family we must entertain on the beach under the sharp eyes of another Signora Lavezzoli? In either case (though it wasn't quite out of the question that they might come somewhere between the two!) I didn't feel I was friendly enough with Deliliers to accept his invitation lightheartedly. If I accepted, I foresaw a day full of regrets and humiliations; and besides, why ever had Deliliers, who had never really liked me or shown any sort of regard for me, suddenly asked me, almost implored me, to go "womanizing" with him? Was it perhaps because he wanted to show me that it wasn't a matter of vice, his being with Fadigati, but just to have his holiday paid for, and that in any case he always preferred a pretty girl?

In the end I stayed behind. And when, a little later, I saw Fadigati on the beach under his big umbrella, abandoned in a solitude that suddenly appeared to me immense and incurable, I felt, deep within me, repaid for what I had given up. I at least had not deceived him, I thought; when I was asked to join someone who was deceiving him and taking advantage of him, I had managed to resist, and kept a minimum of respect for him.

Then I thought he might like a little company.

A moment before I reached his umbrella he turned.

"Oh it's you," he said, but without surprise. "How nice of you to come and see me."

Everything about him showed the weariness and the suffering caused by a recent quarrel. Although very likely he had dragged a promise to stay from Deliliers, the boy had gone to Rimini just the same.

Fadigati shut the book he was reading and laid it down on a stool there beside him, half in shadow and half in the sun. It was not the usual detective story, but a small volume with an old flowered paper cover.

"What were you reading?" I asked, with a gesture at the book. "Is it poetry?"

"Have a look."

It was a school edition of the first canto of the *Iliad*, translated line by line.

"I found it in my suitcase," he said. "Mènin aèide teà peleiadeo Achillèos," he added, with a bitter smile.

My parents arrived just then, my mother holding Fanny's hand. I waved to show them where I was, and whistled the family signature tune: the first line of a Schubert *Lied*.

Fadigati turned, half-rose from his chaise-longue, and raised his panama hat politely. My parents answered together: my mother nodding slightly, my father touching the visor of his brand-new white cloth cap with two fingers. I realized at once that they disliked seeing me with Fadigati. As soon as she saw me, Fanny had turned to ask my mother something, probably permission to join me. But clearly my mother had stopped her.

"How very sweet your sister is," said Fadigati. "How old is she?"

"Twelve: exactly eight years younger than me," I answered, embarrassed.

"But there are three of you altogether, I believe," he said.

"Yes, there are. Two boys and a girl: there are four years between each of us. Ernesto, the second, is in England. . . ."

"What an intelligent little face!" said Fadigati, still looking in Fanny's direction. "And how well that pink bathing dress suits her! She's lucky to have two big brothers, you know."

"Oh, she's still a kid," I said.

"Oh yes, so I see. I'd have thought she was ten or so. But that means nothing. Girls develop all of a sudden. You'll have such a surprise. . . . She's at high school, isn't she?"

"Yes, in the third form."

He shook his head with a kind of melancholy regret, as if he were thinking of all the effort and the pain which every human being must meet to grow, to come to maturity. But his thoughts soon changed.

"And what about Signora Lavezzoli?" he asked.

"Oh, her. I think this morning, because of Mass, we shan't see them before midday."

"Oh that's true, today's Sunday," he said, startled. "Well, in that case," he added, after another pause, as he got to his feet, "let's go and say how d'you do to your parents."

We walked side by side along the sand, already uncomfortably hot.

"I've a feeling," he said to me, "I've a feeling Signora Lavezzoli doesn't like me all that much."

"Oh no, I don't think so."

"All the same, it's not a bad idea to take advantage of her absence."

Without the Lavezzolis, my parents were unable to stick to their obvious resolution to keep him at a distance: especially my father, who was soon talking to him in the friendliest way.

A light wind was coming up from inland, the wind called the *garbino*. The sea had no sails at all on it, and though the sun had not yet reached its zenith, it already looked dark: a thick, leaden colour. Perhaps because he had just read the first canto of the *Iliad*, Fadigati spoke of the Greeks' feeling for nature, and in particular of the meaning he thought we must attribute to adjectives like *purple* and *violet*, applied by Homer to the sea. My father then spoke of Horace, and of Carducci's *Odi Barbare* which he considered—and we argued over it almost daily—his ideal in the field of modern poetry. In fact they chatted so agreeably (the fact that Deliliers was not likely to pop out from the bathing huts from one minute to the next obviously steadied the doctor's nerves), that when the Lavezzoli family, fresh from Mass, landed on us complete towards midday, Fadigati felt strong enough, protected enough, so to speak, to bear Signora Lavezzoli's inevitable remarks quite casually, and even to answer back quite successfully.

We saw no more of Deliliers on the beach: neither that day nor the days that followed. He never returned from his sorties in the car before two o'clock in the morning and Fadigati, left on his own, sought our company more than ever.

And so it was that, apart from spending the morning in our tent (it hardly seemed true to my father that he could discuss music, literature and art with him, instead of politics with Signora Lavezzoli!), he got into the habit of coming to the tennis court behind the café Zanarini in the afternoon when he heard that the Lavezzoli children and I were going there.

There was certainly nothing very exciting about our lazy games, one male couple against one mixed couple. I was a pretty poor player, but Franco and Gilberto Lavezzoli could hardly hold a racket. And as for Cristina, their blonde, rosy and delicate sister of fifteen (she emerged from a convent boarding school in Florence every now and then, and had the entire family running round her), she played even worse than her brothers. Her hair grew in a little crown round her head "like one of Melozzo's singing angels", as Fadigati put it, with fatherly admiration, one day—and rather than disarrange a single curl she would have given up walking. So there was absolutely no question of her bothering about the style of a drive or having a decent backhand!

Yet in spite of all this, Fadigati seemed to be highly interested in our game, however boring and pointless it was.

"Good shot!" "Only just out!" "Bad luck!" He was generous with his praise for all of us, and had some comment, sometimes wildly out, for every shot.

Sometimes our game languished a bit too much even for such an indulgent audience.

"Why don't you play a match?" he would suggest.

"Oh dear," Cristina would protest at once, blushing. "I just can't handle a ball!"

But he refused to listen.

"Order of the Day!" he proclaimed gaily. "Doctor Fadigati will give the winning couple a prize of two superb bottles of San Pellegrino orangeade!"

He ran to the keeper's hut and dragged out a rickety and dangerous umpire's chair at least two yards high, pulled it to one side of the tennis court himself and finally clambered up it. Gradually the air darkened; his hat appeared in the half-light aureoled by a cloud of flies. But, perched up there like a great bird, he stayed and called out the score in a metallic voice, determined to keep up his role as an impartial umpire to the end. Obviously he had no idea what else to do, or how to fill the terrible emptiness of the days.

—*Translated by
Isabel Quigly*

WILLIAM S. BURROUGHS

HASSAN'S RUMPUS ROOM

Gilt and red plush. Rococo bar backed by pink shell. The air is cloyed with a sweet evil substance like decayed honey. Men and women in evening dress sip pousse-cafés through alabaster tubes. A Near East Mugwump sits naked on a bar stool covered in pink silk. He licks warm honey from a crystal goblet with a long black tongue. His genitals are perfectly formed—circumcised cock, black shiny pubic hairs. His lips are thin and purple-blue like the lips of a penis, his eyes blank with insect calm. The Mugwump has no liver, maintaining himself exclusively on sweets. Mugwump push a slender blond youth to a couch and strip him expertly.

"Stand up and turn around," he orders in telepathic pictographs. He ties the boy's hands behind him with a red silk cord. "Tonight we make it all the way."

"No, no!" screams the boy.

"Yes. Yes."

Cocks ejaculate in silent "yes." Mugwump part silk curtains, reveal a teak wood gallows against lighted screen of red flint. Gallows is on a dais of Aztec mosaics.

The boy crumples to his knees with a long "OOOO-OOOOH," shitting and pissing in terror. He feels the shit warm between his thighs. A great wave of hot blood swells his lips and throat. His body contacts into a foetal position and sperm spurts hot into his face. The Mugwump dips hot perfumed water from alabaster bowl, pensively washes the boy's ass and cock, drying him with a soft blue towel. A warm wind plays over the boy's body and the hairs float free. The Mugwump puts a hand under the boy's chest and pulls him to his feet. Holding him by both pinioned elbows, propels him up the steps and under the noose. He stands in front of the boy holding the noose in both hands.

The boy looks into Mugwump eyes blank as obsidian mirrors, pools of black blood, glory holes in a toilet wall closing on the Last Erection.

An old garbage collector, face fine and yellow as Chinese ivory, blows The Blast on his dented brass horn, wakes the Spanish pimp with a hard-on. Whore staggers out through dust and shit and litter of dead kittens, carrying bales of aborted foetuses, broken condoms, bloody Kotex, shit wrapped in bright color comics.

A vast still harbor of iridescent water. Deserted gas well flares on the smoky horizon. Stink of oil and sewage. Sick sharks swim through the black water, belch sulphur from rotting livers, ignore a bloody, broken Icarus. Naked Mr. America, burning frantic with self bone love, screams out: "My asshole confounds the Louvre! I fart ambrosia and shit pure gold turds! My cock spurts soft diamonds in the morning sunlight!" He plummets from the eyeless lighthouse, kissing and jacking off in face of the black mirror, glides oblique down with cryptic condoms and mosaic of a thousand newspapers through a drowned city of red brick to settle in black mud with tin cans and beer bottles, gangsters in concrete, pistols pounded flat and meaningless to avoid short-arm inspection of prurient ballistic experts. He waits the slow striptease of erosion with fossil loins.

The Mugwump slips the noose over the boy's head and tightens the knot caressingly behind the left ear. The boy's penis is retracted, his balls tight. He looks straight ahead breathing deeply. The Mugwump sidles around the boy goosing him and caressing his genitals in hieroglyphs of mockery.

He moves in behind the boy with a series of bumps and shoves his cock up the boy's ass. He stands there moving in circular gyrations.

The guests shush each other, nudge and giggle.

Suddenly the Mugwump pushes the boy forward into space, free of his cock. He steadies the boy with hands on the hip bones, reaches up with his stylized hieroglyph hands and snaps the boy's neck. A shudder passes through the boy's body. His penis rises in three great surges pulling his pelvis up, ejaculates immediately.

Green sparks explode behind his eyes. A sweet toothache pain shoots through his neck down the spine to the groin, contracting the body in spasms of delight. His whole body squeezes out through his cock. A final spasm throws a great spurt of sperm across the red screen like a shootingstar.

The boy falls with soft gutty suction through a maze of penny arcades and dirty pictures.

A sharp turd shoots clean out of his ass. Farts shake his slender body. Skyrockets burst in green clusters across a great river. He hears the faint put-put of a motor boat in jungle twilight. . . . Under silent wings of the anopheles mosquito.

The Mugwump pulls the boy back onto his cock. The boy squirms, impaled like a speared fish. The Mugwump swings on the boy's back, his body contracting in fluid waves. Blood flows down the boy's chin from his mouth, half-open, sweet, and sulky in death. The Mugwump falls with a fluid, sated plop.

Windowless cubicle with blue walls. Dirty pink curtain cover the door. Red bugs crawl on the wall, cluster in corners. Naked boy in the middle of the room twang a two-string ouad, trace an arabesque on the floor. Another boy lean back on the bed smoking keif and blow smoke over his erect cock. They play game with tarot cards on the bed to see who fuck who. Cheat. Fight. Roll on the floor snarling and spitting like young animals. The loser sit on the floor chin on knees, licks a broken tooth. The winner curls up on the bed pretending to sleep. Whenever the other boy come near kick at him. Ali seize him by one ankle, tuck the ankle under the arm pit, lock his arm around the calf. The boy kick desperately at Ali's face. Other ankle pinioned. Ali tilt the boy back on his shoulders. The boy's cock extends along his stomach, float free pulsing. Ali put his hands over his head. Spit on his cock. The other sighs deeply as Ali slides his cock in. The mouths grind together smearing blood. Sharp musty odor of penetrated rectum. Nimun drive in like a wedge, force jism out the other cock in long hot spurts. (The author has observed that Arab cocks tend to be wide and wedge shaped.)

Satyr and naked Greek lad in aqualungs trace a ballet in pursuit in a monster vase of transparent alabaster. The Satyr catches the boy from in front and whirls him around. They move in fish jerks. The boy releases a silver stream of bubbles from his mouth. White sperm ejaculates into the green water and floats lazily around the twisting bodies.

Negro gently lifts exquisite Chinese boy into a hammock. He pushes the boy's legs up over his head and straddles the hammock. He slides his cock up the boy's slender tight ass. He rocks the hammock gently back and forth. The boy screams, a weird high wail of unendurable delight.

A Javanese dancer in ornate teak swivel chair, set in a socket of limestone buttocks, pulls an American boy—red hair, bright green eyes—down onto his cock with ritual motions. The boy sits impaled facing the dancer who propels himself in circular gyrations, lending fluid substance to the chair. "Weeeeeeeeeee!" scream the boy as his sperm spurt up over the dancer's lean brown chest. One gob hit the corner of the dancer's mouth. The boy push it in with his finger and laugh: "Man, that's what I call suction!"

Two Arab women with bestial faces have pulled the shorts off a little blond French boy. They are screwing him with red rubber cocks. The boy snarls, bites, kicks, collapses in tears as his cock rises and ejaculates.

Hassan's face swells, tumescent with blood. His lips turn purple. He strip off his suit of banknotes and throw it into an open vault that closes soundless.

"Freedom Hall here, folks!" he screams in his phoney Texas accent. Ten-gallon hat and cowboy boots still on, he dances the Liquefactionist Jig, ending with a grotesque can-can to the tune of *She Started a Heat Wave*.

"Let it be! And no holes barred!!!"

Couples attached to baroque harnesses with artificial wings copulate in the air, screaming like magpies.

Aerialists ejaculate each other in space with one sure touch.

Equilibrists suck each other off deftly, balanced on perilous poles and chairs tilted over the void. A warm wind brings the smell of rivers and jungle from misty depths.

Boys by the hundred plummet through the roof, quivering and kicking at the end of ropes. The boys hang at different levels, some near the ceiling and others a few inches off the floor. Exquisite Balinese and Malays, Mexican Indians with fierce innocent faces and bright red gums. Negroes (teeth, fingers, toe nails and pubic hair gilded), Japanese boys smooth and white as China, Titian-haired Venetian lads, Americans with blond or black curls falling across the forehead (the guests tenderly shove it back), sulky blond Polacks with animal brown eyes, Arab and Spanish street boys, Austrian boys pink and delicate with a faint shadow of blond pubic hair, sneering German youths with bright eyes scream "Heil Hitler!" as the trap falls under them. Sollubis shit and whimper.

Mr. Rich-and-Vulgar chews his Havana lewd and nasty, sprawled on a Florida beach surrounded by simpering blond catamites:

"This citizen have a Latah he import from Indo-China. He figure to hang the Latah and send a Xmas TV short to his friends. So he fix up two ropes—one gimmicked to stretch, the other the real McCoy. But that Latah get up in feud state and put on his Santa Claus suit and make with the switcheroo. Come the dawning. The citizen put one rope on and the Latah, going along the way Latahs will, put on the other. When the traps are down the citizen hang for real and the Latah stand with the carny-rubber stretch rope. Well, the Latah imitate every twitch and spasm. Come three times.

"Smart young Latah keep his eye on the ball. I got him working in one of my plants as an expeditor.

"Aztec priests strip blue feather robe from the Naked Youth. They bend him back over a limestone altar, fit a crystal skull over his head, securing the two hemispheres back and front with crystal screws. A waterfall pour over the skull snapping the boy's neck. He ejaculate in a rainbow against the rising sun."

Sharp protein odor of semen fills the air. The guests run hands over twitching boys, suck their cocks, hang on their backs like vampires.

Naked lifeguards carry in iron-lungs full of paralyzed youths.

Blind boys grope out of huge pies, deteriorated schizophrenics pop from under a rubber cunt, boys with horrible skin diseases rise from a black pond (sluggish fish nibble yellow turds on the surface).

A man with white tie and dress shirt, naked from the waist down except for black garters, talks to the Queen Bee in elegant tones. (Queen Bees are old women who surround themselves with fairies to form a "swarm." It is a sinister Mexican practice.)

"But where is the statuary?" He talks out of one side of his face, the other is twisted by the Torture of a Million Mirrors. He masturbates wildly. The Queen Bee continues the conversation, notices nothing.

Couches, chairs, the whole floor begins to vibrate, shaking the guests to blurred grey ghosts shrieking in cock-bound agony.

Two boys jacking off under railroad bridge. The train shakes through their bodies, ejaculate them, fades with distant whistle. Frogs croak. The boys wash semen off lean brown stomachs.

Train compartment: two sick young junkies on their way to Lexington tear their pants down in convulsions of lust. One of them soaps his cock and works it up the other's ass with a corkscrew motion. "Jeeeeeeeeeeeeeeesus!" Both ejaculate at once standing up. They move away from each other and pull up their pants.

"Old croaker in Marshall writes for tincture and sweet oil."

"The piles of an aged mother shriek out raw and bleeding for the Black Shit. . . . Doc, suppose it was your mother, rimmed by resident leeches, squirming around so nasty. . . . De-active that pelvis, mom, you disgust me already."

"Let's stop over and make him for an RX."

The train tears on through the smoky, neon-lighted June night.

Pictures of men and women, boys and girls, animals, fish, birds, the copulating rhythm of the universe flows through the room, a great blue tide of life. Vibrating, soundless hum of deep forest—sudden quiet of cities when the junky copes. A moment of stillness and wonder. Even the Commuter buzzes clogged lines of cholesterol for contact.

Hassan shrieks out: "This is your doing, A.J.! You poopa my party!"

A.J. looks at him, face remote as limestone: "Uppa your ass, you liquefying gook."

A horde of lust-mad American women rush in. Dripping cunts, from farm and dude ranch, factory, brothel, country club, penthouse and suburb, motel and yacht and cocktail bar, strip off riding clothes, ski togs, evening dresses, levis, tea gowns, print dresses, slacks, bathing suits and kimonos. They scream and yipe and howl, leap on the guests like bitch dogs in heat with rabies. They claw at the hanged boys shrieking: "You fairy! You bastard! Fuck me! Fuck me! Fuck me!" The guests flee screaming, dodge among the hanged boys, overturn iron lungs.

A.J.: "Call out my Sweitzers, God damn it! Guard me from these she-foxes!"

Mr. Hyslop, A.J.'s secretary, looks up from his comic book: "The Sweitzers liquefy already."

(Liquefaction involves protein cleavage and reduction to liquid which is absorbed into someone else's protoplasmic being. Hassan, a notorious liquefactionist, is probably the beneficiary in this case.)

A.J.: "Gold-bricking cocksuckers! Where's a man without his Sweitzers? Our backs are to the wall, gentlemen. Our very cocks at stake. Stand by to resist boarders, Mr. Hyslop, and issue short arms to the men."

A.J. whips out a cutlass and begins decapitating the American Girls. He sings lustily:

Fifteen men on the dead man's chest
Yo Ho Ho and a bottle of rum.

Drink and the devil had done for the rest
Yo Ho Ho and a bottle of rum.

Mr. Hyslop, bored and resigned: "Oh Gawd! He's at it again." He waves the Jolly Roger listlessly.

A.J., surrounded and fighting against overwhelming odds, throws back his head and makes with the hog-call. Immediately a thousand rutting Eskimos pour in grunting and squealing, faces tumescent, eyes hot and red, lips purple, fall on the American women.

(Eskimos have a rutting season when the tribes meet in short Summer to disport themselves in orgies. Their faces swell and lips turn purple.)

A House Dick with cigar two feet long sticks his head in through the wall: "Have you got a menagerie in here?"

Hassan wrings his hands: "A shambles! A filthy shambles! By Allah I never see anything so downright nasty!"

He whirls on A.J. who is sitting on a sea chest, parrot on shoulder, patch over one eye, drinking rum from a tankard. He scans the horizon with a huge brass telescope.

Hassan: "You cheap Factualist bitch! Go and never darken my rumpus room again!"

ALLEN GINSBERG

A SUPERMARKET IN CALIFORNIA

What thoughts I have of you tonight, Walt Whitman, for I walked down the sidestreets under the trees with a headache self-conscious looking at the full moon.

In my hungry fatigue, and shopping for images, I went into the neon fruit supermarket, dreaming of your enumerations!

What peaches and what penumbras! Whole families shopping at night! Aisles full of husbands! Wives in the avocados, babies in the tomatoes!—and you, Garcia Lorca, what were you doing down by the watermelons?

I saw you, Walt Whitman, childless, lonely old grubber, poking among the meats in the refrigerator and eyeing the grocery boys.

I heard you asking questions of each: Who killed the pork chops? What price bananas? Are you my Angel?

I wandered in and out of the brilliant stacks of cans following you, and followed in my imagination by the store detective.

We strode down the open corridors together in our solitary

fancy tasting artichokes, possessing every frozen delicacy, and never passing the cashier.

Where are we going, Walt Whitman? The doors close in an hour. Which way does your beard point tonight?
(I touch your book and dream of our odyssey in the supermarket and feel absurd.)
Will we walk all night through solitary streets? The trees add shade to shade, lights out in the houses, we'll both be lonely.

Will we stroll dreaming of the lost America of love past blue automobiles in driveways, home to our silent cottage?
Ah, dear father, graybeard, lonely old courage-teacher, what America did you have when Charon quit poling his ferry and you got out on a smoking bank and stood watching the boat disappear on the black waters of Lethe?

BERKELY 1955

PLEASE MASTER

Please master can I touch your cheek
please master can I kneel at your feet
please master can I loosen your blue pants
please master can I gaze at your golden haired belly
please master can I gently take down your shorts
please master can I have your thighs bare to my eyes
please master can I take off my clothes below your chair
please master can I kiss your ankles and soul
please master can I touch lips to your hard muscle hairless
    thigh
please master can I lay my ear pressed to your stomach
please master can I wrap my arms around your white ass
please master can I lick your groin curled with blond soft fur
please master can I touch my tongue to your rosy asshole

please master may I pass my face to your balls,
please master, please look into my eyes,
please master order me down on the floor,
please master tell me to lick your thick shaft
please master put your rough hands on my bald hairy skull
please master press my mouth to your prick-heart
please master press my face into your belly, pull me slowly
    strong thumbed
till your dumb hardness fills my throat to the base
till I swallow & taste your delicate flesh-hot prick barrel veined
    Please
Master push my shoulders away and stare in my eye, & make
    me bend over the table
please master grab my thighs and lift my ass to your waist
please master your hand's rough stroke on my neck your palm
    down my backside
please master push me up, my feet on chairs, till my hole feels
    the breath of your spit and your thumb stroke
please master make me say Please Master Fuck me now
    Please
Master grease my balls and hairmouth with sweet vaselines
please master stroke your shaft with white creams
please master touch your cock head to my wrinkled selfhole
please master push it in gently, your elbows enwrapped round
    my breast
your arms passing down to my belly, my penis you touch
    w/your fingers
please master shove it in me a little, a little, a little,
please master sink your droor thing down my behind
& please master make me wiggle my rear to eat up the prick
    trunk
till my asshalfs cuddle your thighs, my back bent over,
till I'm alone sticking out, your sword stuck throbbing in me
please master pull out and slowly roll into the bottom
please master lunge it again, and withdraw to the tip
please please master fuck me again with your self, please fuck
    me Please
Master drive down till it hurts me the softness the

Softness please master make love to my ass, give body to
  center, & fuck me for good like a girl,
tenderly clasp me please master I take me to thee,
& drive in my belly your selfsame sweet heat-rood
you fingered in solitude Denver or Brooklyn or fucked in a
  maiden in Paris carlots
please master drive me thy vehicle, body of love drops,
  sweat fuck
body of tenderness, Give me your dog fuck faster
please master make me go moan on the table
Go moan O please master do fuck me like that
in your rhythm thrill-plunge & pull-back-bounce & push down
till I loosen my asshole a dog on the table yelping with terror
  delight to be loved
Please master call me a dog, an ass beast, a wet asshole,
& fuck me more violent, my eyes hid with your palms round
  my skull
& plunge down in a brutal hard lash thru soft drip-flesh
& throb thru five seconds to spurt out your semen heat
over & over, bamming it in while I cry out your name I do
  love you
please Master.

May 1968

RAIN-WET ASPHALT

Rain-wet asphalt heat, garbage curbed cans overflowing

I hauled down lifeless mattresses to sidewalk refuse-piles,
old rugs stept on from Paterson to Lower East Side filled with
  bed-bugs,
grey pillows, couch seats treasured from the street laid back
  on the street
—out, to hear Murder-tale, 3rd Street cyclists attacked
  tonite—
Bopping along in rain, Chaos fallen over City roofs,

363

shrouds of chemical vapour drifting over building-tops—
Get the *Times,* Nixon says peace reflected from the Moon,
but I found no boy body to sleep with all night on pavements
    3 AM home in sweating drizzle—
Those mattresses soggy lying by full five garbagepails—
Barbara, Maretta, Peter Steven Rosebud slept on these Pil-
    lows years ago,
forgotten names, also made love to me, I had these mattresses
    four years on my floor—
Gerard, Jimmy many months, even blond Gordon later,
Paul with the beautiful big cock, that teenage boy that lived in
    Pennsylvania,
forgotten numbers, young dream loves and lovers, earthly
    bellies—
many strong youths with eyes closed, come sighing and help-
    ing me come—
Desires already forgotten, tender persons used and kissed
    goodbye
and all the times I came to myself alone in the dark dreaming
    of Neal or Billy Budd
—nameless angels of half-life—heart beating & eyes weeping
    for lovely phantoms—
Back from the Gem Spa, into the hallway, a glance behind
and sudden farewell to the bedbug-ridden mattresses piled
    soggy in dark rain.

Augusт 2, 1969

YUKIO MISHIMA

ONNAGATA

Masuyama had been overwhelmed by Mangiku's artistry; that was how it happened that, after getting a degree in classical Japanese literature, he had chosen to join the kabuki theatre staff. He had been entranced by seeing Mangiku Sanokawa perform.

Masuyama's addiction to kabuki began when he was a high-school student. At the time, Mangiku, still a fledgling *onnagata,* was appearing in such minor roles as the ghost butterfly in *Kagami Jishi* or, at best, the waiting maid Chidori in *The Disowning of Genta.* Mangiku's acting was unassertive and orthodox; nobody suspected he would achieve his present eminence. But even in those days Masuyama sensed the icy flames given off by this actor's aloof beauty. The general public, needless to say, noticed nothing. For that matter, none of the drama critics had ever called attention to the peculiar quality of Mangiku, like shoots of flame visible through the snow, which illuminated his performances from very early in his career. Now everyone spoke as if Mangiku had been a personal discovery.

Mangiku Sanokawa was a true *onnagata,* a species seldom encountered nowadays. Unlike most contemporary *onnagata,* he was quite incapable of performing successfully in male roles. His stage presence was colourful, but with dark overtones; his every gesture was the essence of delicacy. Mangiku never expressed anything—not even strength, authority, endurance, or courage—except through the single medium open to him, feminine expression, but through this medium he could filter every variety of human emotion. That is the way of the true *onnagata* but in recent years this breed has become rare indeed. Their tonal colouring, produced by a particular, exquisitely refined musical instrument, cannot be achieved by playing a normal instrument in a minor key, nor, for that matter, is it produced by a mere slavish imitation of real women.

Yukihime, the Snow Princess, in *Kinkakuji* was one of Mangiku's most successful roles. Masuyama remembered having seen Mangiku perform Yukihime ten times during a single month, but no matter how often he repeated this experience, his intoxication did not diminish. Everything symbolizing Sanokawa Mangiku may be found in this play, the elements entwined, beginning with the opening words of the narrator: 'The Golden Pavilion, the mountain retreat of Lord Yoshimitsu, Prime Minister and Monk of the Deer Park, stands three stories high, its garden graced with lovely sights: the night-lodging stone, the water trickling below the rocks, the flow of the cascade heavy with spring, the willows and cherry-trees planted together; the capital now is a vast, many-hued brocade.' The dazzling brilliance of the set, depicting cherry-trees in blossom, a waterfall, and the glittering Golden Pavilion; the drums, suggesting the dark sound of the waterfall and contributing a constant agitation to the stage; the pale, sadistic face of the lecherous Daizen Matsunaga, the rebel general; the miracle of the magic sword which shines in morning sunlight with the holy image of Fudō, but shows a dragon's form when pointed at the setting sun; the radiance of the sunset glow on the waterfall and cherry-trees; the cherry blossoms scattering down petal by petal—everything in the play exists for the sake of one woman, the beautiful, aristocratic Yukihime. There is nothing unusual about Yukihime's costume, the crimson silk robe customarily worn by young princesses. But a ghostly presence of snow, befitting her name, hovers about this granddaughter of the great painter Sesshū, permeated with snow, may be sensed across the breadth of the scene; this phantom snow gives Yukihime's crimson robe its dazzling brilliance.

Masuyama loved especially the scene where the princess, bound with ropes to a cherry-tree, remembers the legend told of her grandfather, and with her toes draws in the fallen blossoms a rat, which comes to life and gnaws through the ropes binding her. It hardly needs be said that Mangiku Sanokawa did not adopt the puppetlike movements favoured by some *onnagata* in this scene. The ropes fastening him to the tree made Mangiku look lovelier than ever: all the artificial arabesques of this *onnagata*—the delicate gestures of the body, the play of the fingers, the arch of the hand—contrived though they might appear when employed for the movements of daily life, took on a strange vitality when used by Yukihime, bound to a tree. The intricate, contorted attitudes imposed by the constraint of the rope made of each instant an exquisite crisis, and the crises seemed to flow, one into the next, with the irresistible energy of successive waves.

Mangiku's performances unquestionably possessed moments of diabolic power. He used his lovely eyes so effectively that often with one flash he could create in an entire audience the illusion that the character of a scene had completely altered: when his glance embraced the stage from the *hanamichi* or the *hanamichi* from the stage, or when he darted one upward look at the bell in *Dōjōji*. In the palace scene from *Imoseyama*, Mangiku took the part of Omiwa, whose lover was stolen from her by Princess Tachibana and who has been cruelly mocked by the court ladies at the back of the stage saying, 'A groom without peer has been found for our princess! What joy for us all!' The narrator, seated at the side of the stage, declaims in powerful tones, 'Omiwa, hearing this, at once looks back.' At this moment Omiwa's character is completely transformed, and her face reveals the marks of a possessive attachment.

Masuyama felt a kind of terror every time he witnessed this moment. For an instant a diabolic shadow had swept over both the bright stage with its splendid set and beautiful costumes and over the thousands of intently watching spectators. This force clearly emanated from Mangiku's body, but at the same time transcended his flesh. Masuyama sensed in such passages something like a dark spring welling forth from this figure on the stage, this figure so imbued with softness, fragility, grace, delicacy, and feminine charms. He could not identify it, but he thought that a strange, evil presence, the final residue of the actor's fascination, a seductive evil which leads men astray and makes them drown in an instant of beauty, was the true nature of the dark spring he had detected. But one explains nothing merely by giving it a name.

Omiwa shakes her head and her hair tumbles in disarray. On the stage, to which she now returns from the *hanamichi*, Funashichi's blade is waiting to kill her.

'The house is full of music, an autumn sadness in its tone,' declaims the narrator.

There is something terrifying about the way Omiwa's feet hurry forward to her doom. The bare white feet, rushing ahead towards disaster and death, kicking the lines of her kimono askew, seem to know precisely when and where on the stage the violent emotions now urging her forward will end, and to be pressing towards the spot, rejoicing and triumphant even amidst the tortures of jealousy. The pain she reveals outwardly is backed with joy like her robe, on the outside dark and shot with gold thread, but bright with variegated silken strands within.

2

Masuyama's original decision to take employment at the theatre had been inspired by his absorption with kabuki, and especially with Mangiku; he realized also he could never escape his bondage unless he became thoroughly familiar with the world behind the scenes. He knew from what others had told him of the disenchantment to be found backstage, and he wanted to plunge into that world and taste for himself genuine disillusion.

But the disenchantment he expected somehow never came. Mangiku himself made this impossible. Mangiku faithfully maintained the injunctions of the eighteenth-century *onnagata's* manual *Ayamegusa*, 'An *onnagata*, even in the dressing-room, must preserve the attitudes of an *onnagata*. He should be careful when he eats to face away from other people, so that they cannot see him.' Whenever Mangiku was obliged to eat in the presence of visitors, not having the time to leave his dressing-room, he would turn towards his table with a word of apology and race through his meal, so skilfully that the visitors could not even guess from behind that he was eating.

Undoubtedly, the feminine beauty displayed by Mangiku on the stage had captivated Masuyama as a man. Strangely enough, however, this spell was not broken even by close observation of Mangiku in the dressing-room. Mangiku's body, when he had removed his costume, was delicate but unmistakably a man's. Masuyama, as a matter of fact, found it rather unnerving when Mangiku, seated at his dressing-table, too scantily clad to be anything but a man, directed polite, feminine greetings towards some visitor, all the while applying a heavy coating of powder to his shoulders. If even Masuyama, long a devotee of kabuki, experienced eerie sensations on his first visits to the dressing-room, what would have been the reactions of people who dislike kabuki, because the *onnagata* make them uncomfortable, if shown such a sight?

Masuyama, however, felt relief rather than disenchantment when he saw Mangiku after a performance, naked except for the gauzy underclothes he wore in order to absorb perspiration. The sight in itself may have been grotesque, but the nature of Masuyama's fascination—its intrinsic quality, one might say—did not reside in any surface illusion, and there was accordingly no danger that such a revelation would destroy it. Even after Mangiku had disrobed, it was apparent that he was still wearing several layers of splendid costumes beneath his skin; his nakedness was a passing manifestation. Something which could account for his exquisite appearance on stage surely lay concealed within him.

Masuyama enjoyed seeing Mangiku when he returned to the dressing-room after performing a major role. The flush of the emotions of the part he had been enacting still hovered over his entire body, like sunset glow or the moon in the sky at dawn. The grand emotions of classical tragedy—emotions quite unrelated to our mundane lives—may seem to be guided, at least nominally, by historical facts—the world of disputed successions, campaigns of pacification, civil warfare, and the like—but in reality they belong to no period. They are the emotions appropriate to a stylized, grotesquely tragic world, luridly coloured in the manner of a late wood-block print. Grief that goes beyond human bounds, superhuman passions, searing love, terrifying joy, the brief cries of people trapped by circumstances too tragic for human beings to endure: such were the emotions which a moment before had lodged in Mangiku's body, It was amazing that Mangiku's slender frame could hold them and that they did not break from that delicate vessel.

Be that as it may, Mangiku a moment before had been living amidst these grandiose feelings, and he had radiated light on the stage precisely because the emotions he portrayed transcended any known to his audience. Perhaps this is true of all characters on the stage, but among present-day actors none seemed to be so honestly living stage emotions so far removed from daily life.

A passage in *Ayamegusa* states, 'Charm is the essence of the *onnagata*. But even the *onnagata* who is naturally beautiful will lose his charm if he strains to impress by his movements. If he consciously attempts to appear graceful he will seem thorougly corrupt instead. For this reason, unless the *onnagata* lives as a woman in his daily life, he is unlikely ever to be considered an accomplished *onnagata*. When he appears on stage, the more he concentrates on performing this or that essentially feminine action, the more masculine he will seem. I am convinced that the essential thing is how the actor behaves in real life.'

How the actor behaves in real life . . . yes, Mangiku was utterly feminine in both the speech and bodily movements of his real life. If Mangiku had been more masculine in his daily life, those moments when the flush from the *onnagata* role he had been performing gradually dissolved like the high-water mark on a beach into the femininity of his daily life—itself an extension of the same make-believe—would have become an absolute division between sea and land, a bleak door shut between dream and reality. The make-believe of his daily life supported the make-believe of his stage performances. This, Masuyama was convinced, marked the true *onnagata*. An *onnagata* is the child born of the illicit union between dream and reality.

3

Once the celebrated veteran actors of the previous generation had all passed away, one on the heels of the other, Mangiku's authority backstage became absolute. His *onnagata* disciples waited on him like personal servants; indeed, the order of seniority they observed when following Mangiku on stage as maids in the wake of his princess or great lady was exactly the same they observed in the dressing-room.

Anyone pushing apart the door curtains dyed with the crest of the Sanokawa family and entering Mangiku's dressing-room was certain to be struck by a strange sensation: this charming sanctuary contained not a single man. Even members of the same troupe felt inside this room that they were in the presence of the opposite sex. Whenever Masuyama went to Mangiku's dressing-room on some errand, he had only to brush apart the door curtains to feel—even before setting foot inside—a curiously vivid, carnal sensation of being a male.

Sometimes Masuyama had gone on company business to the dressing-rooms of chorus girls backstage at revues. The rooms were filled with an almost suffocating femininity and the rough-skinned girls, sprawled about like animals in the zoo, threw bored glances at him, but he never felt so distinctly alien as in Mangiku's dressing-room; nothing in these real women made Masuyama feel particularly masculine.

The members of Mangiku's entourage exhibited no special friendliness towards Masuyama. On the contrary, he knew that they secretly gossiped about him, accusing him of being disrespectful or of giving himself airs merely because he had gone through some university. He knew too that sometimes they professed irritation at his pedantic insistence on historical facts. In the world of kabuki, academic learning unaccompanied by artistic talent is considered of no value.

Masuyama's work had its compensations too. It would happen when Mangiku had a favour to ask of someone—only,

of course, when he was in good mood—that he twisted his
body diagonally from his dressing-table and gave a little nod
and a smile; the indescribable charm in his eyes at such
moments made Masuyama feel that he wished for nothing
more than to slave like a dog for this man. Mangiku himself
never forgot his dignity: he never failed to maintain a certain
distance, though he obviously was aware of his charms. If he
had been a real woman, his whole body would have been filled
with the allure in his eyes. The allure of an *onnagata* is only a
momentary glimmer, but that is enough for it to exist inde-
pendently and to display the eternal feminine.

Mangiku sat before the mirror after the performance of *The
Castle of the Lord Protector of Hachijin*, the first item of the
programme. He had removed the costume and wig he wore as
Lady Hinaginu, and changed to a bathrobe, not being obliged
to appear in the middle work of the programme. Masuyama,
informed that Mangiku wanted to see him, had been waiting in
the dressing-room for the curtain of *Hachijin*. The mirror suddenly burst into crimson flames as Mangiku returned to the
room, filling the entrance with the rustle of his robes. Three
disciples and dressers joined to remove what had to be
removed and store it away. Those who were to leave departed,
and now no one remained except for a few disciples around
the hibachi in the next room. The dressing-room had all at
once fallen still. From a loudspeaker in the corridor issued the
sounds of stage assistants hammering as they dismantled the
set for the play which had just ended. It was late November,
and steam heat clouded the window-panes, bleak as in a hospital ward. White chrysanthemums bent gracefully in a
cloisonné vase placed beside Mangiku's dressing-table. Mangiku, perhaps because his stage name meant literally 'ten
thousand chrysanthemums', was fond of this flower.

Mangiku sat on a bulky cushion of purple silk, facing his
dressing-table. 'I wonder if you'd mind telling the gentleman
from Sakuragi Street?' (Mangiku, in the old-fashioned
manner, referred to his dancing and singing teachers by the
names of the streets where they lived.) 'It'd be hard for me to
tell him.' He gazed directly into the mirror as he spoke.
Masuyama could see from where he sat by the wall the nape of

Mangiku's neck and the reflections in the mirror of his face still made up for the part of Hinaginu. The eyes were not on Masuyama; they were squarely contemplating his own face. The flush from his exertions on the stage still glowed through the powder on his cheeks, like the morning sun through a thin sheet of ice. He was looking at Hinaginu.

Indeed, he actually saw her in the mirror—Hinaginu, whom he had just been impersonating, Hinaginu, the daughter of Mori Sanzaemon Yoshinari and the bride of the young Satō Kazuenosuke. Her marriage ties with her husband having been broken because of his feudal loyalty, Hinaginu killed herself so that she might remain faithful to a union 'whose ties were so faint we never shared the same bed'. Hinaginu had died on stage of a despair so extreme she could not bear to live any longer. The Hinaginu in the mirror was a ghost. Even that ghost, Mangiku knew, was at this very moment slipping from his body. His eyes pursued Hinaginu. But as the glow of the ardent passions of the role subsided, Hinaginu's face faded away. He bade it farewell. There were still seven performances before the final day. Tomorrow again Hinaginu's features would no doubt return to the pliant mould of Mangiku's face.

Masuyama, enjoying the sight of Mangiku in this abstracted state, all but smiled with affection. Mangiku suddenly turned towards him. He had been aware all along of Masuyama's gaze, but with the nonchalance of the actor, accustomed to the public's stares, he continued with his business. 'It's those instrumental passages. They're simply not long enough. I don't mean I can't get through the part if I hurry, but it makes everything so ugly.' Mangiku was referring to the music for the new dance-play which would be presented the following month. 'Mr. Masuyama, what do *you* think?'

'I quite agree. I'm sure you mean the passage after "How slow the day ends by the Chinese bridge at Seta."'

'Yes, that's the place. How-ow slo-ow the da-ay . . .' Mangiku sang the passage in question, beating time with his delicate fingers.

'I'll tell him. I'm sure that the gentleman from Sakuragi Street will understand.'

373

'Are you sure you don't mind? I feel so embarrassed about making a nuisance of myself all the time.'

Mangiku was accustomed to terminate a conversation by standing, once his business had been dealt with. 'I'm afraid I must bathe now,' he said. Masuyama drew back from the narrow entrance to the dressing-room and let Mangiku pass. Mangiku, with a slight bow of the head, went out into the corridor, accompanied by a disciple. He turned back obliquely towards Masuyama and, smiling, bowed again. The rouge at the corners of his eyes had an indefinable charm. Masuyama sensed that Mangiku was well aware of his affection.

4

The troupe to which Masuyama belonged was to remain at the same theatre through November, December, and January, and the programme for January had already become the subject of gossip. A new work by a playwright of the modern theatre was to be staged. The man, whose sense of his own importance accorded poorly with his youth, had imposed innumerable conditions, and Masuyama was kept frantically busy with complicated negotiations intended to bring together not only the dramatist and the actors but the management of the theatre as well. Masuyama was recruited for this job because the others considered him to be an intellectual.

One of the conditions laid down by the playwright was that the direction of the play be confided to a talented young man whom he trusted. The management accepted this condition. Mangiku also agreed, but without enthusiasm. He conveyed his doubts in this manner: 'I don't really know, of course, but if this young man doesn't understand kabuki very well, and makes unreasonable demands on us, it will be so hard explaining.' Mangiku was hoping for an older, more mature—by which he meant a more compliant—director.

The new play was a dramatization in modern language of the twelfth-century novel *If Only I Could Change Them!* The managing director of the company, deciding not to leave the production of this new work to the regular staff, announced it would be in Masuyama's hands. Masuyama grew tense at the thought of the work ahead of him but, convinced that the play was first-rate, he felt that it would be worth the trouble.

As soon as the scripts were ready and the parts assigned, a preliminary meeting was held one mid-December morning in the reception room adjoining the office of the theatre owner. The meeting was attended by the executive in charge of production, the playwright, the director, the stage designer, the actors, and Masuyama. The room was warmly heated and sunlight poured through the windows. Masuyama always felt happiest at preliminary meetings. It was like spreading out a map and discussing a projected outing: Where do we board the bus and where do we start walking? Is there drinking water where we're going? Where are we going to eat lunch? Where is the best view? Shall we take the train back? Or would it be better to allow enough time to return by boat?

Kawasaki, the director, was late. Masuyama had never seen a play directed by Kawasaki, but he knew of him by reputation. Kawasaki had been selected, despite his youth, to direct Ibsen and modern American plays for a repertory company, and in the course of a year had done so well, with the latter especially, that he was awarded a newspaper drama prize.

The others (except for Kawasaki) had all assembled. The designer, who could never bear waiting a minute before throwing himself into his work, was already jotting down in a large notebook especially brought for the purpose suggestions made by the others, frequently tapping the end of his pencil on the blank pages, as if bursting with ideas. Eventually the executive began to gossip about the absent director. 'He may be as talented as they say, but he's still young, after all. The actors will have to help out.'

At this moment there was a knock at the door and a secretary showed in Kawasaki. He entered the room with a dazed look, as if the light were too strong for him and, without uttering a word, stiffly bowed towards the others. He was rather tall, almost six feet, with deeply etched, masculine—but highly sensitive—features. It was a cold winter day, but Kawasaki wore a rumpled, thin raincoat. Underneath, as he presently disclosed, he had on a brick-coloured corduroy jacket. His

long, straight hair hung down so far—to the tip of his nose—
that he was frequently obliged to push it back. Masuyama was
rather disappointed by his first impression. He had supposed
that a man who had been singled out for his abilities would
have attempted to distinguish himself somehow from the stereotypes of society, but this man dressed and acted exactly in
the way one would expect of the typical young man of the
modern theatre.

Kawasaki took the place offered him at the head of the
table. He did not make the usual polite protests against the
honour. He kept his eyes on the playwright, his close friend,
and when introduced to each of the actors he uttered a word of
greeting, only to turn back at once to the playwright. Masuyama could remember similar experiences. It is not easy for a
man trained in the modern theatre, where most of the actors
are young, to establish himself on easy terms with the kabuki
actors, who are likely to prove to be imposing old gentlemen
when encountered off stage.

The actors assembled for this preliminary meeting managed
in fact to convey somehow their contempt for Kawasaki, all
with a show of the greatest politeness and without an
unfriendly word. Masuyama happened to glance at Mangiku's
face. He modestly kept to himself, refraining from any demonstration of self-importance; he displayed no trace of the
others' contempt. Masuyama felt greater admiration and
affection than ever for Mangiku.

Now that everyone was present, the author described the
play in outline. Mangiku, probably for the first time in his
career—leaving aside parts he took as a child—was to play a
male role. The plot told of a certain Grand Minister with two
children, a boy and a girl. By nature they are quite unsuited to
their sexes and are therefore reared accordingly: the boy
(actually the girl) eventually becomes General of the Left, and
the girl (actually the boy) becomes the chief lady-in-waiting in
the Senyoden, the palace of the Imperial concubines. Later,
when the truth is revealed, they revert to lives more appropriate to the sex of their birth; the brother marries the fourth
daughter of the Minister of the Right, and sister a Middle
Counsellor, and all ends happily.

Mangiku's part was that of the girl who is in reality a man. Although this was a male role, Mangiku would appear as a man only in the few moments of the final scene. Up to that point, he was to act throughout as a true *onnagata* in the part of a chief lady-in-waiting at the Senyoden. The author and director were agreed in urging Mangiku not to make any special attempt even in the last scene to suggest that he was in fact a man.

An amusing aspect of the play was that it inevitably had the effect of satirizing the kabuki convention of the *onnagata*. The lady-in-waiting was actually a man; so, in precisely the same manner, was Mangiku in the role. That was not all. In order for Mangiku, at once an *onnagata* and a man, to perform this part, he would have to unfold on two levels his actions of real life, a far cry from the simple case of the actor who assumes female costume during the course of a play so as to work some deception. The complexities of the part intrigued Mangiku.

Kawasaki's first words to Mangiku were, 'I would be glad if you played the part throughout as a woman. It doesn't make the least difference if you act like a woman even in the last scene.' His voice had a pleasant, clear ring.

'Really? If you don't mind my acting the part that way, it'll make it ever so much easier for me.'

'It won't be easy in any case. Definitely not,' said Kawasaki decisively. When he spoke in this forceful manner his cheeks glowed red as if a lamp had been lit inside. The sharpness of his tone cast something of a pall over the gathering. Masuyama's eyes wandered to Mangiku. He was giggling good-naturedly, the back of his hand pressed to his mouth. The others relaxed to see Mangiku had not been offended.

'Well, then,' said the author, 'I shall read the book.' He lowered his protruding eyes, which looked double behind his thick spectacles, and began to read the script on the table.

5

Two or three days later the rehearsal by parts began, whenever the different actors had free time. Full-scale rehearsals would only be possible during the few days in between the end of this month and the beginning of next month's programme.

Unless everything that needed tightening were attended to by then, there would be no time to pull the performance together.

Once the rehearsal of the parts began it became apparent to everyone that Kawasaki was like a foreigner strayed among them. He had not the smallest grasp of kabuki, and Masuyama found himself obliged to stand beside him and explain word by word the technical language of the kabuki theatre, making Kawasaki extremely dependent on him. The instant the first rehearsal was over Masuyama invited Kawasaki for a drink.

Masuyama knew that for someone in his position it was generally speaking a mistake to ally himself with the director, but he felt he could easily understand what Kawasaki must be experiencing. The young man's views were precisely defined, his mental attitudes were wholesome, and he threw himself into his work with boyish enthusiasm. Masuyama could see why Kawasaki's character should have so appealed to the playwright; he felt as if Kawasaki's genuine youthfulness were a somehow purifying element, a quality unknown in the world of kabuki. Masuyama justified his friendship with Kawasaki in terms of attempting to turn this quality to the advantage of kabuki.

Full-scale rehearsals began at last on the day after the final performances of the December programme. It was two days after Christmas. The year-end excitement in the streets could be sensed even through the windows in the theatre and the dressing-rooms. A battered old desk had been placed by a window in the large rehearsal room. Kawasaki and one of Masuyama's seniors on the staff—the stage manager—sat with their backs to the window. Masuyama was behind Kawasaki. The authors sat on the *tatami* along the wall. Each would go up centre when his turn came to recite his lines. The stage manager supplied forgotten lines.

Sparks flew repeatedly between Kawasaki and the actors. 'At this point,' Kawasaki would say, 'I'd like you to stand as you say, "I wish I could go to Kawachi and have done with it." Then you're to walk up to the pillar at stage right.'

'That's one place I simply can't stand up.'

'Please try doing it my way.' Kawasaki forced a smile, but his face visibly paled with wounded pride.

'You can ask me to stand up from now until next Christmas, but I still can't do it. I'm supposed at this place to be mulling over something. How can I walk across stage when I'm thinking?'

Kawasaki did not answer, but he betrayed his extreme irritation at being addressed in such terms.

But things were quite different when it came to Mangiku's turn. If Kawasaki said, 'Sit!' Mangiku would sit, and if he said 'Stand!' Managiku stood. He obeyed unresistingly every direction given by Kawasaki. It seemed to Masuyama that Mangiku's fondness for the part did not fully explain why he was so much more obliging than was his custom at rehearsals.

Masuyama was forced to leave this rehearsal on business just as Mangiku, having run through his scene in the first act, was returning to his seat by the wall. When Masuyama got back, he was met by the following sight: Kawasaki, all but sprawled over the desk, was intently following the rehearsal, not bothering even to push back the long hair falling over his eyes. He was leaning on his crossed arms, the shoulders beneath the corduroy jacket shaking with suppressed rage. To Masuyama's right was a white wall interrupted by a window, through which he could see a balloon swaying in the northerly wind, its streamer proclaiming an end-of-the-year sale. Hard, wintry clouds looked as if they had been blocked in with chalk against the pale blue of the sky. He noticed a shrine to Inari and a tiny vermilion torii on the roof of an old building near by. Farther to his right, by the wall, Mangiku sat erect in Japanese style on the *tatami*. The script lay open on his lap, and the lines of his greenish-grey kimono were perfectly straight. From where Masuyama stood at the door he could not see Mangiku's full face; but the eyes, seen in profile, were utterly tranquil, the gentle gaze fixed unwaveringly on Kawasaki.

Masuyama felt a momentary shudder of fear. He had set one foot inside the rehearsal room, but it was now almost impossible to go in.

6

Later in the day Masuyama was summoned to Mangiku's dressing-room. He felt an unaccustomed emotional block when he bent his head, as so often before, to pass through the door curtains. Mangiku greeted him, all smiles, from his perch on the purple cushion and offered Masuyama some cakes he had been given by a visitor.

'How do you think the rehearsal went today?'

'Pardon me?' Masuyama was startled by the question. It was not like Mangiku to ask his opinion on such matters.

'How did it seem?'

'If everything continues to go as well as it did today, I think the play'll be a hit.'

'Do you really think so? I feel terribly sorry for Mr. Kawasaki. It's so hard for him. The others have been treating him in such a high-handed way that it's made me quite nervous. I'm sure you could tell from the rehearsal that I've made up my mind to play the part exactly as Mr. Kawasaki says. That's the way I'd like to play it myself anyway, and I thought it might make things a little easier for Mr. Kawasaki, even if nobody else helps. I can't very well tell the others, but I'm sure they'll notice if I do exactly what I'm told. They know how difficult I usually am. That's the least I can do to protect Mr. Kawasaki. It'd be a shame, when he's trying so hard, if nobody helped.'

Masuyama felt no particular surge of emotions as he listened to Mangiku. Quite likely, he thought, Mangiku himself was unaware that he was in love: he was so accustomed to portraying love on a more heroic scale. Masuyama, for his part, considered that these sentiments—however they were to be termed—which had formed in Mangiku's heart were most inappropriate. He expected of Mangiku a far more transparent, artificial, aesthetic display of emotions.

Mangiku, most unusually for him, sat rather informally, imparting a kind of languor to his delicate figure. The mirror reflected the cluster of crimson asters arranged in the cloisonné vase and the recently shaved nape of Mangiku's neck.

Kawasaki's exasperation had become pathetic by the day before stage rehearsals began. As soon as the last private rehearsal ended, he invited Masuyama for a drink, looking as if he had reached the end of his tether. Masuyama was busy at the moment, but two hours later he found Kawasaki in the bar where they had arranged to meet, still waiting for him. The bar was crowded, though it was the night before New Year's Eve, when bars are usually deserted. Kawasaki's face looked pale as he sat drinking alone. He was the kind who only gets paler the more he has had to drink. Masuyama, catcing sight of Kawasaki's ashen face as soon as he entered the bar, felt that the young man had saddled him with an unfairly heavy spiritual burden. They lived in different worlds; there was no reason why courtesy should demand that Kawasaki's uncertainties and anguish should fall so squarely on his shoulders.

Kawasaki, as he rather expected, immediately engaged him with a good-natured taunt, accusing him of being a double agent. Masuyama took the charge with a smile. He was only five or six years older than Kawasaki, but he possessed the self-confidence of a man who had dwelt among people who 'knew the score'. At the same time, he felt a kind of envy of this man who had never known hardship, or at any rate, enough hardship. It was not exactly a lack of moral integrity which had made Masuyama indifferent to most of the backstage gossip directed against him, now that he was securely placed in the kabuki hierarchy; his indifference demonstrated that he had nothing to do with the kind of sincerity which might destroy him.

Kawasaki spoke. 'I'm fed up with the whole thing. Once the curtain goes up on opening night, I'll be only too glad to disappear from the picture. Stage rehearsals beginning tomorrow! That's more than I can take, when I'm feeling so disgusted. This is the worst assignment I've ever had. I've reached my limit. Never again will I barge into a world that's not my own.'

'But isn't that what you more or less expected from the outset? Kabuki's not the same as the modern theatre, after all.' Masuyama's voice was cold.

Kawasaki's next words came as a surprise. 'Mangiku's the hardest to take. I really dislike him. I'll never stage another play with him.' Kawasaki stared at the curling wisps of smoke under the low ceiling, as if into the face of an invisible enemy.

'I wouldn't have guessed it. It seems to me he's doing his best to be cooperative.'

'What makes you think so? What's so good about him? It doesn't bother me too much when the other actors don't listen to me during rehearsals or try to intimidate me, or even when they sabotage the whole works, but Mangiku's more than I can figure out. All he does is stare at me with that sneer on his face. At bottom he's absolutely uncompromising, and he treats me like an ignorant little squirt. That's why he does everything exactly as I say. He's the only one of them who obeys my directions, and that burns me up all the more. I can tell just what he's thinking: "If that's the way you want it, that's the way I'll do it, but don't expect me to take any responsibility for what happens in the performance." That's what he keeps flashing at me, without saying a word, and it's the worst sabotage I know. He's the nastiest of the lot.'

Masuyama listened in astonishment, but he shrank from revealing the truth to Kawasaki now. He hesitated even to let Kawasaki know that Mangiku was intending to be friendly, much less the whole truth. Kawasaki was baffled as to how he should respond to the entirely unfamiliar emotions of this world into which he had suddenly plunged; if he were informed of Mangiku's feelings, he might easily suppose they represented just one more snare laid for him. His eyes were too clear: for all his grasp of the principles of theatre, he could not detect the dark, aesthetic presence lurking behind the texts.

The New Year came and with it the first night of the new programme.

Mangiku was in love. His sharp-eyed disciples were the first to gossip about it. Masuyama, a frequent visitor to Mangiku's dressing-room, sensed it in the atmosphere almost immediately. Mangiku was wrapped in his love like a silkworm in its cocoon, soon to emerge as a butterfly. His dressing-room was the cocoon of his love. Mangiku was of a retiring disposition in any case, but the contrast with the New Year's excitement elsewhere gave his dressing-room a peculiarly solemn hush.

On the opening night, Masuyama, noticing as he passed Mangiku's dressing-room that the door was wide open, decided to take a look inside. He saw Mangiku from behind, seated before the mirror in full costume, waiting for his signal to go on. His eyes took in the pale lavender of Mangiku's robe, the gentle slope of the powdered and half-exposed shoulders, the glossy, lacquer-black wig. Mangiku at such moments in the deserted dressing-room looked like a woman absorbed in her spinning; she was spinning her love, and would continue spinning for ever, her mind elsewhere.

Masuyama intuitively understood that the mould for this *onnagata*'s love had been provided by the stage alone. The stage was present all day long, the stage where love was incessantly shouting, grieving, shedding blood. Music celebrating the sublime heights of love sounded perpetually in Mangiku's ears, and each exquisite gesture of his body was constantly employed on stage for the purpose of love. To the tips of his fingers, nothing about Mangiku was alien to love. His toes encased in white *tabi*, the seductive colours of his under kimono barely glimpsed through the openings in his sleeves, the long, swanlike nape of his neck were all in the service of love.

Masuyama did not doubt but that Mangiku would obtain guidance in pursuing his love from the grandiose emotions of his stage roles. The ordinary actor is apt to enrich his performances by infusing them with the emotions of his real life, but not Mangiku. The instant that Mangiku fell in love, the loves of Yukihime, Omiwa, Hinaginu, and the other tragic heroines came to his support.

The thought of Mangiku in love took Masuyama aback, however. Those tragic emotions for which he had yearned so fervently since his days as a high-school student, those sublime emotions which Mangiku always evoked through his corporeal presence on stage, encasing his sensual faculties in icy flames, Mangiku was now visibly nurturing in real life. But the object of these emotions—granted that he had some talent—was an ignoramus as far as kabuki was concerned; he was merely a young, commonplace-looking director whose only qualification as the object of Mangiku's love consisted in being a foreigner in this country, a young traveller who would soon depart the world of kabuki and never return.

7

If Only I Could Change Them! was well received. Kawasaki,
despite his announced intention of disappearing after opening
night, came to the theatre every day to complain of the performance, to rush back and forth incessantly through the subterranean passages under the stage, to finger with curiosity
the mechanisms of the trap door or the *hanamichi*. Masuyama
thought this man had something childish about him.

The newspaper reviews praised Mangiku. Masuyama made
it a point to show them to Kawasaki, but he merely pouted,
like an obstinate child, and all but spat out the words,
'They're all good at acting. But there wasn't any *direction*.'
Masuyama naturally did not relay to Mangiku these harsh
words, and Kawasaki himself was on his best behaviour when
he actually met Mangiku. It nevertheless irritated Masuyma
that Mangiku, who was utterly blind when it came to other
people's feelings, should not have questioned that Kawasaki
was aware of his good will. But Kawasaki was absolutely
insensitive to what other people might feel. This was the one
trait that Kawasaki and Mangiku had in common.

A week after the first performance Masuyama was summoned to Mangiku's dressing-room. Mangiku displayed on his
table amulets and charms from the shrine where he regularly
worshipped, as well as some small New Year's cakes. The cakes
would no doubt be distributed later among his disciples. Mangiku pressed some sweets on Masuyama, a sign that he was in
a good mood. 'Mr. Kawasaki was here a little while ago,'
he said.

'Yes, I saw him out front.'

'I wonder if he's still in the theatre.'

'I imagine he'll stay until *If Only* is over.'

'Did he say anything about being busy afterwards?'

'No, nothing particular.'

'Then, I have a little favour I'd like to ask you.'

Masuyama assumed as businesslike an expression as he
could muster. 'What might it be?'

'Tonight, you see, when the performance is over . . . I mean, tonight . . .' The colour had mounted in Mangiku's cheeks. His voice was clearer and higher-pitched than usual. 'Tonight, when the performance is over, I thought I'd like to have dinner with him. Would you mind asking if he's free?'

'I'll ask him.'

'It's dreadful of me, isn't it, to ask you such a thing.'

'That's quite all right.' Masuyama sensed that Mangiku's eyes at that moment had stopped roving and were trying to read his expression. He seemed to expect—and even to desire —some perturbation on Masuyama's part. 'Very well,' Masuyama said, rising at once, 'I'll inform him.'

Hardly had Masuyama gone into the lobby than he ran into Kawasaki, coming from the opposite direction; this chance meeting amidst the crowd thronging the lobby during the interval seemed like a stroke of fate. Kawasaki's manner poorly accorded with the festive air pervading the lobby. The somehow haughty airs which the young man always adopted seemed rather comic when set amidst a buzzing crowd of solid citizens dressed in holiday finery and attending the theatre merely for the pleasure of seeing a play.

Masuyama led Kawasaki to a corner of the lobby and informed him of Mangiku's request.

'I wonder what he wants with me now? Dinner together— that's funny. I have nothing else to do tonight, and there's no reason why I can't go, but I don't see why.'

'I suppose there's something he wants to discuss about the play.'

'The play! I've said all I want to on that subject.'

At this moment a gratuitous desire to do evil, an emotion always associated on the stage with minor villains, took seed within Masuyama's heart, though he did not realize it; he was not aware that he himself was now acting like a character in a play. 'Don't you see—being invited to dinner gives you a marvellous opportunity to tell him everything you've got on your mind, this time without mincing words.'

'All the same—'

'I don't suppose you've got the nerve to tell him.'

The remark wounded the young man's pride. 'All right. I'll

go. I've known all along that sooner or later I'd have my chance to have it out with him in the open. Please tell him that I'm glad to accept his invitation.'

Mangiku appeared in the last work of the programme and was not free until the entire performance was over. Once the show ends, actors normally make a quick change of clothes and rush from the theatre, but Mangiku showed no sign of haste as he completed his dressing by putting a cape and a scarf of a muted colour over his outer kimono. He waited for Kawasaki. When Kawasaki at last appeared, he curtly greeted Mangiku, not bothering to take his hands from his overcoat pockets.

The disciple who always waited on Mangiku as his 'lady's maid' rushed up, as if to announce some major calamity. 'It's started to snow,' he reported with a bow.

'A heavy snow? Mangiku touched his cape to his cheek.

'No, just a flurry.'

'We'll need an umbrella to the car.' Mangiku said. The disciple rushed off for an umbrella.

Masuyama saw them to the stage entrance. The door attendant had politely arranged Mangiku's and Kawasaki's footwear next to each other. Mangiku's disciple stood outside in the thin snow, holding an open umbrella. The snow fell so sparsely that one couldn't be sure one saw it against the dark concrete wall beyond. One or two flakes fluttered on to the doorstep at the stage entrance.

Mangiku bowed to Masuyama. 'We'll be leaving now,' he said. The smile on his lips could be seen indistinctly behind his scarf. He turned to the disciple, 'That's all right. I'll carry the umbrella. I'd like you to go instead and tell the driver we're ready.' Mangiku held the umbrella over Kawasaki's head. As Kawasaki in his overcoat and Mangiku in his cape walked off side by side under the umbrella, a few flakes suddenly flew— all but bounced—from the umbrella.

Masuyama watched them go. He felt as though a big, black wet umbrella were being noisily opened inside his heart. He could tell that the illusion, first formed when as a boy he saw Mangiku perform, an illusion which he had preserved intact even after he joined the kabuki staff, had shattered that instant in all directions, like a delicate piece of crystal dropped from a height. At last I know what disillusion means, he thought. I might as well give up the theatre.

But Masuyama knew that along with disillusion a new sensation was assaulting him, jealousy. He dreaded where this new emotion might lead him.

—Translated by
Donald Keene

LEROI JONES

THE TOILET

The *Toilet* was first presented by Leo Garen and Stan Swerdlow at the St. Marks Playhouse, New York, on December 16, 1964. It was directed by Leo Garen, designed by Larry Rivers, and the lighting was by Harold Baldridge. The cast was as follows:

ORA .... James Spruill

WILLIE LOVE .... Gary Bolling

HINES .... D'Urville Martin

JOHNNY BOY HOLMES .... Bostic Van Felton

PERRY .... Norman Bush

GEORGE DAVIS .... Antonio Fargas

SKIPPY .... Tony Hudson

KNOWLES .... Walter Jones

DONALD FARRELL ....Gary Haynes

FOOTS ....Hampton Clanton

KAROLIS ....Jaime Sanchez

CHARACTERS

ORA (Big Shot): *Short, ugly, crude, loud.*

WILLIE LOVE: *Tall, thin. Should have been sensitive. Smiles.*

HINES: *Big, husky, garrulous. He and Love are closest friends.*

JOHNNY BOY HOLMES: *Short, curly hair. Bright, fast, likable.*

PERRY: *Tall, dark, somber, cynical.*

GEORGE DAVIS: *Tall, thin, crudely elegant. Judicious.*

SKIPPY: *Quick. Rather stupid but interested. Someone to be trusted.*

KNOWLES: *Large and ridiculous. A grinning ape.*

DONALD FARRELL: *Tall, thin, blond, awkward, soft.*

FOOTS (Ray): *Short, intelligent, manic. Possessor of a threatened empire.*

KAROLIS: *Medium height. Very skinny and not essentially attractive except when he speaks.*

The scene is a large bare toilet built of gray rough cement. There are urinals along one wall and a partition separating them from the commodes which are along the same wall. The toilet must resemble the impersonal ugliness of a school toilet or a latrine of some institution. A few rolls of toilet paper are spread out on the floor, wet through. The actors should give the impression frequently that the place smells.

Ora breaks through the door grinning, then giggling. Looks around the bleak place, walks around, then with one hand on his hip takes out his joint and pees, still grinning, into one of the commodes, spraying urine over the seat.

LOVE (*sticking his head through the door*): Big Shot! Hey, Big Shot! These guys say come and help them.

ORA (*zipping his fly and wiping the one hand on the back of his pants*): Yeh? (*Turning to* LOVE.) Yeh? They got him, huh?

LOVE (*pushing door open so his arm is straight*): Naw, they don't have him yet. He's on the second floor, running back and forth and hiding in empty rooms. But Knowles said for you to come help.

ORA (*flushing all the commodes and urinals in the row as he walks past*): Sheet! I'll catch that bastid in a second. (*Ducks under* LOVE's *arm to go out.*) Why the hell don't you get up there. You supposed to be faster than me.

LOVE: I'm s'posed to stay here and keep the place clear. (*Making a face.*) Damn. This place smells like hell.

ORA (*without turning around*): Yeh (*giggling*), this must be your momma's house.

LOVE (*slipping inside the door and holding it against* ORA): Shit. At least I got one.

ORA (*thumps against the door, not really angry*): Bastid!

LOVE *waits a few seconds, then pulls the door open slightly. Then lets it shut and walks to a closed commode and noticing it's wet wipes it with some of the strewn toilet paper. He sits down and stretches his legs. Then gets up and opens the commode to pee. There are voices outside and then the door swings open and* HINES *and* HOLMES *come in.*

HINES: Hey, Willie.

LOVE (*still peeing*): What you want? (*Comes out, zipping his pants.*)

HINES (*to* HOLMES): Man, this cat's in here pulling his whatchamacallit.

HOLMES (*to* LOVE): Yeh. Damn, Love, why don't you go get Gloria to do that stuff for you.

LOVE: She-et. (*Grinning.*) Huh. I sure don't need your ol' lady to be pullin' on my joint. (*Laughs.* HOLMES *begins to spar with him.*)

HINES: They didn't even catch that skinny nose punk yet.

LOVE: No? Why in hell not?

HOLMES: He's still running up and down the damn halls. I should go up there and drag that sonofabitch down.

> HOLMES *and* HINES *begin to pee also—in the commodes.*
> LOVE *pulls open the door a small bit and looks out.*

LOVE: Shit. Boy, all you slow ass cats. I'd catch that little skinny paddy boy in a second. Where's that little popeyed Foots?

HINES: Damn if I know. I think he's still in Miss Powell's class. You know if he missed her class she'd beat his head, and then get his ol' lady to beat his head again.

HOLMES: Shit. Skippy should've got hold of that damn Karolis by now. He ain't fast worth a bitch.

LOVE: Yeh, but he's so so goddamned scary he might just jump out a goddamn window.

> HOLMES *finishes peeing and starts pushing* LOVE *and they begin to spar around.* HOLMES *is very funny, making boxer-like sounds and brushing his nose continuously with his thumbs.* LOVE *just stands straight with his left hand stiff and stabbing it out toward Holmes' face.* HINES *finishes and gets in the action too. Both he and* HOLMES *are against* LOVE, *who starts to laugh and curse good naturedly.*

LOVE: Two a' you bastids, huh? I'll take you both. (*He starts kicking at them.*)

HINES: Boy, if you kick me, you'll die just like that . . . with your skinny ass leg up. They'll have to build you a special coffin with a part for your leg.

HOLMES (*backing away, and then turning on* HINES. *Laughing*): Let's get this sum'bitch, Willie.

HINES (*backing away, now kicking and swinging . . . but just timing blows so they won't strike anyone*): Goddamn, Johnny Boy, you a crooked muthafucka. You cats think you can mess with the kid?

> *The two spar against* HINES *and then* LOVE *turns against* HOLMES.

LOVE: Let's get this little assed cat.

> HOLMES *kicks at them, then jumps up on the commodes in order to defend himself more "heroically."*

HOLMES: I'm gonna get your ass, Willie. I'm just trying to help you out and you gonna play wise. Ya' bastid.

HINES: Listen to that cat. (*Runs after* HOLMES.) I'm gonna put your damn head in one of those damn urinals.

> *He and* LOVE *finally grab* HOLMES *and he begins struggling with them in earnest.*

Let's put this little bastard's head in the goddamn urinal!

HOLMES: You bastids! Let me go! I'm gonna cut somebody. Bastids!

> *The door opens and* ORA *comes in. His shirt is torn. But he rushes over laughing and starts punching everyone, even* HOLMES.

HINES: Goddamn it, Big Shot, get the hell out of here.

HOLMES: Get 'em, Big Shot.

ORA (*punches* HOLMES *who's still being held by* LOVE): I'm gonna punch you, you prick. Hold the cocksucker, Love.

LOVE (*releasing* HOLMES *immediately*): I ain't gonna hold him so you can punch him.

> ORA *and* HOLMES *square off, both laughing and faking professional demeanor.*

LOVE: Hey, Big Shot, what happened to your shirt?

ORA (*putting his hands down and handling the torn part of his shirt*): That muthafuckin' Karolis ripped it.

> *The other three yowl.* HINES *puts his fingers to the hole as if to tear it again.*

Get outta here you black ass bastid. (*He squares off at* HINES, *then pushes him away.*) That paddy bastid! I had the cocksucker around the waist, and then he rips my shirt and scratches me. (*He holds up his wounded hand.*)

HINES: You let him get away?

ORA: No, hell. I punched the bastid right in his lip. But he was making so much noise we thought somebody'd come out and see us so Knowles and Skippy took him in the broom closet and I cut down the stairs. The stupid bastid was screaming and biting right outside of ol' lady Powell's room.

HOLMES: Did anybody come outta there?

ORA: You think I was gonna stay around and see? She and Miss Golden after me anyway.

LOVE: Did you see Foots in there?

ORA (*going to the door and peering out*): Yeh. And George Davis and Perry are in there too. (*He pushes door open and leans all the way out.*)

HINES: Shit. They're never gonna bring that sonofabitch down here. We ain't got all day.

ORA: (*letting the door shut*): Yeh, Perry and Foots and them ought to be down here in a few minutes. It's almost 3:00 now.

LOVE (*pretending he has a basketball in his hands, he pretends to dribble and lunges forward simulating a fake at* HINES, *then he sweeps past* HINES *and leaps in the air as if making a layup shot*): Peed on you, just then, buddy.

HINES: Sheet, Man, you what you call a self-checker. I don't even have to block that shot. I just take it off the backboard like this. (*He spins around and leaps up at the imaginary basket and scoops the imaginary ball off, landing and shaking his head as if to shake off imaginary defenders.*) Another rebound! (*Makes motion of long pass down toward opposite "court."*) Now, the fast break (*He moves in position for his own pass, receives it, makes one long stepping dribble and leaps as if dunking the ball in the basket.*) Two!

HOLMES: Boy, you guys sure play a lot of ball . . . off the court.

ORA (*opening the door again*): No shootin', cocksuckas.

LOVE (*still whirling and leaping as if he is making successful hook shots from an imaginary foul line*): Hey, what we gonna do to this cat when he gets here?

ORA (*leaning back in from the door though keeping it open with his fingers*): Damn, Love. You a stupid bastid. (*Peeks out door.*) We gonna kick that little frail bastid's ass.

HINES: In fact, you the one gonna do it, Willie.

HOLMES: Yeh, Love. (*Blocking one of Love's "shots."*)

LOVE: Shit. Karolis never bothered me. (*Faking* HOLMES *and swinging to shoot from the other side.*)

ORA (*looking back in and letting the door swing shut*): Damn, Willie (*in mocking seriousness*), Karolis is always telling everybody how he bangs the hell out of Caroline, every chance he gets. (*Begins to giggle.*)

HOLMES: Is that your mother's name, Love, Caroline?

HINES (*busy trying to lift a back window to look out on the yard*): What you mean, Johnny Boy, is that his mother's name? You the one told me.

LOVE (*swinging around as if to shoot again he suddenly punches* HOLMES *on the shoulder.* HOLMES *lets out a yelp of pain*): Uhhuh ... I told you about messin' with me.

HOLMES (*holding his shoulder*): Shit. Why didn't you hit Big Shot, you bastard? He brought the shit up.

ORA (*has the door propped open again*): Shit. That narrow head bastid know better than to fuck with me. (*He peers out the door and as he does* LOVE *gestures as if to hit him in the back.*)

HOLMES (*to* LOVE): You scared ass bastard. Why don't you do it?

ORA (*turning around and throwing up his hands to defend himself*): Yeh, I wish you would, you bullet head sonofabitch. HOLMES *goes and sits on a radiator next to* HINES.

LOVE: Man, nobody's thinking about you, Big Shot. (*He goes to pee.*)

ORA (*pulling the door open again*): Here come Perry and them.

HOLMES (*jumping off the radiator still holding his shoulder*): Perry and who else?

ORA: George Davis and Donald Farrell.

HINES: Donald Farrell? What the hell's he doin' down here? Where the hell is Foots?

LOVE: Yeh, what the hell is Perry doing bringing Farrell down here with 'em? Shit.

ORA *pulls the door open, and* PERRY, DAVIS *and* FARRELL *come in.*

PERRY: Hey, what's happening?

HOLMES: Shit. I should ask you. Where's Foots?

GEORGE: He had to stay upstairs for awhile. Powell wanted to talk to him ... or something.

ORA (*to* FARRELL): Man, whatta you want down here? Nobody asked you to come.

GEORGE: I told him he could come. Why not?

ORA: Whatta you mean, why not? You know goddamn well, why not. Silly sumbitch!

PERRY: Ah, Big Shot, why don't you be cool for a change, huh?

GEORGE: Yeh, man, Big Shot. Donald's not going to hurt anything.

ORA: No? (*Taking out a much-smoked cigarette butt.*) Maybe you don't think so ... but I do.

GEORGE: Oh, man, shit.

FARRELL: Why don't you want me here, Big Shot?

ORA (*glancing at* FARRELL): Man, don't be asking me questions.

FARRELL: Don't ask you questions? Why the hell not?

ORA (*menacingly at* FARRELL): Cause I said so, that's why. You don't like it, muthafucka?

PERRY (*stepping between them*): Goddamn it, Big Shot, why don't you sit your ass down for awhile and shut the hell up?

ORA (*turning to* PERRY): You gonna make me, muthafucka?

PERRY (*stepping to face* ORA): I can. And you better believe it, baby!

ORA: Shit. (*Disparagingly. Moving away from* FARRELL *and back to the center of the room.*) Well you damn sure got your chance right now, you black sonofabitch.

GEORGE (*moves between* PERRY *and* ORA): Oh, goddamit why don't both you guys sit down. You too, Donald.

FARRELL *moves to sit on a radiator beside* HOLMES *and* HINES. Ora, you wrong, man, and you know it.

ORA: How come I'm wrong, huh? You know goddamn well that skinny cocksucka over there (*at* FARRELL) ain't got no business down here. He ain't gonna do a damn thing but stand around and look.

LOVE (*laughing*): That's all I'm gonna do.

HINES (*hunching* HOLMES *with his elbow*): Yeh, but that's okay for you, Willie. You so black, if you stand still nobody'll know you're standing there anyway.

All laugh. ORA *takes the opportunity to go to the door and crack it open.*

PERRY: Where's the rest of those guys?

HINES: I guess they must still be upstairs in that broom closet.

PERRY: Broom closet?

He and DAVIS *lean against one of the walls and begin to smoke.*

HINES: Yeh, Knowles and Skippy got Karolis upstairs in a

broom closet waiting till everybody leaves the floor I guess.

FARRELL: Jimmy Karolis?

HOLMES: Yeah, that's who we're waiting for. (*Giggles.*)

FARRELL: What the hell's gonna happen then?

ORA (*turning from door*): Man, what the hell you care, huh? Pee-the-bed muthafucka!

HINES: Damn, George!

GEORGE: Damn, what?

HINES: Seems to me like Big Shot's right. You bring this cat down here and he doesn't even know what's happening.

ORA: You goddamn real I'm right. Simple ass cats.

FARRELL: What're you guys gonna gang Jimmy Karolis?

ORA: We gonna break that muthafucka's back.

FARRELL: For what?

ORA: Look man, why don't you shut up and get the hell out of here, huh?

FARRELL: You mean all you guys're gonna jump on Karolis?

ORA (*walking over to* FARRELL *and grabbing him by the shirt*): You gonna stick up for him?

FARRELL *tries to push Ora's hands from his shirt, and though he is much taller than* ORA, ORA *pulls him from his seat.*

FARRELL: Goddamn it, Ora, why don't you cut the shit?

GEORGE: Yeh, Ora, cut it out.

PERRY: Goddamn; that cat's always going for bad.

GEORGE *comes over to restrain* ORA, *but* ORA *succeeds in punching* FARRELL *in the stomach.* FARRELL *clutches his stomach and sinks to the floor groaning.*

PERRY: (*to* ORA): You bastard.

ORA *swings around to confront him.*

ORA: You come on too, if you want to, you black sonofabitch! GEORGE *pushes them apart again and his push sends* ORA *rattling heavily against the door.*

Goddamnit, George, why don't you stay the fuck out of this?

GEORGE: Because there wasn't a goddamn reason in the world for you to hit Donald like that. (*Going to help* FARRELL *up.*) Damn, Ora, you're a wrong sonofabitch, you know that?

FARRELL (*still doubled up and holding his stomach. He pulls his arm back when* GEORGE *tries to help him up*): No, man!

Lemme stay here. (*Still groaning.*) Ora, you dirty cock-sucker.

ORA: Boy, you better shut up before I stomp mudholes in your pissy ass.

The door is suddenly pushed open and KNOWLES *and* SKIPPY *come in holding* KAROLIS *by the arms.* KAROLIS' *head is hanging, and he is crying softly and blood is on his shirt and face. His hair is mussed and standing all over his head.*

LOVE: Ga-uhd damn! What'd you cats do?

KNOWLES (*giggling stupidly*): Love, now what the hell does it look like we did? Broke this muthafucka's jaw.

HINES: Damn. I thought we were just bringing the cat down here to fight Foots. I didn't know you guys were gonna break his head first.

SKIPPY: Well, he didn't wanna come. We had to persuade him.

KNOWLES: Shit, Skippy, whatta you mean "we"? I did all the persuading.

ORA: Aw, shit, Knowles. I bloodied the cat's lip. You trying to take all the credit.

SKIPPY: Yeh, Knowles. You didn't hit the cat but once, and that was on the goddamn shoulder.

Letting KNOWLES *drag* KAROLIS *into a corner where he lets him drop.*

You know what this cat was doing all the time we was in that goddamn broom closet? Tellin' jokes. (*Laughs.*) They must not a been funny either. Karolis didn't laugh once.

KNOWLES: What should I do with this guy. I gotta drag him everywhere.

ORA: Drop him in that goddamn corner. (*Walks over to corner and nudges* KAROLIS *with his foot.*) Hey, muthafucka. Hey! Why don't you straighten up?

SKIPPPY (*noticing* FARRELL, *who is still crumpled in an opposite corner, but stirring*): Damn! What the hell happened to Donald?

PERRY: That goddamn Big Shot had to show how bad he was.

ORA (*laughing paradoxically*): He called me a nigger.

All laugh.

LOVE: Well, what the hell are you? Wha's the matter, you shamed of your people?

ORA: Fuck you! (*He still stands over* KAROLIS, *nudging him with his foot*.) Hey, man, get up! (*Laughs.*)

HINES: Damn, Ora. Why don't you leave the cat alone?

ORA (*bending over as if to talk in* KAROLIS' *ear*): Hey, baby, why don't you get up? I gotta nice fat sausage here for you.

GEORGE: Goddamn, Big Shot . . . You really a wrong sonofabitch!

ORA: Look man. (*Now kneeling over the slumped figure.*) If you want to get in on this you line up behind me. I don't give a shit what you got to say.

LOVE: Man, George, leave the cat alone. You know that's his stick. That's what he does (*laughing*) for his kicks . . . rub up against half-dead white boys.

All laugh.

ORA (*looking over his shoulder . . . grudgingly having to smile too*): I'd rub up against your momma too. (*Leaning back to* KAROLIS.) Come on, baby . . . I got this fat ass sa-zeech for you!

LOVE: Ora, you mad cause you don't have a momma of your own to rub up against.

All laugh.

ORA (*turns again, this time less amused*): Fuck you, you bony head sonofabitch. As long as I can rub against your momma . . . or your fatha' (*laughs of his invention*) I'm doin' alright.

Door is pushed open suddenly and FOOTS *comes in. He is nervous but keeps it hidden by a natural glibness and a sharp sense of what each boy in the room expects, singularly, from him. He is the weakest physically and smallest of the bunch, but he is undoubtedly their leader. When* FOOTS *comes in* KAROLIS *looks up quickly, then slumps again.*

HINES: Man, where the hell you been?

FOOTS: That goddamn Van Ness had me in his office. He said I'm a credit to my race. (*Laughs and all follow.*) He said I'm smart-as-a-whip (*imitating Van Ness*) and should help him to keep all you unsavory (*again imitating*) elements in line.

All laugh again.

LOVE: Yeh? What's he talking about?

FOOTS: Well, he seems to think that you guys . . . particularly that goddam Big Shot and Knowles, are not good influences in this joint.

PERRY: Boy, you can say that again. Nutty muthafuckas!

ORA (*to* PERRY): Fuck you, tar baby!

FOOTS: Well, I'm supposed to make sure that you guys don't do anything bad to anybody. Especially to James Karolis. (*Laughing.*)

GEORGE: Oh yeh? He know about that?

FOOTS: Yeh, somebody told him Knowles said he was gonna kick Karolis' ass. (*Seeing* KAROLIS *in the corner for the first time. His first reaction is horror and disgust . . . but he keeps it controlled as is his style, and merely half-whistles.*) Goddamn! What the fuck happened to him? (*He goes over to* KAROLIS *and kneels near him, threatening to stay too long. He controls the impulse and gets up and walks back to where he was. He is talking throughout his action.*) Damn! What'd you guys do, kill the cat?

PERRY: Heavy handed Big Shot again.

FOOTS (*looks at* ORA *quickly with disgust but softens it immediately to comic disdain*): What the hell you hit him with, Ora, a goddamn train?

ORA (*happy at the notice of his destruction*): No, man, I just bopped him in the mouth with the back of my hand.

FOOTS: Ga-uhd damn! You a rough ass cat, Shot. He sure don't look like he's in any way to fight anybody.

ORA (*laughing*): No, but he might be able to suck you off. Hee, hee.

LOVE: Shit. You the one that look like you want that, Big Shot.

FOOTS: Oh, shit. There wasn't any need of bringing the cat down here if you guys were gonna fuck him up before I got here. He was supposed to fight me. (*Almost angry.*)

HINES: Yeh, that's what I thought. You shouldn't of sent Ora and Knowles up after him then.

FOOTS: The only person I asked to go up was Skippy.

SKIPPY: Well, the sonofabitch wouldn't come . . . so, I got Superduck over there to help me. I didn't ask Ora to come. Knowles did.

KNOWLES: Oh, man, the cat's here. Get him up on his feet

(*laughs*) then knock him down. That's all. That don't seem like no big problem to me. (*Through most of the action* KNOWLES *is drumming on the walls or the window or the door or the floor, in a kind of drum and bugle corps beat . . . also supplying the bugle parts vocally.*)

LOVE: Man, Knowles, why don't you stop being a goddamn Elk all the time. Damn. That cat's always drumming on something. Why don't you get a goddamn drum?

KNOWLES: I'm going to drum on your bony head in a little while if you don't shut up.

FOOTS: Well, I don't see any reason to keep all this shit up. Just pour water on the cat and let's get outta here.

ORA: What? You mean you made us go through all this bullshit for nothing?

FOOTS: Well, what the hell am I gonna do, beat on the guy while he's sprawled on the floor. Damn, Ora, you're a pretty lousy sonofabitch.

HINES: Man, Big Shot'd stomp anybody in any damn condition. He likes it when they're knocked out first, especially.

FOOTS: I'm pushed! There's no reason to stay here. I can't fight the guy like he is.

FARRELL (*who has pushed himself up and is leaning against the wall*): I sure am glad somebody's got some sense here.

FOOTS (*seeing* FARRELL *for the first time*): What the hell you doing here? Who asked you to come here, huh? (*Embarrassed and angry.*)

ORA: That stupid ass Perry brought him.

PERRY: That's right. I just thought there was gonna be a fight. I didn't know you guys were gonna lynch anybody.

FOOTS: Lynch, your ass. Look. Donald, why don't you leave, huh? Nobody needs you here.

FARRELL (*slowly*): Yeh, O.K., Ray. But I just want to know why you're gonna beat up on Jimmy like this. What the hell did he do to you?

FOOTS (*almost indignantly*): None of your goddamn business, Farrell. Just leave!

ORA: Yeh, man. I should've thrown your ass out when you first come in here. Pee-the-bed sonofabitch.

FARRELL: O.K. (*Stands up, still lightly holding his stomach.*) O.K. But I want to take Jimmy out of here with me. He can't fight anybody.

ORA: Man, you better shut your goddamn mouth and get outta here!

FOOTS: Look, Donald, just leave, that's all. You hear? (*Turns his back on* FARRELL *and walks toward* KAROLIS, *then thinking better of it turns toward* FARRELL *again.*)

FARRELL: Ray! You're not gonna beat the guy up when he's like that are you?

FOOTS: I don't need you to tell me what to do. (*He goes over and pulls the door open slightly.*) Just get out of here . . . now!

FARRELL (*takes a step then looks toward* KAROLIS): But look at him, he can't do anything. (*To* FOOTS.) Why do you want to do this?

FOOTS: Goddamn it, get out!

FARRELL: That's no answer.

FOOTS: Man, I'll punch you in the belly myself.

FARRELL: Shit. (*Disparagingly . . . which makes* FOOTS *madder.*)

FOOTS (*in low horrible voice*): Goddamn it. You better get the fuck outta here, right now!

FARRELL: Nobody's gonna tell me why? (*He starts to move for the door.*)

PERRY: Look, Donald, you better cool it, buddy. You heard about that letter didn't you?

FARRELL: Letter? What letter?

FOOTS: Man, I told you to leave. I'm not gonna tell you again.

PERRY (*laughing*): The letter Karolis sent Foots telling him he thought he was "beautiful" . . . and that he wanted to blow him.

All giggle.

FARRELL (*turning sharply toward* FOOTS): A letter?

ORA (*rushing at* FARRELL *from the side and punching him*): Goddamn it! Didn't you hear somebody say leave, pee ass?

FOOTS (*pushing between* FARRELL *and* ORA): Cut it out, Ora!

FARRELL (*hurt again and slumping.* ORA *tries to hit him again and the punch is blocked by* FOOTS *who glares savagely at* ORA): A letter? (*Groaning.*) Oh, Ray, come on. Why don't you come off it? (*He is looking up at* FOOTS.)

ORA (*leaps around* FOOTS *and pushes* FARRELL *into the door*): Get out of here, you dumb bastid!

KNOWLES *pulls the door open and shoves* FARRELL *through it.* Goddamn, what a stupid punk. (*He laughs, as do some of the others.*)

FOOTS (*stares at the closed door for a second, then he turns slowly to the others*): Look, let's get out of here. This stuff is finished.

KAROLIS (*has brought his head up during the preceding scuffle, and has been staring at* FOOTS *As* FOOTS *and the others look over toward him, he speaks very softly, but firmly*): No. Nobody has to leave. I'll fight you, Ray. (*He begins to pull himself up. He is unsteady on his feet, but determined to get up . . . and to fight.*) I *want* to fight you.

FOOTS *is startled and his eyes widen momentarily, but he suppresses it.*

HINES: Damn. Some guys don't know when they're well off.

ORA: Yeh. You little skinny muthafucka. You should've kept your mouth shut, and played dead.

KNOWLES: Goddamn. You mean that sonofabitch wasn' dead? Shit, Big Shot, you must hit like a girl.

ORA (*to* KNOWLES): Yeh? Well, let me hit you, you bastid.

KNOWLES (*disparagingly*): Shit.

KAROLIS (*pushing himself off the wall slightly and wiping his face with his sleeve*): No, Ray. Don't have them leave. I want to fight you.

FOOTS (*very silent and stiff, not wanting to be pushed*): Oh? (*Slowly.*) Well, that's damn fine with me.

ORA (*going behind* KAROLIS *and pushing him toward* FOOTS): You wanna fight? Well, go ahead, dick licker. (*Howls.*)

HINES: Yeh, get it on, fellas.

He lunges at FOOTS *and manages to grab him in a choke hold.*) Ray, you said your name was. You said Ray. Right here in this filthy toilet. You said Ray. (*He is choking* FOOTS *and screaming.* FOOTS *struggles and is punching* KAROLIS *in*

the back and stomach, but he cannot get out of the hold.)
You put your hand on me and said Ray!

SKIPPY: Goddamn, that bastid is choking the shit out of Foots.
The two still struggle, with KAROLIS *continuing to have the advantage.*

HINES: That fuck is trying to kill Foots!

HOLMES: Goddamn it!

ORA (*suddenly leaping on* KAROLIS' *back, puts the same choke hold on him*): You cocksucka . . . how's that feel, huh? (*He pulls* KAROLIS *off of* FOOTS *who falls to his knees.*) Huh?

KNOWLES: Let's kick this cocksucka's ass real good.
He rushes up to help ORA, *and the whole of the crowd surges into the center punching the fallen* KAROLIS *in the face.*
KNOWLES *is screaming with laughter.*

KAROLIS: No no, his name is Ray, not Foots. You stupid bastards. I love somebody you don't even know.
He is dragged to the floor. The crowd is kicking and cursing him. ORA *in the center punching the fallen* KAROLIS *in the face.* KNOWLES *is screaming with laughter.*

FOOTS *is now on his hands and knees but his head hangs limply and he is unaware of what is happening. He slumps again.*

They have beaten KAROLIS *enough.* KAROLIS *is spread in the center of the floor and is unmoving.* ORA *drapes some of the wet toilet paper across his body and face.*

ORA: Let's stick the sonofabitch's head in the damn toilet.

PERRY: Oh, man, fuck you. The cat's completely out. What more can you do to him?

GEORGE: Yeh, let's get Foots, and get outta here before somebody comes in.

ORA: Yeh. Hee, hee. Look at ol' Foots. That fuckin' paddy boy almost kilt him.

LOVE: Yeh (*Laughing.*) I told you Karolis was probably bad!
All laugh.

KNOWLES: Nutty sonofabitch.

LOVE (*picking up* FOOTS, *helped by* HINES *and* HOLMES): Hey, big eye! Get the hell up.

ORA (*takes a paper cup and dips it in the commode and throws*

403

it in FOOTS' *face*) : Yeh, get up, bad ass. (*Laughs.*)
They all leave, as FOOTS *begins to come to. All making noise,*
laughing, cursing. KAROLIS *lies as before in the center of the*
room, motionless.
After a minute or so KAROLIS *moves his hand. Then his head*
moves and he tries to look up. He draws his legs up under
him and pushes his head off the floor. Finally he manages to
get to his hands and knees. He crawls over to one of the
commodes, pulls himself up, then falls backward awkwardly
and heavily. At this point, the door is pushed open slightly,
then it opens completely and FOOTS *comes in. He stares at*
KAROLIS' *body for a second, looks quickly over his shoulder,*
then runs and kneels before the body, weeping and cradling
the head in his arms.

BLACK

LOUIS WILKINSON

THE BETTER END

[*The scene is a Gentleman's Library. A small company, select, is assembled. One gentleman, somewhat elderly, stands bending near the fire, his head parallel to his knees. Another gentleman, younger, stands behind him, unbent. The trousers of both gentlemen lie gathered about their ankles.*]

It was, the advance to that target, heralded by a preamble somewhat more deferring than he, the bender, would, we might suppose, himself have chosen, though he was not—most indubitably he was not—one to be, on any occasion even remotely imaginable, figured as betraying an eagerness that could emerge, in the least discernibly, as "vulgar". He reflected, indeed, how fine, after a manner, this choice of method— of style and mode—was: and how engaging—how really and perfectly, one might even call it, whimsical—was the way of his friend to rearward, who, while he so bristled, stiffly enough, he safely trusted, to satisfy, most admirably, their common great intent, yet with a kind of reluctant—or, it might be, even coy—patience, stretching tangents, he conceived, unexpectedly this way and unexpectedly that, held so strangely aloof, in the very aloofness none the less conveying the sense of an, at any rate not far from, almost vertiginous precipitancy. Ray Lester had, as the phrase is, the horn; but it strained, this nervous pointer, for him, under what was, in a fashion, an intellectual—could it be?—subjugation: those alert anticipatory fibres, with the quite visible quiver that they had —or indeed, if one were brought to the point of admitting it, the swelling and throbbing—hinted, and more than hinted, at some subtle variation, hardly definable, of a tragic mental tensity; while they submitted none the less—indeed, all the more—to the nicest conditions of some remoter and blander— in a way—influence: or perhaps we may conceive of them, in a more romantic view, enskied, as it were, in some far blue extraordinary recess, where vapours curl thinly, too tenuous —hardly that, though—but quite exquisitely communicative their slender—should we say?—smoke-coils and delicate films of mist. This tensity, then, held, under a certain exterior grossness of mere appearance, a quality definable, after all, as frail; something, indeed, quite undeniably shy and sweet, while with a felicity—how rare this was!—it interrelated aether with lowly matter, and revealed—almost you might believe—the secrets—some at least—of such an interrelation, so magically penetrative, and more than a little likely—in fact, "not half" as they say, "bloody likely"—to pass beyond the reach of any interpreting that one could, in the usual "set terms", express. The older man sustained his posture, cherished his—ah!—anticipations; nor did even the indifferent warmth of that slowly dying fire prove, so far as any of the little party assembled could opine, an affliction to the forbearance that he, so incomparably, guarded.

The, as some might have supposed it, dilatoriness of Ray Lester was, rather, a test to him, to the bender, of the fine endurance, the supremely extensive restraint, that he was able —how magnificently well!—to summon and to stand—how beautifully completely!—by; and it brought about, into the, so to speak, bargain, a superlative emergence, unexpected—oh, "a bit"!—of hidden values, the patency of which was quite blithely vivifying, and therefore welcome utterly, at all tangible points, for the assurance that it, in so luminous an enlightenment, conveyed.

Nor did the fact that, in the end, little would seem to have come of it all, break the real, the unquestioned—unquestionable, even—beauty of this "preparedness" that they had had between them, this perfectly outlined preoccupation, either for Lester or for—more strangely, perhaps? or less?—the other. It could not, this especial situation, this lovely little particular phase of theirs, go on, they knew, forever; and if that devolvulent blanching stain now perceivable upon the space of carpet dividing, yet, the two—Lester had "come", as they say, "off" —may have furnished a consummation that they could not too enthusiastically greet as the most appropriate and, wholly, satisfying that might have been looked for, at least they could recognize it as one worthy—and why not?—of their acceptance; one, indeed, to be—you understand?—bowed to.

"Ah, well, my dear," said the elder, turning and straightening, a little, and glancing forth, as he spoke, the most incalculable of comprehending eye-beams towards his—could one say "companion"? "—ah, well, my dear, so there, you see, we are!"

EDUARDO GUDIÑO KIEFFER

A SINNER'S GUIDE BOOK

She knows it, she knows she's the One and Only of Buenos Aires, *rara avis in terris,* she knows there's no other who can do what she does with the skill she does it; she knows she's the Phoenix, the Chosen One, the Incomparable, the heroic Joan of Arc, but no virgin, thank God;

she knows others exist, sure, she knows it because she herself belongs to that garrulous and multicolor fauna, because secret tropisms pushed her toward closed lodges, mysterious clans, guilds whose passwords are smirks, gasps, and sashaying;

she knows others exist but few of them dare to wear the bracelets, necklaces, beads, plumes, high heels, and fake eyelashes except in clandestine mystical phallic ceremonies while she, the One and Only, can strut all that in public, in front of rows and rows of seats packed with hot bodies with lascivious or jeering eyes; the All Defiant, the All Enlightened and not because of some miraculous Celestial Charity but because of Violet Spots describing a centerstage halo at the Orléans; guided not by Voices but by the Sublime Electronic Music;

and she also knows she has almost or completely magical powers; she knows how that audience shouts obscenities at

Leila (Rita Fuad in real life) while she takes off her veils to the tune of "In a Persian Market"; they stamp and whistle while Yoko (Yolanda Cardoza in real life) takes off her kimono to "Poor Butterfly"; they get worked up to fever pitch while Marilyn (Rosita Kluczinsky in real life) takes off her tight-fitting black dress to "Blues in the Night"; but they grow quiet, surprised at first, and then absolutely fascinated, stupefied, bewitched, wrapping her in an almost frightening silence when the esoteric violet aura is switched on and the choral prelude "Jesu, Joy of Man's Desiring" starts up unexpectedly, solemnly, strangely, anagogically;

that's when she comes out of the shadows to station herself under the lights, in her snow-white, floor-length tunic and her jewels like scapulars, like medallions, and her fluttering false silky eyelashes and her ceremonial high heels and the languid wig; she comes forward and hardly begins to move to the contemplative phrasing of the chords;

first raise the right arm then the left in immolation and holocaust let the hair fall forward covering the face bending the head slowly push out the hip advance the leg letting the taut muscle be seen through the furtive slit; oh anointed priestess in the androlatrous ritual of her own adoration, first take off the earrings then the necklaces then the bracelets then one shoe then the other to the beat of the holy sacrifice, and the crowd's silence getting denser moment by moment and the music more overwhelming moment by moment essentially more and more Bach moment by moment interpreted by Walter Carlos on the Moog neosynthesizer and toward the end of the two minutes and fifty-seven seconds which is exactly how long the number lasts let the white tunic drop dramatically turn away from the audience unsnap the bra turn around again facing the thousand-headed monster silenced transported hypnotized modestly covering the breasts with both arms and now without uncovering it with one arm lower the other slllooowllly slloowlly until loosening the small rose on the panties and then with a properly miraculous precision "Jesu, Joy of Man's Desiring" ends and the spots go off and the violet halo is extinguished and the darkness covers her total nudity with mourning clothes and crepe and she runs off between the teasers and quickly puts on the raincoat she left hanging there on a nail just for that purpose;

she also knows that during those two seconds after the lights go out, those two clocked seconds, silence will reign over the orchestra of the Orléans like smoke from the cigarettes, like the echo of that already faded music; and then someone will clap and applause from those who have realized for the very first time that strip tease can be something like a solemn mass, a votive mass, a mass of purification with the body present;

she also knows (although she'd like to forget it) that the applause would roar out of a maddened beast if the light didn't go out at exactly the right moment and if the public discovered the truth, that deceitful truth or, better said, that painful reality she feels between her legs while walking toward the dressing room, oh God, dear God of my soul how mean you were to me when you put this right here, what do I want with something so lovely on men so useless on me, why do you make me feel more of a woman than any woman and you stuck a prick where I'd like to have something else, warm and loving;

sure, the applause would roar out and she would die, crushed by the cheated furious irate iconoclastic crowd and maybe it would be beautiful to die like that with all those sweaty drunken ferocious men on top, stepping on her, spitting on her, and tearing at her;

but the lights always go out on time and she goes to the dressing room (the girls, her associates, say "changing room," but she prefers to say dressing room, it's so much more elegant, so much more aristocratic, dressing room instead of changing room, maybe Sarah Bernhardt had a changing room, no, surely she had a dressing room, maybe Maria Callas has a changing room, but enough of that);

and in the dressing room the noisy chatterboxes talking complaining it's disgraceful three thousand pesos a day and on my last tour of Central America I was earning a thousand dollars a month; shut up what're you talking about Central America for if you never made it past Berazategui; it's easy to see you're blabbing out of jealousy, what's happening is if you keep getting fatter you're not going to be able to strip any more, who's going to pay to see cellulitis, and the laughing and the nasty cracks and did'ja get a load of that and, but what a thing to say;

and when she enters and sits down in front of the mirror and begins to take off her makeup with Aqualane even though Aqualane is used for other necessities, there's a very short silence having nothing to do with the great majestic silence in the theater; a short silence caused by the fact that the others, even doing what she is doing, would love to feel as feminine as she does;

and while she makes the blush and rouge and shadow disappear with a slow and circular massaging of her fingertips on her forehead, on her cheeks, on her neck, the others watch waiting for that ridiculous and sublime moment that is repeated like a sacrament every night;

that moment she waits for too, a martyr facing the lions, a sacrificial victim;

that moment which should also have some background music because it is the moment of true nudity, awesome solemn Wagnerian music that would make the last interior masks fall away:

THE MOMENT OF TAKING OFF THE WIG

now,

like this;

and what is it as if they don't know by heart, as if I haven't repeated it every night these last three years;

take it off suddenly, with a quick jerk, in a defiant gesture that exposes her skull where two or three stray hairs do not cover the miserable premature baldness, sign of a masculinity unchosen but inevitable;

that moment;

she with the wig in her hand looking at the others with a blank stare, the others lowering their eyes as if ashamed suddenly breaking the silence with small talk, something about the weather or about the fat man in the front row, anything;

and little by little the return to normality, she taking off the false eyelashes now with Johnson's Baby Oil, as good for her very delicate eyelids as for very delicate babies' rear ends;

the others beginning to ask her things and she replying as if she were the lonely-hearts column, answering Yoko (Yolanda Cardoza in real life) who consults her about whether it's worthwhile to give up the Orléans and devote herself to studying anthropology, or listening to the moaning of Leila (Rita Fuad in real life) who complains that men are all the same or ducking the innuendos of Marilyn (Rosita Kluczinsky in real life) who attacks her because she's envious, of course;

but the one sure thing is that when all is said and done they all depend on her, all revolve around her, the One and Only of Buenos Aires, *rara avis in terris,* Phoenix, Joan of Arc;

the One and Only capable of imagining that it's possible to strip to Bach put to electronic music;

the One and Only capable of dominating that dragon audience;

the One and Only whose sex is a false sex and yet more genuine than the female bearers of a genuine sex;

the only One and Only;

Corybant at the mad feast of Cybele, druid in the forest of skyscrapers, hierophant officiating at secret ceremonies;

Pope Joan on a canopied throne but on the pyre every day as well, on the sacrificial altar ready to receive a dagger in the center of her breast;

the only One and Only;

who's now entirely clean of makeup, entirely divested of wig, high heels, and false eyelashes, who now stands up, letting the raincoat slip off, who with perfect naturalness walks naked in front of the others who don't even look at her because they're so used to her by now, who walks trying to move her skimpy buns as if they were the mighty buttocks of the others, showing off what she doesn't have and embarrassing herself with what she does have, oh God my God how mean you were to me;

heading toward the locker where the striped pants pink shirt sandals are that she'll wear on the street because obviously, on the street you can't dress like a woman even if you'd like to;

listening to the little cries of the others the goodbyes of the others who and, dressed now, watching them with her head

412

thrown back and the right eyebrow disdainfully raised like Maria Felix as an Aztec deity, sweeping them with a circular gaze, a fiery gaze that could incinerate these other poor women for no more than being just that : women ;

and flinging a half languid, half scornful ciao that drops in the midst of Leila, Yoko, and Marilyn like a wilted carnation that tears out the other carnations, other flowers other ciao sweetheart see you tomorrow, good luck, hope something turns up, hope everything goes well, see ya', good night;

and going out on to the street and crossing over to the bar to dial a number on the payphone;

beep beeep beep beep busy;

then sitting down at the usual table asking Mario for the usual Mario coffee please

Mario attentive bringing her the coffee asking how're you how're things going;

sweetheart, things are always pretty good, justa little tired, you know, when a lady's an artist;

a startled customer who turns around hearing the hoarse voice refer to herself in the feminine gender, when the voice as well as the appearance indicate the masculine;

she winking an accomplice eye at Mario and another devilish eye at the customer and the customer turning red up to here and burying himself in the pages of *La Razón* and Mario's accomplice smile;

the hot coffee does her good, stimulates her stomach, awakens the gratifying memory of her strip tease, the only number of the One and Only, others would've liked to have had the idea, but what were they going to do, so few like classical music, so few who'd think of using Bach for the art of stripping in public;

ten minutes and to the telephone again, once again to dial the number engraved in her memory and now, yes, ringing, one, two, three, then the click and his sleepy voice:

hello who's it;

and she the only One and Only suddenly quaking shivering timid trembling Joan of Arc defeated, handed over letting herself be condemned, yearning for the burning flames, pronouncing just one word:

love;

oh, it's you;

love, tell me that you love me;

shit, you want to be flattered at this hour;

I'm done now, I'm coming out there, I want to see you, please let me in don't be mean;

look, you nut, I'm really tired;

please, sweetheart;

go fuck yourself;

oh cruel stab, oh another click from him when he hangs up, oh injustice, oh pain, oh broken heart;

suddenly wilted, humiliated, repentant, hurt alone

paying for the coffee while Mario looks on sympathetically

going out on to the street alone

walking to the bus stop alone

getting on the bus alone

riding alone

getting off the bus alone

entering her two-room apartment in the Abasto, right there on Gardel Street alone;

looking at the photo of Manfredi under the glass on the bedside table alone;

getting ready for bed alone;

looking at herself in the mirror, seeing herself alone;

alone alone so alone,

and to top it off bald.

—*Translated by*
Ronald Christ and
Gregory Kolovakos

THOM GUNN

MODES OF PLEASURE

New face, strange face, for my unrest.
I hunt your look, and lust marks time
Dark in his doubtful uniform,
Preparing once more for the test.

You do not know you are observed:
Apart, contained, you wait on chance,
Or seem to, till your callous glance
Meets mine, as callous and reserved.

And as it does we recognize
That sharing an anticipation
Amounts to a collaboration—
A warm game for a warmer prize.

Yet when I've had you once or twice
I may not want you any more:
A single night is plenty for
Every magnanimous device.

CALAMUS

Why should that matter? Why pretend
Love must accompany erection?
This is a momentary affection,
A curiosity bound to end,

Which as good-humored muscle may
Against the muscle try its strength
—Exhausted into sleep at length—
And will not last long into day.

FEVER

Impatient all the foggy day for night
   You plunged into the bar eager to loot.
A self-defeating eagerness: you're light,
   You change direction and shift from foot to foot,
Too skittish to be capable of repose
   Or of deciding what is worth pursuit.

Your mother thought you beautiful, I suppose,
   She dandled you all day and watched your sleep.
Perhaps that's half the trouble. And it grows:
   An unattended conqueror now, you keep
Getting less beautiful toward the evening's end.
   The boy's potential sours to malice, deep
Most against those who've done nothing to offend.
   They did not notice you, and only I
Have watched you much—though not as covert friend
   But picturing roles reversed, with you the spy.

The lights go up. What glittering audience
   Tier above tier notices finally
Your ragged defeat, your jovial pretence?
   You stand still, but the bar is emptying fast.
Time to go home babe, though now you feel most tense.
   These games have little content. If you've lost

It doesn't matter tomorrow. Sleep well. Heaven knows
  Feverish people need more sleep than most
And need to learn all they can about repose.

THE MIRACLE

"Right to the end, that man, he was so hot
That driving to the airport we stopped off
At some McDonald's and do you know what,
We did it there. He couldn't get enough."
—"There at the counter?"—"No, that's public stuff:

"There in the rest room. He pulled down my fly,
And through his shirt I felt him warm and trim.
I squeezed his nipples and began to cry
At losing this, my miracle, so slim
That I could grip my wrist in back of him.

"Then suddenly he dropped down on one knee
Right by the urinal in his only suit
And let it fly, saying Keep it there for me,
And smiling up. I can still see him shoot.
Look at that snail-track on the toe of my boot."

—"Snail-track?"—"Yes, there."—"That was six months ago
How can it still be there?"—"My friend, at night
I make it shine again, I love him so,
Like they renew a saint's blood out of sight.
But we're not Catholic, see, so it's all right."

SONG

SAN FRANCISCO STREETS

I've had my eye on you
  For some time now.

417

You're getting by it seems,
   Not quite sure how.
But as you go along
   You're finding out
What different city streets
   Are all about.

Peach country was your home.
   When you went picking
You ended every day
   With peach fuzz sticking
All over face and arms,
   Intimate, gross,
Itching like family,
   And far too close.

But when you came to town
   And when you first
Hung out on Market Street
   That was the worst:
Tough little group of boys
   Outside Flagg's shoes.
You learned to keep your cash.
   You got tattoos.

Then by degrees you rose
   Like country cream—
Hustler to towel boy,
   Bath house and steam;
Tried being kept a while—
   But felt confined,
One brass bed driving you
   Out of your mind.

Later on Castro Street
   You got new work
Selling chic jewelry.
   And as sales clerk

You have at last attained
 To middle class.
(No one on Castro Street
 Peddles his ass.)

You gaze out from the store.
 Watching you watch
All the men strolling by
 I think I catch
Half veiled uncertainty
 In your expression.
Good looks and great physique
 Pass in procession.

You've risen up this high—
 How, you're not sure.
Better remember what
 Makes you secure.
Fuzz is still on the peach,
 Peach on the stem.
Your looks looked after you.
 Look after them.

MAARTEN 'T HART

BROTHERS IN ARMS

We walk in the spacious garden. There is no wind. The summer is almost too hot. The dark-green leaves of the creeper on the wall of the house are drooping, limp and heavy. The humming of the insects sounds dull and menacing, but very summery. The woman strolling with Arthur in the summer sunlight among blooming flowers is me. What a marvelous feeling!

We sit down at the bottom of the garden in the tall grass beside a broad ditch. The grass gives way to reeds. The ditch is completely overgrown with green-brown duckweed. Flowering rush and bur reed are growing in the ditch. Further down I see arrowhead and water crowfoot. Two eyes peer at me from the surface of the water. I move. The frog vanishes. In the place where it has dived into the depths there is, for a brief moment, a small, dark opening in the duckweed that quickly closes again. On the other side of the water there is a hedge with hedge-bells growing along it. The brilliant white flowers stand out sharply against the green leaves.

"Sweet girl," Arthur says mockingly but cheerfully, tenderly. He strokes my blond hair. He puts his arm round me. I don't move. His caresses grow more intense and I submit to them without guilt. I think of the shower. When he caressed me for the first time, I found it wonderful, but I felt guilty. Men doing shameful things with other men. Even though I am not religious, the guilt feelings remain. Later, too, I always felt guilty: in bed in the dormitory when we lay next to each other while the others slept, in the tent during the field exercise. I thought I would always experience it as something wonderful that would nonetheless make you feel sinful. But not now. The more he caresses me the more I feel myself a woman. It is now easier, too, for me to overcome my fear at my own actions. Feeling guilty made me passive. I am still not as active as he is; I shall never be able to be very active because I am a woman. I know it is a myth, passive women. But in my case the myth is true. I still feel a vague kind of remorse because I cannot honestly and brutally live out my homosexuality but have to make use of this subterfuge, a subterfuge through which I place myself even further outside the world of ordinary, healthy people who are repelled by everything they do not understand. It will probably never be possible without guilt, without remorse. Maybe it would not be as good then, either.

I lie on my belly and press my face into the prickly, aromatic grass. A grasshopper is sitting on a blade of grass close to me. I gaze at the leaves of a buttercup as if I had never seen them before. Do they have feather-shaped veins, I think, are they pinnate-veined? Are the leaves crenate? It is curious that I cannot think of anything but pinnate-veined and crenate leaves when I reach the climax and Arthur's hands disappear, and I remain still and I am not tired.

We lie side by side in the grass. Arthur hums a tune. The sun is warm on my face. The clouds hang threateningly over us. Who was it who said that man is sad after an orgasm?

"Arthur, are you sad?"

"No," he says, "why should I be?" The sound of his voice is almost tender. His eyes are closed. He laughs easily.

"Were you thinking about the famous proverb that everyone is sad after coitus? But that wasn't coitus."

"No," I say, "that's true."

"That saying was probably invented by the dutifully married who went whoring."

He falls silent, I think about the future. I still have another year and a half in the army with Arthur. And after that? Why should I not be able to go on living with Arthur afterwards?

"Are we going to live together, Arthur, when we get out of the army?"

"That's still a long way off," he says.

Does my question irritate him? I get that impression from the slight wrinkling of his eyebrows. But I am dreaming of my future with Arthur, I am lost in a reverie and see him and myself in the same house, where I am living as a woman. My imagination goes no further. I dare not let it go any further even if I should like to. Other images rise up before me, images of long ago, and I notice with astonishment that even my memories are different now that I am wearing these clothes. I go far back in time, I am four years old and I am walking from our house to the Nieuwe Weg. Along the Nieuwe Weg are a great many poppies. I have often gathered flowers for my mother. I love my mother even if she is often ill-tempered and unfriendly. I had picked dandelions and daisies for her and she had said, "Thank you," but she was never really happy with the flowers. But then they had only been small flowers, weeds. Now I can pick poppies for her. How lovely she will think the poppies are! Big, red flowers, no common, everyday flowers. I gather poppies for my mother, a great bunch. I also pick buds, lots of buds. They will open at home. I run back with my bunch of flowers. I can hardly carry the big bouquet. I am very happy to be able to give my mother these poppies. How excited she will be. She will say, "What pretty flowers, Ammer, I have never seen such pretty flowers." Perhaps my mother will give me a kiss for bringing her flowers. After all, other mothers also kiss when they receive something nice from their children. I reach home. I can scarcely carry the bouquet any longer. In the corridor of our house I call, "Mother, flowers!"

My mother opens the door of the living-room. "What are those? Poppies? Nasty, poisonous flowers. They make opium from them. Dangerous flowers! Throw those flowers away at once! Throw them in the trash pit in front of the house. And the buds? What are they?"

"Poppies, too."

"Into the pit. Out with the flowers. Not in my house. Out with them!" She pushes me along the corridor. She shows me the trash pit beside the edge of the steps. A lid with small square holes lies on top of the pit. "In here," she says imperiously.

I cannot thrust many of the flowers into the trash pit at the same time. I do not want to, either. I take each flower separately in my right hand. Slowly I let it drop into the pit, first the long stem and then the red flower. With each flower that I let fall, a part of the love for my mother disappears. How I had loved my mother! But the bouquet is so big—so many flowers that they use up all my love for my mother.

I sit on the edge of the steps for a long time, looking at the flowers under the grating. They are wilting. Perhaps she would have taken the buds if I had not said that they were poppies, too.

I had never before realized that I loved my mother so much. Now I discover it, now that I am a woman myself and see such indistinct images before me. I am sitting with my mother and my aunts on a Sunday afternoon in the sunlight beside the canal. Are there other little nephews and nieces as well? My mother is wearing a white dress, white as the billowing sails of the boats that sail by, and I look at my mother, I cannot keep my eyes off my mother and I stroke the white cloth of her dress with my hands. I cannot remember any more. What a discovery! I loved my mother.

I was cured of loving her because she did not want my flowers. Could my lying here in the grass with a blond wig on my head be the result of this perverted love?

Arthur puts an end to these reminiscenses. He says, "Dressing in women's clothes goes very deep, I think. Do you know the story of the two men in Auschwitz who were missing from rollcall? They had dressed themselves as women. Of course it wasn't very difficult, everybody was naked and so thin that the breasts had gone. A few rags were enough. Terrific consternation among the camp leaders: two men were missing. When it was eventually discovered what the two men had done, everyone laughed and thought it a good joke. But the Nazi killers executed the whole group the two had belonged to. Yes, you never knew if it was in fact only for fun that the guys had dressed as women. It began as a joke but the result was to be killed. It can never be a joke, I think, it always has serious consequences. Come, let's go indoors. We'll listen to Wagner now."

"Wagner?"

"Yes, it's lacking in your education."

"Flashy, pretentious music."

"You don't know what you're talking about."

As we go back into the house we tease each other, the kind of quarreling that can exist only between people who are very fond of each other. I do not protest when he wants to listen to *Die Walküre,* and before we can begin we first have to look for the score. Searching through piles of old music is a delightful occupation, especially on a Sunday afternoon in summer when, from time to time, with a nonchalant, absentminded feminine gesture you have to tuck your hair back because it keeps falling over your eyes. When doing it you hear the clinking of the bracelet and feel the movement of the earrings.

"What a collection of music," I say.

"Not bad," Arthur says, "yes, we have quite a lot."

"But no Bach," I say.

"Boy, you and your everlasting Bach."

"I'm not a boy."

"That's true. You're a woman in a man's body that you have managed to camouflage very well. It is really crazy that now you're like this you're much more natural than in normal circumstances, you're less inhibited than normally, less turned into yourself. I should feel like saying, take them off. Now that you've done it, it's going to be harder to play your usual role. Each time you dress up makes it more impossible to live normally."

"Then there is a better solution, I must go on living as a woman, I must let my hair grow. I think it will be a success."

"Yes, I'm sure it would work very well," says Arthur, "too well. You'd have to go to the Johns Hopkins Institute in Baltimore. You can have an operation that will change you into a woman. You go to Baltimore and come back with Nobalmore. I bet you would be very good in the role of a housewife. Still, it's an idiotic idea. But tell me something, would you really want to be a woman?"

"I have never thought very deeply about it. There were always dreams of being a woman; but now that I've seen how happy I am, I have discovered how much I'd like to be a woman."

"So you see that by dressing as a woman you have made yourself conscious of a desire that scarcely existed before. With each succeeding disguise it will grow stronger, the longing to be a woman, and finally you will be a hopeless transsexual, somebody who, no matter what the cost, will want to be freed from his manhood, first from his sexual organs and then all the rest. You are still happy now, but then you will be so miserable! And supposing it succeeds, in Baltimore or Casablanca or wherever, afterwards there will be the difficulties with the registration authorities. And why would you want to be a woman now?"

"I could be married to a strong man, mentally strong, I mean, and then I could be a bit protected."

"Jesus, Ammer, what a nineteenth-century ideal: the strong man, the weak woman. Put the clock back and make everything that women are fighting for undone. That's really a sign of weakness in you, of impotence. But I accept it from you because it is real. You are simply that way, you really do have something of a helpless child that makes people like you. I truly believe it is a pity for you that you weren't born a woman. But you can also look after yourself perfectly well, you don't need the protection of a strong man at all."

"You say that, but right from the first days in the army you always stood up for me when the others were putting me down."

"Is that true? Give me an example."

"At breakfast on the second day a boy from an earlier draft

said that when I was on the assault course I lay down dead after the first obstacle. He was putting me down but you began . . ."

"Yes, I remember. Now that you mention it, situations like that cropped up later, too. And with Marijke . . . How crazy, I never realized it. But it's my fault, I'm always talking out of turn, I never give you a chance to say anything."

"I thought it was very nice of you to stand up for me like that."

"You should have protested! I'll have to think about it. Let's listen to Wagner, though.''

The music of *Die Walküre* is just as pathos-laden, heavy and barbaric as I imagine Wagner to be. I don't like Wagner, I shall never like Wagner. But Arthur is sitting beside me on a low bench and he holds the score with one hand while I turn the pages and with his other hand he holds me pressed against him except when he changes a record. How long the opera is! I lose consciousness of time, I look at the staves of music but hardly listen to the music, I am lost in a reverie. I imagine things that cannot happen: I have an operation in Baltimore and come back and live in this house with Arthur and see children before me and am ashamed of these naive fantasies that rise up unhindered and easily within me; a kind of crystalline dreaming, slightly sad, slightly mournful and not intense but with a sudden affinity with the music at the point when the opera is almost finished and Arthur has said, "Now for the most beautiful part." The music is a soft whispering. A constantly repeated motif, with a horn suddenly playing a related motif, and I am completely amazed because it is so inexpressibly beautiful. It is a lyrical instrumental intermezzo, a fragment of music that conjures up lights gliding past over dark waters. Afterwards a male voice sings the motif of a moment ago and it is repeated again but faster now, more passionately, so that my dreams, too, grow more rapid and the former sadness turns to melancholy and I feel the tears welling up in my eyes. For two days now I have been living as a different person. Am I unable to bear it? I cry without making a sound. I feel the make-up mixing with the moisture from my eyes.

Arthur looks at me. "Ammer, you're crying! Why are you crying?"

"I don't know. The music . . . It's because it's so overwhelming, to be sitting here, and being a woman . . ."

But that is not it, it is not because of what I am now but because of what I have never been, because of my unhapy youth, because of all the possibilities that have never been realized and also because of the farewell to youth, because of the sudden weight of a genuine relationship with another person, an undertaking that has been so difficult for me, which is why I am wearing these clothes and have run away from my true self, not having dared simply to be myself.

I let myself fall back on the bench and cry like a child with long, racking sobs. My body is convulsed.

"Are you crazy, Ammer? Stop it!"

"Let me," I say. "I need to have a good cry, I have never had a friend with whom I could listen to music like this. Can't we stay here, Arthur, can't I stay with you always? I would like to do that so much . . ." Crying makes it difficult to speak.

"Are you as over-sensitive, too?" Arthur says.

"As who?"

"As the girl, Marijke. She also sat here one evening, in the same place, she also cried and said, 'Arthur, when are we going to get married? I want to stay with you always.' Do I have to keep on running into hysterical women who want to change a pleasant friendship into a kind of eternal marriage? You're howling as hysterically as that girl. Goddamn it, Ammer, these clothes haven't done you any good. They show you for what you are—a spineless, hysterical woman. I think it's disgusting. In my opinion you're crying because it's too much for you. You simply can't take the luxury of a simple relationship with another person; you're behaving exactly like someone who is experiencing a homosexual friendship for the first time. I believe it would be better for us to give each other more freedom. We're chained together like two love-sick fools. The others are noticing it and making fun of us. It wouldn't be so bad if you weren't always talking about the future. 'I always want to be with you.' I find that so damned boring. To

427

tie yourself down now for more than a year and a half. Stop it, you crybaby. What is it now?"

"Why do you always say that?"

"I've had enough of it. You cling to me as if I were saving your life. You really behave just like those dumb girls."

"Dumb girls?"

"Yes. Marijke was not my first girl friend and I hope she won't be the last, either. The only thing is, from now on I must be sure they won't immediately start talking about 'for always' and adorable things like that. Do you know what I'll do with the stupid girls? I'll throw them out. I shouldn't have to do that. But between two sobs they tell you they love you. God, what a lousy kind of love. That anyone could humiliate himself like that before someone else. Love! Rubbish. People should have fun with each other and not make use of the big words and especially not want to tie each other up in a permanent relationship. I hate crying women, Ammer, and anyway I think we've been much too intimate with each other. We sit feeding each other on childhood memories like love-sick turtle doves. Do you know what we'll do? We'll give it a rest from now on, we'll both look for someone else. One of these days they're going to throw us out of the army because we . . . That's something I certainly want to prevent. You have all sorts of problems afterwards, too. I don't intend letting my life be wrecked by you, letting some homosexual or other who has never had a relationship with anyone and clings to me like a madman and sits howling like a child screw up my future. Howling like a child. But why, actually?"

Although I hear his outburst, I can barely grasp the sense of what he says, even if the words that generate new and stronger expressions engrave themselves deeply in my memory. The words do not yet have any connection with the strange, uncontrollable grief, this sudden, appallingly clear glimpse of my past. But the misery is also because of the pent-up tension of the past six weeks, it is because of Arthur, walking with Sergeant Eelwout and talking about the girl Marijke, it is because of the hopeless transformation that has taken place and through which, now that I am a woman, I am suddenly able to give expression to all my repressed feelings. Now I have a right to my jealousy, a right to my friendship with Arthur. But he does not understand it, he is shocked by the tears, he is only talking and in him, too, repressed emotions come to the surface, but of a different kind than mine. I am crying in order to express my feelings, he talks, but you don't exorcize demons with words.

He is still talking. "I am almost certain they all know already. Sergeant Eelwout made an insinuation about our friendship when we were playing billiards in the café and I think they're only waiting for a suitable opportunity to catch us. But you have never done anything to hide it, and neither have I, like the idiot I am, because somehow I felt sorry for you, you were such a damned nice fellow . . . But now I see it all differently, now I see the other side of the niceness: cowardice, pettiness. Now I see that you're just like everyone else, that you'll be damned if you'll accept that all friendship is a thing that remains free, not some kind of passion like Tristan and Isolde. We haven't swallowed a love potion. Man, pull yourself together. Take off those clothes, you have given yourself away in them."

"Arthur, don't say any more now, shut up now . . ."

"I, shut up?" My request releases new rage. He continues, "I will not shut up, I should have told you much sooner, I was only waiting for the right moment. I hadn't intended to be so hard on you but tears scare me to death. I keep on seeing the girls in front of me, especially Marijke. They throw themselves, they lie at your feet crying. 'Arthur,' they say, 'I love you, say something. Why don't you say something?' I'm expected to talk, too. They try to cage you in with their heart-rending sobbing, to tie you to them and you, you're no different with your inane whining, your jealous hysterics. I must say, it suits you, that part of the drag show is very well done."

I am not really surprised at his words. I have always sensed a menacing undertone in his speech. He had often talked about Marijke Reehorst, a sort of veiled warning. And yet, his words hurt now. He cannot take them back, they have been spoken. They will go on sinking more deeply into me, go on tormenting me more and more. Why is he saying all this? Is it due to my hysterical crying or has he, now that I've let myself go like this, seized the opportunity of ridding himself of me, something he has wanted to do for a long time but has not dared? Arthur not dare anything? Could that be true? Could he really have been afraid of hurting me? That could only be true if he had liked me. This last thought intensifies the pain caused by his words.

"Listen," he says, "you have got to stop now, enough is enough. Drink some water. Wash your face. I can't bear to look at you. I'm leaving, I'll go and fetch us something to eat at a Chinese place in Amsterdam. Meanwhile you can get hold of yourself a bit and take off those clothes, that seems the best thing to do. I'll fetch your uniform from the car and put it in the kitchen. I'll be back soon."

In the bathroom I look at my face in the mirror. A wreck. But with my puffy eyes and smeared make-up I am a real woman. I stare at the reflection. I comb the hair. I cannot take leave of myself. The tears start to flow again, now because of Arthur's monologue. An hysterical woman! I let cold water run down beside my eyes. I have a headache. My eyes sting. I walk back into the living-room. I sit down by the window. Spineless, hysterical woman. Two love-sick fools. The stupid girls. I throw them out. What a lousy sort of love! I don't intend letting my life be ruined by you, my life . . . We have already been too intimate with each other. Why not? I think, why must you not be too intimate with each other? Can you ever be too intimate? A jealous hysteric. Why has he insulted me like this? Why did he have to touch that sensitive spot? I felt so happy in this disguise, even if a little insecure, and was only waiting for some recognition of its genuineness. "Hysterical woman," he said. In this way he acknowledged its authenticity. I go to the kitchen, I pick up the uniform from a chair and walk to the bathroom. I get undressed, wash the make-up from my face and take off the wig. Slowly I transform myself into a soldier and loathe the sloppy trousers, the beige shirt, the stock and the jacket that I do not put on yet. I carry the clothes and the wig to the kitchen. I lay them carefully down on a chair. In a little while we will take them back to the Zwanenburgerstraat. I take my artificial fingernails and fake eyelashes into the garden. With my hands I make a hole in the ground next to a rosebush. I bury the nails and the eyelashes.

—*Translated by*
Derek Yeld

YVES NAVARRE

LUC

The bigger the city, the more the young men feel at home there. This is the biggest cradle Luc has ever known. Yet get lost in it. A cradle of corners of streets and avenues, with toy boxes all over the place and shady nooks where baby can go to sleep with his arms spreadeagled or held outstretched. Papa is there, tall as tall, with something sticking out in front of him. Everything starts again from scratch. It is raining and in a few seconds the city becomes human: it looks at its reflection and assesses its own beauty. The cradle is wet and Luc is happy. He exists.

He will take the Downtown road again, trudging through the rain. He will arrive there soaked, clammy, feverish. He will arrive behind the evening trucks ahead of all the others. He will wait there in a corner, sitting on an oil-drum with his feet on a pile of planks. He will watch the rain disturb the surface of the puddles. He will tap his fists against the palms of his hands, as though he's messed up one appointment and was sure he'd miss out on the next. What had Rasky meant when he left him? 'Go away, Luc, I don't want to see you any more...' Was he to come back tomorrow or the day after? Or true to their pattern of parallel affinities, should he go on alone with hands in pockets and a truant conscience, never asking any more questions, with the vague remembrance of a friend he once met on the way, his travelling companion for nearly fifteen years? The rain fell twice as hard. Luc took cover under a truck and squatted down with his hands clasped under his chin. It is Saturday. He counts up the days, then works them out again, it's Saturday night all right, a time for rendezvous of all kinds. Everyone's out. Cramp. Luc shifts his position. A handsome Negro comes and crouches next to him. He stuffs a popper up his nose, then holds it out to Luc, who contemplates the two-pronged capsule. Luc sticks it into his nose like a plug into a socket and inhales ferociously. The effect is instantaneous: the city becomes a pin-cushion spinning around in the troubled sky of the puddles. And the raindrops turn into bloodstains. Beneath the truck the ground is hard and dry: Luc lies full length. The guy crawls right up against him, opening his jacket, bare-chested. Luc pinches his nipples, two large pieces of confetti, pink against the black skin. 'Harder!' Luc bites them. The guy groans, with his left hand undoes Luc's clothing and plants one prong of the popper in Luc's nostril. 'Go on, have a good sniff!'

The truck, childhood, that gigantic piano which Luc would hide under with his special treats, a lump of cane sugar or a piece of quince cheese, on Thursday afternoons when he was bored, with all his lessons learnt and all his homework done, and it was raining and the visit to the Musée Carnavalet was off and Maman would ask Nanny where Luc was. 'I don't know, Madame.' Luc was hiding under the piano, in the drawing-room under the piano, that musical coffin on which nobody played, forsaken, out of tune, a memorial in a room for the living. Luc hid there with his afternoon snack. At school he was a good pupil. A well-behaved child. On the day of his First Holy Communion the chaplain gave him an art-book, *The Shrine of Saint Ursula,* fifteen reproductions in colour, with the following inscription on the fly-leaf: 'For Luc, who I am sure will always be as good as these pictures.' Pictures of fire, of pin-cushions, blood and martyrdom. Luc was to tear out the fly-leaf and then hide the beautiful book so that no-one should ever know what it was that he secretly refused and desired. Pictures of towns going up in flames . . .

The guy slaps Luc, 'Hey, man!' He is biting Luc's ear and Luc grasps him by the hair and twines himself round him. With concertinaed trousers masking their shoes and their clothes scattered about they lie face to face, outspread hand clamped on outspread hand, and they kiss as if kissing their own image in a mirror. Poppers again. Luc pulls himself up and bangs his head against the steel casing of this travelling piano. He is bleeding. The other guy licks the graze on his forehead. Luc is not sure whether he has hurt himself or whether it is his heart that has leapt into his head and is drumming a tattoo. He lies flat and the guy takes him like a woman, from the front, gently, very gently. Canoeing down the Mississippi. Watch out, don't rock the boat or it's going to capsize in that river of rain. This time Luc shuts his eyes, he no longer belongs anywhere. He can feel this boy on top of him, plunging. And the boy puts a yellow pill on Luc's tongue. 'Come on, swallow it, get that saliva flowing and swallow.' Silence. 'Come on, come on!' The fellow braces his back. With one fingertip he strokes the wounded brow, there under the piano that hides you and kills. And wounds. 'If the truck moved off, if the truck ran over me, I'd be a puddle.'

Caresses. Afterwards. The guy lights a cigarette. He rolls his jacket into a ball and slips it under Luc's neck. Luc opens his eyes. Crouching all round them, new arrivals are taking everything in. Motionless. Scared. Dazed. Conniving. Speechless. The great *soirée* is about to begin. Luc feels his trouser pockets. He has lost his keys, his wallet. Now he cannot even raise a smile. He lies back. His partner licks his navel, then all round it in ever-widening circles. Every now and again he moistens his tongue and then resumes. Concentric circles. Luc feels himself swept into the vortex. Hudson. Deep waters in the Port of New York. Black waters. Negro.

Negro is sitting cross-legged. Luc is sprawling in front of him, his head resting between the other fellow's legs, the back of his neck against his fly. It is still raining. The truck makes a

curious canopy, which could start in New York and finish in
the inner suburbs of Mexico City: the biggest truck in the
world, the biggest Big Top on earth, the Lucus Sexus Circus
and its whipping pricks, a new show every half-hour. It is
played out on a north-south axis, in the recumbent position,
the head clamped between the folded legs of the other creature, the black-jacketed scurbius with its black penis and shiny
black skin. Negro, chocolate blackamoor: coarse-grained,
vanilla-scented skin, lips like little cushions of tender flesh, a
body veiled for a funeral. The ceremony is beginning. Crawl-
ing, on their knees, or with their legs upright but bending at
the waist, arms hanging limply or jerking into action, here
come the robots, the others, the voyeurs, visitors to the inter-
minable truck, a steel umbrella which could cover the whole
earth. But what was that yellow pill which grows and grows
inside Luc's head, exploding into a thousand colours, distorting the world with its firework display? Luc is naked, but who
has removed his trousers, his shoes and socks? Who is sucking
at his toes, first one mouth, then two, then three? He wants to
buck and wriggle and break the hold these mouths have on the
Downtown end of his body, but the sensation is too acute, the
sweetness of it too much like pain, too intense for him to take
evasive action. He plays dead. Pretends that nothing is happening. Negro's knees are squeezing his shoulders, crushing
him; he can hardly breathe, a fine mess, there'll be nothing left
of him, he knows that, and the thought of it overwhelms him.
Bye-bye to the dolly boys of Paris, the lonely gropers of the
Tuileries, the gigolos of the Pincio and the tea-room trade of
the Tivoli Gardens. The trucks of the United States are the
biggest trucks in the world. They breed men like insects and
the elite is hatched out on Saturday and Sunday nights. They
lay their eggs when it's raining. And they do it on a patch of
wasteland when the earth is dry, with puddles near at hand so
the grubs will have something to drink. The congregation has
gathered, worshippers shaking their left wrists. And they spit
in your eye and all over. Downtown.

'Oh, cool it!' Negro waves them off. They move aside and
make room. He puts Luc's socks on again, pulling them tight
over Luc's feet, each gesture slow and deliberate, with a gleam

of passion that flares up in Luc's mind and dazzles him. 'Don't move, I'll take care of you.' He pulls Luc's trousers back on. 'Fuck off, leave us alone.' His voice sounds far away, hoarse, velvety, dusky, at one and the same time rasping and caressing. Luc tries to get up but a shaft of light nails him to the ground. 'Police!' The glare of headlights, the thrill of fear, dispersal and flight. Negro flattens himself over Luc. 'Don't move.' The squad car remains facing the trucks for a long, a very long time, long enough to drive out of one's mind all memory of history books and wars and fine mornings on the way to school when you don't feel like going but you go all the same and through the classroom window gaze at the sky that is pretending to be the sea with islands of cloud and currents of wind and men drowning unseen. 'Don't move.' The squad car turns around. No-one left under the trucks but Luc and Negro. 'Help me, they'll be back.' Luc slips on his shirt and buttons it up. The wrong buttons. He undoes them and does them up again. 'O.K.?' 'O.K., hurry!' Negro ties up Luc's shoelaces. 'What got into you, wearing shoes with laces, *here*!' They crawl out behind the trucks as the others begin to creep back. 'My name's Andrew, what's yours?' 'Luc.' 'Luck?' 'No, Luc, without a K at the end, I'm French.' Luc has the feeling that someone else has answered for him, another self. 'Come on.' In places Luc's shirt is sticking to his chest. In places Luc's trousers are sticking to his legs. 'Here,' says Andrew, 'here's your keys, a good thing you've got me with you.' Luc shrugs his shoulders, takes the keys and puts them in the left pocket of his jacket. 'I saw the guy who stole your billfold. Did you have much with you?' Luc shrugs his shoulders. 'Come on, we'll get a drink in here. Gay bar.' In the restroom Luc strips to the waist. He dries his shoulders and his stomach with paper towels. He spits in the wash-basin, soaks his face, fills his mouth with water and spits again and again. Then he puts his shirt on, pushes open the door of a W.C. behind him, lowers his trousers and wipes the slime from his legs, that spittle of rain and larvae, those tears from under the trucks. There is no lock on the door. Someone pushes at it. 'Wait.' 'It's Andrew, everything O.K.?' 'O.K.' Latrines, a cul-de-sac, no exit. The wall carries a constellation of addresses and telephone numbers, a matter of discipline, lovers of bondage and leather and chains. Luc smiles. The first smile of the evening.

They are celebrating the anniversary of the bar. On a platform a coffin on which is written in large letters ONE MORE YEAR FOLKS. Flashing lights, fairground décor, sprays of flowers and, hanging from their necks from the ceiling, strangled dolls, each one bearing the name of a rival establishment. The bartenders wear leather tee-shirts with the words: 'Mrs. Nixon is expected at any moment. Do her proud.' Andrew offers Luc a tankard of beer. 'You're crazy.' 'Which of us is the crazier?' Andrew pinches Luc's ear and strokes the back of his neck. 'I felt a bit scared, those guys were beginning to do just anything.' 'What's anything?' 'Well, they'd gotten out of control. I don't trust those trucks. Still, you can trust me.' Silence. 'You do trust me, don't you?'

'My father's black, my mother's Puerto Rican. I have an Irish name, I'm a Baptist, and I work for a Jewish florist. And you're the first Frenchman I've ever met.' Andrew spoke in a dry tone. 'Listen', he says, pinching Luc's arm. The noise of steel-studded boots, the creak of leather jackets, the smell of badly tanned hide, sounds and smells battling together, bruised and battered faces, everyone waiting, lashing out at each other with their eyes. A night of brutality. 'I don't go for this dump, come on back to my place.'

80th Street, Westside. 'This is my ghetto,' Andrew admits, 'I love it and you're sure gonna love it too.' Andrew squeezes the words out through clenched teeth. 'Don't you know how to smile?' 'It makes me tired.' A ramshackle staircase with tall steps, steeply pitched. 'You go first.' 'Which floor is it?' 'Way up at the top, last door.'

The walls are leprous. Broad patches of yellowish paint have scaled off. 'I don't even sweep it, I like it like this, I like it to look neglected,' says Andrew, tossing his leather jacket on the floor. Short-sleeved tee-shirt, ebony arms: Luc remembers that book of strip cartoons which he had read and re-read as a child. *The Adventures of Chocolate,* the nice little black boy who wants to learn to read and write, gets taken up by the Missionary Priest and finally lands up in Paris where he feels cold, very cold, but where a very rich old lady offers him a pullover and has suits made for him out of old frock-coats that belonged to her husband, who died in the war. So Chocolate becomes an engineer, learns how to build dams and goes back to his own country. His own village is doomed by the very first dam he constructs (all alone?). The Missionary dies in his arms and gives him his blessing. To be continued in our next. 'Right, get moving.' 'I'd like to take a shower.' 'If you want to, but there's no hot water.'

Luc gets undressed. It is a huge room with a high ceiling and over the fireplace a picture of Louis XIV on a prancing horse. Pinned to the picture are photographs of Andrew, naked, front view, back view, sprawling, in chains, and with a sailor's cap on his head. 'Come on, move.' Socks screwed into a ball left lying on the floor, dirty briefs and threadbare shirts. 'Right, yeah, O.K., it's my mess, I like it that way.' Luc is warily folding his blue jeans, then his shirt and his socks. 'What the hell are you doing?' Andrew snatches the clothes out of Luc's hands and hurls them to the ground. Chocolate is getting cross. He grips Luc by the shoulder. 'If you want that shower, buddy, get on with it!'

Luc crosses the bedroom. The bed is unmade, ravaged, filthy, quite filthy with stains all over. It is framed between two large wardrobes, like giant strong-boxes. Instead of a canopy over the bed, a mirror slung from the ceiling. 'Bathroom's in there.' Andrew is giving orders, pushing Luc at arm's length in front of him. 'What are you gaping at? You scared?' 'Those insects . . .' 'Oh, they're all over the place, gotta get used to them, man. The bathroom belongs to them.' Standing in the bath-tub Luc turns on the hot water and hears the empty pipes shudder and croak like someone vomiting. Andrew cuts it off. 'I told you, cold water, that's all.' And he turns that on. Luc is caught in a glacial jet. 'No soap: better just scrub yourself.' The water is green and then yellow, and the stink of chlorine fills the bathroom. Luc's hair gets plastered over his face and blinds him. The cold water beats down on the top of his head like hail and re-echoes inside him. He kneels in the bath: this time the powerful jet pins him down. It's raining pebbles. It seems to Luc as if the whole building is

vibrating with him. Niagara. Chocolate is getting his own
back. Chocolate has learned his lesson. Luc feels he'd like to
claw off the discoloured enamel of the tub, but in the five days
since he arrived in New York City he has conscientiously
bitten his nails right down. He clenches his fists. Andrew stops
the cold water. 'O.K., move, out! No towels, so you'll have to
jump around.' Andrew takes hold of him and sets him on his
feet. Luc mutters: 'What was that yellow thing you gave me
just now?' Nothing, man, nothing, a fun thing.' 'Tell me,'
murmurs the shivering Luc, 'tell me.' Happiness, buddy, happiness, and now we're going to have a ball.' 'No.' 'What d'ya
mean, no? Come on . . .' Dripping wet, Luc stretches out on the
bed. Andrew dries him with the dirty sheets. Luc is thinking
how the dirt will make him filthy again. He closes his eyes.
Lets it happen. Andrew is whispering: 'I'm your friend, you
hear me, your friend . . .' And in the mirror over the bed Luc
watches Andrew bend over him and nibble at his navel. A
fringe of frizzy hair tickles his stomach. The black hands take
a grip on his thighs. Andrew is still wearing his trousers and
tee-shirt. He is breathing heavily, and then more and more
noisily. 'It's what you wanted, eh? This is what you were looking for? Tell me it's what you were looking for. Here, you
see!' Andrew gets up and opens the doors of the wardrobes on
either side of the bed. In each of them a strip of neon lights
up: what a collection, an untidy array of whips, plastic gad-
gets and studded corsets. 'Which would you like? Tell me what
you want.' 'But . . .' 'Come on, you know damn well what you
want.' Luc shuts his eyes. Andrew leaps up, straddling him
and pinches Luc's cheeks between the thumb and forefinger of
both hands. 'Come on, talk, you can choose, open your eyes
and look!' Luc tries to sit up. Andrew clobbers him with a
good resounding slap. Luc falls back on the Missionary's lap.
The Missionary blesses him. The wardrobe doors creak. Sound
of metal, sound of leather. In the bathroom columns of insects
were marching up the wall, insects like enormous ants with
strange nightcaps on their heads and hairy legs, eight, ten,
twelve hairy legs. An electric light bulb hung from the ceiling.
Attracted by the light, the insects were making for it, avoiding
the leprous patches of flaking paint, selecting the routes which

they could best adhere to, though sometimes they fell with an unpleasant smack on the tiled floor. As he had stepped out of the bath, Luc had taken care not to tread on them, for they could still have been alive. Then he had told himself that 'he was inside Rasky's body' and that he'd really like to 'make a go of it with Rasky and pick up where they left off', but Andrew's arm was pushing him towards the bed. Ceremonial.

A whip, like a dog's lead. Andrew strikes his legs, then his thighs, harder and harder, then his stomach and his chest. Luc bites his lips. He would like to cry out, but sharp as the pain is it also seems remote, so unbearable that it can in fact be borne. Who is striking whom? Yes, this pain will save Rasky. And the insects in the bathroom will be the first to witness his recovery. The trip to New York will at least have served some purpose. Rasky will return to Paris his old self again, with his smile, and his luggage full of bits and pieces and his gilded life of vacuity and his talent for farewell letters and telephone calls in the middle of the night. 'Come to me, I need you.' With his eyes wide open Luc is watching in the mirror canopied above him the black shadow bent on hurting him: 'You're white, anyone can see that, look and you can see. When I get beaten it leaves no marks behind. Aha!' The laughter of Chocolate returning home to find his village is going to be submerged. What a lot of things he has learnt from him, thanks to him! After the whip, then the chains and the corset, Luc is hardly conscious of anything. Except, above him, the finest picture he has seen in his life, a picture which would go on being finished off forever. No longer will he see that fixed, precise, unmoving image of himself, which used to bring him comfort and despair. He no longer belongs to himself. He is emerging from a cocoon of pain and distress.

Then Luc tells himself that he has missed out on everything. Every chance of courtesy or contemplation, all the great truths. There is nothing moral about his life anyway, just one long record of misconduct. He has missed everything on the way. So that was his body, that white thing with the over-large hips and the fine-boned angular shoulders, the rather weak chin and the rather slack face, a body ready to resign. Andrew makes a bound and grips him round the throat: 'What's on your mind?' Luc is suffocating, he is going to faint. Andrew loosens his hold. Luc gets his breath back. 'What were you thinking?' Silence. 'Answer!' Again Andrew squeezes, more and more tightly. Luc gets the feeling that his eyes are going to swivel round and look into his brain. He tries to cry out. Andrew slackens his grip. Luc gets his breath back. 'Well, answer!' 'I . . .' 'Talk.' '. . . stop a moment.' 'I'll stop if you answer.' Silence. Andrew chucks on the floor all the sheets that encumber the bed, the pillows and the blankets, and shifting Luc round lengthwise on the smooth surface of the mattress, pulls out the straps level with his feet, his genitals and his neck. 'There, that'll stop you moving.' 'Let me go.' 'Where to?' 'Home.' 'Where's home?' 'To Rasky's.' 'Who's Rasky?' 'My friend.' 'He'll wait.' 'Let me alone . . .' 'What are you thinking about, what?' 'I was thinking about Tom, he's coming with his leather cushion. He'll protect me.' 'How do you expect him to get here? No-one knows where you are.' 'Tom and Bill are coming, I know they are.' Andrew smiles. 'Wait, we're gonna celebrate their arrival.' He stands up and goes to the left-hand wardrobe where he makes a choice among several knives. 'We're gonna play a little game, it's only a game, but I hope it's gonna scare you.' He sharpens a large kitchen knife, bends over Luc, bears down on Luc's stomach, and caresses Luc with the cutting edge of the blade. 'Don't move now, or you might get a little scratch.' Andrew puts down the knife, pulls a popper from his pocket and sticks it up Luc's nostrils. 'Come on, take a deep breath, come on, that's it, this'll help you take it easy, do you good, that's the way . . .'

'Wake up, so I can hit you.' That fourth article of yours, we've been waiting for your fourth article. And now, at the last moment, you think you can turn out a piece that shows you're a genius. Oh no! I'll have nothing to do with genius. I'll fling it back in your face. There's no sale for genius. We'd only get another pile of letters. And don't tell me that we only publish the readers' letters that suit us, complimentary ones if they're snappy enough and critical ones if they're stupid. Get on with that article. You have half an hour . . .

'Come on, baby, on your feet, there's plenty more for us to

441

do.' On the corner of a table in the editor's office Luc is scribbling away on white sheets of paper, sweeping over them with his fountain pen. He twists the nib, tries to scratch it straight, wipes it on a piece of blotting-paper and licks it with the tip of his tongue. Then he shakes the pen and attempts to write, but nothing happens. Out of ink? But he has just filled it! So he squeezes out a blob of ink and dips the nib in it, but apart from the blob the ink fails to make a mark. He tries writing the words without ink, but one by one he digs a hole in every sheet. Hurry up. Only twenty minutes left. You ought to have a moment to think. Luc picks up a pencil, a piece of wood with no lead in it. So he takes a paper-knife, makes a nick in the forefinger of his left hand, squeezes out two drops of blood and dips the nib in that: at last it writes, makes a mark, he spreads the globule out and tries to form a word, but the word refuses to take shape . . .

'On your feet, beauty, on your feet.' Andrew undoes the straps and lifts Luc up. The editor enters the office. Ah! there you are, you might have let us know you were back. That article, it's time! Luc holds out a sheet of paper with one spot of blood on it. Is that all? Yes, sir, that's all. So that's what New York means to you. You promised us a piece on the Presidential elections. Is this it? Yes, sir. Since when have you been calling me sir? Yes, sir . . . Come on, stop fooling around, give me the article. You're hiding it. No. Luc, what's got into you? Grasping him with both hands, the editor squares up to Luc, pinches his cheeks, tugs his hair and upbraids him. Come on, give me that article! What's your little game? We've no time to lose. Rasky is dead? What's that? Rasky is dead, there, he just died, I know, I can feel it. Who is Rasky? A friend, my friend. What are you going on about? My private life. I've got a private life too, old man, but I don't blurt it out. I keep it to myself. He slaps Luc. Wake up, good God, what's happened to you? It was a trap! What's that? I've been caught in a trap . . .

Andrew pushes Luc into the living-room and flings him on the floor. Rolled-up socks and dirty briefs. Luc's head is full of flashing colours, meteors that explode, meadows soaked in dew, too lush and too green, blue canopies torn asunder:

through the port-hole of a plane he stretches out his arm and snatches at the blue cloth and the clouds. The editor keeps coming back to him, holding out the blood-stained page. What do you think I'm going to do with this then, eh? What am I going to do with this mark? You're a dead duck, Luc, a dead duck. And Luc wonders how he could ever have been the friend of such a bastard. He holds out his arms to his boss. He holds out his arms to Andrew. Andrew yanks his head back by the hair. 'Here, swallow this.' Two pills, a glass of water. 'Come on, swallow.' Luc gulps. 'Again.' The water trickles down his chin, forming bubbles at the corners of his mouth. 'Good, right, that's good.' He takes a grip on the nape of Luc's neck, forces him up and drives him back into the bedroom. 'This time, we're gonna have fun, you wanna have fun?' Luc can feel a ball of fire growing in his stomach. He is dazzled by too many lights: he flies off into the infinite immensity of the palms of Andrew's black hands. The pages of the *Collected Adventures of Chocolate* are turning furiously, creating a violent wind. In a daze, Luc can neither see nor feel anything now. He makes one last effort and tries to explain to his boss that it is not his fault. He cries to Rasky for help, but on the pavement outside his school there is no-one waiting for him. Luc is sinking.

Only then does Andrew strip naked. Luc can no longer see him. An ebony totem streaming with sweat, he is rubbing his left fist and forearm all over with viscous jelly from a tube. Long minutes the ritual lasts. His forearm becomes a second member, which slowly, very slowly, twisting like a trepan, forces a passage into Luc, plunges and takes him. Luc is lying on his stomach, his face embedded in a pillow. When Andrew's foream has been lodged in its most comfortable position, without loosening his hold Andrew pulls himself up over Luc's body and with his right hand, using all his force, he presses the face of the white boy down into the white pillow. He stays that way for several long minutes, holding his breath, waiting for the other to die. Death arrives on the scene unannounced. She was concealed in the pillow. Epitaph for a life: asphyxia.

—Translated by
Donald Watson

CHRISTIAN KAMPMANN

FEELINGS

The priest said on the telephone that if I want to turn Catholic I must first attend instruction. A new class is beginning soon, and he will decide whether I'll be allowed to join the group after he has had a personal conversation with me. I can come to see him fifteen minutes before the class begins.

It's what I want to do. I'm sure of it. It's what I've always been looking for, without realizing it. I sense new meanings and connections. There is a reason for my being so depressed during the first months of this year: I needed to be forced to understand the innermost purpose of my longing.

The priest receives me in a friendly yet somewhat sceptical manner. He observes me with more than his eyes. He is wearing a black suit with a clerical collar, and there is a crucifix hanging on the wall. But that doesn't seem strange, here. He must be about ten years older than my father.

We seat ourselves one on each side of the desk. My heart is pounding. The moment is filled to the bursting point with meaning.

He asks why I don't want to continue being a Protestant. I try to describe what my childhood was like—the purely religious aspects of it—and why Confirmation classes didn't change a thing. He seems to have heard the story often.

"But what makes you think that Catholicism will be any better for you?"

My restlessness. Books. None of these things provide real proof.

"My life has been lacking something," I say, "as do the lives of most Danes, it seems to me. If you compare our lives with those of people in southern Europe . . ." I make a vague gesture which I immediately regret.

The priest wants to know what I plan to do when I've completed my military service. When I reply that I want to try to become a journalist, he makes a slight grimace.

"In that case, you'll have to be even better informed than others. It will take time."

"I'm prepared for that—now."

He smiles a little. When the doorbell rings he says, "Perhaps you'll help me set up the chairs."

In the class are three women and one other man, all much older than I. Apparently it usually takes people half their lives to begin to find their way.

The priest seems somewhat different now, more relaxed. He pays less attention to me than to the others. That's fine with me.

"Let's begin with the reason why we are here on earth," he says very calmly. "We are here to do God's will, so we can be saved and go to heaven. That is the purpose of our lives."

Aside from my grandfather, no one has ever told me that life has a purpose, or what that purpose is. I like the priest's explanation better than my grandfather's.

I guard my secret. Everything will be changed. At least, I feel that's what will happen. My perspective has been altered—or created; up to now, I haven't had any perspective. The hope of change is in itself a change.

Sometimes I'm afraid that it's all just something I'm imagining. Then I think about the millions of people on earth who profess the same faith I'll soon have, and I keep on reading.

I'm amazed by the fact that Christianity hasn't made a greater impact—true Christianity, I mean. Of course, I've always been aware of the gulf between the way everything could be and the way everything, unfortunately, is. But now I can accept this without the disgust I previously felt, because now I know there is hope.

In order for change to occur, I must help—and not just spiritually. I try to drink less without stopping completely, which might call attention to myself. I try to be more friendly toward other people, both at the office on the military base and at home. This doesn't seem to make much difference to anyone; I'm probably still so reserved that people barely notice the change in my behavior. But in time it will be noticed.

And then there's her. Here too, something has to be changed. I've always thought that, in a country like Denmark that sort of thing is permissible, especially when two people are fond of each other—but no. I've read it, and I've heard the priest say it: "When a young man marries a young woman they must both be virgins." I know what I have to do, and I want to do it. But I wish I could avoid hurting her. I'm going to have to break off our relationship. She isn't the one I eventually want to marry after all.

Until I'm ready to get married, I'll just have to get used to being alone. In a way, I'm already alone. So I'm sure I'll manage.

I arrange to meet her in town as usual. She thinks it's just an ordinary date. While we sit waiting for our drinks I wish it were she who was getting ready to say something unpleasant. I would make sure I acted surprised and unhappy, and then I would forgive her and wish her happiness and good luck.

We raise our glasses and say *skål,* then lapse into quietness. The silence is stifling.

"What's wrong?" she finally asks.

With a sense of relief, I realize that I can do what has to be done after all. She has reached out to take what's coming. I hardly need to do anything myself.

"There's nothing wrong," I reply. "I mean—yes, there is."

"What is it?"

"You know perfectly well. Don't you? I'm really sorry. But I'm sure it will be best for you too, at least in the long run."

Her look grows more and more intense, and then suddenly weakens. She leans back.

I have to explain. Try to explain. To some extent. "It doesn't have anything to do with you."

"But with someone else?"

"Not at all. No, no. Just with me. If you see what I mean?"

"Maybe I do," she says slowly. And then, a little later: "How long have you felt this way?"

"Let's not go into it."

"Since New Year's Eve?"

"Well . . . yes. Sort of. Please don't misunderstand."

"I'm trying not to," she says, as she reaches for her purse and stands up.

"Don't feel bad about it," I say. "I still like you a lot."

Fortunately, she pretends not to have heard me. After she has left I sit for a while without moving or thinking about anything at all. I finish her drink and order another. I'm free.

I go to mass each Sunday. Look forward to it all week. No one knows what I'm doing except the priest, who sometimes gives me an impassive look. The first Saturday night I sleep at the barracks, even though I've always got a weekend pass, but after that I prefer to find an excuse. I tell my parents that I'm going to a museum or, if I stay in town afterwards, that I'm going to visit her.

It's over a month since the last time I was really with her. During the first two weeks I managed to be "chaste," to use the embarrassing term the priest often uses in dead seriousness. Then I "satisfied myself," to use an expression that over-evaluates the act. From now on I'll let it happen in my sleep. ("Angel pussy," they call it in the barracks.) That's the way it will have to be for the time being. Other things are more important to me.

I want to guard my secret until my faith is even stronger. But one evening when I'm at home alone with my mother and we've had a little more than usual to drink, I suddenly feel that she will understand.

"There's something I'd like to talk to you about," I say, and regret having started with that stupid old sentence. It's generally used in order to ward off the consequences of small, painful disclosures, and I can see by my mother's face—before she assumes a neutral expression—that this is in fact what she fears.

"Something good," I hasten to add.

My mother tries to appear as though she had not expected anything different. She lights another cigarette.

Then I say it. It's out. At first my mother looks as though she is going to cry. Then she gives me a strange smile.

"I can understand very well," she says. "But whether your father will understand—that's another question. Your grandmother will be happy."

"I don't want her to know yet."

"What about other people?"

"No."

"Nobody?"

"Not yet. Don't you agree?"

My mother shakes her head, a faraway look in her eyes. Then she says, "You haven't definitely made up your mind, have you?"

"Yes," I say. And with that the decision is made.

I explain about the time it will take before I'm accepted into the Church, about all the things in my life I must get in order first.

"Danes think they know the answers to everything," she says. "Like I say to your father: Wait till you die—you'll get the surprise of your life."

Eternal life is something I'll wait to decide about until later. I'll think about it when my faith is stronger.

"That way out," says my mother," is closed to me, of course."

"Why?"

"Because of your father."

"Would *you* want to?"

Although she says nothing, my mother responds nevertheless, with one of the wordless communications I've experienced since earliest childhood, a secret look into her that we both are supposed to pretend we're not aware of.

"What's most important to me, of course," she says, "is how things are between your father and me."

I nod. I want to add that she is free to do whatever she wants in her thoughts and feelings, but I don't say it, because I know I would not be satisfied with so little either. One can't be a Catholic in secret.

"Do you know anyone who is a Catholic?" asks my mother. "Have you met any?"

"It's something that just happened inside me. I can't explain it any better."

"I really do understand. When one is a child, one has one's parents. That is, if one has both parents. Later—Yes, one gets married, but—anyway, I do understand."

"I'm glad."

"Do you love your mother?" my mother asks in English.

We hug each other and have something more to drink.

One day while running errands for the office I stop in front of a movie theater to look at the stills. The sun warms my back —it is spring—and as I'm standing there one of my old classmates from high school comes riding by on his bicycle. We talk together a while and then go our separate ways. The next time I'm at home I find a letter there from him asking if I'd like to meet him in town some evening.

If I'm going to spend an evening with another fellow I'd rather have it be my friend from the barracks; but until that happens, I can certainly sacrifice one evening. The fact that my classmate was never among the few I regarded as my friends in high school is probably all the better.

We meet in Tivoli and get drunk. Then we wander around the amusement park. I find myself in that mellow state I sometimes achieve: I seem to flow together with everything around me. A squeeze on my arm isolates me again. He wants to know what we should do now. I wish I could get rid of him so I could once again become part of the sounds and the movements. On the other hand, I certainly don't want to be rude. How about a ride on the roller coaster? Once I suggest it and he says "yes," I start to feel like doing it myself. I decide that soon I'll ask my friend at the barracks if he wants to spend an evening in town with me, and immediately it's easier to reconcile myself to the fact that he's not the one I'm walking beside now. When my classmate says something, I turn toward him and smile, and the electric lights twinkling in the trees flow into me and give a rhythm to my expectation.

We're lucky—we get the back car on the roller coaster.

"Are you scared?" he asks.

"Are you?"

"Not as much as usual."

The row of cars starts with a jolt. We slowly glide into a tunnel. The tracks curve upward, carrying us into the open air. We turn toward each other, as though impelled by a common movement, and kiss each other. For a moment everything is still, all movement stops. Then the sounds burst out again, louder than ever, and the car climbs higher, abruptly, and we ride the entire trip without reacting to it, or to the other thing.

He overtakes me at the bottom of the stairs.

"Let's go somewhere and talk."

"No. I have to get back," I say.

"Already?"

"Yes. Thanks for the nice time."

"Wait! If you think that I—that we—have done anything wrong . . ."

"There's nothing to talk about."

"Yes there is!"

"I don't think so."

"Yes, but we both—we agreed like two sparrows."

I see how confused and unhappy he is. As for me, I feel totally calm. I hurry off, grateful that each person I pass puts me farther away from him. At the heart of my calmness I feel a kernel of anger, directed only at myself. I don't feel a thing for him, and of course I won't ever have anything to do with him again.

What happened to me? It wasn't even a genuine desire that I gave in to. Had it happened in the right way, it should have been with someone else, a fellow I really like.

I catch myself with a start. What have I just admitted? Something I've known for a long time. Yes, of course. But until now I've blocked off my knowledge from the rest of me.

Outside Tivoli I discover I've got to take a piss so badly that I can't wait until I get back to the barracks, not even if I take a taxi. I know there are public toilets at Radhuspladsen —the square is just a few blocks away—and even though I prefer to avoid that type of dirty, smelly place, I'm going to have to make an exception.

The area outside the toilets, where there are telephones and a coatroom, looks relatively clean. I'm about to go inside when the door swings open and my classmate comes out.

We stop and look at each other. It appears that the situation is so unexpected he can't even react to it, rather than that he's feeling bad about things the way he was before. I myself feel nothing at all, except an even stronger need to take a piss.

I walk the whole way home. I've got to straighten out my thoughts and feelings.

I've always known something like this would happen. That much I'm quite willing to admit. I've been longing for it, at the same time as I've tried to prevent myself from having such feelings. How much it actually means, I don't know. Truly. I'm being completely honest.

I hate him for comparing us to a couple of sparrows. The next time I go home I find a letter from him. In it he asks me to forgive him if he has done anything wrong and says he can't be as strong as I am, he's tried, and if I change my mind, there's nothing he'd rather do than see me again. I tear up the letter and flush it down the toilet.

"I've told him," says my mother. "I had to tell him."

I give a slight nod, understanding what she means.

"I think he wants to talk to you," she continues. "He's your father, after all."

Of course I've known that such a conversation between my father and myself would have to take place. I've rehearsed fragments of it. Although they have varied in tone and major points, all the versions have had one thing in common: they surprise my father, and thereby prevent him from going around shaking his head disapprovingly in advance.

"Did I do anything wrong?" asks my mother.

"No, no." I would have preferred to have been even stronger in my faith. The "episode"—I see mocking quotation marks whenever my thoughts are forced back to that evening —also made it necessary to wait a little. I have to be completely sure about everything, including those things I keep secret.

"You *are* certain," says my mother, "aren't you?"

My anxiety is a false alarm. She is referring to something else after all.

"More certain than ever," I say.

My mother, who normally sits and waits for my father to come home from the office, turns her head, listens.

"That's him." She puts out her cigarette and smoothes her skirt.

My father comes in whistling. My mother runs over and gives him a hug. I greet him in my usual way. My friends who have witnessed it have been surprised to see me greet my father with a kiss on the cheek—they don't do anything like that even to their mothers—and I've felt myself to be rather lucky. But since "it" happened that stupid evening I've begun to notice that my father obviously prefers to just shake hands.

My father goes upstairs to take a bath and change his clothes. I go up to my room. I sit by the window looking out at the backyards and at the water far away; beyond the water a strip of land shines in the sunlight. Something within me is trying to burst out, but for my own sake I repress it.

While we're eating dinner I get an idea: I can refuse to discuss the subject with my father. That's my right, after all. For a while I sit relishing the idea, but then all its dangerous aspects bubble to the surface and corrode it away. When we've drunk our after-dinner coffee, when my brothers and sisters have gone upstairs to do their homework and my mother gets up and closes the glass doors to the room where my father and I are sitting, I try to pull myself together. I'm the one who has the upper hand, not he.

"Your mother told me that—"

"Yes," I say, "I know."

"Do you want to explain anything about it to me?"

"All right. But either you understand, in which case you don't need an explanation, or else—"

"I'd like you to try anyway."

"I've been looking for something. And I've found it."

"I see. How did you find it? Forgive me for asking. But that sort of thing has always seemed so foreign to me."

"And irrelevant?"

"It would be strange if it were otherwise, wouldn't it? Is it because you know some?"

"Know some . . . ?"

"Some Catholics."

I shake my head. Now is when I have to be most careful if I don't want my father to think I've fallen prey to weird ideas.

"Who would that be?"

"It could be you've met somebody. You must have come in contact with it somehow or other."

"That's true, of course. But it's not exactly a small, obscure sect we're talking about after all. It's hard to overlook Catholicism if one is the least bit observant."

My father pretends to ponder this line of reasoning. Then he slowly draws in his breath and expels it with a sudden, violent puff.

"So this is something you've thought of all by yourself?" he says.

"I didn't think of it."

"Then who did?"

I'm about to reply that it's essentially a matter of feelings, and that feelings aren't something you "think of." But I let it go. He neither can nor wants to understand. He may as well direct the conversation however he wants to; I'll act like I'm still taking part in it. That way we can both feel satisfied afterwards.

"It must be self-suggestion," he says.

I give him a slight smile.

"What do you expect it to offer you?" he asks.

The true, spontaneous answer—a meaning in life and a desire to live—I keep to myself.

"Is that so hard to figure out?" I say.

He mulls that over. I wonder if he has ever before been so intensely interested in me.

"What will you do on Fridays," he asks teasingly, "you who don't like any fish except lobster?"

"Eat just potatoes. Like I already do. Actually, there are more important things than that."

"And they're even more impossible to accept."

"Who says it's supposed to be easy?"

"You've already learned something, I see."

"I don't think it will be so hard," I argue. "Besides, I'm tired of all that 'bed-hopping.'"

The final word elicits a look of mild surprise on my father's face. He wants me to think that the expression is deliberately assumed and that he's done it to deal gently with me. What kind of stupid word is that to use anyway? Does such a word even exist? Why did I blurt that out?

"I don't imagine you've tried too much of that sort of thing yet," he says.

"Enough to know I'd rather—I'd rather be serious about it."

In order to avoid the word "love" I say: "I don't want to be with someone unless it's really serious."

"And do you think you can tell when it's serious?"

"Couldn't you?"

"With your mother? Yes. But that was far from the first time. For her too. You already know that. If you want to enjoy life, why join a group that says you shouldn't do it?"

I shrug my shoulders. It's not particularly convincing, but I can't come up with anything better. I'm tired. I want the conversation to end so I can go up to my room and figure out what it meant.

"I guess you know about the Catholics' humane, up-to-date attitudes toward things like divorce and contraception."

"Yes. But what does that matter, if people really care about each other?"

My father smiles. Things have gone exactly as I figured they would. That's obvious. My father can't understand me, and therefore hopes that I can't understand myself either. Otherwise, in his opinion, I must be a little crazy.

"I've got to go to the bathroom," I explain.

"Go ahead."

I'm about to close the glass doors again. "Leave them open," my father says. "It's a bit stuffy in here."

A short time later my mother steals up to my room.

"How did it go?"

"Fine."

"I thought it would. He isn't so—what word should I use? —unreasonable after all, is he?"

"You can use that word. No, he isn't unreasonable."

"But he couldn't really understand, could he?"

I shake my head, and my mother smiles contentedly.

"Still, I love him," she says. "And you know what? The most important thing isn't what a person believes. It's got to do with something else entirely."

When, in the following days, I try to figure out where I stand now, I get a strange feeling. It seems as though most of my thoughts are already so muddled by the time they reach my consciousness that there's nothing left of the true, original impulse. But the sun is shining, there are new leaves on all the trees, and when I ride off on my bicycle in the sunshine, my movements melting into those of everything around me, I'm closer to an explanation than when I try to think.

A witty, light-hearted friend of mine from officers' training school invites me and my friend from the barracks to have dinner at his stepmother's home. She's very anxious to meet a couple of his military friends, and he can't invite just anybody. Not that his stepmother is a snob; it would just be too bad if she unintentionally made someone feel he was using his knife and fork incorrectly.

I look forward to it. I call up a girl, whom I've thought about before too—we went together for a while in high school —and ask her if she'd like to go out with me some evening. She'd like to very much. We agree to talk more about it later. Now everything is in order. In the meantime, I'm going to spend a whole long evening with my friend from the barracks and my other friend from officers' training school, toward whom I must always act equally friendly. Nobody can tell what I really feel.

We all three take the streetcar together to the stepmother's home. Each building we jolt past gleams with hidden meaning. I'm careful to pay exactly the same amount of attention to each of my companions. I see the way small dark hairs curl up over the neck of the undershirt that my friend from the barracks is wearing. Quickly, I look away.

We get off in an area I'm not familiar with. "My stepmother's mailing address is Copenhagen V.—the Vesterbro district," says my friend, "but it *is* the Frederiksberg district. At least, I know the Nørrebro district doesn't start until way over there. And the apartment itself is very nice." We all know, of course, that Frederiksberg is a better district than either Vesterbro or Nørrebro.

His stepmother is in her late thirties, but looks younger. Naturally she tries to hide the fact that she's nervous. She is from Sweden and speaks with a slight accent, and I realize this makes me feel that she's a little—what should I call it?—different. Even though I understand why she seems that way. When it's so easy to appear different without really being so, how can one ever keep from seeming different when one really is?

After we've had a couple of drinks and are seated at the dinner table I stop worrying. I become part of something light and bubbling: a cultivated atmosphere. It's impossible to say anything wrong. Each new comment binds us gently together, and I'm careful to treat everyone exactly the same.

I make a pleasant observation about a piece of furniture. Suddenly my friend's stepmother is on her guard; something has to be defended.

"We all know, of course, that when my husband died he left us nothing. I was forced to disclaim the assets and liabilities of the estate. I had to buy our furniture back at auction with my own savings. Sometimes I wonder: what is that furniture doing *here*? It would certainly fit in better somewhere else. But what would I put here instead? What *would* fit in? And besides, when I get home from the office I'm simply too tired to do anything about it."

We talk some more about various tasteless ways to furnish the living room. The fact that my friend from the barracks doesn't understand, that he thinks the rest of us are only having fun, makes my tender feelings for him break through my usual defenses. He's better than we are, finer. Which is why I—Nothing.

I'm drunk, but in a manner that my father would approve: witty, brilliant. My friend's stepmother tells about the manor house she had visited with her husband. She gets out a book about the family she married into and reads one of her favorite passages. It's something about a captain who successfully survives a dangerous situation sometime around the end of the eighteenth century, and how he thereby earns some sort of title. I try to keep my attention focused on the conversation, but the entire time I'm aware of a radiance surrounding my friend. In a little while I'm going to do something terrible: put my arm around him or something. I've got to get away.

I look at my watch several times. The thin smile on my hostess's face when I say I must leave indicates that, no matter how fortunate I'd been in making the right impression up to that point, I've now ruined everything. In my mind I take from the corner cupboard some of the antique goblets I've just been admiring and smash them through a couple of glass panes. Then I thank the hostess and say a polite goodbye.

When I get outside, my friend asks if we're heading in the same direction. I tell him I'm going to sleep overnight at my grandparents; I can't stand to be near him, and yet I hope he will insist on accompanying me. Pain is better than nothing. He says he will just be in time to catch the streetcar. I let him go.

I'm relieved. I've never been so much on the verge of revealing myself. Fortunately, he's too drunk to notice anything. And besides, he doesn't have any suspicion, of course. I've got to make sure at all costs that he keeps a good impression of me. Nobody's respect means more to me than his.

I hail a taxi and it stops at the curb. Where do I want to go? The main entrance of Tivoli. I have to tell the driver something after all. I'm so excited that my undershirt is soaked with sweat. Out in the bluish summer darkness the lights rush past and flow together into a glowing, pulsating pattern. A faint scent of lemon detaches itself from the smell of old tobacco in the taxi.

We arrive at the entrance to Tivoli. I wait until the taxi has disappeared. Then I turn and walk slowly toward the central square at Radhuspladsen. Each face I pass is so intense that I gasp for breath. Everything is trembling on the edge of transformation. In front of the townhall I decide that if someone should seem startled that I'm standing here I can just look up at the words of the "news in lights" that flash constantly outside the Politiken newspaper building. I try. The words flickering past have no meaning to me. I walk around a little. There's no law against a person doing that.

Gradually I become aware that something is going on at the other side of the square. I see how it happens. Either one stands still, or one moves around. The person who is moving passes close to the one standing still. He walks a short distance, looks back, continues a bit further, then turns and goes back and holds out a cigarette to get a light. A little later they go off together, or the one who was moving walks away alone and begins all over again with someone else.

I'm on the verge of fainting the whole time. I sit down on a bench. All around me advertisements in neon lights blink: Do it now! A clear, deep violet sky arches the entire scene, indifferent to my small actions.

It's too early, or else maybe the moment when I felt brave enough is already past. I've got to get away from the square for a while. I walk by the building where my grandfather has his office. I don't want to think about him or anyone else. As I continue walking away I know with growing certainty that I'll soon go back to the square. Nothing else has any meaning to me now.

I go into a courtyard and take a leak. Might as well get it over with. I am calm. What is supposed to happen, and will happen, is something I've been waiting for always.

On the way back, I pass a man and look directly into his eyes. At first all I can see is a haze; then his expression comes into focus. I can't understand the look at first, it seems so contradictory. But a little later, after I've walked over to some shop windows, I realize what his expression meant: first, curiosity that gives rise to an urge to do something audacious and is, in turn, penetrated by a deeper-lying despair and loneliness; then, an immediate camouflage of indifference which, in the end, turns into something roguish and noncommittal. The man must be forty years old, or even older. At the same time he seems almost boyish. If he has misunderstood my look and is on his way over here, I'll leave. Then I'll just have to come back another night. Besides, I'm so exhausted that I'm sick to my stomach. Fortunately, he seems to have understood.

Eventually I've looked at all the books in the windows. For the third or fifth time I decide to go home. Then I discover that someone has stopped a short distance away from me.

I stand motionless and stare straight ahead until I can catch my breath. I turn my head just slightly. The other fellow has done the same. He is younger than the first one, much younger —in his early twenties. His hair is dark and curly. He is good-looking. His light-colored pants and dark suede jacket are an inconspicuous outfit. There is nothing strange about him, except that no one has ever attracted me so powerfully.

He smiles a little. I try to do the same, but the muscles of my face are too stiff to smile. Nonetheless, he comes closer and stands a few steps away from me.

"Hi," he says.

I manage to make a weak, hoarse sound.

"Want to take a walk?"

I clear my throat. "O.K." I don't understand what he means. Maybe he's using code words.

He wants to go down a side street off the main shopping street. Fine with me. He asks what my name is, and how old I am. I tell him that I'm eighteen and that my name is Peter. That's my middle name too. When he hears that I'm in the military he laughs.

"I'm Tom."

I've never known anyone by that name before. I'm glad to have waited until now. Tom is exactly the right name. Nice, friendly, safe. A lot of unpleasant qualities are unthinkable in a person with that name. I want to tell him everything about myself immediately, and to hear all about him.

"What do you do?" I ask.

"Hairdresser."

I'm just about to say that he doesn't look like one. But obviously I still have to think twice before saying things, at least at the start. Later we'll be able to say everything to each other without fear of being misunderstood.

He radiates the same type of calmness as my friend at the barracks. And there's something wise about him. Suddenly I realize why he doesn't fit my idea of a hairdresser. The idea isn't my own. I've never known, or even talked with, a hairdresser; I've never been inside one of those places where women get their hair done. My impression of hairdressers hasn't had anything to do with my personal experience. And this can hardly be the only area where that is true.

As we are crossing a deserted square he touches my arm briefly. A warm feeling spreads throughout my entire body. We come to Rundetarn, the Round Tower. He stops, looks around. Not a person in sight. The only sound, other than that of his breathing next to me, is the faint hum of a car far away. The silence and the empty streets increase my sense of being in a dream, where everything is both surprising and obvious at the same time.

"Come," he says in a low voice.

I follow him through a gate and then on into a courtyard. He looks carefully all around, including upwards. The courtyard is surrounded by gray-painted buildings. All of the darkened windows are closed, except for one on the top floor which is half-open.

"Do you think anyone lives here?" I whisper.

He shakes his head. "Offices," he says, and turns toward me.

We move, in unison, into each other's arms. For the first time in my life I really feel another person's body, and my own. Stronger than the smell of either his tobacco or his suede jacket is the smell of Tom himself. It's the key to everything I've been longing for. We begin to kiss each other. This way is the right way for me. There's nothing wrong with me: I can feel what the songs and the novels praise; I can get out of myself and flow into another person. The other way was pleasant, and I felt something during it—no doubt about that—but it was always shadowed by the longing for this. I understand everything. I'm glowing inside.

We look at one another. I put my arms around his neck and curve my fingers down into his thick hair. All the caresses I've given in the sleepwalker existence of my past I can now experience in reality. I touch his forehead with the tip of a finger. We smile at each other. He takes hold of my thighs, between my legs. It's the most exciting thing I've ever felt.

He unzips my pants and puts his hand inside. I feel its warmth around my cock, which he tries to take out without success. I want to help him, but am too shy. Yet when he squats down and begins to pull at my pants I manage to get them and my undershorts pulled down around my thighs. He pulls them down even further with a caressing movement along my legs, then carefully takes hold of my cock and puts it in his mouth; suckles, sucks. I've never tried anything like this before, or ever read or heard about it, but that doesn't make it either strange or surprising. It's the most wonderful physical sensation I've ever had. The only problem is that I get more and more excited so quickly that I'm afraid I'll come before he lets go of me. I've already started—in my head too, in every part of my body. I come in a wave of light. The next thing I'm aware of is the sound of a small splash on the asphalt as he spits out my sperm, and then the feeling of the chilly air on my rear end and thighs.

For the time being it's probably best that I put on my pants. I do it hurriedly. He has lit a cigarette. He looks at his watch, shakes himself a little.

"What time do you have to be at the base tomorrow?" he asks.

"Six-thirty."

"Ugh! I don't have to be at work until nine."

"What time is it now?"

"Almost two-thirty. Should we head off together?"

I ask what direction he's going before the meaning of his words hits me.

"Vanløse. I'll take a taxi from Radhuspladsen."

"I'll walk that far with you then."

The question of why he shouldn't get to have a come too is

461

pushed aside, because he has put his arms around me. We kiss each other again and again. Somewhere nearby a few birds have started to sing, and when I look up I see that the panes in the half-opened window are reflecting the dawn.

The street is still deserted except for the two of us. Light filters down over it, there is a smell of salt water, and when we come out into an open square a breeze wafts over us and he puts his arm around me for a moment.

In the past I've always thought I could never be really alive, or even just be completely involved in the attempt, and, furthermore, I've accepted that. Why? I can't understand it, now that it's ended. Everything has become simple and real. And if I were holding his hand now there would be nothing left to wish for.

A shrill, foolish laughter reaches us, and two men come around the corner and walk quickly past us—mince past us, in the case of the younger one, the one who continues laughing.

Tom quickens his pace. "I can't stand people like that," he says, making some exaggerated movements with his arms and hips that look like a gross parody of a woman who considers herself extremely high-class. He abruptly becomes himself again and, after lighting another cigarette, continues talking about his dislike of that type of person. I nod, agreeing with him. Relief and pride stream through me, until suddenly I start to be afraid that he has the same opinion about me but is just hiding it carefully. In spite of everything, what we did together was pretty limited after all. Maybe he lost his desire during it, or even before.

"You feel the same way?" he asks.

I venture a slight nod.

"That's easy to see," he adds, and I hide my relief.

We have come to Radhuspladsen. It mustn't end. I nod eagerly when he says that perhaps we'll see each other again.

"Are you in town a lot?" he asks.

"What do you mean?"

"At all the places."

I'm about to explain about places that are off-limits for the military. He pats my arm.

"Stay happy," he says, and turns and walks away quickly and gets into a taxi. We wave to one another.

I walk a little further and then take a taxi. The sun is up. I ask the driver to stop a short distance from the house, out of consideration for my sleeping grandparents. The smell of the sea is stronger out here and blends with the fragrance from all the gardens. My feeling of having broken through to reality has increased; I'm even more intensely a part of it than before. Everything is incredibly obvious and, at the same time, full of secrets.

The grandfather clock in the hall shows twenty minutes after four. I've only got one hour to sleep, if I want time to eat some breakfast before I leave for the base. I tiptoe up the stairs, stepping in and out of broad bands of sunshine which I've never seen here on the stairway before. I can hear my grandfather's heavy breathing. He must have fallen asleep again after his late-night reading. On the table beside my bed is a glass and a bottle of mineral water. Next to a bottle opener are some aspirin and a piece of paper on which my grandmother has written: "Sleep well. Take one if necessary." I do that, drink some mineral water, and hear her turn in bed in the next room before sleep unites me with him.

—*Translated by*
Nadia Christensen

DARCY PENTEADO

THE ICE-CREAM FAIRY

Dr. Chrisóstomo Mascarenhas was mayor of Riacho Escuro in the state of São Paulo. He and his wife were a fine, upstanding couple of irreproachable moral, religious, civic and sexual principles, an honor and adornment to their town and state—in fact, to every fortunate spot they had ever chosen to grace with their illustrious presence. As a consequence, this worthy gentleman had been elected to three consecutive terms as president of the Riacho Escuro Recreation Association, fashionable gathering place for the cream of local society. That he should in due course be appointed mayor as well was only the logical culmination of a social and political career solidly based on a lifetime of perfect propriety.

Shortly after the new mayor took office, Silvio Santos, the producer of a popular weekly television series, began promoting a "Tournament of Towns" in which Riacho Escuro was invited to participate. Before replying, Dr. Chrisostomo passed on the invitation to the city councilmen, who would base their decision on how much support they thought they could expect from local industry and the Chamber of Commerce, as well as the sports clubs and cultural and social organizations. If they entered the contest at all, they would have to go the whole hog; if they tried to cut corners they would be pushed out of the running by the other towns. As it happened, money was no problem, for they were in the middle of a boom. Tax revenue was rolling in, Riacho Escuro produced all its own food supply, and there was even a labor shortage because the town was growing so rapidly.

The mayor's pride at the thought of showing off his home town on a nationwide television program proved infectious. The city council voted unanimously to participate, if the sponsors would give them a reasonable length of time to prepare. In the end it was decided that Riacho Escuro would be the eighth town to appear on the program. As soon as that point was settled the mayor called a meeting of local industrialists, prominent businessmen, sports club directors, the presidents of the Lions and Rotary Clubs (inevitably) and the vicar of the mother church, together with several members of the Marian Congregation. The meeting resulted in a finance committee, a ways and means committee on which the vicar would serve, and a committee of society matrons and debutantes to look after the finer details.

By this time most of the population of Riacho Escuro—excited, argumentative and fearful by the turns—were eagerly following the competition among the other towns. Imagine the excitement there would be when their home town joined in! The rivals were actually bringing in all the strange and improbable things they were being asked to produce, and a mere point or two might spell the difference between glory and defeat. The contenders were all doing their damnedest, and Riacho Escuro could do no less. The mayor's house became battle headquarters, where major and minor decisions were made and announced. As the working group with its friends and hangers-on grew more numerous, Dr. Chrisóstomo had a massive color television installed in the den so they could all watch the Sunday program together. During the breaks for commercials and while everyone was vigorously dissecting the show after it was over, snacks were served, with whisky for the men and tangerine cordial or soda-water for the ladies.

Riacho Escuro's turn to go into action came in the eighth week of the Tournament of Towns. That Sunday morning at six an imposing cortège set out for São Paulo. It was composed of three buses, several private cars, a moving van loaded with sports equipment, ballet costumes and miscellaneous props, and finally a cattle truck conveying the most important entry for the shows—a Brahma bull which had won prizes in five livestock competitions, to be displayed on television with all his blue ribbons and medals. That hadn't been much of a challenge since Riacho Escuro was prime cattle country; the mayor's wife had just asked her second cousin to lend them one of the fine animals from his herd.

The entire presentation had been planned to perfection; there was even a youthful cheering section waving streamers, banners and balloons stamped with "Riacho Escuro" in large letters. That part had been planned and rehearsed by the debutantes of the ladies' auxiliary. After an athletics display the real show began, with a parade of rare items and an artistic program complete with ballet, folk songs, instrumental music and a poetry recital. Thanks to the mayor and the city council —and perhaps still more to the keen discussion and thoughtful analysis of the rivals' performance by the ways and means committee and the ladies' auxiliary—Riacho Escuro scored a resounding victory in that first encounter.

The triumphal procession returned in the wee hours of the morning. The whole town had stayed up to welcome the champions, and the celebration went on until dawn. From that Sunday on Riacho Escuro thought, ate and slept "Tournament of Towns." It was the topic of conversation for every group in every social class; people thought of nothing but learning about or hunting for the curious objects required by the program's producers. The objects would become more exotic and the quest more and more arduous, they knew, particularly since every item had to be produced in a scant week's time. The rare object demanded for the second show was an antique image of a female saint which would shed tears on Corpus Christi. It wouldn't have been so hard to find one if the rules hadn't called for making it cry on cue before the cameras. Naturally, the mayor turned this problem over to the vicar, who served as chairman of the ways and means committee.

Not a single old figure remained in any of the churches in Riacho Escuro. All had been sold to antique dealers and plaster ones put in their place, but perhaps there were a few left in nearby villages or on some old *fazenda*. The priest and all the members of the sodality set out to beat the bushes. On Friday afternoon, when the committee was beginning to lose hope, a sodalist walked in triumphantly with a carved figure in his arms. The old woman who cared for the little chapel where he had found it had assured him that the saint shed tears not only on the feast of Corpus Christi but on various other holy days scattered throughout the calendar.

That Sunday morning the cortège set off again with the mayor and his lady, the vicar bearing the precious image, an honor guard of twelve men from the sodality with their sky-blue sashes and flag, plus the athletes, singers, musicians, recitalists, little girls from the ballet school, and the claque of liberated young people already high on marijuana and primed to yell their lungs out from the audience.

That Dr. Chrisóstomo's team would walk away with the prize on the second show was a foregone conclusion when Riacho Escuro's image not only wept before the cameras but smiled immediately afterwards to show its support for the town. The young fans, who by then were feeling no pain, shouted out, "It's the greatest, the greatest, the greatest!" and the audience went wild with agreement.

The main attraction Riacho Escuro was asked to contribute to the next show, the semi-final round, was a pair of adult Siamese twins, preferably a male and a female. (Really, the imagination of Silvio Santos and his team knew no bounds!) Luckily, a member of the finance committee recalled having read in a magazine, years before, a feature article about two babies who were born together in a village 150 miles away, off near the border of Minas Gerais. This time the mayor and his wife went to search for the hidden treasure themselves and found a pair of black Siamese twins living in a decrepit shack. They were seventeen and could therefore be considered adult. The only difficulty was that both of them were girls. What to do? The mayor thought a few minutes, consulted his wife, and with one accord, thinking of the difficulty of finding any more suitable Siamese twins in the short time remaining, took the pair away with them.

Because the Siamese twins were the same sex, Riacho Escuro came within an inch of losing, but led by two points in the final voting because the singing toad from the rival town forgot the words to the second verse of "Bésame Mucho" and was booed.

This time the celebration in Riacho Escuro was more restrained. On the way home the mayor admitted to his wife and to the vicar that he had misgivings about the finals, for which they were required to present a transvestite who had been born and raised in Riacho Escuro (a firm stipulation) and could do a perfect imitation of Carmen Miranda. In any other town this would have presented no problem, but it was an impossibility in Riacho Escuro because the mayor himself, immediately after taking office, had ordered the police chief to make a clean sweep of all public places suspected of harboring vice and to throw all unsavory characters out of town in the name of decency and morality. In one fell swoop the police closed down the whore houses, the motels on the edge of town, and a nightclub that alternated a timid drag show with the routine strip-tease numbers. Now it looked as if the mayor's impulsive cleanup campaign would ruin the town's chances of winning the contest. But they *had* to win, or the civic pride of Riacho Escuro would be dragged in the dust.

When he started out for City Hall on Monday morning the mayor was deeply troubled. Passing the Two Fatherlands Bar and Ice Cream Parlor on the courthouse square, he decided a cup of coffee might help him collect his thoughts. A few minutes later, as he raised the steaming cup to his lips, he noticed a young man behind the counter stirring sherbet in a mixer with a wooden paddle. While he distractedly stirred the thick mass of sherbert, the youth sang to himself in time with the mixer, *"You say I've come back an American, that I'm rich and got money to burn? . . ."* Leaning on the paddle, the youth swayed seductively, making sinuous movements with his free arm. Dr. Chrisóstomo could hardly believe his eyes. When the ice-cream maker noticed the mayor watching him he turned up his eyes, waved coquettishly and finished the verse: *". . . now don't talk so bad about me.*" Then he smiled, a dazzling white smile that narrowed his mischievous eyes into almond-shaped slits. It was as though Carmen Miranda herself had come to life again!

"Hey, young fellow, were you born around here?"

The youth put his hands on his hips and flung the mayor a scornful look and a saucy retort: "Yes I was, if you want to know. Do the authorities think they can shut me up? This is a democracy!"

Without thinking twice, a jubilant Dr. Chrisóstomo seized the young man by the arm, dragged him down the street to City Hall and showed him off to all the municipal employees and city councilmen he could find. The verdict was unanimous: tart him up a little and he'd be the spitting image of the great entertainer. The mayor phoned his wife and told her to call a meeting of the ladies' auxiliary without delay. Then he gave orders that every last detail should be settled then and there in the conference room in City Hall, so that Claudinho (that was the young man's name) would be ready for Sunday's grand finale.

Everyone scurried around being helpful. The mayor's wife insisted on taking Claudinho to São Paulo that very afternoon to be fitted for a frilly Bahiana costume and start being coached by a choreographer, a music arranger, a voice teacher and an expert in bodily expression. (They could have managed without the last, but just to be on the safe side, they thought their new star ought to be drilled in the fine points of walking on platform shoes and holding his wrists a little limper.) Dr. Chrisóstomo, pleased as punch at having unearthed such a treasure on his own, called in the reporter and photographer from the Riacho Escuro *Post* to have his picture taken with Claudinho. He also contributed the headline for the story that appeared the following day: "Thanks to Dr. Chrisóstomo Mascarenhas, His Honor the Mayor, the Next Carmen Miranda Makes His Debut in Riacho Escuro and Will Soon Belong to Brazil and the World."

The next five days were the most hectic Claudinho had ever spent in his life. He was rushed from choreographer to voice coach, from there to the dressmaker, next to the hairdresser, then to the makeup artist, and back to the choreographer without a break. At night he fell into his hotel bed and slept like a log until the next morning, when the same dizzy round began again. By Saturday, though, he was perfectly primed and sure of himself, belting out his songs with verve and pizazz, gyrating expertly on his platform shoes, swinging his hips saucily, moving his arms with incredible grace and rolling his eyes in a way that provoked enthusiastic applause from the soberest citizen. The grand finale was a triumph. Riacho Escuro easily surged ahead of its last rival and was awarded top honors in the Tournament of Towns.

That night Claudinho, still in his makeup and gorgeous costume, rode home in the mayor's car between that dignitary and the vicar, the mayor's wife having gone in the other car with the police chief and his wife. They were welcomed in glory at dawn in the courthouse square by a brass band, ovations, applause, confetti and streamers. (The young cheering section, thoroughly stoned, even risked a sniff of illegal ether spray.) The owner of the Two Fatherlands treated everyone to ice cream and Claudinho, borne aloft on the shoulders of the cheering crowd, had to repeat his triumphal number on top of the mayor's car.

The award ceremony, with the handing over of countless medals, trophies and a scroll with gold letters commemorating the victory, took place the following Sunday at the end of Silvio's program. It was a bang-up show. A special stage set had been designed with circular platforms and elaborate lamps that blinked on and off. On the first platform stood the prize Brahma bull who had won the first competition for Riacho Escuro, nobly bedecked with all his ribbons and medals, with the girls from the ballet class poised like sylphs in a semi-circle around him. On the second platform were the Siamese twins, dressed as Princess Isabel the emancipator and José do Patrocinio the abolitionist, and behind them the athletes forming an allegorical frieze of the freeing of the slaves. On the ramps leading up to the platforms were grouped the authorities of Riacho Escuro—the mayor and his wife, the vicar, the chief of police, the district judge, the presidents of the Lions and Rotary Clubs and the city councilmen. At the apex, rising from the second platform and ending in an imposing metallic curtain, was a huge open fan with its ribs illuminated by more blinking lights. Framed in each section of the fan was a member of the Marian Sodality and at the very top, in a blaze of light from slowly revolving mirrored globes and a shower of glittering tinsel, Claudinho struck a pose in his magnificent Carmen Miranda garb, holding in his arms the image that shed tears on Corpus Christi and on other, less sanctified days.

But that was only the beginning of Claudinho's brilliant career. No sooner had he stepped down from the fan at the end of the show than he was offered a contract by Waldemar Issa as the star of a musical revue at São Paulo's Medieval Theater. And it looks as if it will be Claudinho and not a famous television actress (as had been rumored), who will get the title role in the million-dollar film Luiz Carlos Barreto is currently negotiating with an American producer: "The Life and Loves of Carmen Miranda."

—*Translated by*
Barbara Shelby Morello

ANNA RHEINSBERG

VISITING

Ruth stands in the bathroom before the mirror and scrubs the lilac lipstick from her mouth. "Johannes comes tomorrow," she says, then turns her head and gives Thomas a quizzical glance. "We won't have much time for each other!" Thomas, with one foot on the floor and the other on the side of the bath, is drying his thighs with a towel. She loves it when his legs are slightly spread and his body bent forward so that she can see the twin spheres sway to and fro as he dries himself. In that position he has firm buttocks, like milk and honey, and his hips are wide. Thomas has hips like a woman, and a slender waist.

Ruth adores being in the bathroom: here it is damp and warm, and after a shower they stand rubbing cream into each other until the skin becomes silken and fragrant. She always wants to stand behind him, and at the moment he stoops forward she bends her head and sinks her white teeth into his bottom. Each time he jerks up, flinging his damp hair across his shoulders, then whirls about, and they kiss until both are gasping for breath.

But tomorrow Johannes is coming.

She senses, even though he makes a dismissing gesture with his hand, how pleased he really is. Johannes has been a friend for many years, but now has time to visit them only every couple of months. Johannes is his lover.

She still remembers vividly how it all began three years before. How Johannes sat on the old plush sofa in the kitchen with weary eyes and slightly trembling hands and finally, finally had to tell them something about himself, something they could have no idea of, could never have guessed for themselves. He had remained silent for such a long time. Out of fear, as he later admitted, that they might turn away from him, leave him alone forever.

It took a long while before the whole thing was out. Ruth had become impatient. She had no love for such endless wrestling with words, always wanted to have everything stated quickly and straightforwardly, and without the long, oppressive silences. A strange atmosphere surrounded the kitchen sofa that day. Johannes with his soft lips that seemed unable to speak, even though she already knew what they wanted to say. It had caught her attention the instant he entered the apartment.

He moved differently, he spoke softly to her as he took off his jacket, and he wore his hair longer than before. But it wasn't merely the external clues that caught her attention, it was more the feeling that this man whom she had known for so many years and who was her friend had altered in some way or other.

And then Thomas. He was restless the whole afternoon, smoked too much and had a look in his eyes which always gave her delight when she saw it. But this time it was not meant for her.

That evening Thomas was agitated, he stared greedily and had the same expression around his mouth as when he was about to kiss her after spending an hour together in the bath. But he did not take her in his arms.

He sat fumbling with his tobacco and gazed at Johannes, gazed at his slender face, at the full, sensuous lips, which sometimes gave him the appearance of a fretful sleepy child about to burst into tears; he stared at Johannes's slanting eyes, at the brown page-boy hair, the ring in his right earlobe, and Ruth realized that Thomas was randy.

That night she observed him carefully. The way he looked up when Johannes went to the stove to put on more water for tea. The way he sized up the long legs, mesmerized by the way Johannes's tight jeans parted his buttocks and outlined their firm shape.

Thomas's constant staring escaped neither her nor the friend. "So you're a fag," she said suddenly, to give a name to the unspoken. Thomas and Johannes both recoiled at the same instant. "And Thomas is randy," she said with a laugh, sprang to her feet, embraced the friend and kissed him lightly on the mouth. "You can't fool Ruth!"

They sat for a long time then and discussed it, though no one referred to Thomas's desire with even a single sentence. Later, as Ruth lay in bed beside him, with Johannes in the adjoining room, she cuddled against him and he kissed her, stroking her with his hands, until she told him he should go to his friend.

"I can't do that!" Thomas shook his head, but the idea haunted him; his entire body desired it, and yet he dared not. He was afraid. "What would you say to that," he asked her, sitting up in the bed. "I find you so desirable—your breasts, your cunt, your legs . . ."

Thus he sought to justify himself in a way that was completely unnecessary. "If you want it," she said to him, "then go. He may already be asleep. Don't miss your chance."

"And you?" he asked, his eyes seeking her face in the darkness.

"I'll come with you!" she said. "I'll sit with my back to the wall and watch!"

And that was precisely what happened. Ruth pulled on her socks, dragged her quilt and Thomas behind her; he held back timidly, protesting each time she was about to knock on Johannes's door. "No, no, we can't do that," he whispered. "Pssst—don't be so loud." Finally her patience was worn out. She rapped her knuckles briskly on the door, pressed down on the handle even before Johannes could answer, and pushed the resisting Thomas into the room.

A streetlamp that glowed outside the window cast its light over the friend; his bluntly cut hair flowed softly across his shoulders, and he had thrown aside the sheet so that he lay naked before them, a dream.

Ruth sat on the floor, drew her legs up, and wrapped herself in the quilt. Come what may, she was prepared! She snuggled the quilt about her shoulders. Suddenly Thomas was left standing alone in the room, and his first thought was to rush to her, to crawl under the quilt. But it couldn't be done. She stared stubbornly ahead, as she always did when there was a decision to be reached that he didn't feel confident to make.

Johannes, not quite understanding the charade, but guessing whose idea it was, took a deep breath, and after that resistance faded quickly.

Ruth sat in her corner, fascinated, while the two men reached for each other, first uncertainly, with erratic movements, then more and more sure of themselves. Confidently they stroked each other's bodies, exploring, touching, running their hands wherever pleasure led them. When they finally rolled apart and lay still, not knowing where to look, Ruth shuffled across to them. She pulled the quilt behind her like a child, stumbled over it, and sprawled across the naked pair.

They all laughed with relief and each of the men kissed her on the mouth and on the neck, tickled her behind the ears and pulled her between them. Thomas put his arms around her, cradled her so that her rump pressed against his stomach, while Johannes buried his head in her hair. They slept.

"Johannes is coming today," she says, but Thomas's eyes are still tightly shut, and she presses her lips against his forehead. She points at his penis, which has raised itself as it always does after sleep, standing boldly upright and quivering. Quickly he turns on his side and grumbles something incomprehensible, but once she is awake there is no more dreaming for him, either.

He finally gets up and begins to paint his eyes with kohl.

Carefully he pulls the skin taut and skillfully outlines the lids in black. He had had to practice often before he succeeded in doing it without tears flowing and smearing everything. Then he shaves with great care, letting no single hair escape; all fall to the merciless blade. He wants to be beautiful. Wants to smell of cinnamon and to be as supple as a young cat.

"You're a goose," says Ruth, who perches on the toilet seat and watches him. "What a vain, silly goose!"

"You're jealous—envious is what you are. I do just the same for you." And Thomas squares his shoulders, so that he seems taller than usual.

"I'll put a book on your head," she nags, "and until he comes you can spend your time walking up and down the hall —straight as a candle, head up. It improves the posture." She stands on her toes and gives him a demonstration. "That's the way young ladies learn how to walk properly," she says, and snorts contemptuously. But he splashes so much water that she shrieks in protest. Today no one can spoil his mood. Let the woman across the way stick her twentieth note of the week into the mailbox about finally cleaning the stairs! He also declines to fetch the breakfast-rolls; his hair is wet, he says, and getting the sniffles is unthinkable.

Silently Ruth curses Johannes for turning everything upside down. When the bell rings she at first doesn't want to open the door. That can't be him yet, they think, and who knows what sort of nuisance it could mean. They want to have a cozy breakfast together, taking their time, and afterwards go back to bed to read and make love.

When she opens the door, someone is standing there. In the first instant she thinks it is a woman, but then she recognizes Johannes. He is wearing a dress covered with ruffles and frills, a yellow dress with a beaded collar, and he has painted his mouth scarlet. "How fabulous you look," he warbles as he enters. "There was almost an accident in the street, *chérie,*" he says, and extends her a cheek so that she can give him a peck—but very carefully, so as not to spoil his make-up. "How do I look?" It sounds like three question marks, and while they float through the air he arches his eyebrows. They stand there in the hall, Ruth with her hands on her hips and staring critically, Johannes in high drag and with rouged cheeks, his hair teased into a bouffant cloud.

"Well?" he asks, and minces toward her, a complete parody. He wiggles his fanny, swings an imaginary purse. "I'm Johannes," he says with a nasal twang, sugar-sweet and twittering, "don't you know me any more?"

Then she gives a joyful yelp, takes a running start, as she always did when he returned—takes a running start and leaps into his arms. Johannes has strong arms. Now, as he catches her, holds her, they protrude from the wide sleeves of his dress. Arms downed with pale hair, blue veins lacing the backs of his hands. They contract as he holds her, bulging, and she can see that the little fingernail of his right hand is lacquered black.

Johannes is beautiful. Like a child she clings to him and gazes into his face. The sloping eyes are as full of expression as before. They gleam beneath lids dusted with golden powder. Then the nose, so firmly aquiline, and the full bottom lip which once so gently caressed her. He is half man, half woman, with strong arms and a flat chest, wearing a brilliant yellow dress and the face of a primadonna.

"What have you got under your dress? Show me, Johannes!" As he lowers her to her feet, she reaches under and raises the skirt. "You're wearing underpants? Goodness gracious! You're not supposed to be wearing anything underneath," she teases. "How's anybody supposed to get a hand in if you've got panties on?"

Johannes pretends to be embarrassed, as if the whole thing were frightfully distressing. "But you mustn't," he pipes. "Don't touch me there, don't you dare!"

Thomas enters from the kitchen. His mouth, that had curved in an impish smile when Ruth asked him how he had enjoyed himself with Johannes, is now clamped firmly shut.

"Hell." He stands there stiff as a poker, his legs welded together.

"He's here." Ruth, enjoying herself thoroughly, draws the friend forward. "Johannes is finally here." She is delighted, but Thomas only raises the corners of his mouth disdainfully.

"What a sight you are!" He gestures at the dress. "Like a scarecrow. You really dare to go out on the street like that?"

Ruth drops the friend's hand, bites her lip. Why is he saying such things?

"Don't you like it?" Johannes conceals his bewilderment. "Look!" Again he waggles his fanny and swings an imaginary purse. "Just look, sweetie. I'm beautiful!" He parades around Thomas, and pauses to give him a quick kiss on the nose.

Thomas shrinks back. "You look like a . . . woman . . . like a real faggot. I always thought you didn't go in for that kind of thing. I thought you were a . . . man! And now you look like something out of the comics. A real freak!"

He doesn't want a friend like that—or so he tells himself, and tries to look cold, imperious. But that isn't honest. For Johnnes is indeed beautiful, and this combination of penis and woman, the lure of manly arms with their faint down, and the long skirt trapping the powerful legs and preventing them from striding out—it is all exciting, arousing.

Thomas knows that. Like Ruth, he has the desire to see what Johannes is wearing under his skirt, but he controls himself. Instead, he heats water for tea, arranges cups and saucers on the flowered tablecloth, takes out spoons and sugar. He has forgotten the penciled lines on his own lids, the scent of cinnamon and the morning shave. He is doing this for her as well, he thinks to himself, and that is nothing out of the ordinary.

They sit around the table in silence. Ruth wants somehow to break through the barrier, and begins to question Johannes about everything that can possibly be questioned. About the life he leads, about the clothes he wears—the why and wherefore, the method of it all. Johannes at first replies only in monosyllables, but the old familiarity between them is still there, though Thomas broods gloomily and wrinkles his forehead.

They sit through the whole morning, the afternoon. Toward evening Thomas prepares something to eat. He remains silent, ignores Johannes's appearance, refuses to acknowledge that there is anything his timid heart cannot tolerate or comprehend.

Ruth suffers. She fails in her efforts to lead Thomas back to his friend. Well, that's that, she thinks. Let him sulk, but he'll get a hard-on anyhow.

That, of course, is up to her. She coos and flirts and finally brings in her make-up so that she can paint Johannes's face to her own liking, with heavy black circles around his eyes, high cheekbones and lilac lips. Lilac is her own color. The whole thing is a wonderful game between them, and it takes her breath away. She drags in the most outrageous things—a picture-hat with a veil, yards of colored tulle, her great-grandmother's mink collar, spike-heeled shoes.

Johannes must try everything on. Let's play dress-up is her motto, and she adores seeing him slipping into the most wildly different roles. At one moment he is the *grande dame,* then the dandy with top-hat and cane. Johannes gives everything a touch of the bizarre: he is a gentleman who menaces her even as he gallantly tips his hat, he is a villainess who purrs and entices her.

Ruth sits with her legs spread, her arms resting on the back of the chair, and holds first one hand and then the other over her mouth as she plunges into renewed fits of laughter.

Thomas can't tear himself away. There is something fascinating about Johannes: he takes on a thousand different personalities—is simultaneously conqueror and conquered, is hustler, ladies' man, clod.

They no longer take any notice of Thomas. He kneels on the sofa and lets the film unreel. They don't look toward him. Or? Ruth watches him from the corner of her eye, knowing he is not unaffected by their presentation. Indeed, she knows he is randy and can't comprehend Johannes, can't fit him into the pigeonholes of man or woman. And there should be nothing in between. Far from it, Thomas. The show goes on.

Ruth brings wine from a shop on the corner. They sip from mother-of-pearl cups and play their game. Indefatigably.

They continue to drink. Ruth has put on a negligee of rose-colored silk, so deeply cut in the front that the tops of her small breasts are visible. She smells of some heavy perfume, has dabbed musk behind her ears and her wrists. She has also drawn up her long dark dair, and a few stray locks curl down her neck.

She is wearing a fine gold chain at her throat. The rose-colored negligee reaches to her feet, cut voluptuously narrow in the hips and slit in the center up to the knee. What is further up one must imagine. And so she sits again on her chair, legs spread, but from the waist up a lady.

Johannes is naked; his chest is almost hairless and his nipples small as the heads of pins. His deeply tanned skin is stretched taut across his biceps, his stomach, and Ruth wants to bury her head there. She wants to do it at once, and she spends little time considering whether he might dislike it. She is already there, slips onto his knees and presses her cheek beneath his left nipple, where she hears the heart pounding. Thomas now accepts Johannes's glances. Relaxed, he sprawls on the sofa, his hands folded over his crotch. He has stretched out his legs, and he shifts them slightly to draw Johannes's attention. And so they exchange glances. Ruth, with her arms flung around the friend's neck, feels his penis stirring. Although she knows it is not meant for her, she is excited by it. Johannes rocks her without taking his eyes from Thomas. Or Thomas from him. The make-up is beginning to flake away; Johannes's eyelids are no longer so golden as in the morning, the kohl has gathered in the corners of Thomas's eyes, and he wipes it with the back of his hand.

The three stand up. They seem to proceed in slow-motion into the next room, approach the wide wooden bed that Thomas built for Ruth when she was away from him for a few days and telephoned almost every hour, desperate with yearning for him.

It is her bed. Thomas pulls off his linen shirt and overalls. He stands before them with his wide, womanly hips. Johannes is already naked. Now it is Ruth's turn. The friends draw her to the bed and she sits between them as they run their hands up her arms, press their mouths first against her right breast, then the left. They kiss the flesh around her brown nipples, suck at them until her thighs begin to spread, she feels her body opening and a hand probing her fleece. But to whom does she belong—Thomas or Johannes? Johannes kisses Thomas on the lips, and Thomas does the same to Ruth. Is that him kissing her on the mouth, between the legs?

Burrowing in Ruth's hair, Thomas nibbles at her ear lobes while a hand tenderly strokes her belly, then slides down to massage her where she has grown firm and moist with passion. She seizes Thomas vigorously by the hips, pulls him up and into her, while Johannes braces her back. He runs his fingers along her neck, braces her so that she can sit firmly and hold Thomas inside her.

She cries out slightly, groans loudly, arches her body until her head is so far back that she sees Johannes. His penis is close to her, she can feel the silken skin and rub her cheek against it, and still he is the one who holds her so that she doesn't sink back against the pillows.

Even when they change positions, Ruth on top of Thomas now, locking him tightly with her thighs, the friend kneels behind her, runs his hands down her back and then along Thomas's legs. Ruth knows that Johannes does not desire her, even though he fondles her; it is only a way of showing his affection. Then she lies still. Johannes kisses her fingers. Suddenly needing to feel his mouth against her once more, she pulls him to her, flings her arms around him, and offers him her lips. She holds him tightly, rumples his hair, tastes his salt. And yet it can last only a second, it must be over before the spark jumps once more and he turns away from her, disappointed that she refuses to acknowledge the real direction of his lust.

Then she rolls into a corner against the wall and remains still. Thomas has laid his head on Johannes's chest. His mouth makes a damp trail across his skin and burrows beneath Johannes's arm while with one hand he strokes the damp tip of the friend's penis until his entire body begins to tremble. There is no longer anything here for Ruth, and she makes no use of the position Johannes had taken before. Masculine arms grasp each other, legs are buried in pillows, and mouths grind together; their tongues dart and lick between the thighs, on the ass, along the spine. Thomas's hair gives off a sweet smell, and Johannes moans softly.

They rock together, rub and bite each other's nipples, their bodies gliding up and down. For Thomas it is all as it was then, a long while ago.

CALAMUS

As morning dawns they wearily raise their heads. Golden make-up shimmers from the pillows, and some corner of the sheet has long since wiped the last traces of lilac lipstick from Johannes's mouth.

—*Translated by*
David Galloway and
Christian Sabisch

NOTES ON AUTHORS

SHERWOOD ANDERSON, born in the town of Camden, Ohio, in 1876, was strongly shaped by his midwestern boyhood, which supplied the major themes and settings and strongly influenced the language of his writings. Like many American authors of the period, he was largely self-educated, and was forty at the time his first novel appeared. After a series of odd jobs and military service in Cuba during the Spanish-American War, Anderson married and settled down in Elyria, Ohio, as the manager of a paint factory. When he walked out one day, left his family behind and headed for Chicago to pursue a literary career, he created for numerous writers and intellectuals a symbol for the plight of the artist in materialistic America. Anderson first attracted wide attention with the collection of interlocked short stories entitled *Winesburg, Ohio* (1919), a kind of *Bildüngsroman* in which a young reporter peers behind the polite, ordered facades of small-town America. In a series of epiphanies he encounters the loneliness, yearning and sexual frustration that make up the secret life of Winesburg. The book's critical success assured Anderson's reception by the literati of New York and Paris, where for a time he joined the celebrated circle of Gertrude Stein, who strongly influenced his novel of Negro life, *Dark Laughter* (1925). In his last years Anderson lived with his fourth wife in a simple cottage in rural Virginia; he died in 1941 during an unofficial goodwill tour of South America. Anderson once enjoyed a kind of notoriety as a writer on sex, the focal theme of many of his stories, and his name was frequently linked to that of D.H. Lawrence. It is true that he viewed sexual experience as an opportunity to escape the ruthless standardization of the modern age, the confinement of the regulated life; and he believed that the primal, instinctive forces of human behavior must not be denied. On the other hand, sexuality ultimately has a mystical rather than an erotic dimension in Anderson's work, and properly viewed is only one aspect of the struggle for identity and personal dignity chronicled in his writings.

GIORGIO BASSANI was born in Bologna, Italy, in 1916, and educated at the University of Bologna, but his most famous writings are set in the medieval town of Ferrara. In a series of interlocking short stories and novels, including *The Gold-Rimmed Spectacles* (1958) and *The Garden of the Finzi-Continis* (1963), he has recorded the destinies of dozens of families, from the working class to the faded aristocracy, focusing on the period from 1930 to 1945. Characters appear and reappear, threading the works together into a dense and vivid tapestry as noteworthy for its refined social and political observations as for its elegantly spare, lyric style. The figure of the homosexual Doctor Athos Fadigati plays a central role in *The Gold-Rimmed Spectacles*, not only because of his influence on the young narrator's vision of life, but also because his double existence is a key to other characters in the novel who are compelled to mask their inner feelings and desires. Revealing his true nature to his fellow citizens eventually leads to Dr. Fadigati's suicide; similarly, opening up their enchanted garden leads to the death of the Finzi-Continis in a Nazi concentration camp. In addition to novels and short stories, Giorgio Bassani has also published several volumes of poetry, lectured on drama, and served as vice-president of Italian Radio and Television.

WILLIAM BURROUGHS was born in St. Louis in 1914, the grandson of the inventor of the famous Burroughs adding-machine. After graduation from Harvard College, he studied medicine in Vienna, worked at a variety of odd jobs, and served briefly in the U.S. Army. While living in Mexico shortly after World War II, Burroughs killed his wife in a game of "William Tell," attempting to shoot a champagne glass balanced on her head. In the following years he became legendary as a haunted, drug-addicted homosexual who wandered between Tangiers, London and Paris. His highly autobiographical first novel, *Junkie* (1953), is a painful, straightforward account of the tormented underground life of an addict, but incorporates vignettes of sexuality and police action that anticipate the themes of his later, more experimental work. *The Naked Lunch* (1959) also begins as a first-person narrative by an addict, but quickly breaks with linear discourse in favor of a kind of hallucinatory continuum where the viewpoint is in continuous flux. The book blends fragmentary narratives, violent images, satirical effects and raw sexual encounters—usually of a sensationally homosexual nature. In the works that followed, including *Nova Express* (1964), Burroughs developed "cut-up" and "fold-up" techniques of random composition that sometimes resemble surrealist collages; he also showed a growing interest in science fiction. An admirer of de Sade, Kafka and Genet, he is by turns fiendishly comic, coldly surreal; he has repeatedly attacked technological power groups, corporate capitalism and medical tyranny. William Burroughs is often seen as the "Guru" of the Beat Generation, and his extreme formal experimentation has been a major influence on contemporary American writing.

MATEI CARAGIALE was born in Bucharest, Rumania, in 1885, and died there in 1936. He was the son of Ion Luca Caragiale, a brilliant and eccentric dramatist whose comic plays mocked bourgeois pretension and political rhetoric. Ion Caragiale had a deep and passionate love for Germany, and he exiled himself in Berlin in 1904. His impressionable son Matei was deeply influenced by his own stay in the German capital as a young man; when he returned to Bucharest he worked as a miniature painter, heraldist and civil servant. Although Caragiale produced relatively little in his lifetime, he is remembered as a consummate stylist whose meticulous language evoked a submerged world hovering between reality and dream. His models included Poe, Oscar Wilde and Baudelaire, but the exotic lessons he learned from them were given his own distinctive stamp. In his most famous work, *The Four from the Old Court* (1929), he explored the city of Bucharest from the mud of unpaved alleys to the airy drawing-rooms of the nobility. He began the novel in 1910 and worked at it, meticulously revising and rewriting, for nearly two decades. Other than sonnets, a few sketches and an extensive diary, Caragiale published only one other work—the remarkable novella *Remember* (1924), which drew heavily in mood and atmosphere on his own stay in Berlin.

CONSTANTIN CAVAFY was born to a prosperous Greek merchant family in 1863 in Alexandria, where he lived for most of his life and died in 1933. At school he developed such a deep love for ancient Greek civilization that he eventually became a Greek citizen. When anti-European, anti-Christian riots broke out in Alexandria in 1882, Cavafy went to Constantinople to live for three years in the home of his grandfather; there he discovered the delights of modern, demotic Greek, and composed his first poems. His linguistic gifts were a prime recommendation for the clerical post he received in Egypt's Ministry of Irrigation in 1892, and held for the next thirty years. Cavafy was a rigorous aesthetician, whose work underwent continuous revision; he wrote as many as seventy poems a year, but usually destroyed all but four or five. His first book of verse, published in 1904, contained a mere fourteen titles, and a later edition added only twelve more; though various poems appeared in periodicals in Greece and Egypt, these were the sole book-length publications in Cavafy's lifetime. The poet once identified the three principal modes of his verse as the erotic, the philosophical and the historical; the first two are frequently interwoven, and all three sometimes come together in a single work. The erotic poems are almost all frankly homosexual. These frequently set up a dialogue between the imagination of the artist-speaker and the realities—often sordid or disillusioning—of the flesh; yet Cavafy insists that the imagination must always be rooted in physical reality. In the original Greek, Cavafy's poems were revolutionary in their mingling of classical and modern voices—an aspect lost in any translation. Nonetheless, his work has had a profound impact on other writers, including E.M. Forster, who introduced Cavafy's poems to T.S. Eliot and D.H. Lawrence, among others; W.H. Auden also acknowledged that many of his own poems were shaped by his reading of Cavafy.

JEAN COCTEAU was born in 1891 into a social milieu whose members presumed the arts to be an essential part of the good life, and as a child he formed a life-long passion for the theater, which he described as "the fever of crimson and gold." A sense for theatrical illusion and flair is one of the elements uniting his amazingly versatile work. Shortly after his seventeenth birthday Cocteau published his first volume of poems, *Aladin's Lamp*, and for more than half a century would explore not only every existing literary genre but the cinema, ballet, the circus and jazz. He made his debut as a novelist with *Thomas the Impostor* in 1923, and perfected his fictional expressionism with *The Grand Ecart* (1923) and *Enfants Terribles* (1929). Cocteau made a firm distinction between his "sleeping books" and his "waking books," the latter composed after the new self-awareness he learned through contact with friends like André Gide. Thus, he dated his own literary beginnings from the publication of the prose fantasy *Le Potomak*, which became even more imaginative, more baroque, in the revised edition that appeared in 1919. The same spirit would inform films like *Blood of a Poet* and *Beauty and the Beast,* his most successful plays, his paintings and drawings, and the sensuous little novella—a kind of prose poem—which Cocteau published anonymously in 1928 under the title *Le livre blanc.* It has been said that of the artistic generation whose daring vision gave birth to twentieth-century art, Cocteau came closest to being a Renaissance man. As his own posthumous tribute to that phenomenal range of talent, following his death in 1963 he was buried in the garden of the chapel of Saint-Blaise-des-Simples which he had designed himself.

LONNIE COLEMAN was born in 1920 in Barstow, Georgia, which provided him with much of the setting for his most popular work, the trilogy of novels entitled *Beulah Land.* This complex saga of the destinies of a nineteenth-century plantation family became a television mini-series, and established the author's international reputation. Following work as an editor for *Collier's* magazine, Coleman lived for seven years in England and Ireland, and since 1979 has made his home in Savannah. He is the author of more than a dozen novels, and has frankly explored homosexual themes in *Ship's Company* (1955), *Sam* (1959) and *Mark* (1981). *Sam* was a pioneering work in its conscious opposition to the formula whereby homosexual experience inevitably ends in suicide or murder; the portrayal of a successful relationship between two men is saved from sentimentality by the author's restrained style and his flair for dry, witty dialogue.

OTTO VILHELM EKELUND, the son of a blacksmith, was born in 1880 in Scania, the southernmost province of Sweden, and died in 1949. His first book of verse, *Varbris (Spring Breeze),* appeared in 1900, and from that year he devoted himself exclusively to a literary career. Ekelund's early collections were lyrical and impressionistic, drawing chiefly on the experiences of his own country childhood. With *Elegier (Elegies,* 1903), his mature style was formed—a distinctive amalgam of influences from classical Greek poetry, Expressionism, and Swedish and German Romanticism—most notably, the free verse of Hölderlin and Platen. The links with Platen were not only formal but thematic, for the subject of homosexual love was important to them both. Largely because of his frank treatment of this subject, Ekelund soon found himself without either a publisher or an audience, and almost entirely abandoned the writing of verse. In 1908 he was sentenced to a month in prison for obstructing justice. Rather than serve the sentence, he spent the next twelve years in exile in Germany and Denmark. Ekelund married in 1914, and his daughter was born in the same year; in 1921 he returned to Sweden, and the last collection of his poetry was released. Ekelund's marriage and his abandonment of homosexual subjects was not a recantation, but a deliberate remaking of the self. The choice facing him, as his letters show, was either a heterosexual "transformation" or destruction both as a writer and as an individual. A few aphorisms from his later years testify to a continuing sympathy for the dilemmas facing homosexuals in a hostile society.

JAMES (THOMAS) FARRELL was born in 1904 on the South Side of Chicago, where he lived until he moved to New York in 1931; the city would provide the setting for his most important fiction, which in an urgent, naturalistic style exposes the boredom, violence and isolation of modern urban life. While a student at Chicago University, Farrell wrote a sketch that would eventually grow into a trilogy of novels about Studs Lonigan. For *Young Lonigan* (1932) the author drew heavily on his own experiences as a pupil in a Catholic school and the numerous odd jobs he held as a young man —including that of a newspaper reporter. *The Young Manhood of Studs Lonigan* (1934) and *Judgment Day* (1935) continue the dispassionate record of the brutalized life and pathetic death of the inarticulate hero. Farrell's vision was shaped by the Great Depression, and he never lost a sense of indignation at social and economic inequalities. In a tetralogy of novels about Danny O'Neill, Farrell holds out hope that the hero can escape the destructive forces of his environment, and in a trilogy focused on novelist Bernard Carr, the author seems to have vicariously fulfilled some of his own aesthetic ambitions. But Farrell's most characteristic writings show man caught in a trap formed by the familiar naturalistic forces of heredity and environment. Though he remained incredibly prolific, producing essays, novels and more than 200 short stories, most critics agree that Farrell's work shows little real development, and that his proletarian-naturalistic aesthetic tends to produce a flat, self-conscious prose. The work of the 1930's, however, made a substantial contribution to the school of urban fiction in America.

EDWARD MORGAN FORSTER was born in London in 1879 and educated at King's College, Cambridge, where he was appointed honorary fellow in 1946. His years in Italy provided background for his earliest novels, *Where Angels Fear to Tread* (1905) and *A Room with a View* (1908). In 1910 Forster published *Howards End*, which dramatizes his ideal of effecting harmony between the discordant elements within man himself and between man and the universe. During World War I the author served as a Red Cross volunteer, visiting both India and Egypt, where he met Constantin Cavafy. His most celebrated novel, *A Passage to India* (1924), masterfully blends symbolic suggestion, psychological insight and social realism. Forster borrowed his title from the famous poem of the same name by Walt Whitman, and like Whitman he stressed the need to combine the technical triumphs of Western civilization with a new exploration of man's spiritual resources. The novel documents the struggles of individuals to reach out across barriers of race, culture and social convention. Figuratively, the predicament of the isolated individual analyzed in *A Passage to India* offers a key to understanding the situation of the homosexual in British society of the same period. E.M. Forster suppressed his own homosexual novel *Maurice,* composed in 1913, and the seven explicitly homosexual short stories he wrote between 1922 and 1958; it was only after his death in 1970 that what the author called his "indecent writings" first appeared in print. Perhaps it was in part his reluctance to explore the sexual manifestations of his philosophical vision that blocked Forster in his later years; he produced essays and occasional writings and collaborated on the libretto for Benjamin Britten's opera *Billy Budd,* but there was no more major fiction, though Forster lived for nearly a half-century after the publication of *A Passage to India.*

JEAN GENET, born in Paris as an illegitimate child in 1910, only learned the name of his mother when he was issued a birth certificate at the age of twenty-one. As a ward of the *Assistance Publique* he developed a precocious sympathy for the outcast and the criminal, and was himself first sentenced to a reformatory at the age of ten; he would spend the next thirty years in and out of the most notorious prisons in Europe. It was in the Fresnes prison is 1942 that he completed his first book, *Our Lady of the Flowers,* composed on the sheets of coarse brown paper with which prisoners produced paper bags. The novel described the life of a young man who, like the author, had spent his childhood in the provinces and became a male prostitute in Paris, changing his name to Divine and his identity from masculine to feminine. Such inversions are typical of Genet's work, which repeatedly mocks the values and assumptions of bourgeois society; the homosexual, the murderer and the thief become the "angels" of this underworld, their lives startlingly transformed by the incantatory power of Genet's narrative voice. By 1948 Genet had published three novels, two plays and two long poems when he was sent to prison for the tenth time and thus received an automatic life-sentence. France's leading intellectuals —including Gide, Sartre and Jean Cocteau—successfully petitioned the government for his release. Particularly for the Existentialists, Genet's life and his writings seemed symbolic of the condition of modern man, and Sartre made him the subject of a mammoth biography entitled *Saint Genet*. Genet's most characteristic work—including the highly autobiographical *Thief's Journal* (1949)—blends motifs of eroticism, religious ecstasy and anarchy, fused in a poetic language of startling vividness and inventiveness.

ALLEN GINSBERG was born in 1926 in Newark, New Jersey, the son of the poet and teacher Louis Ginsberg; his mother Naomi was a Russian Jewish immigrant active in the politics of the Left. After school in Paterson and study at Columbia University, Ginsberg worked at a variety of odd jobs, began to experiment with drugs, to explore Zen Buddhism, and intensely absorbed the inspiration of other poets—including Blake, Whitman and Pound. He exploded onto the literary scene in 1956 with a collection of poems entitled *Howl,* apocalyptically chanting the alienation of "the best minds of my generation." The slim volume, with an introduction by another New Jersey poet, William Carlos Williams, was indicted in California for obscenity and thus won the author instant notoriety. Together with Jack Kerouac and William Burroughs, Ginsberg would be celebrated as a pioneer of the Beat Generation; both his work and his life—including his exuberant proclamation of homosexuality—were a protest against the conformity of the Eisenhower decade, and a herald of the youth revolution of the 1960's. In *Kaddish* (1960) he produced a painfully frank autobiographical elegy on the illness and death of his mother, in which her recurrent madness becomes a metaphor for the fall of Western civilization. Most of his later volumes are part of a single long, discursive, socially critical work based on his own travels and composed with the assistance of a tape-recorder. Ginsberg's characteristic poems are either short, intensely personal lyrics or long, rhapsodic discourses blending personal confession, social criticism, prophetic utterance and quasi-religious rituals. Above all, this egocentric and visionary poetry celebrates individual experience, pacifism and the need for human tenderness; its appeal is personal and immediate, and much of it only achieves its full effect through the poet's energetic public performances.

WITOLD GOMBROWICZ, born in Poland in 1904 to a prominent noble family, studied in Warsaw and Paris, and as a young man became a celebrated member of the Polish avant-garde. He made his literary debut with a collection of seven short stories entitled *Memoirs of Immaturity* (1933). When war broke out in Europe, Gombrowicz was visiting Buenos Aires, and he remained in Argentina for the next twenty-four years, isolated and unknown, but continuing to write. In 1958 his satirical novel *Ferdydurke*, originally published in 1937, appeared in a French translation and immediately established the author's European reputation. Gombrowicz described the book, which parodied in form the popular Polish novel of an earlier time, as "the struggle for maturity by a man in love with immaturity." The "myth of immaturity" also informs the grotesque satire on Polish nationalism, *Trans-Atlantyk* (1950), and *Pornografia* (1960), his best-known novel. In the latter two old men, intrigued and then indecently excited by the innocence of an adolescent boy and girl, conspire to bring about the consummation of the young people's imagined love. In seeking to make their fantasies real, the conspirators are figuratively participating in an elaborate homo-erotic charade. Here, as in most of his writings, Gombrowicz demonstrated his fascination with the fusion of contraries. Like Gide, he felt the diary to be the form best suited to contemporary narration; his own diaries, which he began to publish in 1953, describe Proust as ineffectual, praise Genet as the greatest French writer, and acknowledge his close ties to the Existentialists. In 1963 Gombrowicz returned to Europe, settling in Vence in the South of France, where he died in 1969.

THOM(SON) GUNN, born in Gravesend, England, in 1929, studied at Cambridge University and at Stanford, and has for many years made his home in California. His first book of poems appeared in 1953, and he was early recognized as a gifted proponent of the "new" poetry in Britain. Unlike his English contemporaries, however, he did not cultivate a distanced, neutral poetic tone, but experimented widely with poetic forms and frequently explored violent themes, praising action over sensibility. In a poem on the bomb plot against Hitler, he stressed that violence may often be both rational and necessary; he has given heroic status to the black-jacketed motorcyclist, and bestowed his blessing on "all the toughs through history." But Gunn is also capable of immense tenderness, subtlety and intellectual complexity; his powerful images and compelling rhythms can vivify even the banal and commonplace subject. Among his most influential collections of verse are *The Sense of Movement* (1957), *My Sad Captains* (1961), *Touch* (1967) and *Jack Straw's Castle* (1976). *Touch* contains a remarkable sequence of poems entitled "Misanthropos" which deals with the plight of the last man alive after an atomic holocaust, and which richly illustrates the poet's tough humanism. Homosexual allusion has often played a role in Gunn's verse, but it has become more overt and more central in recent years.

MAARTEN 'T HART was born in 1944 in the small Dutch town of Maassluis, and presently teaches ethnology at the University of Leiden. While still studying biology at the university, he published his first novels—*Steenen voor een ransuil* (*Stones for a Horned Owl*, 1971) and *Ik had een wapenbroeder* (*I Had a Brother in Arms*, 1973); in these penetrating studies of psychological development, he focused on a working-class milieu indelibly stamped by the Reformed Church of Holland. The poverty, obsessive religiosity and sexual prudery he records were elements he knew well from his own childhood. In addition to various scholarly papers, Maarten 't Hart has written essays on music, feminism and the behavioral sciences; his short-story collection *Mammoet op Zondag* (*Mammoth on Sunday*) received the Dutch Literary Award for 1977.

ERNEST HEMINGWAY was born in upper-middle-class Oak Park, Illinois, in 1899, but his boyhood and youth were strongly influenced by the northern Michigan woods, where his doctor father introduced him to the rituals of the sportsman. After working briefly for the famous *Kansas City Star* as a cub reporter, Hemingway served in France and Italy as honorary lieutenant in the Red Cross ambulance corps. The wound he received on the Italian front became a central metaphor in his work, and he went on to become the leading spokesman for the so-called "lost generation." Hemingway's work as a newspaper reporter had a profound impact on his lean, understated prose; Sherwood Anderson, Gertrude Stein and Ezra Pound also helped shape his early style. In 1921 Hemingway and the first of his four wives settled in Paris, and in 1923 his first book, *Three Stories & Ten Poems,* appeared there, followed in 1925 by the American publication of *In Our Time.* These early stories record a midwestern boy's initiation into the duplicities of the adult world; they also show Hemingway's sympathy for the soldier, hunter and professional athlete. Later the bullfighter would be added to the galaxy of Hemingway heroes faced with elemental tests of dignity and courage; in the famous Hemingway "code," the hero was a stoic who never flinched at danger, never falsified his emotions, and always observed the rules of the game. In 1926 Hemingway published *The Sun Also Rises,* the definitive portrait of the lost generation, and in 1929 *A Farewell to Arms.* In the decades that followed, the legends of his escapades as drinker, lover and daredevil sportsman often overshadowed the work he produced. Though Hemingway sometimes aggressively projected the supermasculine "macho" image in both his prose and his life, many of his heroes reveal a surprising tenderness and emotional vulnerability. Homosexual characters are central to four of his stories: both "The Light of the World" and "The Mother of a Queen" are savage in their indictments, extending the negative tones with which a giddy crowd of homosexuals is presented in *The Sun Also Rises;* "Homage to Switzerland," though archly condescending, takes a somewhat more objective view; and "A Simple Enquiry" shows genuine compassion for the confused, sexually frustrated young officer. Ernest Hemingway was awarded the Nobel Prize for Literature in 1954, and in 1961 committed suicide at his ranch near Ketchum, Idaho.

WILLIAM INGE, born in Independence, Kansas, in 1913, was fascinated by the theater from childhood. While majoring in drama at the University of Kansas, he also acted with stock companies; though he then became a schoolteacher, he yearned for some connection with the theater, and in 1943 became drama and film critic for the St. Louis *Star Times.* The job gave Inge a life-long respect for the well-made play, and his own full-length dramas show a careful sense of craftsmanship, though his themes are conventional and his essentially realistic style can verge toward melodrama. Encouraged by Tennessee Williams, whom he greatly admired, Inge produced his first play in 1947, but his first real success was *Come Back, Little Sheba* (1950); it was rapidly followed by three other box-office hits —*Picnic* (1953), which received the Pulitzer Prize, *Bus Stop* (1955) and *The Dark at the Top of the Stairs* (1957). Inge's most important plays are psychodramas focusing on the lives of seemingly ordinary midwestern characters who, in the author's own words, suddenly reveal "surprising depths of feeling that lie far below the public surface of human personality." Inge's later works tend to be rather flat and repetitious, with an unhappy inclination toward platitudinous self-analysis; their seriousness is too often stated rather than demonstrated. The one-act plays—including *The Boy in the Basement*—are less polished and their dramatic mechanisms are sometimes clumsy, but they often reveal a raw power obscured in the realistic dramas critics praised so highly in the 1950's. William Inge died in 1973.

CHRISTOPHER ISHERWOOD was born in Cheshire, England, in 1904, and educated at Cambridge University. After a year of medical study in London, he went to Berlin in 1929 and remained there for the next four years—until "Hitler's coming to power made me an honorary refugee." Though his first novel, *All the Conspirators*, had appeared in 1928, it was with the publication of two impressionistic, highly episodic novels of the Berlin years—*Mr. Norris Changes Trains* (1935) and *Goodbye to Berlin* (1939)—that Isherwood established his reputation as a subtle, gifted social observer. In the 1930's Isherwood collaborated with W.H. Auden, his friend since boarding-school days, to produce three plays and a travel book describing their visit to China. In 1939 he went to California to work for the film industry and eventually became an American citizen. In his earlier writings Isherwood showed a pronounced fascination for eccentrics; his narrators take mischievous delight in depicting characters whom polite society would shun—including a series of older men obsessed by heterosexual youths. In later works the homosexual becomes more central and is far more complexly portrayed—as in *Down There on a Visit* (1962) and *A Single Man* (1964). In the autobiographical volume *Christopher and His Kind* (1976), Isherwood analyzed the period from his departure for Berlin to his arrival in America and acknowledged the deep conflict then existing between his sexual and social selves; his youthful homosexual existence was, he reasoned, one way of expressing his reaction against the stuffy Puritanism of his own class. His perennial themes of the multiplicity of self, loneliness and separation, and the search for a homeland can all be related to a fundamental rebellion against the "Others"—above all, against what Isherwood labels "the heterosexual dictatorship."

LEROI JONES was born in Newark, New Jersey, in 1934, and studied at Rutgers, Howard and Columbia universities, as well as the New School for Social Research, where he earned an M.A. in German literature. In 1964 three of his plays were produced in New York; one of them, *Dutchman*, spoke fiercely but lucidly to black Americans about the merciless destruction of their cultural identity. The works that followed—plays, poetry, short stories, essays and novels—became increasingly revolutionary, and Jones was the acknowledged new leader of the black cultural awakening. His semi-autobiographical novel, *The System of Dante's Hell* (1965), impressionistically equated the Newark slums with Dante's Inferno. To create a showcase for black theatrical talent, Jones founded the Black Arts Repertory Theater, but economic problems and his own continuing difficulties with the law forced its closing; in 1968 he formed the Black Community Development and Defense Organization, dedicated to the creation of new values for Afro-Americans. The organization encouraged the adoption of the Muslim faith and Arabic names; Jones himself assumed the name Amiri Baraka, preceded by the title "Imamu" for spiritual leader. His more recent writings continue to urge Afro-Americans to root out white values from their hearts, including the hypocrisy of Christianity. Rite and ritual play important roles here, and the voice is one of fierce, lyric urgency. Homosexual themes are present in several of Jones's works, including *Experimental Death Unit # 1* (1965), in which two homosexuals are beheaded by a black liberation army. In *The Toilet* Jones hints that the races may someday come together, but only after the black has earned his manhood by defeating the white.

CHRISTIAN KAMPMANN was born in Hellerup, Denmark, in 1939, and trained as a journalist. His novelistic career began in 1962 with *Blandt venner* (*Among Strangers*), but he first achieved major critical recognition with a complex tetraology of novels on the Gregersen family, published between 1973 and 1975. Beginning in the 1950's and continuing through the early 1970's, this chronicle traces the way in which a prosperous bourgeois family copes with the decay of older traditions, of the family as a self-contained and self-defining unit. Although neurosis often results from the new "freedom" of the post-war decades, Kampmann implies in the conclusion of the fourth volume that there is now hope for the individual's discovery of more fulfilling modes of self-expression. One of the central characters of the tetralogy is a homosexual who acts as spokesman for the novelist—thus anticipating the homosexual focus of Kampmann's autobiographical novel *Fornemmelser* (*Feelings,* 1978), which explores the conflicts aroused by the narrator's awakening recognition of his homosexual impulses. *Fornemmelser* is the first of a trilogy of novels that includes *Videre Trods Alt* (*Proceed in Spite of All,* 1979) and *I Glimt* (*In Flashes,* 1980). Kampmann himself has been an outspoken advocate for the social rights of homosexuals in Denmark.

STANLEY KAUFFMANN is the quintessential New Yorker. He was born in the city in 1916, studied at New York University, and has pursued a remarkably versatile career there in publishing, journalism and the theater. His early love for the theater led to work as actor, stage-manager and director, chiefly with the Washington Square Players. Following World War II he held editorial positions with several major publishers, and meanwhile began to write both plays and novels; most of the latter were concerned with the world of artists, writers and musicians he knew so well. *The Philanderer* (1954) became the subject of a famous obscenity case in the

English courts. As film critic for the *New Republic* and a member of the board of *Film Quarterly*, Kauffmann made an important contribution to the development of a new critical aesthetics for the motion picture, but he became best known as drama critic for the *New York Times;* his uncompromising standards and urbane style have made him one of the most feared and influential critics in America.

EDUARDO GUDIÑO KIEFFER, born in 1935 in Esperanza, Argentina, is a novelist and journalist distinguished by his passionate social engagement. For many years he served as foreign correspondent for numerous magazines and newspapers in Argentina. Newspaper headlines and captions frequently play a role in the collage-like structure of his novels, which seek to reveal the absurdity and grotesqueness, the quality of dread which he sees as a continuous element of contemporary experience. After the sensational *Para comerte mejor* (*The Better to Eat,* 1968), Kieffer published a picaresque novel in 1972 that explored the lives of the poor and the oppressed living in the underworld of Buenos Aires. It is from this work, *Guia de pecadores* (*Handbook for Sinners*), that the startling monologue of ''Rara avis in terra'' is extracted.

MIKHAIL ALEKSEYEVICH KUZMIN was born in St. Petersburg, Russia, in 1875. Little is known about his childhood, but as a young man he toured Italy and visited Alexandria—events that made a deep impression on his literary imagination. His first sonnets were published in 1905, and in 1906 he scandalized the literary *beau monde* of Russia by publishing a novel entitled *Wings,* clearly autobiographical in content and forthright in its portrayal of homosexual experience. Several of his ''Alexandrian Songs'' also explored homosexual themes; like *Wings,* the poems first appeared in *The Scales,* a symbolist journal, but were collected in a separate edition in 1921. In 1920 Kuzmin privately printed a collection of homoerotic poems, together with drawings by his friend Vladimir Milashevski. Strongly influenced by both the *fin-de-siècle* Aesthetes and the theories of Walter Pater, Kuzmin created a resonant poetic mythology focused on Alexandria. Mingling eroticism, an exquisite artificiality and the quest for Gnostic wisdom, the city of his poems has numerous parallels to the writings of Constantin Cavafy. Though later officially suppressed as ''bourgeois-decadent,'' Kuzmin's *Alexandrian Songs* had an immense impact on his contemporaries. His uncanny sense for the avant-garde persists in the later poetry collections, *Parabolas* (1923) and *The Trout Breaks the Ice* (1929). During the Stalinist purges of the 1930's, Kuzmin's lover was executed, and he himself was reportedly on the list of those to be eliminated when he died in 1936.

DAVID HERBERT LAWRENCE was born in 1885 in the coal-mining village of Eastwood in Nottinghamshire, one of five children of a miner and a former schoolteacher. The conflict of sensibilities between his parents, the poverty and boredom and alcoholism that surrounded the family, would be documented in Lawrence's first mature novel, *Sons and Lovers* (1913). Lawrence nearly died of pneumonia in childhood, and his weakened lungs disqualified him for service in World War I; they also accounted for numerous later illnesses and his death from tuberculosis in 1930. Encouraged by his mother, Lawrence developed a deep love for books and a determination to receive a good education; he attended Nottingham University and after graduation worked as a schoolteacher. Meanwhile, he had already begun to write poetry, and in 1911 published his first novel, *The White Peacock*. Lawrence and his German wife Frieda spent most of their tempestuous married life abroad, chiefly in Italy and New Mexico. In one of his most famous novels, *Women in Love* (1920), the author described his central concern as "the passionate struggle into conscious being." Repeatedly, he showed men and women grappling with their inmost needs—often against the restrictions and conventions of society—and struggling to give them both emotional and intellectual fulfillment. Frequently, he contrasted a passionate, instinctive, "southern" temperament with an intellectual, icily controlled "northern" one. In Lawrence's ideal, the better qualities of the two were fused. The full articulation of the inner self also included sexual expression, and Lawrence's direct treatment of the theme often caused problems with the authorities. The entire first edition of *The Rainbow* (1915) was seized and destroyed, and *Lady Chatterley's Lover* (1928) was not legally published in England until 1960. In Lawrence's fiction and poetry there are often strong homoerotic implications, but his frankest treatment of homosexual yearning, the "Prologue" to *Women in Love,* seems to have been suppressed by the author himself.

FEDERICO GARCÍA LORCA spent most of his childhood on the farm outside Granada, Spain, where he was born in 1899; his most characteristic poetry and plays were deeply rooted in Spanish landscape and folklore. Lorca published his first book at the age of nineteen, and after a brief stay at the university devoted himself entirely to his literary endeavors, which included the transcription of Castilian folksongs, public readings of his own verse, and the organization of an annual folksong festival at the Alhambra. In

1929 Lorca departed for New York, where he lived at Columbia University for a year, though never formally attending classes. He spent hours each day wandering the streets, gathering images of the great city plagued by the Depression; in particular, he was drawn to Harlem, finding in the rhythms of Negro street life and music something that recalled the gypsy traditions of Spain. The isolated poems Lorca began to compose in his dormitory room gradually fitted together into the complex mosaic of *Poet in New York,* the visionary work first published four years after his death. The poem's imagery and tone differ considerably from those made familiar by *Gypsy Ballads* (1928), *Lament for the Death of a Bullfighter* (1937) and his plays, so frequently concerned with the tragic lot of women in rural Spain. Yet Lorca's obsession with primitive passions, earthy emotions and the omnipresence of death are central elements in the New York poems as well. Many have a feeling of hallucination, of a world in permanent metamorphosis—in part, at least, the result of recent exposure to the tenets of Surrealism. But Lorca's vision was also reshaped by the work of Walt Whitman, by a sense of the betrayal of Whitman's democratic faith. The year in America was clearly a period of emotional crisis for Lorca, and he may also have turned to Whitman as a fellow-poet who had successfully come to terms with his own homosexuality. In 1933 Lorca's most famous play, the stark rural tragedy of *Blood Wedding*, was first produced in Madrid. Shortly after the outbreak of the Civil War in 1936, Lorca was murdered by Franquist soldiers, and his books were burned in Granada's Plaza del Carmen.

WILLEM DE MERODE was born Willem Eduard Keuning in 1887, in the village of Groningen, Holland. In the orthodox Calvinistic household where he grew up, pleasure of every sort was regarded as sinful. De Merode began to teach in the village school in 1906, and nourished a deep love for literature—particularly the writings of the Decadents; Aestheticism, with its stress on individuality and "l'art pour l'art," had an immense appeal, and inspired his own youthful, pseudonymous writings. The early poems he published in literary reviews brought him new contacts and acquaintances, as well as the courage to live more openly with his own homosexuality. In 1924 he was sentenced to eight months in prison for allegedly seducing a minor; after serving the sentence he officially withdrew from the church and retired to a small farm, where he lived obscurely until his death in 1939. De Merode's writings are shaped by his own long spiritual conflict with religious dogma and by the seemingly antagonistic demands of the flesh and the spirit. Only in recent years has he been given proper critical recognition as a writer of poetry distinguished both by its rich contemplative mood and its refined lyricism.

YUKIO MISHIMA was the pen-name of the brilliant Japanese novelist, dramatist and short-story writer born in Tokyo in 1925. His real name was Kimitake Hiraoka, and he adopted his pseudonym at the age of sixteen, when his first fiction was published; so successful was he in promoting the dynamic popular image of warrior-writer that the Japanese public was unaware of his true identity until after his death. Mishima was a sickly, delicate child, dominated by a severe grandmother who instilled in him a fanatical reverence for the family's ancient Samurai tradition. One of his obsessions was the beauty of the violent or painful death of a handsome youth; later he himself posed for photographs as St. Sebastian, and his writings were frequently preoccupied with blood, death and suicide. Rejected as physically unfit for service in World War II, he worked in a munitions factory and later studied at the University of Tokyo. After a brief career in banking, he devoted himself completely to literature, producing both serious novels and popular romances, plays for the No and Kabuki theaters, film scenarios, short stories and essays. Though influenced by European writers and devoted to Greek culture, he deplored the corruption of Japanese tradition by the introduction of Western values. Soon after his marriage in 1959 Mishima began a rigorous campaign of kendo and bodybuilding, seeking to make his physique conform to the Samurai ideal. Eventually he founded a private army, the *Tate no kai* (Shield Society), dedicated to the military arts and defense of the Emperor. In 1970 the *Tate no kai* stormed the military headquarters near downtown Tokyo; after a ten-minute speech from the balcony, Yukio Mishima committed harakiri and was decapitated by one of his followers.

ROBERT MUSIL was born in 1880 in the small but prosperous city of Klagenfurth, Austria. As a boy he was trained for a military career and spent some time in the same grim academy where the poet Rilke had been so desperately unhappy. While Musil adapted well to such rigors, he quit the military academy in Vienna shortly before being commissioned in favor of studying civil engineering. Ultimately, mathematics and machines failed to satisfy him, and he enrolled as a student of philosophy at the University of Berlin, earning his Ph.D. in 1908. Meanwhile, Musil had completed *Young Törless,* whose publication in 1906 won wide acclaim as a sensitive, complex study of the psychology of puberty. Through an adolescent's painful initiation into the mechanisms of sexuality and power, Musil examined the thin tissues of convention separating the rational world from the dangerous but alluring world of the irrational. Musil rejected a promising academic career to pursue his literary ambitions, and in 1911 published *Vereinigungen,* a pair of stories minutely scrutinizing the emotional and psychological consequences of adultery. From 1914 to 1918 he served as an officer in the Austrian Army, first at the front and later as a military journalist. From 1922 he lived in Vienna as a free-lance novelist, playwright and critic, devoting his most intense energies to a vast novel entitled *The Man without Qualities,* which established his international reputation. The first volume appeared in 1930, the second in 1933, but the work was still unfinished in 1942 when Musil died in Geneva, where he lived in exile after the affiliation of Austria with Nazi Germany. Some critics see the ambitious novel as a product of German Expressionism; others liken its unhurried sweep and bristling detail, its wit and verbal dexterity, to the work of James Joyce. It offers a breathtaking, constantly shifting panorama of a culture and shows a continuous refinement of the concern with psychology that characterized all Musil's writings.

YVES NAVARRE, born in Gascogne, France, in 1940, made a spectacular novelistic debut in 1971 with *Lady Black,* the memoirs of a transvestite. He soon established himself as one of the most prolific writers of his generation, as well as an articulate advocate of homosexual experience. *Evolène* (1972), the story of the solitude of a seven-year-old child, confirmed his talent, but the book most enthusiastically received by the critics was *Sweet Tooth* (1973). Set in New York, the novel's fragmented narrative presents the bizarre, interlocking stories of three characters doomed by obsession and disease. Like most of Navarre's fiction—including *Killer* (1975)—the novel blended tender intimacy with raw candor; the city itself is seen as predatory, and the scenes in New York's sexual underground are brutally explicit. Yves Navarre has not only produced a novel a year since *Lady Black,* but numerous pieces for the theater; he has been actively involved in the homosexual rights movement, and took a leading part in creating the *Syndicat des Ecrivains de la Langue Française* in 1976. His most recent novel, *Le jardin d'acclimatation,* received the Prix Goncourt in 1980.

FRANK O'HARA was born in 1926 in Baltimore, Maryland, and the following year his family moved to Massachusetts, where he attended school. At the precocious age of fifteen he was admitted to the New England Conservatory as a piano student. After two years in the Navy, O'Hara entered Harvard College; there he majored in music and began to compose poetry. He had already developed a passionate interest in American painting, and when he moved to New York in 1951, was employed at the Museum of Modern Art; his first collection of poems, *A City Winter* (1952), was published by the Tibor de Nagy Gallery. At the Club of New York Painters he met Franz Kline, Willem de Kooning and Jackson Pollock, and also cultivated a broad circle of friendship in the musical and literary worlds of New York. Among the most influential volumes of poetry published during his lifetime were *Lunch Poems* (1964) and *Love Poems* (1965), the latter including several of the remarkable love poems written to Vincent Warren from 1959 to 1961. O'Hara's verse had little in common with American literary traditions; it was influenced by Rimbaud, Mallarmé and Mayakovsky, but even more fundamentally shaped by the poet's love for music and painting. The Abstract Expressionists helped him develop a concept of art as process, of the poem as living chronicle of the creative act. Most of his subjects were provided by New York, with its surrealistic accumulations of imagery, its nightmares and delights and paradoxes; the poems have a consistent visual precision, though their moods range from exuberance to melancholy. O'Hara also produced verse dramas, incidental music and distinguished art criticism—including *Jackson Pollock* (1959) and *Robert Motherwell* (1965). He died as a result of a beach accident in 1966.

DARCY PENTEADO was born in São Roque (São Paulo), Brazil, in 1926, and started to work as a commercial artist at the age of eighteen. In 1945 he began to illustrate books, and later would design costumes for both the theater and television. Penteado's lyrically romantic paintings, which often have a clear homosexual content, have been exhibited not only throughout Brazil, but also in Europe and the United States. The sense of delicate fantasy that characterizes his visual art is also a prominent element in Penteado's three collections of short stories—*The Goal* (1976), *Crescilda and the Spartans* (1977) and *Theoremambo* (1979). In the form of contemporary fables and inverted fairy-tales, they frequently employ motifs of transformation: a married homosexual permanently altered by an affair with a transvestite, a transsexual couple who have sex changes before their marriage, a naive fairy godmother who punishes her beautiful godson by turning him into a heterosexual, a leading intellectual revealed as a transvestite rhumba-dancer. Penteado repeatedly seeks to demystify sexual, religious and social taboos; his comic inventiveness and incisive irony have led Brazilian critics to compare Penteado to Mark Twain.

ANNA RHEINSBERG was born in Berlin in 1956 and spent her childhood in a small town in Niedersachsen. At the University of Marburg she studied folklore and German literature, and continues to live in Marburg as a free-lance writer. Her first book, a collection of poems entitled *Marlene in den Gassen* (*Marlene in the Alleys*) appeared in 1979, the same year in which she helped found a new feminist journal in Germany. Rheinsberg's recent novel, *Die Reise nach Jerusalem* (*The Journey to Jerusalem*, 1981), is the story of a pregnant fourteen-year-old as related by an objective narrator, the girl herself, and a diary covering the months of her pregnancy. Anna Rheinsberg worked for a time for *Don*, one of Germany's most successful magazines for male homosexuals, and there she published numerous erotic stories, as well as critical articles. "Visiting" originally appeared in a volume entitled *Wo die Nacht den Tag umarmt* (*Where the Night Embraces the Day*, 1980), a collection of stories in which women were invited to explore their own sexual fantasies.

H.H. VON W. was the pseudonym of an author who contributed to Adolf Brand's *Der Eigene* (*The Special*), a periodical of "masculine art and culture" that first appeared in 1896. Adolf Brand, its founder, was a member of the so-called "Community of the Special," a homosexual rights organization active in the campaign to repeal discriminatory legislation, but equally concerned with the promotion of cultural achievements. In 1907 Brand himself wrote a courageous attack on the notorious "Paragraph 175," but his claim that Chancellor von Bülow was a homosexual brought him a prison sentence. Following World War I *Der Eigene* became an important literary forum, and began to publish its own books. Among them was a collection of stories entitled *Armer Junge!* (*Poor Boy!*), edited by German author Hanns Heinz Ewers in 1927. That volume provides the source for the anonymous "Marquis de Saint-Brissac." Publication of *Der Eigene* was suppressed by the National Socialists, and Brand himself was killed during an air-raid on Berlin in 1945.

LOUIS WILKINSON was born in Aldeburgh, Suffolk, in 1881, the son of a clergyman who afterwards kept a school in the town. According to Frank Harris, Wilkinson "sucked in rebellion with his mother's milk," and throughout his life remained highly critical of convention. Expelled from Pembroke College, Oxford, for what the authorities described as blasphemy, he completed his education at the more liberal St. John's College, Cambridge. A small inheritance gave him the freedom to travel widely, supplementing his income by lecturing and writing. Married four times, he had three daughters and a son, and as one of the last great cosmopolitans was equally at home in London, Berlin, New York and Rome. In addition to numerous shorter pieces, he published ten novels, three biographical works and two volumes of autobiography. Some of these, including "The Better End," appeared under the nom-de-plume of Louis Marlow. Wilkinson died on September 13, 1966.

WILLIAM CARLOS WILLIAMS attended preparatory schools in Geneva and Paris and did postgraduate study in pediatrics at the University of Leipzig, but his name is permanently linked with the town of Rutherford, New Jersey, where he was born in 1883 and spent all his professional life. As a student at the University of Pennsylvania, Williams came to know Ezra Pound, and his earliest poems show a clear debt to the Imagist school, which stressed the need for a new poetry that relied on clear, precise and concentrated images to express its meaning, much in the manner of Japanese Haiku. The tenets of Imagism were clearly etched in Williams's first books, *Poems* (1909) and *The Tempers* (1913). As his own poetic voice matured, Williams found the Imagist formula restricting, and developed the thesis of "Objectivism," in which the poem itself was regarded as an object projecting its meaning primarily through form. His technique became freer and more vernacular, but was still characterized by vivid observation restricted almost entirely to sensory experience—in such volumes as *Collected Poems* (1934), *Pictures from Brueghel* (1963) and the four parts of an ambitious, structureless epic entitled *Paterson* published between 1946 and 1951. Williams practiced medicine until a few years before his death in 1963; seen in terms of his demanding career as a pediatrician, his literary output was truly prodigious—embracing not only more than twenty volumes of poetry, but essays, novels, plays and autobiographical works. Among them is a collection of impressionistic essays, *In the American Grain*, widely regarded as one of the most remarkable prose works in modern English. Williams's particular gift for reducing experience to its essence and holding emotion at arm's length is also richly evident in short stories like "The Sailor's Son," collected in *The Knife of the Times* in 1932.